Copyright 2020 by Dane Flores-All rights reserved.

No part of this book may be reproduced or transmitted in any form or by any means, electronic or mechanical, including photocopying and recording, or by any information storage and retrieval system, without permission in writing from the publisher. This is a work of fiction. Names, places, characters and incidents are either the product of the author's imagination or are used fictitiously, and any resemblance to any actual persons, living or dead, organizations, events or locales is entirely coincidental. The unauthorized reproduction or distribution of this copyrighted work is ilegal.

Disclaimer Notice:

Please note the information contained within this document is for educational and entertainment purposes only. All effort has been executed to present accurate, up to date, reliable, complete information. No warranties of any kind are declared or implied. Readers acknowledge that the author is not engaged in the rendering of legal, financial, medical, or professional advice. The content within this book has been derived from various sources. Please consult a licensed professional before attempting any techniques outlined in this book.

By reading this document, the reader agrees that under no circumstances is the author responsible for any losses, direct or indirect, that are incurred as a result of the use of the information contained within this document, including, but not limited to, errors, omissions, or inaccuracies.

CONTENTS

- INTRODUCTION ... 9
- Breakfasts ... 11
  - 1. Salsa Eggs ... 11
  - 2. Banana Oats ... 11
  - 3. Jalapeno Popper Egg Cup ... 11
  - 4. Breakfast Frittata ... 11
  - 5. Easy French Toast ... 11
  - 6. Scrambled Eggs ... 11
  - 7. Turkey Burrito ... 12
  - 8. Bread Pudding ... 12
  - 9. Ham Cups ... 12
  - 10. Breakfast Calzone ... 12
  - 11. Morning Salad ... 13
  - 12. Coconut Pudding ... 13
  - 13. Loaded Cauliflower Bake ... 13
  - 14. Easy Granola ... 13
  - 15. Fennel Frittata ... 13
  - 16. Chicken Spinach Casserole ... 13
  - 17. Cheese Sausage Quiche ... 14
  - 18. Salsa Chicken Burrito ... 14
  - 19. Morning Oats Casserole ... 14
  - 20. Cheesy Bread Bake ... 14
  - 21. Cream Cheese Omelet ... 14
  - 22. Roasted Peppers Frittata ... 15
  - 23. Blackberries Cornflakes Bowl ... 15
  - 24. Egg Paprika Scramble ... 15
  - 25. White Mushroom Pie ... 15
  - 26. Morning Cauliflower Bake ... 15
  - 27. Cheese Bread Pizza ... 16
  - 28. Cherry Tomato Omelet ... 16
  - 29. Polenta Bites ... 16
  - 30. Blueberry Cream Cheese with French Toast ... 16
  - 31. Bread Cups Omelets ... 16
  - 32. Air Fried Potato Pancakes ... 17
  - 33. Exquisite Dutch Pancake ... 17
  - 34. Clean Breakfast Sandwich ... 17
  - 35. Craving Cinnamon Toast ... 17
  - 36. Wow! Feta Breakfast ... 18
  - 37. Cinnamon Flavored Grilled Pineapples ... 18
  - 38. The Great Japanese Omelet ... 18
  - 39. Air Fried Hash brown ... 18
  - 40. Breakfast Turkey Melt Sandwich ... 18
  - 41. Deserving Cheesy Omelet ... 19
  - 42. Air Fried Cheese Soufflé ... 19
  - 43. Chicken and Potato Nuggets ... 19
  - 44. Fluffy Cheesy Omelet ... 20
  - 45. Crust-Less Quiche ... 20
  - 46. Milky Scrambled Eggs ... 20
  - 47. Toasties and Sausage in Egg Pond ... 20
  - 48. Banana Bread ... 20
  - 49. Flavorful Bacon Cups ... 21
  - 50. Crispy Potato Rusty ... 21
  - 51. Stylish Ham Omelet ... 21
  - 52. Healthy Tofu Omelet ... 21
  - 53. Peanut Butter Banana Bread ... 21
  - 54. Yummy Savory French Toasts ... 22
  - 55. Aromatic Potato Hash ... 22
  - 56. Pumpkin and Yogurt Bread ... 22
  - 57. Zucchini Fritters ... 22
  - 58. Bacon Bombs ... 23
  - 59. Morning Potatoes ... 23
  - 60. Breakfast Pockets ... 23
  - 61. Avocado Flautas ... 23
  - 62. Cheese Sandwiches ... 23
  - 63. Sausage Cheese Wraps ... 24
  - 64. Chicken Omelet ... 24
  - 65. Sausage Burritos ... 24
  - 66. Sausage Patties ... 24
  - 67. Spicy Sweet Potato Hash ... 25
  - 68. Cinnamon Cream Doughnuts ... 25
  - 69. Sausage Frittata ... 25
  - 70. Potato Jalapeno Hash ... 25
  - 71. Bread Rolls ... 25
- BRUNCH RECIPES ... 27
  - 72. Perfect Breakfast Frittata ... 27
  - 73. Indian Cauliflower ... 27
  - 74. Zucchini Salad ... 27
  - 75. Healthy Squash ... 27
  - 76. Spinach Frittata ... 27
  - 77. Lemon Dill Scallops ... 27
  - 78. Herb Mushrooms ... 28
  - 79. Easy & Tasty Salsa Chicken ... 28
  - 80. Fish and Chips ... 28
  - 81. Hash Brown Toasts ... 28
  - 82. Delicious Beef Cubes ... 28
  - 83. Pasta Salad ... 29
  - 84. Philadelphia Chicken ... 29
  - 85. Tasty Cheeseburgers ... 29
  - 86. Stuffed Mushrooms ... 29
- MAINS ... 30
  - 87. Air-Fried Chicken Recipe ... 30
  - 88. Air Fried Chinese Pineapple Pork ... 30
  - 89. Cauliflower and Chickpea Tacos ... 30
  - 90. Perfect Air Fryer Salmon ... 31
  - 91. Air Fryer Buffalo Cauliflower ... 31
  - 92. Air Fryer Mexican-style Stuffed Chicken Breast 31
  - 93. Lemon Pepper Shrimp ... 31
  - 94. Air Fried Crumbed Fish ... 32
  - 95. Air Fryer Meatloaf ... 32
  - 96. Air Fryer Shrimp a La Bang Bang ... 32
  - 97. Crumbed Chicken Tenderloins ... 32
  - 98. Caribbean Spiced Chicken ... 33
  - 99. Air Fryer Jalapeno Popper Hassel back Chicken 33
  - 100. Air Fryer Steak & Asparagus ... 33
  - 101. Lettuce Salad with Beef Strips ... 33
  - 102. Cayenne Rib Eye Steak ... 34
  - 103. Beef-Chicken Meatball Casserole ... 34
  - 104. Juicy Pork Chops ... 34
  - 105. Chicken Goulash ... 35
  - 106. Chicken & Turkey Meatloaf ... 35
  - 107. Turkey Meatballs with Dried Dill ... 35
  - 108. Chicken Coconut Poppers ... 35
  - 109. Parmesan Beef Slices ... 36
  - 110. Chili Beef Jerky ... 36
  - 111. Spinach Beef Heart ... 36
  - 112. Paprika Pulled Pork ... 36

113. Paprika Whole Chicken.. 37
114. Pork Almond Bites.. 37
115. Panda Coconut Chicken 37
116. Air Fryer Raspberry Balsamic Smoked Pork
Chops 38
117. American Air Fried Cheese Sandwich 38
118. Midnight Nutella Banana Sandwich................... 38
119. Air Fried Pork Chops with Brussels Sprouts.... 38
120. Air Fryer Fish and Fries... 39
121. Air Fried Broccoli with Cheese Sauce................. 39
122. Air Fryer Chicken Sandwich 39
123. Air Fryer Orange Turkey Burgers......................... 40
124. Cheesy Ravioli Lunch.. 40
125. Carrots & Shallots with Yogurt 40
126. Grandma's Ratatouille 40
127. Amazing Macadamia Delight 41
128. Veggie Mix Fried Chips 41
129. Cheese Stuffed Green Peppers with Tomato
Sauce 41
130. Basil White Fish... 41
131. Cajun Salmon with Lemon 41
132. Lemon Salmon 42
133. Saucy Cod with Green Onions 42
134. Parmesan Tilapia Fillets 42
135. Party Cod Nuggets 42
136. Lemon Pepper Tilapia Fillets.................................. 42
137. Citrus Cilantro Catfish 42
138. Salmon & Caper Cakes 43
139. Lunch Egg Rolls... 43
140. Veggie Toast.. 43
141. Stuffed Mushrooms 43
142. Quick Lunch Pizzas.. 43
143. Lunch Gnocchi 44
144. Tuna and Zucchini Tortillas 44
145. Squash Fritters 44
146. Lunch Shrimp Croquettes 44
147. Lunch Special Pancake... 45
148. Scallops and Dill 45
149. Chicken Sandwiches 45
150. Hot Bacon Sandwiches... 45
151. Tasty Air Fried Cod 45
152. Delicious Catfish... 46
153. Cod Fillets with Fennel and Grapes Salad......... 46
APPETIZERS AND SIDES 47
154. Parmesan Zucchini Rounds..................................... 47
155. Green Bean Casserole.. 47
156. Zucchini Spaghetti 47
157. Cabbage and Radishes Mix...................................... 47
158. Jicama Fries.. 47
159. Kale Chips 48
160. Coriander Artichokes 48
161. Spinach and Artichokes Sauté 48
162. Green Beans... 48
163. Balsamic Cabbage 48
164. Herbed Radish Sauté 48
165. Roasted Tomatoes... 48
166. Kale and Walnuts... 49
167. Bok Choy and Butter Sauce 49
168. Turmeric Mushroom 49
169. Broccoli Gratin 49
170. Coleslaw...49
171. Roasted Zucchini and Pumpkin Cubes 49
172. Chile Casserole 50
173. Pickled Jalapeno...50
174. Sautéed Tomato Cabbage 50
175. Tender Radicchio 50
176. Green Salad with Walnuts.......................................50
177. Jicama Slaw..51
178. Peanut Slaw...51
179. White Mushroom Sauté 51
180. Caesar Salad 51
181. Cranberry Relish..52
182. Vegetable Tots..52
183. Kale Chips...52
184. Air Fried Pickles...52
185. Air Fried Green Tomatoes.......................................52
186. Chives Radishes 53
187. Kale and Pine Nuts..53
188. Cabbage and Radishes Mix......................................53
189. Turmeric Mushroom..53
190. Cheesy Garlic Biscuits..53
191. Green Bean Casserole..53
192. Roasted Garlic...54
193. Coriander Artichokes...54
194. Herbed Radish Sauté 54
195. Mexican Style Cauliflower Bake............................54
196. Curry Cabbage..54
197. Brussels Sprouts..55
198. Kale and Walnuts 55
199. Pesto Zucchini Pasta..55
200. Kale and Cauliflower Mash 55
201. Zucchini Gratin...55
202. Spiced Cauliflower 56
203. Roasted Tomatoes...56
204. Cauliflower and Artichokes 56
205. Zucchini Noodles and Sauce...................................56
206. Broccoli Mash 56
207. Cream Cheese Zucchini 56
208. Parmesan Zucchini Rounds 57
209. Zucchini Spaghetti...57
210. Pac Cheri Cramoisy Alla Sorrentino 57
211. Fast Mashed Speck and Stracchino without
Yeast 57
212. Baked Potatoes and Fennels 57
213. Baked Fennels 58
214. Baked Crisp Fennels..58
215. Free Fennel Ham and Mozzarella.........................59
216. Meat Rolls with Bacon and Camorra 59
217. Pineapple with Honey and Coconut 59
218. Ratatouille..60
219. Potatoes with Paprika Powder and Greek
Yogurt...60
220. Pork Satay with Peanut Sauce 60
221. Spicy Roulades 60
222. Spicy Chicken Legs with Grilled Marinade........61
223. Thick French Fries - Spicy.......................................61
224. Minced Beef Steak with Ham 61
225. Saltimbocca - Veal Rolls with Sage.......................61
226. Salmon Quiche..62
227. Cinnamon Maple Chickpeas 62

228. Parmesan Carrot Fries.................................. 62
229. Tater Tots 62
230. Chili Lime Chickpeas.................................. 63
231. Salted Peanuts... 63
232. Potato Wedges... 63
233. Ranch Chickpeas 63
234. Radish Chips 63
235. Beef Olive Balls 63
236. Easy Salmon Bites..................................... 64
237. Air Fried Cauliflower Bites......................... 64
238. Air Fried Simple Tofu Bites 64
239. Roasted Almonds 64
240. Healthy Eggplant Chips............................. 65
241. Crispy Roasted Cashews 65
242. Grilled Pineapple with Cinnamon.............. 65
243. Bell Peppers with Potato Stuffing 65

SEAFOOD 66
244. Coconut Shrimp... 66
245. Air Fryer Salmon.. 66
246. Healthy Fish and Chips 66
247. 3-Ingredient Air Fryer Calf........................ 66
248. Bang Bang Panko Breaded Fried Shrimp.. 66
249. Louisiana Shrimp Po Boy 66
250. Air Fryer Salmon Patties 67
251. Fried Calamari... 67
252. Panko-Crusted Tilapia 67
253. Salmon Croquettes 67
254. Air Fryer Fish Tacos................................... 68
255. Bacon Wrapped Scallops........................... 68
256. Parmesan Shrimp 68
257. Honey Glazed Salmon 68
258. Crispy Air Fried Sushi Roll 68
259. Crab Legs 69
260. Crusty Pesto Salmon................................. 69
261. Buttery Cod 69
262. Sesame Tuna Steak................................... 69
263. Lemon Garlic Shrimp................................. 69
264. Foil Packet Salmon.................................... 70
265. Foil Packet Lobster Tail............................. 70
266. Avocado Shrimp 70
267. Lemon Butter Scallops 70
268. Cheesy Lemon Halibut 70
269. Spicy Mackerel 71
270. Thyme Scallops... 71
271. Crispy Calamari... 71
272. Filipino Bistek.. 71
273. Saltine Fish Fillets..................................... 71
274. Air Fried Cod with Basil Vinaigrette 72
275. Almond Flour Coated Crispy Shrimps....... 72
276. Another Crispy Coconut Shrimp Recipe ... 72
277. Apple Slaw Topped Alaskan Cod Filet...... 72
278. Baked Cod Fillet Recipe from Thailand 73
279. Baked Scallops with Garlic Aioli 73
280. Basil 'n Lime-Chili Clams 73
281. Bass Filet in Coconut Sauce...................... 73
282. Beer Battered Cod Filet 73
283. Buttered Baked Cod with Wine 73
284. Buttered Garlic-Oregano on Clams.......... 74
285. Butterflied Prawns with Garlic-Sriracha... 74
286. Cajun Seasoned Salmon Filet................... 74
287. Cajun Spiced Lemon-Shrimp Kebabs.................74
288. Cajun Spiced Veggie-Shrimp Bake 74
289. Sweet Cod Fillets 75
290. Pecan Cod 75
291. Balsamic Cod..75
292. Garlic Salmon Fillets..75
293. Shrimp and Veggie Mix......................................75
294. White Fish with Peas and Basil 76
295. Cod and Chives..76
296. Paprika Salmon Fillets.......................................76
297. Thyme Tuna 76
298. Buttery Shrimp...76
299. Maple Salmon 77
300. Balsamic Orange Salmon 77
301. Crunchy Pistachio Cod......................................77
302. Roasted Parsley Cod..77
303. Salmon with Almonds..77
304. Crispy Paprika Fish Fillets 78
305. Air Fryer Salmon..78
306. Sweet and Savory Breaded Shrimp..................78
307. Quick Paella...78
308. Coconut Shrimp 79
309. Cilantro-Lime Fried Shrimp 79
310. Lemony Tuna..79
311. Grilled Soy Salmon Fillets.................................79
312. Old Bay Crab Cakes...80
313. Scallops and Spring Veggies.............................80
314. Fried Calamari..80
315. Soy and Ginger Shrimp.....................................80
316. Halibut and Sun Dried Tomatoes Mix...............80
317. Black Cod and Plum Sauce 81
318. Fish and Couscous...81
319. Chinese Cod...81
320. Cod with Pearl Onions.......................................81
321. Hawaiian Salmon..81
322. Salmon and Avocado Salad 82
323. Salmon and Greek Yogurt Sauce......................82
324. Spanish Salmon...82
325. Marinated Salmon..82
326. Delicious Red Snapper......................................83
327. Snapper Fillets and Veggies.............................83
328. Air Fried Branzino 83
329. Lemon Sole and Swiss Chard 83
330. Salmon and Blackberry Glaze 83
331. Persian Mushrooms..84

POULTRY...85
332. Chicken Tears..85
333. Breaded Chicken with Seed Chips...................85
334. Salted Biscuit Pie Turkey Chops 85
335. Lemon Chicken with Basil.................................85
336. Fried Chicken Tamari and Mustard..................85
337. Breaded Chicken Fillets 86
338. Dry Rub Chicken Wings.....................................86
339. Chicken Soup...86
340. Ginger Chili Broccoli...86
341. Chicken Wings with Garlic Parmesan 86
342. Jerk Style Chicken Wings..................................87
343. Tasty Chicken Tenders......................................87
344. Chicken Skewers with Yogurt...........................87
345. Fried Lemon Chicken...87

346. Chicken's Liver ... 88
347. Chicken Parmigiana with Fresh Rosemary ... 88
348. Chicken Pinchos with Salsa Verde ... 88
349. Paprika Chicken Breasts ... 88
350. Spinach Loaded Chicken Breasts ... 89
351. Texas BBQ Chicken Thighs ... 89
352. French-Style Chicken Thighs ... 89
353. Sweet Chili & Ginger Chicken Wings ... 89
354. Spice-Rubbed Jerk Chicken Wings ... 89
355. Juicy Chicken with Bell Peppers ... 90
356. Quinoa Chicken Nuggets ... 90
357. Tarragon & Garlic Roasted Chicken ... 90
358. Comfort Chicken Drumsticks ... 90
359. Greek-Style Chicken Tacos ... 91
360. Cheesy Chicken Thighs with Parmesan Crust . 91
361. Pretzel Crusted Chicken with Spicy Mustard Sauce ... 91
362. Chinese-Style Sticky Turkey Thighs ... 91
363. Easy Hot Chicken Drumsticks ... 92
364. Crunchy Munch Chicken Tenders with Peanuts ... 92
365. Tarragon Turkey Tenderloins with Baby Potatoes ... 92
366. Mediterranean Chicken Breasts with Roasted Tomatoes ... 92
367. Thai Red Duck with Candy Onion ... 93
368. Rustic Chicken Legs with Turnip Chips ... 93
369. Easy Ritzy Chicken Nuggets ... 93
370. Asian Chicken Filets with Cheese ... 93
371. Paprika Chicken Legs with Brussels Sprouts ... 94
372. Asian Spicy Turkey ... 94
373. Spicy Chicken Drumsticks with Herbs ... 94
374. Classic Chicken with Peanuts ... 94
375. Turkey with Paprika and Tarragon ... 95
376. Italian-Style Chicken with Roma Tomatoes ... 95
377. Duck Breasts with Candy Onion and Coriander ... 95
378. Turkey Burgers with Crispy Bacon ... 95
379. Turkey Tenderloins with Gravy ... 96
380. Old-Fashioned Turkey Chili ... 96
381. Rustic Chicken Drumettes with Chives ... 96
382. Chicken Sausage in Dijon Sauce ... 96
383. Parsley & Lemon Turkey Risotto ... 96
384. Chicken with Vegetables & Coconut Milk Stew ... 97
385. Grilled Chicken Drumsticks with Summer Salad ... 97
386. Tuscan Vegetable Chicken Stew ... 97
387. Hot Chicken with Garlic & Mushrooms ... 97
388. Sage Chicken in Orange Gravy ... 98
389. Awesome Spicy Turkey Casserole with Tomatoes ... 98
390. Easy Italian Chicken Stew with Potatoes ... 98
391. Quick Swiss Chard & Chicken Stew ... 98
392. Delicious Turkey Burgers ... 99
393. Easy Primavera Chicken Stew ... 99
394. Dijon Mustard Chicken Breast ... 99
395. Bell Pepper & Chicken Stew ... 99
396. Weekend Turkey with Vegetables ... 99
397. Cranberry Turkey with Hazelnuts ... 100

398. Pork Tenders with Bell Peppers ... 100
399. Dijon Garlic Pork Tenderloin ... 100
400. Pork Neck with Salad ... 100
401. Cajun Pork Steaks ... 101
402. Wonton Taco Cups ... 101
403. Cajun Sweet-Sour Grilled Pork ... 101
404. Chinese Braised Pork Belly ... 101
405. Air Fryer Sweet and Sour Pork ... 101
406. Pork Loin with Potatoes ... 102
407. Fried Pork Scotch Egg ... 102
MEAT ... 103
408. Spicy Pork Tenderloin with Broccoli ... 103
409. Mexican Hot Meatloaf ... 103
410. Garlicky Pork Belly with New Potatoes ... 103
411. Spanish Pork Kabobs (Pinchos Moreno's) ... 104
412. Simple Greek Pork Sirloin with Tzatziki ... 104
413. Beef Sausage and Veggie Sandwiches ... 104
414. Cheese and Sausage Pepper Pocket ... 105
415. Sizzling Beef Steak Fajitas ... 105
416. Pork Belly ... 105
417. Sirloin Steak ... 106
418. Vietnamese Grilled Pork ... 106
419. Meatloaf ... 106
420. Herbed Lamb Chops ... 106
421. Spicy Lamb Sirloin Steak ... 107
422. Pork Chops ... 107
423. Steak ... 107
424. Meatloaf Slider Wraps ... 108
425. Homemade Beef Liver Soufflé ... 108
426. Rib Eye Steak with Avocado Sauce ... 108
427. Hot Flank Steaks with Roasted Peanuts ... 108
428. Authentic Wiener Beef Schnitzel ... 109
429. Dreamy Beef Steak with Rice, Broccoli and Green Beans ... 109
430. Mustard Pork Chops with Lemon Zest ... 109
431. Herbed Beef Roast ... 109
432. Roast Pork Belly with Cumin ... 109
433. Ginger Rack Rib Steak ... 110
434. Sunday Night Garlic Beef Schnitzel ... 110
435. Meatballs with Parsley and Thyme ... 110
436. Garlic Lamb Chops with Thyme ... 110
437. Bacon-Wrapped Stuffed Pork Tenderloin ... 111
438. Basil Meatloaf with Parmesan ... 111
439. Cheesy Ground Beef and Mac Taco Casserole ... 111
440. Beefy Steak Topped with Chimichurri Sauce 111
441. Beef Ribeye Steak ... 112
442. Air Fryer Roast Beef ... 112
443. Beef Korma ... 112
444. Cumin-Paprika Rubbed Beef Brisket ... 112
445. Chili-Espresso Marinated Steak ... 112
446. Crispy Mongolian Beef ... 113
447. Beef & Lemon Schnitzel for One ... 113
448. Crispy Beef Schnitzel ... 113
449. Simple Steak ... 113
450. Garlic-Cumin and Orange Juice Marinated Steak ... 113
451. Beef Taco Fried Egg Rolls ... 114
452. Beef with Beans ... 114
453. Flavors Herb Lamb Chops ... 114

454. Simple & Quick Lamb Chops 114
455. Breaded Pork Chops 114
456. Cheese Garlic Pork Chops 115
457. Creole Pork Chops 115
458. Tender Pork Chops 115
459. Simple Dash Seasoned Pork Chops 115
460. Jerk Pork Butt 115
461. Asian Lamb 116
462. Beef Stew 116
463. Mushroom Beef Stew 116
464. Spicy Pepper Beef 116
465. Slow Cooked Beef Brisket 117
466. Slow Cooked Pork Chops 117
VEGETABLE RECIPES 118
467. Sweet Potato Casserole 118
468. Delicious Roasted Garlic Mushrooms 118
469. Roasted Cauliflower, Olives and Chickpeas 118
470. Fruit and Vegetable Skewers 118
471. Roasted Sweet Potatoes with Rosemary 119
472. Tangy Roasted Broccoli with Garlic 119
473. Roasted Carrots with Garlic 119
474. Savory Roasted Balsamic Vegetables 119
475. Baked Macaroni and Cheese 119
476. Curried Zucchini Chips 119
477. Lemony Okra 120
478. Buttered Broccoli 120
479. Baked Sweet Potatoes 120
480. Beetroot Chips 120
481. Buffalo Cauliflower 120
482. Buttermilk Fried Mushrooms 121
483. Chinese Spring Rolls 121
484. Onion Pakoras 121
485. Onion Rings 122
486. Roasted Green Beans 122
487. Basil Tomatoes 122
488. Pesto Tomatoes 122
489. Sweet & Spicy Parsnips 123
490. Caramelized Baby Carrots 123
491. Carrot with Spinach 123
492. Broccoli with Sweet Potatoes 124
493. Vegetable Air Fryer with Beans, Peppers and Carrots 124
494. Roasted Avocado in Bacon 124
495. Fried Cauliflower with Fresh Herbs 124
496. Fried Liver with Onion and Herbs 125
497. Green Asparagus with Salmon Fillet and Dill Butter 125
498. Chicken Breast Strips with Green Asparagus of Asian Style 125
499. Salmon Fillet on Green Asparagus and Kohlrabi 125
500. Roasted trout with butter and lemon 126
501. Steak on spring onions with cherry sauce 126
RICE RECIPES 127
502. Cheesy Rice with Artichoke Hearts 127
503. Salty Jasmin Rice 127
504. Rice with Salmon Fillets 127
505. Savory Beef Soup Rice 127
506. Black Rice Pudding 127
507. Buttered Brown Rice 128

508. Hawaiian Style Rice 128
509. Brown Rice with Black Beans 128
510. Rice Combo 128
511. Breakfast Rice 128
512. Rice Veggies Stew 129
513. Easy Brown Rice 129
514. Rice and Vegetables Mix 129
515. Spiced Natural Rice 129
SOUP AND STEW RECIPES 130
516. Creamy Pumpkin Soup 130
517. Goulash 130
518. Mushroom and Wild Rice Soup 130
519. Loaded Potato Soup 131
520. Italian Sausage, Potato, and Kale Soup 131
521. Butternut Squash, Apple, Bacon and Orzo Soup 131
522. Braised Pork and Black Bean Stew 132
523. Fish Chowder and Biscuits 132
524. Coconut and Shrimp Bisque 132
525. Roasted Tomato and Seafood Stew 133
526. Chicken Enchilada Soup 133
527. Chicken Noodle Soup 133
528. Chicken Potpie Soup 134
529. Tex-Mex Chicken Tortilla Soup 134
530. Chicken Tomatillo Stew 135
SNACKS RECIPES 136
531. Classic French Fries 136
532. Olive Oil Sweet Potato Chips 136
533. Parmesan Breaded Zucchini Chips 136
534. Low-Carb Cheese-Stuffed Jalapeño Poppers .136
535. Vidalia Onion Blossom 137
536. Crispy Fried Pickle Chips 137
537. Spiced Nuts 137
538. Pigs in a Blanket 138
539. Breaded Artichoke Hearts 138
540. Crunchy Pork Egg Rolls 138
541. Air Fry Bacon 139
542. Crunchy Bacon Bites 139
543. Easy Jalapeno Poppers 139
544. Perfect Crab Dip 139
545. Spinach Dip 139
546. Sweet Potato Tots 139
547. Herb Zucchini Slices 140
548. Ranch Kale Chips 140
549. Curried Sweet Potato Fries 140
550. Roasted Almonds 140
551. Pepperoni Chips 140
552. Crispy Eggplant 141
553. Steak Nuggets 141
554. Cheese Bacon Jalapeno Poppers 141
555. Cabbage Chips 141
556. Fried Calzones 141
557. Reuben Calzones 142
558. Popcorn 142
559. Mexican-Style Corn on the Cob 142
560. Salt and Vinegar Chickpeas 142
561. Curry Chickpeas 143
562. Buffalo-Ranch Chickpeas 143
563. Whole-Wheat Pizzas 143
564. Basic Hot Dogs 143

- 565. Feta Cheese Dough Balls 144
- 566. Flourless Crunchy Cheese Straws 144
- 567. Veggie Wontons 144
- 568. Avocado Rolls 145
- 569. Fried Ravioli 145
- 570. Corn Fritters 145
- 571. Mushroom Pizza 145
- 572. Onion Appetizers 146
- 573. Crispy Brussels Sprouts 146
- 574. Sweet Potato Tots 146
- 575. Popcorn Tofu 146
- 576. Black Bean Burger 147
- 577. Crisp Sweet Potato Fries 147
- 578. Snack-Sized Calzones 147
- 579. Jalapeno and Cheese Balls 148
- 580. Parmesan Chicken Nuggets 148
- 581. Date Tapas 148
- 582. Hush Puppies 149
- 583. Flavorful Salsa 149
- 584. Cheddar Cheese Dip 149
- 585. Creamy Eggplant Dip 149
- 586. Delicious Nacho Dip 150
- 587. Spinach Dip 150
- 588. Chipotle Bean Dip 150
- 589. Asian Boiled Peanuts 150
- 590. Mexican Pinto Bean Dip 151
- 591. Perfect Cinnamon Toast 151
- 592. Easy Baked Chocolate Mug Cake 151
- 593. Angel Food Cake 151
- 594. Fried Peaches 151
- 595. Easy Donuts 152
- 596. Apple Pie in Air Fryer 152
- 597. Raspberry Cream Roll-Ups 152

BREAD RECIPES 154
- 598. Sourdough Bread 154
- 599. Cream Bread 154
- 600. Sunflower Seeds Bread 154
- 601. Date Bread 154
- 602. Banana Bread 155
- 603. Nutty Banana Bread 155
- 604. Yogurt Banana Bread 155
- 605. Peanut Butter Banana Bread 156
- 606. Soda Brad 156
- 607. Baguette Bread 156
- 608. Yogurt Bread 157
- 609. Banana & Raisin Bread 157
- 610. Brown Sugar Banana Bread 158
- 611. Date & Walnut Bread 158

DESSERTS RECIPES 159
- 612. Easy Lava Cake 159
- 613. Tasty Cheese Bites 159
- 614. Apple Chips with Dip 159
- 615. Delicious Spiced Apples 159
- 616. Easy Cheesecake 159
- 617. Coconut Pie 160
- 618. Strawberry Muffins 160
- 619. Pecan Muffins 160
- 620. Chocolate Brownie 160
- 621. Blueberry Muffins 160
- 622. Pumpkin Muffins 161
- 623. Cappuccino Muffins 161
- 624. Moist Cinnamon Muffins 161
- 625. Cream Cheese Muffins 161
- 626. Cinnamon Apple Chips 162
- 627. Sweet Pumpkin Loaf 162
- 628. Milky Egg Custard 162
- 629. Raisins Carrot Pie 162
- 630. Cracker Cheesecake 163
- 631. Ginger Apricot Tart 163
- 632. Banana Oatmeal Bites 163
- 633. Honey Pumpkin Delights 163
- 634. Nutmeg Blueberry Crumble 164
- 635. Cherry Crust Pie 164
- 636. Cream Cheesecake Soufflé 164
- 637. Creamy Chocolate Profiteroles 165
- 638. Oats Cookies 165
- 639. Avocado Cream 165
- 640. Cocoa Brownies 165
- 641. Cocoa Cream 165
- 642. Coconut Ramekins 166
- 643. Carrot Bars 166
- 644. Pecan Bars 166
- 645. Chocolate Cream 166
- 646. Walnut and Pecan Bars 166
- 647. Yogurt and Berries Cream 166
- 648. Cream Cheese Pudding 167
- 649. Rhubarb Cake 167
- 650. Mango and Plums Bowls 167
- 651. Rhubarb Cream 167
- 652. Lime Cake 167
- 653. Cinnamon Apple Bowls 167
- 654. Instant Pot Chocolate Chip Cookie in Air Fryer 168
- 655. Air Fried Chocolate Chips 168
- 656. Flourless Chocolate Almond Cupcakes ... 168
- 657. Air Fryer Gluten-Free Chocolate Lava Cake ... 169
- 658. Air Fried Sweet Potato Dessert 169
- 659. Gluten-Free Easy Coconut Pie in Air Fryer ... 169
- 660. Air Fryer Brownies 170
- 661. Air Fryer Doughnuts 170
- 662. Perfect Cinnamon Toast 171
- 663. Easy Baked Chocolate Mug Cake 171
- 664. Angel Food Cake 171
- 665. Fried Peaches 171
- 666. Apple Dumplings 172
- 667. Apple Pie in Air Fryer 172
- 668. Raspberry Cream Roll-Ups 172
- 669. Air Fryer Chocolate Cake 172
- 670. Banana-Choco Brownies 173
- 671. Chocolate Donuts 173
- 672. Easy Air Fryer Donuts 173
- 673. Chocolate Soufflé for Two 173
- 674. Fried Bananas with Chocolate Sauce 173
- 675. Apple Hand Pies 174

OTHER OMNI AIR FRYER LID FAVORITES 175
- 676. Deviled Eggs with Bacon 175
- 677. Quick Greek Revithokeftedes 175
- 678. Baked Philadelphia Mushroom Omelet ... 175
- 679. Spiced and Baked Mixed Nuts 175
- 680. Fingerling Potatoes with Cashew Sauce ... 176

- 681. Brown Rice Bowl 176
- 682. Greek-style Fruit Skewers 176
- 683. Yummy Hot Fruit Bake 176
- 684. Cornmeal Puddings with Jamaican Flair 177
- 685. Mushroom Frittata with Mozzarella 177

DEHYDRATOR AND CASSEROLE RECIPES 178
- 686. Eggplant Jerky 178
- 687. Dehydrated Pear Slices 178
- 688. Sausage Casserole 178
- 689. Squash Casserole 178
- 690. Apple Chips 178
- 691. Apple Sweet Potato Fruit Leather 179
- 692. Dehydrated Mango 179
- 693. Sausage Zucchini Casserole 179
- 694. Broccoli Rice Casserole 179
- 695. Cheesy Mashed Potato Casserole 179
- 696. Corn Gratin 179
- 697. Flavors Crab Casserole 180
- 698. Broccoli Chicken Casserole 180
- 699. Asian Mushroom Jerky 180
- 700. Banana Fruit Leather 180

INTRODUCTION

The Instant Omni Toaster Oven Air Fryer is ideal for home cooks who need quick, nutritious, simple dinners consistently—at the bit of a catch. Its extra-enormous limit fits six cuts of toast or a 12" pizza, and lets you air fry, dry out, cook, toast, heat, and sear all the nourishment you have to take care of your family and your companions. Brisk and in any event, warming guarantees firm, brilliant outcomes without fail. With an assortment of one-contact cooking choices, there's no compelling reason to compute temperature, weight, or time. Select one of the seven Smart Programs and click start. Be that as it may, for you foodies out there, the Omni Toaster Oven gives the adaptability to alter settings to tweak your culinary experience.

This air fry toaster oven likewise accompanies all the embellishments your requirement for rotisserie cooking. The superior convection oven, alongside the rotisserie work, conveys succulent, flavorful rotisserie dishes.

So get together those different apparatuses coating your counter and account for the Omni Toaster Oven today.

Understanding Instant Omni Plus Toaster Oven

The Instant Omni plus toaster oven is the perfect oven to use in the home kitchen or in a professional setting. Its range of cooking programs and easy to use control panel will definitely make cooking a convenient job for you. This toaster oven is a breeze for those who want to cook large servings at a time. It is an advanced version of the previously launched Instant Omni, and it provides greater capacity and additional cooking functions.

Advantages of Using Instant Omni

The following features of the Instant Omni make this toaster a must to keep cooking appliance:

Eight Smart Functions

This toaster oven combines all the cooking functions of an oven, broiler, air fryer, and a toaster. Imagine you have one single appliance that can carry out all such functions.

Each smart program comes with a preset temperature and timer settings, which are also adjustable as per the needs.

Two Cooking Modes

One feature that makes Instant Omni a toaster oven different from other toaster ovens is its two cooking modes. This feature is rare or impossible to find in other toaster ovens. There are two cooking modes which can be used to cook different types of meals. The two modes are:

Rotate

Using this mode, a user can cook or roast its chicken, duck, or any other meat on the rotisserie. The heat is provided to the food as it rotates on the rotisserie stick.

Convection

This mode is suitable for all other cooking functions in which food is placed in a fixed position. The heat is produced and regulated inside the oven through convection.

XL Capacity

The size of Instant Omni takes it to the top of the list when compared to other toaster ovens. Its great capacity to accommodate all food types, whether you want to cook a whole chicken inside or what to Air fryer a large batch of French fries, the appliance is capable of carrying them all at a time. So, it is perfect to use for large families. The XL capacity of the Instant Omni can cook the following in a single layer:

- 12" Pizza
- Six Toast Slices

Easy to Read Display screen

The display panel of the Instant Omni is easy to understand. It has a display at the center, which is surrounded by the touch keys for all the smart programs, the cooking modes, and the on/off functions.

There are separate knobs attached at the two ends of the touch panel, which can be used to adjust the cooking programs, time, and temperature manually.

Intuitive Customizable Programs

All the smart programs of Instant Omni are customizable. Even when the cooking program is running, the settings can be changed using the temperature and time knobs.

The adjustable programs allow the users to switch from one cooking settings to another with its super flexible heating system.

Even-Heat: Toasts Both Sides

Due to its convection heating mechanism, the Instant Omni toaster oven is capable of heating the food from all sides. This feature ensures even heating. When bread slices or bagels are toasted inside this toaster oven, they are cooked both from the top and the bottom. Without flipping a single slice, a user can get evenly cooked and crispy toasts.

When it comes to electric appliances, it is important to inspect all the parts of the appliance before giving it a test run. The Instant Omni toaster oven comes with the following basic elements and the accessories.

The Oven Base Unit
- Rack tray
- Crumb Tray
- Oven Door
- Rotisserie Catch
- Rotisserie Spit & Forks Rotisserie Lift
- Air Fry Basket
- Baking pan
- Baking trays
- Power plug

Inside the Instant Omni plus oven, there are three grooves on both sides. These grooves are used to insert three rack trays in the oven. The uppermost grooves can be used to insert the trays when the food needs to be broiled. The center grooves are for Air frying and roasting purposes.

The lowermost level is used to place the food which needs to be baked, reheated, or dehydrated. Crumb tray is inserted at the bottom to protect the bottom of the oven from the food particle during cooking.

The rotisserie stick can be inserted and used to fix the meat of chicken. This stick can be fixed on the inner side of the center portion of the oven into the rotisserie catch. Air fryer basket can be placed on the lower rack when required.

Control Panel
The control panel of the appliance is fixed on the front top portion of the oven. The center black panel consists of the touch screen, which shows all the functions. This panel is placed in between two knobs which are used to adjust the time and cooking temperature:

Smart Program Keys: The seven smart program keys are located at the bottom of the black panel. Any of the programs can be selected by rotating the preset dial.

Display: right above the keys, there is a display which lights in blue colored figures indicating the time, temperature, and other indicators like Start, Cancel, Door, Warm, Flip or turn, etc.

Cooking Modes: There are two keys to the cooking modes, indicated by the: Rotate and Convection marks.

Start and Cancel Key: At the two corners of the display screen, there are keys to start or cancel a selected program.

Dials: The Temp/time dial can be used to adjust the cooking time and temperature. Rotate the dial to the right to increase the value of rotate it to the left to decrease the values. The Preset dial is used to switch the cooking modes.

Breakfasts

1. Salsa Eggs
Preparation Time: 10 minutes
Cooking Time: 20 minutes
Servings: 2
Ingredients:
- 1/2 cup grated cheese
- Pepper
- Salt
- 1/2 tbsp. of chopped chives
- 1 tbsp. of mild salsa
- 2 Eggs, whisked
- 1/2 chopped Bell pepper
- 1/2 chopped Green pepper

Directions:
1. Turn the air fryer to 360 degrees. Prepare two ramekins with some cooking spray and divide the bell peppers into each. Whip together pepper, salt, chives, salsa, and eggs. Divide between the ramekins and sprinkle the cheese on top.
2. Pour into lined frying basket and allow it to cook. After twenty minutes, take these out and cool down before enjoying.

Nutrition: Calories 142 Fat 9g Carbs 5g Protein 10g

2. Banana Oats
Preparation Time: 10 minutes
Cooking Time: 20 minutes
Servings: 2
Ingredients:
- 1/2 cup milk
- 1/2 cup heavy cream
- 1 banana, peeled and mashed
- 1/2 tbsp. of vanilla
- 2 tbsp. sugar
- 1 cup old fashioned oats
- Cooking spray
- 1/2 tbsp. baking powder
- 1 tbsp. butter
- 1 Egg, whisked

Directions:
1. Turn on the air fryer to 340 degrees. Bring out a bowl and mix together all the ingredients except the cooking spray.
2. Divide this between the ramekins. Grease the air fryer up.
3. Add the ramekins inside and cook for a bit. After 20 minutes, they are done and ready to serve.

Nutrition: Calories 533 Fat 26g Carbs 58g Protein 113g

3. Jalapeno Popper Egg Cup
Preparation Time: 5 minutes
Cooking Time: 10 minutes
Servings: 2
Ingredients:
- 1/2 cup shredded cheddar cheese
- 1/4 cup cream cheese
- 1/2 cup pickled jalapenos
- 4 Eggs

Directions:
1. Beat the eggs inside a bowl before adding to muffin cup.
2. In another bowl, mix the cheddar, jalapenos and cream cheese.
3. Place the microwave-proof bowl into the microwave and heat up for half a minute.
4. Take a bit of the mixture and put it into one egg cup. Repeat with the rest of the mixture.
5. Add these into the air fryer basket and heat it up to 320 degrees.
6. After ten minutes, these are done, and you can serve.

Nutrition: Calories 354 Fat 25g Carbs 2g Protein 21g

4. Breakfast Frittata
Preparation Time: 10 minute
Cooking Time: 15 minutes
Servings: 2
Ingredients:
- Pepper and salt
- 2 tbsp. milk
- 1/2 cup chopped tomato
- 1/4 cup sliced mushrooms
- 2 tbsp. chopped chives
- 1 cup egg whites

Directions:
1. Turn the air fryer on to 320 degrees.
2. Whisk everything above in a bowl until combined.
3. Coat a frying pan using some cooking spray.
4. Pour the frittata mixture into the pan.
5. Move this to the air fryer and let it bake.
6. After 15 minutes, take out and serve.

Nutrition: Calories 79 Carbs 3g Fat 1g Protein 14g

5. Easy French Toast
Preparation Time: 5 minutes
Cooking Time: 6 minutes
Servings: 2
Ingredients:
- 2 Eggs
- 2/3 cup milk
- 1 tbsp. vanilla
- 1 tbsp. powdered Cinnamon
- 4 Bread slices

Directions:
1. Turn on the air fryer to 320 degrees.
2. Take out a bowl and combine the milk, cinnamon, vanilla, and eggs.
3. Dip each bread slice into this, shaking off the extra and add to a pan.
4. Place the pan into the air fryer.
5. After three minutes, flip the bread around and cook a bit longer before serving.

Nutrition: Calories 166 Carbs 161g Fat 7g Protein 10g

6. Scrambled Eggs

Preparation Time: 5 minutes
Cooking Time: 9 minutes
Servings: 2
Ingredients:
- Pepper and salt
- 2 Bread slices
- 4 Eggs

Directions:
1. Turn on the air fryer to 400 degrees. Warm up the slices of bread inside for a bit.
2. Toss your eggs to a pan and season with both of your seasonings to taste. Place the pan within the air fryer and cook. After two minutes, stir and cook a bit longer.
3. Four minutes later, take the eggs out of the air fryer and add them to the bread slices before enjoying.

Nutrition: Calories 150 Carbs 5g Fat 9g Protein 12g

7. Turkey Burrito
Preparation Time: 5 minutes
Cooking Time: 10 minutes
Servings: 2
Ingredients:
- Tortillas to serve
- 1/4 cup grated mozzarella cheese
- Pepper
- Salt
- 2 tbsp. salsa
- 1 avocado, sliced
- 2 Eggs
- Red bell pepper, halved, sliced
- 4 slices of cooked turkey breast

Directions:
1. Bring out a bowl and whisk the pepper, salt, and eggs. Put them into a pan and then into the air fryer. Cook these for five minutes at 400 degrees. When this is done, add the eggs to a plate.
2. Add the tortillas onto a counter and divide all the ingredients between them. Roll these up and set to the side. Turn the temperature of the air fryer to 300 degrees. Line the basket with tin foil and add the burritos inside.
3. After 3 minutes of cooking, these are ready to serve.

Nutrition: Calories 349 Carbs 20g Fat 23g Protein 21g

8. Bread Pudding
Preparation Time: 10 minutes
Cooking Time: 22 minutes
Servings: 2
Ingredients:
- 1 1/4 cup soft butter
- 3/4 cup flour
- 1 tsp. Powdered cinnamon
- 1/2 tsp. vanilla
- 20 1/2 tbsp. Honey
- 3 tbsp. peeled and roughly chopped apple
- 1 tbsp. cornstarch
- 6 tbsp. water
- 1/3 cup of brown Sugar
- 6 tbsp. milk
- 25 lb. white bread, cubed

Directions:
1. Bring out one bowl and combine the water, milk, honey, cinnamon, vanilla, cornstarch, apple, and bread, whisking well. In a second bowl, mix together your butter, flour, and sugar to create a crumble.
2. Press half of your crumble mixture into the air fryer bottom and add the apple mixture on top. Add the rest of the first mixture. Turn the air fryer on to 350 degrees and cook this for a bit. After 22 minutes, divide the pudding onto some plates and serve.

Nutrition: Calories 261 Fat 7g Carbs 8g Protein 5g

9. Ham Cups
Preparation Time: 10 minutes
Cooking Time: 12 minutes
Servings: 2
Ingredients:
- 1/2 cup of shredded cheese
- 2 tablespoons of white onion
- 2 tablespoons of diced red bell pepper
- 4 Eggs
- 3 tablespoons of diced green bell pepper
- 2 tablespoon of sour cream
- 4 slices of Deli ham

Directions:
1. Take one piece of ham and add it to the bottom of four baking cups. In another bowl, whisk the eggs with the sour cream before adding the green and red pepper and onion.
2. Pour this mixture of eggs into the baking cups and top with the cheddar. Add to the basket in the air fryer. Turn the air fryer on to 320 degrees. Cook the ham cups for the next 12 minutes before serving.

Nutrition Calories 382 Carbs 5g Fat 24g Protein 29g

10. Breakfast Calzone
Preparation Time: 10 minutes
Cooking Time: 15 minutes
Servings: 2
Ingredients:
- 4 tbsp. cheddar cheese
- 0.25 lb. breakfast sausage, cooked and crumbled
- 2 Scrambled eggs
- 1 whole egg
- 1/2 oz. cream cheese
- 1/4 cup almond flour
- 3/4 cup shredded mozzarella

Directions:
1. Put the cream cheese, mozzarella cheese, and almond flour into a bowl. Add to the microwave for sixty seconds. Stir this until it is smooth and can form a ball. Add the egg and stir to make nice dough.
2. Put this between sheets of parchment paper and use a rolling pin to make a crust. Cut into four rectangles.

3. In another bowl, mix the scrambled eggs and sausage. Divide this between the pieces of dough, putting on the lower part of the rectangle. Sprinkle on the cheddar. Fold this over and seal up the edges. Cover the basket of the air fryer with some parchment paper and add these inside. Turn the air fryer to 380 degrees and then add the calzone inside. Flip halfway through.
4. After 15 minutes, these are done, and you can serve.
Nutrition: Calories 560 Carbs 4g Fat 42g Protein 34g

11. Morning Salad
Preparation Time: 5 minutes
Cooking Time: 15 minutes
Servings: 4
Ingredients:
- 1 tsp. olive oil
- 2 tbsp. chives, chopped
- 2 cups mustard greens
- 0.5 lb. Cherry tomatoes, cubed

Directions:
1. Turn the air fryer on to 360 degrees.
2. Place all of the ingredients inside to cook.
3. After fifteen minutes, and shaking around halfway through, divide into a few bowls and serve.
Nutrition: Calories 224 Carbs 2g Fat 8g Protein 7g

12. Coconut Pudding
Preparation Time: 15 minutes
Cooking Time: 20 minutes
Servings: 5
Ingredients:
- 1/2 cup shredded coconut
- 1 cup cauliflower rice
- 3 cups coconut milk
- 2 tbsp. stevia

Directions:
1. Add the ingredients into a pan that will fit with the air fryer. Whisk to combine.
2. Turn the air fryer on to 360 degrees. Add the pan into the air fryer to cook.
3. After 20 minutes, this is done, and you can divide into between four bowls and enjoy for breakfast.
Nutrition: Calories 211 Carbs 4g Fat 11g Protein 8g

13. Loaded Cauliflower Bake
Preparation Time: 5 minutes
Cooking Time: 15 minutes
Servings: 4
Ingredients:
- 8 tbsp. sour cream
- 6 eggs
- 10 1/2 cup cauliflower, chopped
- 1/4 cup heavy whipping cream
- 1 avocado, peeled and pitted
- 1 cup cheddar cheese
- 12 slices bacon, cooked and crumbled
- 2 Sliced scallions

Directions:
1. Turn on the air fryer to heat up to 320 degrees.
2. Take out a bowl and whisk the cream and eggs together.
3. Pour into a round baking dish that can hold four cups.
4. Add the cauliflower to mix and top with the cheddar before adding to the basket of the air fryer.
5. After 20 minutes of cooking, this will be done. Take it out and slice into four pieces.
6. Slice the avocado and split between the portions. Top with some sour cream, bacon, and scallions before serving.
Nutrition: Calories 512 Carbs 73g Fat 38g Protein 27g

14. Easy Granola
Preparation Time: 5 minutes
Cooking Time: 15 minutes
Servings: 6
Ingredients:
- 1 tsp cinnamon, ground
- 2 tbsp. butter
- 1 cup coconut flakes
- 1/4 cup Granular erythritol
- 1/3 cup sunflower seeds
- 1 cup almond slivers
- 1/4 cup chocolate chips
- 1/4 cup golden flaxseed
- 2 cup chopped pecans

Directions:
1. Take out a bowl and meld everything listed above.
2. Turn the air fryer to 320 degrees.
3. Pour the mixture into a baking dish and add it to the basket in the air fryer.
4. After five minutes, take this out of the air fryer and give it time to cool down before serving.
Nutrition: Calories 617 Carbs 63g Fat 10g Protein 11g

15. Fennel Frittata
Preparation Time: 13 minutes
Cooking Time: 20 minutes
Servings: 6
Ingredients:
- Cooking spray
- 1 tbsp. sweet paprika
- 2 tsp cilantro, chopped
- 6 eggs, whisked
- 1 fennel bulb, shredded

Directions:
1. Turn on the air fryer to 370 degrees. Mix together all of the ingredients besides the cooking spray.
2. Bring out a baking pan and prepare it before pouring the frittata mix inside. Place this pan into your hot air fryer and let it bake. After 15 minutes, divide between the six plates and serve.
Nutrition: Calories 200 Carbs 5g Fat 12g Protein 8g

16. Chicken Spinach Casserole
Preparation Time: 10 minutes
Cooking Time: 25 minutes
Servings: 4

Ingredients:
- 1-pound chicken meat, ground
- 1 tablespoon olive oil
- ½ tablespoon sweet paprika
- 12 eggs, whisked
- 1 cup baby spinach
- Salt and black pepper to taste

Directions:
1. Beat eggs with paprika, salt, and pepper in a large bowl. Stir in spinach and chicken. Pour the egg spinach mixture into a small casserole dish and place it inside the Instant Pot. Put on the Instant Air Fryer lid and cook on Bake mode for 25 minutes at 35 1.0 degrees F. Once done, remove the lid and serve warm.

Nutrition: Calories: 270 Protein 7g Carbs: 14g Fat 1g

17. Cheese Sausage Quiche

Preparation Time: 10 minutes
Cooking Time: 20 minutes
Servings: 6

Ingredients:
- 4 bacon slices, cooked and crumbled
- a drizzle olive oil
- 2 cups of coconut milk
- 2½ cups cheddar cheese, shredded
- 1-pound breakfast sausage, chopped
- 2 eggs
- Salt and black pepper to taste
- 3 tablespoon cilantro, chopped

Directions:
1. Beat eggs with cheese, milk, salt, cilantro, and pepper in a suitable bowl.
2. Pour eggs into the Instant Pot and top it with sausage and bacon. Put on the Instant Air Fryer lid and cook on Bake mode for 20 minutes at 350 degrees F. Once done, remove the lid and serve warm.

Nutrition: Calories: 244 Protein 9g Carbs: 15g Fat 11g

18. Salsa Chicken Burrito

Preparation Time: 10 minutes
Cooking Time: 14 minutes
Servings: 4

Ingredients:
- 4 chicken breast slices, cooked and shredded
- 1 green bell pepper, sliced
- 2 eggs, whisked
- 1 avocado, peeled, pitted and sliced
- 2 tablespoons mild salsa
- Salt and black pepper to taste
- 2 tablespoon cheddar cheese, grated
- 2 tortillas

Directions:
1. Take a pan, small enough to fit the Instant. Whisk eggs with salt and pepper, pour it into the pan. Transfer this pan in the Instant Pot.
2. Put on the Instant Air Fryer lid and cook on Bake mode for 5 minutes at 400 degrees F. Once done, remove the lid and serve warm. Cook for exactly 5 minutes at 400 degrees F. Crumble the cooked egg and toss it with chicken, avocado, bell peppers and cheese in a bowl. Spread the tortillas on the working surface and divide the egg mixture.
3. Roll the tortillas to make the burritos. Layer the Air fryer basket with a foil sheet and place the burritos in the basket. Put on the Instant Air Fryer lid and cook on Air Fry mode for 4 minutes at 400 degrees F. Once done, remove the lid and serve warm.

Nutrition: Calories: 329 Protein 8g Carbs: 20g Fat 13g

19. Morning Oats Casserole

Preparation Time: 10 minutes
Cooking Time: 20 minutes
Servings: 6

Ingredients:
- 2 cups old fashioned oats
- 1 tablespoon baking powder
- ⅓ cup of Sugar
- 1 tablespoon cinnamon powder
- 1 cup blueberries
- 1 banana, peeled and mashed
- 2 cups of milk
- 2 eggs, whisked
- 2 tablespoon butter
- 1 tablespoon vanilla extract
- Cooking spray

Directions:
1. Beat eggs with sugar, cinnamon, baking powder, blueberries, banana, and vanilla in a suitable bowl. Pour it into the Instant Pot and top it with oats. Put on the Instant Air Fryer lid and cook on Bake mode for 20 minutes at 320 degrees F. Once done, remove the lid and serve warm.

Nutrition: Calories: 260 Protein 10g Carbs: 9g Fat 4g

20. Cheesy Bread Bake

Preparation Time: 10 minutes
Cooking Time: 30 minutes
Servings: 6

Ingredients:
- 1-pound white bread, cubed
- 1-pound smoked bacon, cooked and chopped
- ¼ cup avocado oil
- 1 red onion, chopped
- 30 oz. canned tomatoes, chopped
- ½ pound cheddar cheese, shredded
- 2 tablespoon chives, chopped
- ½ pound Monterey jack cheese, shredded
- 2 tablespoon chicken stock
- Salt and black pepper to taste
- 8 eggs, whisked

Directions:
1. Grease the baking pan with oil. Add everything to this pan except the chives. Place the pan in the Instant Pot and Put on the Instant Air Fryer lid and cook on Bake mode for 30 minutes at 350 degrees F. Once done, remove the lid and serve warm.

Nutrition: Calories: 211 Protein 3g Carbs: 14g Fat 8g

21. Cream Cheese Omelet

Preparation Time: 10 minutes
Cooking Time: 20 minutes
Servings: 6
Ingredients:
- 1½ pounds hash browns
- 1 cup almond milk
- Olive oil a drizzle
- 6 bacon slices, chopped
- 8 oz. cream cheese, softened
- 1 yellow onion, chopped
- 1 cup cheddar cheese, shredded
- 6 spring onions, chopped
- Salt and black pepper to taste
- 6 eggs

Directions:
1. Whisk everything in a bowl except the spring onions.
2. Pour this mixture into the Instant Pot. Put on the Instant Air Fryer lid and cook on Bake mode for 20 minutes at 350 degrees F. Once done, remove the lid and garnish with spring onions. Serve fresh.

Nutrition: Calories 231Protein 12gCarbs 8gFat 9g

22. Roasted Peppers Frittata

Preparation Time: 10 minutes
Cooking Time: 20 minutes
Servings: 6
Ingredients:
- 6 oz. jarred roasted red bell peppers, chopped
- 12 eggs, whisked
- ½ cup parmesan cheese, grated
- 3 garlic cloves, minced
- 2 tablespoon parsley, chopped
- Salt and black pepper to taste
- 2 tablespoon chives, chopped
- 6 tablespoon ricotta cheese
- A drizzle olive oil

Directions:
1. Whisk eggs with bell peppers, parsley, garlic, pepper, salt, ricotta and chives in a suitable bowl.
2. Transfer the egg mixture into the pan and drizzle the parmesan on top.
3. Place this pan in the Instant Pot. Put on the Instant Air Fryer lid and cook on Bake mode for 20 minutes at 350 degrees F. Once done, remove the lid and serve warm.

Nutrition: Calories: 262Protein 8gCarbs: 18gFat 6g

23. Blackberries Cornflakes Bowl

Preparation Time: 10 minutes
Cooking Time: 10 minutes
Servings: 4
Ingredients:
- 3 cups of milk
- 1 tablespoon Sugar
- 2 eggs whisked
- ¼ tablespoon nutmeg, a ground
- ¼ cup blackberries
- 4 tablespoon cream cheese, whipped
- 1½ cups of corn flakes

Directions:
1. Add everything to a suitably sized bowl and stir well. Add this prepared mixture to the Instant Pot. Put on the Instant Air Fryer lid and cook on Air Fryer mode for 10 minutes at 350 degrees F. Once done, remove the lid and serve warm.

Nutrition: Calories 180Protein 5gCarbs 12gFat 5g

24. Egg Paprika Scramble

Preparation Time: 10 minutes
Cooking Time: 10 minutes
Servings: 6
Ingredients:
- 4 eggs, whisked
- A drizzle olive oil
- Salt and black pepper to taste
- 1 red onion, chopped
- 2 teaspoons sweet paprika

Directions:
1. Add everything to a suitably sized bowl and stir well. Add this prepared mixture to the Instant Pot. Put on the Instant Air Fryer lid and cook on Bake mode for 10 minutes at 200 degrees F. Once done, remove the lid and serve warm.

Nutrition: Calories: 190Protein 4gCarbs: 12gFat 7g

25. White Mushroom Pie

Preparation Time: 10 minutes
Cooking Time: 10 minutes
Servings: 6
Ingredients:
- 1 tablespoon olive oil
- 9inch pie dough
- 6 white mushrooms, chopped
- 2 tablespoon bacon cooked and crumbled
- 3 eggs
- 1 red onion, chopped
- ½ cup heavy cream
- Salt and black pepper to taste
- ½ tablespoon thyme, a dried
- ¼ cup cheddar cheese, grated

Directions:
1. Grease a pie pan with oil, suitable to fit the Instant Pot. Spread the dough in the pie pan. Beat everything in a bowl except the cheese.
2. Pour this mixture over the dough and drizzle cheese on top.
3. Put on the Instant Air Fryer lid and cook on Bake mode for 10 minutes at 400 degrees F.
4. Once done, remove the lid and serve warm.

Nutrition: Calories 192Protein 7gCarbs 14gFat 6g

26. Morning Cauliflower Bake

Preparation Time: 10 minutes
Cooking Time: 20 minutes
Servings: 4
Ingredients:
- 1 cauliflower head stems removed, florets separated and steamed

- 3 carrots, chopped and steamed
- 2 oz. cheddar cheese, grated
- 3 eggs
- 2 oz. milk
- 2 teaspoon cilantro, chopped
- Salt and black pepper to taste

Directions:
1. Beat eggs with salt, pepper, parsley, and milk in a bowl. Spread the carrots and cauliflower in the Instant Pot. Pour the egg mixture over them. Put on the Instant Air Fryer lid and cook on Bake mode for 20 minutes at 350 degrees F. Once done, remove the lid and serve warm.

Nutrition: Calories 194Protein 6gCarbs 11gFat 4g

27. Cheese Bread Pizza

Preparation Time: 15 minutes.
Cooking Time: 8 minutes
Servings: 4
Ingredients:
- 6 bread slices
- 5 tablespoon butter, melted
- 3 garlic cloves, minced
- 6 teaspoon basil and tomato pesto
- 1 cup mozzarella cheese, grated

Directions:
1. Spread the bread slices on the working surface. Whisk butter with garlic and pesto in a bowl. Spread this mixture over the slices. Set the air fryer basket in the Instant Pot and place the pizza slices in the Air fryer basket and drizzle half of the cheese over them. Put on the Instant Air Fryer lid and cook on Air Fry mode for 8minutes at 350 degrees F. Once done, remove the lid and serve warm.

Nutrition: Calories 187Protein 5gCarbs 13gFat 6g

28. Cherry Tomato Omelet

Preparation Time: 15 minutes
Cooking Time: 11 minutes
Servings: 4
Ingredients:
- 1 sausage link, sliced
- 2 eggs, whisked
- 4 cherry tomatoes halved
- 1 tablespoon cilantro, chopped
- 1 tablespoon olive oil
- 1 tablespoon cheddar cheese, grated
- Salt and black pepper to taste

Directions:
1. Add sausage and tomatoes to the Instant Pot. Put on the Instant Air Fryer lid and cook on Bake mode for 5 minutes at 350 degrees F. Once done, remove the lid and serve warm. Take a pan, suitable to fit the Instant Pot. Add the sausage and tomatoes to the pan. Whisk remaining things in a bowl and pour it over the tomatoes. Place this pan in the Instant pot and put on the Instant Air Fryer lid and cook on Bake mode for 6minutes at 360 degrees F. Once done, remove the lid and serve warm.

Nutrition: Calories: 270Protein 16gCarbs: 23gFat 14g

29. Polenta Bites

Preparation Time: 10 minutes
Cooking Time: 15 minutes
Servings: 4
Ingredients:
- 1 cup cornmeal
- 3 cups of water
- Salt and black pepper to taste
- 1 tablespoon butter softened
- ¼ cup potato starch
- A drizzle vegetable oil
- Maple syrup for serving

Directions:
1. Add water and cornmeal to a pot and cook for 10 minutes on medium heat. Stir in butter and mix well, then put off the heat. Once the cornmeal is cooled, make small balls out of it. Place them in a greased baking pan and flatten them with a press of your hand.
2. Drizzle oil over them then place the pan in the Instant Pot. Put on the Instant Air Fryer lid and cook on Bake mode for 15 minutes at 380 degrees F. Once done, remove the lid and allow the bites to cool.
3. Garnish with maple syrup and serve.

Nutrition: Calories: 170Protein 4gCarbs: 12 Fat 2g

30. Blueberry Cream Cheese with French Toast

Preparation Time: 10 minutes
Cooking Time: 15 minutes
Servings: 4
Ingredients:
- 2 eggs, beaten
- 4 slices bread
- 3 tsp sugar
- 1½ cup corn flakes
- 1/3 cup milk
- ¼ tsp nutmeg
- 4 tbsp. berry-flavored cheese
- ¼ tsp salt

Directions:
1. Preheat the fryer to 400 degrees F.
2. In a medium bowl, mix together sugar, eggs, nutmeg, salt, and milk.
3. In a separate bowl, mix the blueberries and cheese.
4. Take 2 slices of bread and gently pour the bacon mixture over the slices.
5. Fill with the milk mixture. Top with the remaining two slices to make a sandwich. Dip the sandwiches over cornflakes to coat well.
6. Put the sandwiches in the freezer kitchen and cook for 8 minutes.
7. Serve with berries and syrup.
8. Enjoy!

Nutrition: Calories: 428 Fat 11.3g Carbs: 53.7g Protein 23.4g

31. Bread Cups Omelets

Preparation Time: 8 minutes

Cooking Time: 5 minutes
Servings: 4
Ingredients:
- 4 crusty rolls
- 5 eggs, beaten
- Pinch salt
- ½ tsp dried thyme
- 3 strips precooked bacon, chopped
- 2 tbsp. heavy cream
- 4 Gouda or Swiss cheese mini wedges, thin slices

Directions:
1. Preheat your air fryer 330 degrees F.
2. Chop off the rolls' tops, and get rid of the inside with your fingers.
3. Line a slice of cheese to the rolls and gently press down, so the cheese conforms to the inside of the roll. In a medium-sized bowl, mix eggs with heavy cream, bacon, thyme, salt, and pepper.
4. Fill the rolls with the egg mixture.
5. Place the rolls in your pan and cook for 8 to 12 minutes or until the eggs are puffy and the roll shows a golden texture. Enjoy!

Nutrition: Calories: 499 Fat 24g Carbs: 46g Protein 26g

32. Air Fried Potato Pancakes

Preparation Time: 15 minutes
Cooking Time: 10 minutes
Servings: 4
Ingredients:
- 200g potatoes, cleaned and peeled
- 1 chopped onion
- 1 egg, beaten
- ¼ c. low-Fat milk
- 2 tablespoons of unsalted butter
- ½ teaspoon of garlic powder
- ¼ tablespoon of kosher salt
- 3 tablespoon of all-purpose flour
- Ground black pepper

Directions:
1. Shred the peeled potatoes and then transfer in a bowl filled with cold water to wash off excess starch.
2. Drain the potatoes and the use of paper towels to dry off the potatoes.
3. In a mixing bowl, combine together egg, butter, garlic powder, salt and pepper, and lastly the flour. Stir well. Add in shredded potatoes.
4. Preheat Air Fryer to 390°F.
5. Pull out the Air Fryer cooking basket and then place ¼ cup of the potato pancake batter in the cooking basket.
6. Cook until golden brown for approximately 10 minutes.
7. Serve and enjoy!

Nutrition: Calories: 255 Fat 8.4 g Carbs 42 g Protein 7.1g

33. Exquisite Dutch Pancake

Preparation Time: 5 minutes
Cooking Time: 10 minutes
Servings: 4
Ingredients:
- 3 eggs, beaten
- 2 tablespoons of unsalted butter
- ½ c. flour
- 2 tbsp. powdered sugar
- ½ c. milk
- 1½ c. freshly sliced strawberries

Directions:
1. Preheat your Air Fryer to 330 degrees F.
2. Set a pan on low heat and melt butter.
3. In a medium-sized bowl, mix flour, milk, eggs, and vanilla until fully incorporated. Add the mixture to the pan with melted butter.
4. Place the pan in your air fryer's cooking basket and bake for 12-16 minutes until the pancake is fluffy and golden brown.
5. Drizzle powdered sugar and toss sliced strawberries on top.
6. Serve and enjoy!

Nutrition: Calories 196 Fat 9g Carbs: 19g Protein 16g

34. Clean Breakfast Sandwich

Preparation Time: 5 minutes
Cooking Time: 5 minutes
Servings: 1
Ingredients:
- 1 whole egg
- 1 slice English bacon
- Salt and pepper
- 1 slice bread
- ½ c. butter

Directions:
1. Heat your Fryer to 402 degrees F.
2. To one side of the bread slice, apply butter. Add the cracked egg on top and season with salt and pepper.
3. Place bacon on top.
4. Place the bread slice in your Air Fryer's cooking basket and bake for 3-5 minutes.
5. Serve and enjoy!

Nutrition: Calories: 320 Fat 13g Carbs: 33g Protein 17g

35. Craving Cinnamon Toast

Preparation Time: 5 minutes
Cooking Time: 8 minutes
Servings: 6
Ingredients:
- 12 slices bread
- Pepper
- ½ c. sugar
- 1 stick butter
- 1½ tsp vanilla extract
- 1½ tsp cinnamon

Directions:
1. Preheat your Air Fryer up to 400 degrees F.
2. In a microwave proof bowl, mix butter, pepper, sugar, and vanilla extract. Warm the mixture for 30 seconds until everything melts as you stir.
3. Pour the mixture over bread slices.

4. Lay the bread slices in your air fryer's cooking basket and cook for 5 minutes.
5. Serve with fresh banana and berry sauce.
6. Enjoy!
Nutrition: Calories 81 Fat 5g Carbs 8g Protein 3g

36. Wow! Feta Breakfast
Preparation Time: 5 minutes
Cooking Time: 10 minutes
Servings: 3
Ingredients:
- 3½ lbs. feta cheese
- Pepper
- 1 whole chopped onion
- 2 tbsp. chopped parsley
- 1 egg yolk
- Olive oil
- 5 sheets frozen filo pastry

Direction
1. Preheat the Air Fryer to 400 degrees F.
2. Cut each of the 5 filo sheets into three equal sized strips.
3. Cover the strips with olive oil.
4. In a bowl, mix onion, pepper, feta, salt, egg yolk, and parsley.
5. Make triangles using the cut strips and add a little bit of the feta mixture on top of each triangle.
6. Place the triangles in your air fryer's cooking basket and cook for 3 minutes.
7. Serve alongside green onions and a drizzle of olive oil.
8. Enjoy!
Nutrition: Calories: 426 Fat 14g Carbs: 65g Protein 9g

37. Cinnamon Flavored Grilled Pineapples
Preparation Time: 10 minutes
Cooking Time: 5 minutes
Servings: 2
- **Ingredients** 1 tsp. cinnamon
- 5 pineapple slices
- ½ c. brown sugar
- 1 tbsp. chopped basil
- 1 tbsp. honey

Directions:
1. Preheat your fryer to 340 degrees F. Using a bowl, combine the cinnamon and brown sugar. Dampen the sugar mixture on the pineapple slices and leave it for about 20 minutes.
2. Place the pineapple rings in the pan and cook for 10 minutes. Turn the pineapple over and cook for another 10 minutes.
3. Serve with basil and chopped honey.
Nutrition: Calories: 480 Fat 18g Carbs: 71g Protein 13g

38. The Great Japanese Omelet
Preparation Time: 15 minutes
Cooking Time: 20 minutes
Servings: 1
Ingredients:
- 1 cubed Japanese tofu
- 3 whole eggs
- Pepper
- 1 tsp. coriander
- 1 tsp. cumin
- 2 tbsp. soy sauce
- 2 tbsp. chopped green onion
- Olive oil
- 1 chopped onion

Directions:
1. Preheat your Air Fryer up to 400 degrees F. Using a medium bowl, mix the eggs, soy sauce, pepper, oil, and salt. Add cubed tofu to baking forms and pour the egg mixture on top. Place the prepared forms in the air fryer cooking basket and cook for 10 minutes. Serve with a sprinkle of herbs.
2. Enjoy!
Nutrition: Calories: 300 Fat 40g Carbs: 19g Protein 72g

39. Air Fried Hash brown
Preparation Time: 10 minutes
Cooking Time: 11 minutes
Servings: 4
Ingredients:
- 4 (200g) potatoes, cleaned and peeled
- 3 tbsp. butter, melted
- ½ tsp. cayenne pepper
- ½ tsp. ground cumin
- Salt and black pepper

Directions:
1. Slice the peeled potatoes and then soak in cold water. Add the potatoes and let them soak until the water is clean; this is the starch of the potatoes. Drain the water and then pour another batch of cold water. Repeat the method again.
2. Transfer the potatoes to a flat tray and then pat dry with paper towels.
3. Preheat fryer to 390 ° F.
4. In a bowl, combine the butter, cayenne pepper, cumin, salt, and black pepper. Add the chopped potatoes and mix.
5. Remove the cooking basket from the fryer. Spoon about 2 tablespoons. of the potato mixture and then format it to the desired shape. Place in the cooking basket.
6. Cook hash brown until golden brown for 15 minutes.
7. Serve and enjoy!
Nutrition: Calories: 207 Fat 9.3 g Carbs 30.1 g Protein 3.2 g

40. Breakfast Turkey Melt Sandwich
Preparation Time: 15 minutes
Cooking Time: 10 minutes
Servings: 4
Ingredients:
- 28g whole wheat bread, sliced
- 56g lean turkey ham, sliced
- 28g cheese slices
- 15g tomato, sliced
- Butter, unsalted

Directions:
1. Each bread slice should be spread with 1 teaspoon butter on one side.
2. Top the buttered bread with cheese, turkey ham, and tomato slices. Cover with remaining bread slices. Take two breads together and then place them together to make 4 sandwiches.
3. Preheat Air Fryer to 360°F.
4. Place sandwiches inside the Air Fryer cooking basket and then cook for 7-10 minutes or until bread turns golden brown.
5. Serve and enjoy!

Nutrition: Calories 294 Fat 15g Carbs 25.3g Protein 16.8g

41. Deserving Cheesy Omelet

Preparation Time: 10 minutes
Cooking Time: 8 minutes
Servings: 1
Ingredients:
- 2 eggs, beaten
- Pepper
- 1 c. shredded cheddar cheese
- 1 chopped onion
- 2 tbsp. soy sauce

Directions:
1. Preheat the fryer to 340 degrees F. Pour the soy sauce over the chopped onions.
2. Put the onions in your pan and cook for 8 minutes.
3. In a medium bowl, mix beaten eggs with salt and pepper.
4. Pour the egg mixture over the onions (in the cooking basket) and cook for 3 minutes.
5. Add cheddar cheese to eggs and cook for another 2 minutes.
6. Serve with fresh basil and enjoy!

Nutrition: Calories: 396 Fat 32g Carbs: 1g Protein 27g

42. Air Fried Cheese Soufflé

Preparation Time: 15 minutes
Cooking Time: 20 minutes
Servings: 6
Ingredients:
- 1 oz. panko breadcrumbs
- 2 oz. unsalted butter
- 56g all-purpose flour
- 1¼ c. skim milk
- 4 eggs
- ½ c. grated cheddar cheese
- ¼ c. grated parmesan cheese
- ½ tsp. nutmeg
- ½ tsp. vanilla extract
- Powdered Sugar
- Olive oil spray

Directions:
1. Preheat your Air Fryer to 330°F.
2. I wrote soufflé with greasy spray and sprinkle with crumbs.
3. In a small saucepan, melt the butter and then add the flour. Mix both ingredients until smooth. Transfer to a small bowl. Clean the pot for the next steps.
4. Heat the milk and add the vanilla extract to the clean pot. Boil. Add the flour and butter mixture. Mix well until smooth. Simmer the sauce until it thickens. Immediately transfer the pot to ice water for 10 minutes to cool.
5. In a bowl, separate the yolks from the whites.
6. Add the egg yolks to the thick sauce. Mix the cheddar and parmesan. Sprinkle with nutmeg.
7. In another bowl, beat the egg whites until they reach the top, which can keep its shape. Then, with a metal spoon, gradually mix the egg whites into the sauce mixture.
8. Divide the mixture into soufflé plates. Use a knife to smooth the top of the soufflé plate.
9. Place the soufflé in the Air Fryer cooking basket. Cook for about 15-18 minutes.
10. Sprinkle powdered sugar over the cooked soufflé cheese.
11. Serve and enjoy!

Nutrition: Calories: 238 Fat 12g Carbs: 15.3g Protein 11.9g

43. Chicken and Potato Nuggets

Preparation Time: 12 minutes
Cooking Time: 8 minutes
Servings: 4
Ingredients:
- 1 lb. minced chicken breast fillet
- 1 c. mashed potato
- 1 egg
- Salt and pepper
- Olive oil spray
- For the breading:
- 2 beaten eggs
- ¾ c. breadcrumbs
- Salt and pepper

Directions:
1. Combine chicken, mashed potatoes, and egg in bowl. Spice with salt and pepper. Spoon about 1. tablespoon of the mixture and form into 1-inch-thick pieces (breadcrumbs). Place in a large bowl. Set aside while preparing bakery ingredients.
2. In a bowl, put the crumbs and season with pepper.
3. Place the breadcrumbs and eggs in separate bowls.
4. Top each chicken and potato nugget with beaten eggs and then in crumbs.
5. Preheat fryer to 390 ° F.
6. Place the chicken nuggets and potatoes in the cooking basket. Spray with oil. Do not overdo it for even heat distribution during cooking.
7. Cook for about 7-10 minutes, or until golden brown.
8. Serve and enjoy!

Nutrition: Calories: 271 Fat 12.2g Carbs: 16.1g Protein 24.2g

44. Fluffy Cheesy Omelet

Preparation Time: 10 minutes
Cooking Time: 15 minutes
Servings: 2
Ingredients:
- 4 eggs
- 1 large onion, sliced
- 1/8 cup cheddar cheese, grated
- 1/8 cup mozzarella cheese, grated
- Cooking spray
- ¼ teaspoon soy sauce
- Freshly ground black pepper, to taste

Directions:
1. Preheat the Air fryer to 360 o F and grease a pan with cooking spray.
2. Whisk together eggs, soy sauce and black pepper in a bowl.
3. Place onions in the pan and cook for about 10 minutes.
4. Pour the egg mixture over onion slices and top evenly with cheese.
5. Cook for about 5 more minutes and serve.

Nutrition: Calories: 216 Fat 13.8gCarbohydrates: 7.9g Protein 15.5g

45. Crust-Less Quiche

Preparation Time: 5 minutes
Cooking Time: 30 minutes
Servings: 2
Ingredients:
- 4 eggs
- ¼ cup onion, chopped
- ½ cup tomatoes, chopped
- ½ cup milk
- 1 cup Gouda cheese, shredded
- Salt, to taste

Directions:
1. Preheat the Air fryer to 340 o F and grease 2 ramekins lightly.
2. Mix together all the ingredients in a ramekin until well combined.
3. Cook for about 30 minutes in the air fryer.
4. Dish out and serve.

Nutrition: Calories: 348 Fat 23.8gCarbohydrates: 7.9gProtein 26.1g

46. Milky Scrambled Eggs

Preparation Time: 10 minutes
Cooking Time: 9 minutes
Servings: 2
Ingredients:
- ¾ cup milk
- 4 eggs
- 8 grape tomatoes, halved
- ½ cup Parmesan cheese, grated
- 1 tablespoon butter
- Salt and black pepper, to taste

Directions:
1. Preheat the Air fryer to 360 o F and grease an Air fryer pan with butter.
2. Whisk together eggs with milk, salt and black pepper in a bowl.
3. Transfer the egg mixture into the prepared pan and place in the Air fryer.
4. Cook for about 6 minutes and stir in the grape tomatoes and cheese.
5. Cook for about 3 minutes and serve warm.

Nutrition: Calories: 351 Fat 22gCarbohydrates: 25.2g

47. Toasties and Sausage in Egg Pond

Preparation Time: 10 minutes
Cooking Time: 22 minutes
Servings: 2
Ingredients:
- 3 eggs
- 2 cooked sausages, sliced
- 1 bread slice, cut into sticks
- 1/8 cup mozzarella cheese, grated
- 1/8 cup Parmesan cheese, grated
- ¼ cup cream

Directions:
1. Preheat the Air fryer to 365 o F and grease 2 ramekins lightly.
2. Whisk together eggs with cream in a bowl and place in the ramekins.
3. Stir in the bread and sausage slices in the egg mixture and top with cheese.
4. Transfer the ramekins in the Air fryer basket and cook for about 22 minutes.
5. Dish out and serve warm.

Nutrition: Calories: 261Fat 18.8gCarbohydrates: 4.2gProtein 18.3g

48. Banana Bread

Preparation Time: 10 minutes
Cooking Time: 20 minutes
Servings: 8
Ingredients:
- 1 1/3 cups flour
- 1 teaspoon baking soda
- 1 teaspoon baking powder
- ½ cup milk
- 3 bananas, peeled and sliced
- 2/3 cup sugar
- 1 teaspoon ground cinnamon
- 1 teaspoon salt
- ½ cup olive oil

Directions:
1. Preheat the Air fryer to 330 o F and grease a loaf pan.
2. Mix together all the dry ingredients with the wet ingredients to form dough.
3. Place the dough into the prepared loaf pan and transfer into an air fryer basket.
4. Cook for about 20 minutes and remove from air fryer.
5. Cut the bread into desired size slices and serve warm.

Nutrition: Calories: 295Fat 13.3gCarbohydrates: 44gProtein 3.1g

49. Flavorful Bacon Cups
Preparation Time: 10 minutes
Cooking Time: 15 minutes
Servings: 6
Ingredients:
- 6 bacon slices
- 6 bread slices
- 1 scallion, chopped
- 3 tablespoons green bell pepper, seeded and chopped
- 6 eggs
- 2 tablespoons low-Fat mayonnaise

Directions:
1. Preheat the Air fryer to 375 o F and grease 6 cups muffin tin with cooking spray.
2. Place each bacon slice in a prepared muffin cup.
3. Cut the bread slices with round cookie cutter and place over the bacon slices.
4. Top with bell pepper, scallion and mayonnaise evenly and crack 1 egg in each muffin cup.
5. Place in the Air fryer and cook for about 15 minutes.
6. Dish out and serve warm.

Nutrition: Calories: 260 Fat 18gProtein 16.7g

50. Crispy Potato Rusty
Preparation Time: 10 minutes
Cooking Time: 15 minutes
Servings: 2
Ingredients:
- ½ pound russet potatoes, peeled and grated roughly
- 1 tablespoon chives, chopped finely
- 2 tablespoons shallots, minced
- 1/8 cup cheddar cheese
- ounces smoked salmon, cut into slices
- 2 tablespoons sour cream
- 1 tablespoon olive oil
- Salt and black pepper, to taste

Directions:
1. Preheat the Air fryer to 365 o F and grease a pizza pan with the olive oil.
2. Mix together potatoes, shallots, chives, cheese, salt and black pepper in a large bowl until well combined.
3. Transfer the potato mixture into the prepared pizza pan and place in the Air fryer basket.
4. Cook for about 15 minutes and dish out in a platter.
5. Cut the potato rusty into wedges and top with smoked salmon slices and sour cream to serve.

Nutrition: Calories: 327 Fat 20.2g Carbohydrates: 23.3gProtein 15.3g

51. Stylish Ham Omelet
Preparation Time: 10 minutes
Cooking Time: 30 minutes
Servings: 2
Ingredients:
- 4 small tomatoes, chopped
- 4 eggs
- 2 ham slices
- 1 onion, chopped
- 2 tablespoons cheddar cheese
- Salt and black pepper, to taste

Directions:
1. Preheat the Air fryer to 390 o F and grease an Air fryer pan.
2. Place the tomatoes in the Air fryer pan and cook for about 10 minutes.
3. Heat a nonstick skillet over medium heat and add onion and ham.
4. Shake for about 5 minutes and transfer to the pan.
5. Whisk the eggs, salt, and black pepper in a bowl and pour into the pan.
6. Set the Air fryer to 335 o F and cook for about 15 minutes.
7. Dish out and serve warm.

Nutrition: Calories: 255Fat 13.9gCarbohydrates: 14.1gProtein 19.7g

52. Healthy Tofu Omelet
Preparation Time: 10 minutes
Cooking Time: 29 minutes
Servings: 2
Ingredients:
- ¼ of onion, chopped
- 12-ounce silken tofu, pressed and sliced
- 3 eggs, beaten
- 1 tablespoon chives, chopped
- 1 garlic clove, minced
- 2 teaspoons olive oil
- Salt and black pepper, to taste

Directions:
1. Preheat the Air fryer to 355 o F and grease an Air fryer pan with olive oil.
2. Add onion and garlic to the greased pan and cook for about 4 minutes.
3. Add tofu, mushrooms and chives and season with salt and black pepper.
4. Beat the eggs and pour over the tofu mixture.
5. Cook for about 25 minutes, then poking the eggs twice in between.
6. Dish out and serve warm.

Nutrition: Calories: 248Fat 15.9gCarbohydrates: 6.5gProtein 20.4g

53. Peanut Butter Banana Bread
Preparation Time: 15 minutes
Cooking Time: 40 minutes
Servings: 6
Ingredients:
- 1 cup plus 1 tablespoon all-purpose flour
- 1¼ teaspoons baking powder
- 1 large egg

- 2 medium ripe bananas, peeled and mashed
- ¾ cup walnuts, roughly chopped
- ¼ teaspoon salt
- 1/3 cup granulated sugar
- ¼ cup canola oil
- 2 tablespoons creamy peanut butter
- 2 tablespoons sour cream
- 1 teaspoon vanilla extract

Directions:
1. Preheat the Air fryer to 330 o F and grease a non-stick baking dish.
2. Mix together the flour, baking powder and salt in a bowl.
3. Whisk together egg with sugar, canola oil, sour cream, peanut butter and vanilla extract in a bowl.
4. Stir in the bananas and beat until well combined.
5. Now, add the flour mixture and fold in the walnuts gently.
6. Mix until combined and transfer the mixture evenly into the prepared baking dish.
7. Arrange the baking dish in an Air fryer basket and cook for about 40 minutes.
8. Remove from the Air fryer and place onto a wire rack to cool.
9. Cut the bread into desired size slices and serve.

Nutrition: Calories: 384Fat 2.6gCarbohydrates: 39.3gProtein 8.9g

54. Yummy Savory French Toasts

Preparation Time: 10 minutes
Cooking Time: 4 minutes
Servings: 2
Ingredients:
- ¼ cup chickpea flour
- 3 tablespoons onion, chopped finely
- 2 teaspoons green chili, seeded and chopped finely
- Water, as required
- 4 bread slices
- ½ teaspoon red chili powder
- ¼ teaspoon ground turmeric
- ¼ teaspoon ground cumin
- Salt, to taste

Directions:
1. Preheat the Air fryer to 375 o F and line an Air fryer pan with a foil paper.
2. Mix all ingredients together in a large bowl, except bread slices.
3. Spread the mixture over both sides of the bread slices and transfer into the Air fryer pan.
4. Cook for about 4 minutes and remove from the Air fryer to serve.

Nutrition: Calories: 151Fat 2.3gCarbohydrates: 26.7gProtein 6.5g,

55. Aromatic Potato Hash

Preparation Time: 10 minutes
Cooking Time: 42 minutes
Servings: 4
Ingredients:
- 2 teaspoons butter, melted
- 1 medium onion, chopped
- ½ of green bell pepper, seeded and chopped
- 1½ pound russet potatoes, peeled and cubed
- 5 eggs, beaten
- ½ teaspoon dried thyme, crushed
- ½ teaspoon dried savory, crushed
- Salt and black pepper, to taste

Directions:
1. Preheat the Air fryer to 390 o F and grease an Air fryer pan with melted butter. Put onion and bell pepper in the Air fryer pan and cook for about 5 minutes.
2. Add the potatoes, thyme, savory, salt and black pepper and cook for about 30 minutes.
3. Meanwhile, heat a greased skillet on medium heat and stir in the beaten eggs.
4. Cook for about 1 minute on each side and remove from the skillet. Cut it into small pieces and transfer the egg pieces into the Air fryer pan. Cook for about 5 more minutes and serve warm.

Nutrition: Calories: 229 Fat 7.6gProtein 10.3g

56. Pumpkin and Yogurt Bread

Cooking Time: 15 minutes
Servings: 4
Ingredients:
- 2 large eggs
- 8 tablespoons pumpkin puree
- 6 tablespoons banana flour
- 4 tablespoons plain Greek yogurt
- 6 tablespoons oats
- 4 tablespoons honey
- 2 tablespoons vanilla essence
- Pinch of ground nutmeg

Directions:
1. Preheat the Air fryer to 360 o F and grease a loaf pan.
2. Mix together all the ingredients except oats in a bowl and beat with the hand mixer until smooth.
3. Add oats and mix until well combined.
4. Transfer the mixture into the prepared loaf pan and place in the Air fryer.
5. Cook for about 15 minutes and remove from the Air fryer.
6. Place onto a wire rack to cool and cut the bread into desired size slices to serve.

Nutrition: Calories: 212Fat 3.4gCarbohydrates: 36gProtein 6.6g

57. Zucchini Fritters

Preparation Time: 15 minutes
Cooking Time: 7 minutes
Servings: 4
Ingredients:
- 10½ ounces zucchini, grated and squeezed
- 7 ounces Halloumi cheese
- ¼ cup all-purpose flour
- 2 eggs

- 1 teaspoon fresh dill, minced
- Salt and black pepper, to taste

Directions:
1. Preheat the Air fryer to 360 o F and grease a baking dish.
2. Mix together all the ingredients in a large bowl.
3. Make small fritters from this mixture and place them on the prepared baking dish.
4. Transfer the dish in the Air Fryer basket and cook for about 7 minutes.
5. Dish out and serve warm.

Nutrition: Calories: 250 Fat 17.2gCarbohydrates: 10gProtein 15.2g

58. Bacon Bombs

Preparation Time: 10 minutes
Cooking Time: 16 minutes
Servings: 4
Ingredients:
- 3 center-cut bacon slices
- 3 large eggs, lightly beaten
- 1 oz. 1/3-less-Fat cream cheese, softened
- 1 tbsp. chopped fresh chives
- 4 oz. fresh whole wheat pizza dough
- Cooking spray

Directions:
1. Sear the bacon slices in a skillet until brown and crispy then chop into fine crumbles. Add eggs to the same pan and cook for 1 minute then stir in cream cheese, chives and bacon. Mix well, then allow this egg filling to cool down. Spread the pizza dough and slice into four -5inches circles. Divide the egg filling on top of each circle and seal its edge to make dumplings. Place the bacon bombs in the Air Fryer basket and spray them with cooking oil. Set the Air Fryer basket inside the Air Fryer toaster oven and close the lid. Select the Air Fry mode at 350 degrees F temperature for 6 minutes. Serve warm.

Nutrition: Calories 278Protein 7.9gCarbs 23gFat 3.9g

59. Morning Potatoes

Preparation Time: 10 minutes
Cooking Time: 23 minutes
Servings: 4
Ingredients:
- 2 russet potatoes, washed & diced
- ½ tsp salt
- 1 tbsp. olive oil
- ¼ tsp garlic powder
- Chopped parsley, for garnish

Directions:
1. Soak the potatoes in cold water for 45 minutes; then drain and pat dry. Toss potato cubes with garlic powder, salt, and olive oil in the Air Fryer basket. Set the Air Fryer basket inside the Air Fryer toaster oven and close the lid. Select the Air Fry mode at 400 degrees F temperature for 23 minutes. Toss them well when cooked halfway through then continue cooking. Garnish with chopped parsley to serve.

Nutrition: Calories 146 Protein 6.2gCarbs 41.2gFat 5g

60. Breakfast Pockets

Preparation Time: 10 minutes
Cooking Time: 10 minutes
Servings: 6
Ingredients:
- 1 box puff pastry sheet
- 5 eggs
- ½ cup loose sausage, cooked
- ½ cup bacon, cooked
- ½ cup cheddar cheese, shredded

Directions:
1. Stir cook egg in a skillet for 1 minute then mix with sausages, cheddar cheese, and bacon. Spread the pastry sheet and cut it into four rectangles of equal size. Divide the egg mixture over each rectangle. Fold the edges around the filling and seal them. Place the pockets in the Air Fryer basket. Set the Air Fryer basket inside the Air Fryer toaster oven and close the lid. Select the Air Fry mode at 370 degrees F temperature for 10 minutes. Serve warm

Nutrition: Calories 387 Protein 14.6gCarbs 37.4gFat 6g

61. Avocado Flautas

Preparation Time: 10 minutes
Cooking Time: 24 minutes
Servings: 8
Ingredients:
- 1 tbsp. butter
- 8 eggs, beaten
- ½ tsp salt
- ¼ tsp pepper
- 1 ½ tsp of cumin
- 1 tsp chili powder
- 8 fajita-size tortillas
- 4 oz. cream cheese, softened
- 8 slices cooked bacon
- Avocado Crème:
- 2 small avocados
- ½ cup sour cream
- 1 lime, juiced
- ½ tsp salt
- ¼ tsp pepper

Directions:
1. In a skillet, melt butter and stir in eggs, salt, cumin, pepper, and chili powder, then stir cook for 4 minutes. Spread all the tortillas and top them with cream cheese and bacon.
2. Then divide the egg scramble on top and finally add cheese. Roll the tortillas to seal the filling inside. Place 4 rolls in the Air Fryer basket.
3. Set the Air Fryer basket inside the Air Fryer toaster oven and close the lid. Select the Air Fry mode at 400 degrees F temperature for 12 minutes.
4. Cook the remaining tortilla rolls in the same manner. Meanwhile, blend avocado crème ingredients in a blender then serve with warm flautas.

Nutrition: Calories 212 Protein 17.3gCarbs 14.6g

62. Cheese Sandwiches

Preparation Time: 10 minutes
Cooking Time: 10 minutes
Servings: 2
Ingredients:
- 1 egg
- 3 tbsp. half and half cream
- ¼ tsp vanilla extract
- 2 slices sourdough, white or multigrain bread
- 2½ oz. sliced Swiss cheese
- 2 oz. sliced deli ham
- 2 oz. sliced deli turkey
- 1 tsp butter, melted
- Powdered sugar
- Raspberry jam, for serving

Directions:
1. Beat egg with half and half cream and vanilla extract in a bowl. Place one bread slice on the working surface and top it with ham and turkey slice and Swiss cheese.
2. Place the other bread slice on top, then dip the sandwich in the egg mixture, then place it in a suitable baking tray lined with butter.
3. Set the baking tray inside the Air Fryer toaster oven and close the lid. Select the Air Fry mode at 350 degrees F temperature for 10 minutes. Flip the sandwich and continue cooking for 8 minutes. Slice and serve.

Nutrition: Calories 412 Protein 18.9gCarbs: 43.8gFat 24.8g

63. Sausage Cheese Wraps
Preparation Time: 10 minutes
Cooking Time: 3 minutes
Servings: 8
Ingredients:
- 8 sausages
- 2 pieces' American cheese, shredded
- 8-count refrigerated crescent roll dough

Directions:
1. Roll out each crescent roll and top it with cheese and 1 sausage. Fold both the top and bottom edges of the crescent sheet to cover the sausage and roll it around the sausage. Place 4 rolls in the Air Fryer basket and spray them with cooking oil. Set the Air Fryer basket inside the Air Fryer toaster oven and close the lid. Select the Air Fry mode at 380 degrees F temperature for 3 minutes. Cook the remaining rolls in the same manner. Serve fresh.

Nutrition: Calories 296 Protein 34.2Carbs 17gFat 22.1g

64. Chicken Omelet
Preparation Time: 10 minutes
Cooking Time: 18 minutes
Servings: 4
Ingredients:
- 4 eggs
- ½ cup chicken breast, cooked and diced
- 2 tbsp. shredded cheese, divided
- ½ tsp salt, divided
- ¼ tsp pepper, divided
- ¼ tsp granulated garlic, divided
- ¼ tsp onion powder, divided

Directions:
1. Spray 2 ramekins with cooking oil and keep them aside. Crack two large eggs into each ramekin then add cheese and seasoning. Whisk well, and then add ¼ cup chicken. Place the ramekins in a baking tray. Set the baking tray inside the Air Fryer toaster oven and close the lid. Select the Bake mode at 330 degrees F temperature for 18 minutes. Serve warm.

Nutrition: Calories: 322 Protein 17.3gCarbs: 4.6gFat 21.8g

65. Sausage Burritos
Preparation Time: 10 minutes
Cooking Time: 10 minutes
Servings: 6
Ingredients:
- 6 medium flour tortillas
- 6 scrambled eggs
- ½ lb. ground sausage, browned
- ½ bell pepper, minced
- 1/3 cup bacon bits
- ½ cup shredded cheese
- Oil, for spraying

Directions:
1. Mix eggs with cheese, bell pepper, bacon, and sausage in a bowl. Spread each tortilla on the working surface and top it with ½ cup egg filling. Roll the tortilla like a burrito then place 3 burritos in the Air Fryer basket. Spray them with cooking oil. Set the Air Fryer basket inside the Air Fryer toaster oven and close the lid. Select the Air Fry mode at 330 degrees F temperature for 5 minutes. Cook the remaining burritos in the same manner. Serve fresh.

Nutrition: Calories: 197 Protein 7.9gCarbs: 58.5gFat 15.4g

66. Sausage Patties
Preparation Time: 10 minutes
Cooking Time: 20 minutes
Servings: 4
Ingredients:
- 1 1.5 lbs. ground sausage
- 1 tsp chili flakes
- tsp dried thyme
- 1 tsp onion powder
- ½ tsp each paprika and cayenne
- Sea salt and black pepper, to taste
- 2 tsp brown sugar
- 3 tsp minced garlic
- 2 tsp Tabasco
- Herbs for garnish:

Directions:
1. Toss sausage ground with all the spices, herbs, sugar, garlic and tabasco sauce in a bowl and then make 1.5-inch-thick and 3-inch round patties out of the mixture. Place the sausage patties in the Air Fryer basket. Set the Air Fryer basket inside the Air Fryer toaster oven and close the lid. Select the Air Fry mode at

370 degrees F temperature for 20 minutes. Flip the patties when cooked halfway through then continue cooking.
Nutrition: Calories: 208 ProtCarbs: 9.5gFat 10.7g

67. Spicy Sweet Potato Hash
Preparation Time: 10 minutes
Cooking Time: 16 minutes
Servings: 4
Ingredients:
- 2 large sweet potatoes, diced
- 2 slices bacon, cooked and diced
- 2 tbsp. olive oil
- 1 tbsp. smoked paprika
- 1 tsp of sea salt
- 1 tsp ground black pepper
- 1 tsp dried dill weed

Directions:
1. Toss sweet potato with all the spices and olive oil in the Air Fry basket. Set the Air Fryer basket inside the Air Fryer toaster oven and close the lid. Select the Air Fry mode at 400 degrees F temperature for 16 minutes. Toss the potatoes after every 5 minutes. Once done, toss in bacon and serve warm.
Nutrition: Calories: 134 Protein 6.6gCarbs: 36.5gFat 6g

68. Cinnamon Cream Doughnuts
Preparation Time: 10 minutes
Cooking Time: 8 minutes
Servings: 4
Ingredients:
- 1/2 cup Sugar
- 2 1/2 tbsp. butter
- 2 large egg yolks
- 2 1/4 cups all-purpose flour
- 1 1/2 tsp baking powder
- 1 tsp salt
- 1/2 cup sour cream
- To garnish
- 1/3 cup white Sugar
- 1 tsp cinnamon
- 2 tbsp. butter, melted

Directions:
1. Beat egg with sugar and butter in a mixer until creamy, then whisk in flour, salt, baking powder, and sour cream. Mix well until smooth then refrigerate the dough for 1 hour. Spread this dough into ½ inch thick circle then cut 9 large circles out of it. Make the hole at the center of each circle. Place the doughnuts in the Air Fryer basket. Set the Air Fryer basket inside the Air Fryer toaster oven and close the lid. Select the Air Fry mode at 350 degrees F temperature for 8 minutes. Cook the doughnuts in two batches to avoid overcrowding. Mix sugar, cinnamon, and butter and glaze the doughnuts with this mixture. Serve.
Nutrition: Calories: 387 Carbs: 26.4gFat 13g

69. Sausage Frittata
Preparation Time: 15 minutes
Cooking Time: 20 minutes
Servings: 4
Ingredients:
- 1/4-pound sausage, cooked and crumbled
- 4 eggs, beaten
- 1/2 cup shredded Cheddar cheese blend
- 2 tbsp. red bell pepper, diced
- 1 green onion, chopped
- 1 pinch cayenne pepper
- Cooking spray

Directions:
1. Beat eggs with cheese, sausage, cayenne, onion, and bell pepper in a bowl. Spread the egg mixture in a 6x2 inch baking tray, greased with cooking spray. Set the baking tray inside the Air Fryer toaster oven and close the lid. Select the Bake mode at 360 degrees F temperature for 20 minutes. Slice and serve.
Nutrition: Calories: 212 Protein 17.3gCarbs: 14.6gFat 11.8g

70. Potato Jalapeno Hash
Preparation Time: 15 minutes
Cooking Time: 24 minutes
Servings: 4
Ingredients:
- 1 1/2 lbs. potatoes, peeled and diced
- 1 tbsp. olive oil
- 1 red bell pepper, seeded and diced
- 1 small onion, chopped
- 1 jalapeno, seeded and diced
- 1/2 tsp olive oil
- 1/2 tsp taco seasoning mix
- 1/2 tsp ground cumin
- Salt and black pepper to taste

Directions:
1. Soak the potato in cold water for 20 minutes then drain them. Toss the potatoes with 1 tbsp. olive oil. Spread them in the Air Fryer basket. Set the Air Fryer basket inside the Air Fryer toaster oven and close the lid. Select the Air Fry mode at 370 degrees F temperature for 18 minutes. And meanwhile, toss onion, pepper, olive oil, taco seasoning, and all other ingredients in a salad bowl. Add this vegetable mixture to the Air Fryer basket, and return it to the oven. Continue cooking at 356 degrees F for 6 minutes. Serve warm.
Nutrition: Calories: 242 Protein 8.9gCarbs: 36.8gFat 14.4g

71. Bread Rolls
Preparation Time: 10 minutes
Cooking Time: 39 minutes
Servings: 8
Ingredients:
- 8 Bread Slices
- 2 Potatoes boiled and mashed
- 1 tsp Ginger grated
- 1 tbsp. Coriander powder
- 1 tsp Cumin powder
- 1/2 tsp Chili powder

- 1/2 tsp Garam Masala
- 1/2 tsp Dry Mango powder
- 1&1/2 tsp Salt
- 1 Large Bowl of Water
- Cooking Oil

Directions:

1. Mix mashed potatoes with ginger and all the spices. Divide this mixture into 16 balls and keep them aside. Slice the bread slices into half to get 16 rectangles. Dip each in water for 1 second, then place one potato ball at the center and wrap the slice around it. Place half of these wrapped balls in the Air Fryer basket and spray them with cooking oil. Set the Air Fryer basket inside the Air Fryer toaster oven and close the lid. Select the Air Fry mode at 390 degrees F temperature for 18 minutes. Flip the balls after 10 minutes of cooking then continue cooking. Cook the remaining balls in the same manner. Serve fresh.

Nutrition: Calories: 331 Protein 14.8gCarbs: 46gFat 2.5g

BRUNCH RECIPES

72. Perfect Breakfast Frittata
Preparation Time: 10 minutes
Cooking Time: 32 minutes
Servings: 2
Ingredients:
- 3 eggs
- 2 tbsp. parmesan cheese, grated 2 tbsp. sour cream
- 1/2 cup bell pepper, chopped 1/4 cup onion, chopped
- 1/2 tsp pepper 1/2 tsp salt

Directions:
1. Add eggs in a mixing bowl and whisk with remaining ingredients.
2. Spray air fryer baking dish with cooking spray.
3. Pour egg mixture into the prepared dish and place in the air fryer and cook at 350 F for 5 minutes.
4. Serve and enjoy.

Nutrition: Calories 227 Fat 15.2 g Carbohydrates 6 g Sugar 2.6 g Protein 18.2 g Cholesterol 271 mg

73. Indian Cauliflower
Preparation Time: 10 minutes
Cooking Time: 20 minutes
Servings: 2
Ingredients:
- 3 cups cauliflower florets 2 tbsp. water
- 2 tsp fresh lemon juice
- ½ tbsp. ginger paste 1 tsp chili powder
- ¼ tsp turmeric
- ½ cup vegetable stock Pepper
- Salt

Directions:
1. Add all ingredients into the air fryer baking dish and mix well.
2. Place dish in the air fryer and cook at 400 F for 10 minutes.
3. Stir well and cook at 360 F for 10 minutes more.
4. Stir well and serve.

Nutrition: Calories 49 Fat 0.5 g Carbohydrates 9 g Sugar 3 g Protein 3 g Cholesterol 0 mg

74. Zucchini Salad
Preparation Time: 10 minutes
Cooking Time: 25 minutes
Servings: 4
Ingredients:
- 1 lb. zucchini, cut into slices
- 2 tbsp. tomato paste
- ½ tbsp. tarragon, chopped 1 yellow squash, diced
- ½ lb. carrots, peeled and diced 1 tbsp. olive oil
- Pepper Salt

Directions:
1. In air fryer baking dish mix together zucchini, tomato paste, tarragon, squash, carrots, pepper, and salt. Drizzle with olive oil.
2. Place in the air fryer and cook at 400 F for 25 minutes. Stir halfway through.
3. Serve and enjoy.

Nutrition: Calories 79 Fat 3 g Carbohydrates 11 g Sugar 5 g Protein 2 g Cholesterol 0 mg

75. Healthy Squash
Preparation Time: 10 minutes
Cooking Time: 25 minutes
Servings: 4
Ingredients:
- 2 lbs. yellow squash, cut into half-moons 1 tsp Italian seasoning
- ¼ tsp pepper
- 1 tbsp. olive oil
- ¼ tsp salt

Directions:
1. Add all ingredients into the large bowl and toss well.
2. Preheat the air fryer to 400 F.
3. Add squash mixture into the air fryer basket and cook for 10 minutes.
4. Shake basket and cook for another 10 minutes.
5. Shake once again and cook for 5 minutes more.

Nutrition: Calories 70 Fat 4 g Carbohydrates 7 g Sugar 4 g Protein 2 g Cholesterol 1 mg

76. Spinach Frittata
Preparation Time: 10 minutes
Cooking Time: 8 minutes
Servings: 6
Ingredients:
- 8 eggs
- 1/4 cup mushrooms, sliced 1 tbsp. olive oil
- 1 cups spinach
- 1 tbsp. curry powder 1/4 cup onion, diced Pepper
- Salt

Directions:
1. Preheat the air fryer to 325 F.
2. Heat the oil in a pan over medium-high heat.
3. Add onion and mushrooms to the pan and sauté for 5-8 minutes.
4. Add spinach and cook for 2 minutes.
5. In a large bowl, whisk eggs, curry powder, pepper, and salt.
6. Transfer pan mixture into the air fryer baking dish. Pour egg mixture over vegetables and stir well.
7. Place dish in the air fryer and cook for 8 minutes or until eggs are set
8. Serve and enjoy.

Nutrition: Calories 116 Fat 8 g Carbohydrates 2 g Sugar 1 g Protein 8 g Cholesterol 218 mg

77. Lemon Dill Scallops
Preparation Time: 10 minutes

Cooking Time: 5 minutes
Servings: 4
Ingredients:
- 1 lb. scallops
- 2 tsp olive oil
- 1 tsp dill, chopped
- 1 tbsp. fresh lemon juice Pepper
- Salt

Directions:
1. Add scallops into the bowl and toss with oil, dill, lemon juice, pepper, and salt.
2. Add scallops into the air fryer basket and cook at 360 F for 5 minutes.
3. Serve and enjoy.

Nutrition: Calories 121 Fat 3.2 g Carbohydrates 2.9 g Sugar 0.1 g Protein 19 g Cholesterol 37 mg

78. Herb Mushrooms
Preparation Time: 10 minutes
Cooking Time: 12 minutes
Servings: 2
Ingredients:
- 10 mushrooms, stems remove
- 1 tbsp. dill, chopped
- 1 tbsp. olive oil
- 1 tbsp. parmesan cheese, grated
- ½ tbsp. oregano
- ½ tsp dried basil Pepper
- Salt

Directions:
1. Add mushrooms into the bowl and toss with oil, oregano, basil, pepper, and salt.
2. Add mushrooms into the air fryer basket and cook at 360 F for 6 minutes.
3. Add dill and cheese and toss well and cook for 6 minutes more.
4. Serve and enjoy.

Nutrition: Calories 87 Fat 7 g Carbohydrates 4 g Sugar 1 g Protein 3 g Cholesterol 0 mg

79. Easy & Tasty Salsa Chicken
Preparation Time: 10 minutes
Cooking Time: 30 minutes
Servings: 4
Ingredients:
- 1 lb. chicken thighs, boneless and skinless
- 1 cup salsa
- Pepper Salt

Directions:
1. Preheat the air fryer to 350 F.
2. Place chicken thighs into the air fryer baking dish and season with pepper and salt. Top with salsa.
3. Place in the air fryer and cook for 30 minutes.
4. Serve and enjoy.

Nutrition: Calories 233 Fat 8 g Carbohydrates 4 g Sugar 2 g Protein 33 g Cholesterol 101 mg

80. Fish and Chips
Preparation Time: 10 minutes
Cooking Time: 12 minutes
Servings: 2
Ingredients:
- 2 medium cod fillets, skinless and boneless
- Salt and black pepper to the taste
- ¼ cup margarine milk
- 3 cups kettle chips, cooked

Directions:
1. In a bowl, mix fish with salt, pepper and margarine milk, toss and leave aside for 5 minutes.
2. Put chips in your food processor, crush them and spread them on a plate.
3. Add fish and press well on all sides.
4. Transfer fish to your air fryer's basket and cook at 400 °F for 12 minutes.
5. Serve hot for lunch.

Nutrition: Calories 113 Fat 8.2 g Carbohydrates 0.3 g Sugar 0.2 g Protein 5.4 g Cholesterol 18 mg

81. Hash Brown Toasts
Preparation Time: 10 minutes
Cooking Time: 7 minutes
Servings: 4
Ingredients:
- 4 hash brown patties, frozen
- 1 tablespoon olive oil
- ¼ cup cherry tomatoes, chopped
- 3 tbsp. mozzarella, shredded
- 2 tbsp. parmesan, grated
- 1 tablespoon balsamic vinegar
- 1 tablespoon basil, chopped

Directions:
1. Put hash brown patties in your air fryer, drizzle the oil over them and cook them at 400 °F for 7 minutes.
2. In a bowl, mix tomatoes with mozzarella, parmesan, vinegar and basil and stir well.
3. Divide hash brown patties on plates, top each with tomatoes mix and serve for lunch.

Nutrition: Calories 113 Fat 8.2 g Carbohydrates 0.3 g Sugar 0.2 g Protein 5.4 g Cholesterol 18 mg

82. Delicious Beef Cubes
Preparation Time: 10 minutes
Cooking Time: 12 minutes
Servings: 4
Ingredients:
- 1-pound sirloin, cubed
- 16 ounces jarred pasta sauce
- 1 and ½ cups bread crumbs
- 2 tbsp. olive oil
- ½ tsp. marjoram, dried
- White rice, already cooked for serving

Directions:
1. In a bowl, mix beef cubes with pasta sauce and toss well.
2. In another bowl, mix bread crumbs with marjoram and oil and stir well.
3. Dip beef cubes in this mix, place them in your air fryer and cook at 360 °F for 12 minutes.

4. Divide among plates and serve with white rice on the side.
Nutrition: Calories 113 Fat 8.2 g Carbohydrates 0.3 g Sugar 0.2 g Protein 5.4 g Cholesterol 18 mg

83. Pasta Salad
Preparation Time: 10 minutes
Cooking Time: 12 minutes
Servings: 6
Ingredients:
- 1 zucchini, sliced in half and roughly chopped
- 1 orange bell pepper, roughly chopped
- 1 green bell pepper, roughly chopped
- 1 red onion, roughly chopped
- 4 ounces' brown mushrooms, halved
- Salt and black pepper to the taste
- 1 tsp. Italian seasoning
- 1 pound penne rig ate, already cooked
- 1 cup cherry tomatoes, halved
- ½ cup Kalamata olive, pitted and halved
- ¼ cup olive oil
- 3 tbsp. balsamic vinegar
- 2 tbsp. Basil, chopped

Directions:
1. In a bowl, mix zucchini with mushrooms, orange bell pepper, green bell pepper, red onion, salt, pepper, Italian seasoning and oil, toss well, transfer to preheated air fryer at 380 °F and cook them for 12 minutes.
2. In a large salad bowl, mix pasta with cooked veggies, cherry tomatoes, olives, vinegar and basil, toss and serve for lunch.

Nutrition: Calories 113 Fat 8.2 g Carbohydrates 0.3 g Sugar 0.2 g Protein 5.4 g Cholesterol 18 mg

84. Philadelphia Chicken
Preparation Time: 10 minutes
Cooking Time: 30 minutes
Servings: 4
Ingredients:
- 1 tsp. olive oil
- 1 yellow onion, sliced
- 2 chicken breasts, skinless, boneless and sliced
- Salt and black pepper to taste
- 1 tablespoon Worcestershire sauce
- 14 ounces' pizza dough
- 1 and ½ cups cheddar cheese, grated
- ½ cup jarred cheese sauce

Directions:
1. Preheat your air fryer at 400 °F, add half of the oil and onions and fry them for 8 minutes, stirring once.
2. Add chicken pieces, Worcestershire sauce, salt and pepper, toss, air fry for 8 minutes more, stirring once and transfer everything to a bowl.
3. Roll pizza dough on a working surface and shape a rectangle.
4. Spread half of the cheese all over, add chicken and onion mix and top with cheese sauce.
5. Roll your dough and shape into a U.
6. Place your roll in your air fryer's basket, brush with the rest of the oil and cook at 370 °F for 12 minutes, flipping the roll halfway.
7. Slice your roll when it's warm and serve for lunch.

Nutrition: Calories 113 Fat 8.2 g Protein 5.4 g Cholesterol 18 mg

85. Tasty Cheeseburgers
Preparation Time: 10 minutes
Cooking Time: 20 minutes
Servings: 2
Ingredients:
- 12 ounces' lean beef, ground
- 4 tsp ketchup
- 3 tbsp. yellow onion, chopped
- 2 tsp mustard
- Salt and black pepper to the taste
- 4 cheddar cheese slices
- 2 burger buns, halved

Directions:
1. In a bowl, mix beef with onion, ketchup, mustard, salt and pepper, stir well and shape 4 patties out of this mix.
2. Divide cheese on 2 patties and top with the other 2 patties.
3. Place them in preheated air fryer at 370 °F and fry them for 20 minutes.
4. Divide cheeseburger on 2 bun halves, top with the other 2 and serve for lunch.

Nutrition: Calories 113 Fat 8.2 g Carbohydrates 0.3 g Sugar 0.2 g Protein 5.4 g Cholesterol 18 mg

86. Stuffed Mushrooms
Preparation Time: 10 minutes
Cooking Time: 20 minutes
Servings: 4
Ingredients:
- 4 big Portobello mushroom caps
- 1 tablespoon olive oil
- ¼ cup ricotta cheese
- 5 tbsp. parmesan, grated
- 1 cup spinach, torn
- 1/3 cup bread crumbs
- ¼ tsp. rosemary, chopped

Directions:
1. Rub mushrooms caps with the oil, place them in your air fryer's basket and cook them at 350 °F for 2 minutes.
2. Meanwhile, in a bowl, mix half of the parmesan with ricotta, spinach, rosemary and bread crumbs and stir well.
3. Stuff mushrooms with this mix, sprinkle the rest of the parmesan on top, place them in your air fryer's basket again and cook at 350 °F for 10 minutes.
4. Divide them on plates and serve with a side salad for lunch.

Nutrition: Calories 113 Fat 8.2 g Carbohydrates 0.3 g Sugar 0.2 g Protein 5.4 g Cholesterol 18 mg

MAINS

87. Air-Fried Chicken Recipe
Prepare Time: 15 minutes
Cooking Time: 51 minutes
Servings: 10
Ingredients:
For the Chicken:
- Chicken: 4 pound, cut into 10 parts (2 halved breasts, 2 legs, 2 wings, 2 thighs)
- 1 tsp kosher salt
- 1 tsp black pepper
- 2 cups buttermilk
- For chicken coating:
- 2 cups all-purpose flour
- 1 tbsp. seasoned salt
- 1 tsp kosher salt:
- 1 tsp ground black pepper
- 1 tbsp. garlic powder
- 1 tbsp. paprika
- Olive oil spray to cook

Directions:
1. When marinating the chicken: Use salt and pepper to season the chicken. Take a bowl and add buttermilk and well-seasoned chicken in it. The bits of chicken should be brushed with buttermilk. Rest aside for an hour or until overnight.
2. Bread the chicken: Stir together flour, seasoned salt, salt, pepper, garlic powder, and paprika to prepare the breading mixture.
3. Remove pieces of chicken from buttermilk, shake off any excess, and then dip in the flour mixture and cover well. Put pieces of breaded chicken onto a clean plate or wire rack to rest.
4. Air-frying the chicken: If you're doing a full chicken, you'll need to work in two lots. Spray nonstick spray into your air fryer bowl.
5. Place half the pieces in your air fryer bowl. Try to make sure that there is enough space between the pieces. Air must be circulating around them.
6. Sprinkle gently the spray oil on the chicken pieces. Place the basket in the air fryer and change to 350 ° F for the air fryer.
7. Cook for 15 minutes, then flip the fried chicken with tongs, sprinkle lightly on the chicken's bottom side with oil a second time, and cook for another 8 to 10 minutes.
8. On the low end of the time scale, the half-breast pieces and the wings will be cooked, and the dark meat pieces will require a full 24 to 26 minutes to cook through. The pieces of dark meat will hit 175°F.
9. Spray those spots lightly with oil if you pull the chicken out and notice any dry flour spots on the chicken during the air frying process.
10. If it has no tiny bit of oil to hydrate it, the breading will never crisp up. It just is going to burn.
11. **Servings:** Let the fried chicken rest on a plate a few minutes before serving. Serve with salad, coleslaw, mashed potatoes, or your favorite side of fried chicken right away!
Nutrition: Calories 332 Fat 9g Protein 18 Carbs 25

88. Air Fried Chinese Pineapple Pork
Preparation Time: 20 Minutes
Cooking Time: 20 Minutes
Servings: 4
Ingredients:
- Pork Loin: 450 grams cut in cubes
- 1/2 tsp Sal:
- 1/2 tsp pepper
- Half Pineapple, cut into cubes
- Green Pepper: 1 cut in cubes
- 1 Clove of garlic, chopped
- 1 tsp of fresh ginger, chopped
- 2 tbsp. Soy sauce
- 1 tbsp. Brown sugar
- 1 Spoon vegetable oil
- 1 Small bunch of fresh, chopped coriander leaves
- Sesame seeds, toasted

Directions:
1. Use salt and pepper for seasoning the pork.
2. To the Air Fry basket, add the seasoned pork, pineapple, green pepper, garlic, and ginger.
3. In a cup, add the soy sauce and brown sugar. Pour the ingredients over the pork—drizzle ingredients over vegetable oil.
4. Turn on your Air Fry and set a 17-minute cooking timer. After you have completed the cooking process, test to ensure that all ingredients are cooked to your specifications. Garnish with sesame seeds and chopped coriander. Serve with rice and enjoy!
Nutrition: Calories 372 Fat 18.3 g Cholesterol 71 mg Sodium 806 mg Carbohydrates 28.6 g Protein 24.4 g

89. Cauliflower and Chickpea Tacos
Preparation Time: 15 minutes
Cooking Time: 25 minutes
Servings: 6
Ingredients:
- 1 tbsp. olive oil
- 1 tablespoon lime juice
- 1 tsp chili powder
- 1 tsp ground cumin
- 1 tsp sea salt
- ¼ tsp garlic powder
- 1 cans (15 ounces) canned chickpeas
- 1 little head of cauliflower, cut into pieces of bite-size
- For the sauce:
- Sour cream: 1 cup
- Freshly chopped coriander: ¼ cup
- Lime juice: 1/8 cup
- 1 tbsp. sriracha
- Salt to taste
- 6 (6 inches) corn tortillas

Directions:
1. Preheat an air fryer to 370 °F (190 °C).
2. In a large bowl, whisk together olive oil, lime juice, chili powder, cumin, salt, and garlic powder. Add the chickpeas and cauliflower and mix until coated evenly.
3. Stir sour cream, Cilantro, lime juice, and Sriracha together in a bowl until mixed evenly. Season it with salt.
4. Place cauliflower mixture in the air fryer basket. Cook and shake after 10 minutes, then cook for another 10 minutes. Remove again and cook for about 5 minutes, until desired crispness.
5. Use a spoon to put the mixture over the corn tortillas and spread the sauce on the top.
Nutrition: Calories 232 Fat 11.8 g Carbohydrates 27.6 g Protein 6.1 g

90. Perfect Air Fryer Salmon
Prepare Time: 5 Minutes
Cooking Time: 7 Minutes
Servings: 2 people
Ingredients:
- Wild salmon fillets: 2 fillets of similar thickness, 1-1/12-inches thick
- Avocado oil or olive oil: 2 teaspoons
- Paprika: 2 teaspoons
- Salt and black pepper for seasoning
- Lemon wedges

Directions:
1. If possible, remove any bones from your salmon, and allow the fish to sit on the counter for an hour. Season each filet with olive oil and paprika, salt, and pepper.
2. Place filets in the air fryer basket. Set air-fryer at 390 degrees and air fry for 7 minutes.
3. When the timer leaves, open the basket and check the filets with a fork to ensure that they are done to your desired doneness.
Nutrition: Calories 288 Fat 18.9g Carbohydrates 1.4g Protein 28.3g

91. Air Fryer Buffalo Cauliflower
Prepare Time: 5 minutes
Cooking Time: 15 minutes
Servings: 2
Ingredients:
- Cauliflower: ½ head
- Red hot buffalo wing sauce with 1/2 cup buffalo sauce, 120 ml
- 2 tbsp. olive oil:
- 1 tsp garlic powder:
- ½ tsp salt
- To **servings**: creamy dip and celery stalks (like ranch or bleu cheese).

Directions:
1. Cut the cauliflower into florets of bite-size.
2. Gently stir cauliflower and all remaining ingredients together in a large bowl. Fill your air fryer basket or rack with light grease.
3. Arrange cauliflower in one layer (working in batches if not all of them suit in one layer).
4. Cook for 12 to 15 minutes at 375 °F (190 °C) or until tender and slightly brown. Serve warm with your favorite celery sticks and dipping sauce.
Nutrition: Calories: 141 Carbohydrates: 4.5g Protein 1.6g Fat 14.1g

92. Air Fryer Mexican-style Stuffed Chicken Breast
Preparation Time: 20 Minutes
Cooking Time: 10 Minutes
Servings: 2
Ingredients:
- 4 inches extra-long toothpicks
- 4 tsp chili powder, divided
- 4 tsp ground cumin, divided
- 1 chicken breast skinless and boneless
- 2 tsp chipotle flakes:
- 2 tsp of mexican oregano
- Salt and ground pepper to taste
- 1/2 red pepper, cut into thin strips
- 1/2 onion cut in thin stripes
- 1 fresh jalapeno pepper cut in thin stripes
- 2 tsp corn oil:
- Juice of 1/2 lime

Directions:
1. Place the toothpicks in a small bowl and cover with water; let them soak for a while so they won't burn during cooking.
2. In a shallow dish, mix together 2 teaspoons of chili powder and 2 teaspoons of cumin.
3. Preheat the air fryer to 400 °F (200 °C).
4. Place the breast on a flat working surface. Horizontally cut through the middle. Pound up to around 1/4-inch thickness per half using a kitchen mallet or rolling pin.
5. Sprinkle with remaining chili powder, remaining cumin, chipotle flakes, oregano, salt, and pepper evenly on each breast portion. Fill up the center of 1 half of the breast with 1/2 of the bell pepper, onion, and jalapeno. Roll the chicken upwards from the tapered end and use 2 toothpicks to secure it. Repeat with other breasts, spices, and vegetables and use the remaining toothpicks to secure it. In the shallow bowl, roll each roll-up into the chili-cumin mixture while drizzling with olive oil until coated evenly.
6. Place roll-ups with the toothpick side facing up, in the air-fryer basket. Set a 6-minute timer.
7. Turn over roll-ups. Continue cooking in the air fryer until the juices run clear, and an instant-read thermometer reads at least 165 degrees F (74 degrees C) when inserted into the center, about 5 minutes more.
8. Drizzle with the lime juice evenly before serving onto roll-ups.
Nutrition: Calories 185.3 Protein 14.8 g Carbohydrates 15.2 g Cholesterol 32.3 mg Sodium 170.8 mg

93. Lemon Pepper Shrimp
Preparation Time: 5 Minutes

Cooking Time: 10 Minutes
Servings: 2
Ingredients:
- 1 tsp olive oil
- Juice of 1 lemon
- Lemon pepper
- 1/4 tsp paprika
- 1/4 tsp garlic powder
- Uncooked medium shrimp: 12 ounces, washed and deveined
- 1 sliced lemon

Directions:
1. Preheat an air fryer to 400 °F (200 °C).
2. In a cup, mix olive oil with lemon juice, lemon pepper, paprika, and garlic powder. Add the shrimps and then toss in the mixture until fully coated.
3. Open the air fryer and put the shrimp on the air fryer basket and cook for 6 to 8 minutes, until pink and strong. Serve with sliced lemon.

Nutrition: Calories 214.9 Protein 28.9 g Carbs 12.6 g Cholesterol 255.4 mg Sodium 528 mg

94. Air Fried Crumbed Fish

Preparation Time: 10 Minutes
Cooking Time: 12 Minutes
Servings: 4
Ingredients:
- Bread crumbs: 1 cup
- Vegetable oil: ¼ cup
- 4 Flounder fillets
- 1 Beaten egg
- 1 Sliced Lemon

Directions:
1. Preheat an air fryer to 350 °F (180 °C).
2. In a cup, add the bread crumbs and the oil. Stir until the mixture becomes crumbly and loose.
3. Dip the fish fillets in the egg mixture; shake off any excesses. Dip the fillets into a mixture of bread crumbs; until evenly and thoroughly coated.
4. Gently lay coated fillets in the preheated air fryer. Cook, about 12 minutes, with a fork, until fish flakes easily. Garnish with sliced lemon.

Nutrition: Calories 354 Fat 17.7 g Carbohydrates 22.5 g Protein 26.9 g

95. Air Fryer Meatloaf

Preparation Time: 10 Minutes
Cooking Time: 25 Minutes
Servings: 4
Ingredients:
- 1-pound lean beef
- 1 lightly beaten egg
- 3 tbsp. bread crumbs
- 1 small, finely chopped onion
- 1 tbsp. chopped fresh thyme
- 1 tsp salt
- 1 pinch ground black pepper to taste
- 2 thickly sliced mushrooms
- 1 tbsp. olive oil

Directions:
1. Preheat an air fryer up to 200 degrees C (392 degrees F).
2. In a bowl, combine ground beef, egg, bread crumbs, ointment, thyme, salt, and pepper. Knead and mix well.
3. Move the mixture of beef into a baking pan and smooth the rim—press chestnuts into the top and coat with olive oil. Place the saucepan in the basket of the air fryer and slide into the air fryer.
4. Set 25-minute air fryer timer and roast meatloaf until well browned.
5. Set aside the meatloaf for at least 10 minutes before slicing and serving into wedges.

Nutrition: Calories 296.8 Protein 24.8 g Carbohydrates 5.9 g Cholesterol 125.5 mg

96. Air Fryer Shrimp a La Bang Bang

Preparation Time: 10 minutes
Cooking Time: 12 minutes
Ingredients:
- 1/2 cup mayonnaise
- 1/4 cup sweet chili sauce
- 1 tbsp. sriracha sauce
- 1/4 cup all-purpose flour
- 1 cup panko bread crumbs
- Raw shrimp: 1 pound, peeled and deveined
- 1 leaf lettuce
- 2 green, chopped onions or to taste (optional)

Directions:
1. Set temperature of air fryer to 400 degrees F (200 degrees C).
2. In a bowl, stir in mayonnaise, chili sauce, and sriracha sauce until smooth. Put some bang bang sauce, if desired, in a separate bowl for dipping.
3. Take a plate and place flour on it. Use a separate plate and place panko bread crumbs on it.
4. First coat the shrimp with flour, then mayonnaise mixture, then panko. Place shrimp covered on a baking sheet.
5. Place shrimp, without overcrowding, in the air fryer basket.
6. Cook for approximately 12 minutes. Repeat with shrimp leftover.
7. Use lettuce wraps for serving, garnished with green onion.

Nutrition: Calories 415 Fat 23.9 g Carbohydrates 32.7 g Protein 23.9 g

97. Crumbed Chicken Tenderloins

Preparation Time: 15 Minutes
Cooking Time: 12 Minutes
Servings: 8
Ingredients:
- 1 Egg
- ½ cup dry bread crumbs
- 2 tbsp. vegetable oil:
- 8 chicken tenderloins

Directions:
1. Preheat an air fryer to 350 °F (175 °C).

2. Whisk the egg in a bowl.
3. In a second bowl, mix the bread crumbs and oil until the mixture becomes loose and crumbled.
4. Dip the tenderloin of chicken into the egg bowl shake off any remaining egg.
5. Dip the chicken into the crumb mixture, ensuring it is evenly and thoroughly coated. Place the chicken tenderloins into the air fryer basked. Cook, about 12 minutes, until the center, is no longer pink. A center-inserted instant-read thermometer should read at least 165 degrees F (74 degrees C).
Nutrition: Calories 252.7 Protein 26.2 g Carbohydrates 9.8 g

98. Caribbean Spiced Chicken
Preparation Time: 10 minutes
Cooking Time: 10 minutes
Servings: 8
Ingredients:
- Chicken thigh fillets: 3 Lbs., boneless and skinless
- Ground black pepper
- 1 tbsp. Ground coriander seed
- Salt
- 1 tbsp. Ground cinnamon
- 1 tbsp. Cayenne pepper
- 1 ½ teaspoons ground ginger
- 1 ½ tsp ground nutmeg
- 3 tbsp. coconut oil

Directions:
1. Take chicken off the packaging and pat dry. To soak up any residual liquid, place on a large baking sheet covered with paper towels. Chicken is salted and peppered on both sides. Let the chicken sit for 30 minutes, so when you go into the air fryer, it isn't that cold.
2. Combine cilantro, cinnamon, cayenne, ginger, and nutmeg in a small bowl. Coat the spice mixture on each piece of chicken and brush both sides with coconut oil.
3. Place four pieces of chicken in your air fryer basket (they shouldn't overlap). Air fry for 10 minutes at 390 degrees F. Remove the chicken from the basket and place it in a safe stove dish, tightly covered with foil.
4. Keep the chicken in the oven to keep it warm until the remaining chicken is done — repeat the **directions:** for air frying with the rest of the chicken.
Nutrition: Calories 202 Fat 13.4g Carbohydrates 1.7g Protein 24.9g

99. Air Fryer Jalapeno Popper Hassel back Chicken
Preparation Time: 10 minutes
Cooking Time: 15 minutes
Servings: 2
Ingredients:
- Sugar-free bacon: 4 slices, cooked and crumbled
- 2 ounces softened cream cheese
- ¼ cup chopped pickled jalapenos:
- 1/2 cup shredded and sharp cheddar cheese, split
- Chicken: 2 breasts, boneless and skinless

Directions:
1. Stir bacon, cream cheese, jalapenos, and 1/4-cup shredded cheddar cheese together in a medium bowl.
2. Use a knife and cut about 6 slits across the top of the chicken, and be careful not to cut through all the way.
3. Stuff the mixture with cream cheese into the slits.
4. Place the chicken in the air-fryer basket and set for 15 minutes to Air Fry at 350. Open the Air Fryer with 1-minute left, and sprinkle the remaining cheese on top. Last-minute Air Fry.
Nutrition: Calories 530 Fat 30g Saturated Fat 12g Carbohydrates 2g Protein 41g

100. Air Fryer Steak & Asparagus
Preparation Time: 10 minutes
Cooking Time: 5 minutes
Servings: 2
Ingredients:
- 1 bunch asparagus:
- 1 tbsp. Olive oil:
- 1 tsp sea salt
- 2 sirloin steaks with a boneless chuck eye
- Steak marinade of your choice

Directions:
1. Marinate the steak in your favorite steak marinade for 1-8 hours. Trim asparagus and place in the air fryer's bottom. Drizzle with coarse sea salt and olive oil.
2. Remove steak from marinade and top with asparagus set the air fryer temperature to 350 °F, fry for 5 minutes. Remove and serve the asparagus warm you can cook the steak for another 3-8 minutes, depending on your taste.
Nutrition: Calories: 245 Protein 3.9g Carbs: 46.8g Fat 12.4g

101. Lettuce Salad with Beef Strips
Preparation Time: 10 minutes
Cooking Time: 12 minutes
Servings: 5
Ingredients:
- 2 cup lettuce
- 10 oz. beef brisket
- 2 tbsp. sesame oil
- 1 tbsp. sunflower seeds
- 1 cucumber
- 1 tsp ground black pepper
- 1 tsp paprika
- 1 tsp Italian spices
- 2 tsp butter
- 1 tsp dried dill
- 2 tbsp. coconut milk

Directions:
1. Cut the beef brisket into strips.

2. Sprinkle the beef strips with the ground black pepper, paprika, and dried dill.
3. Preheat the air fryer to 365 F.
4. Put the butter in the air fryer basket tray and melt it.
5. Then add the beef strips and cook them for 6 minutes on each side.
6. Meanwhile, tear the lettuce and toss it in a big salad bowl.
7. Crush the sunflower seeds and sprinkle over the lettuce.
8. Chop the cucumber into the small cubes and add to the salad bowl.
9. Then combine the sesame oil and Italian spices together. Stir the oil.
10. Combine the lettuce mixture with the coconut milk and stir it using 2 wooden spatulas.
11. When the meat is cooked – let it chill to room temperature.
12. Add the beef strips to the salad bowl.
13. Stir it gently and sprinkle the salad with the sesame oil dressing.
14. Serve the dish immediately.

Nutrition: Calories 199 Fat 12.4g Carbs 3.9g Protein 18.1g

102. Cayenne Rib Eye Steak

Preparation Time: 10 minutes
Cooking Time: 13 minutes
Servings: 2
Ingredients:
- 1-pound rib eye steak
- 1 tsp salt
- 1 tsp cayenne pepper
- ½ tsp chili flakes
- 3 tbsp. cream
- 1 tsp olive oil
- 1 tsp lemongrass
- 1 tbsp. butter
- 1 tsp garlic powder

Directions:
1. Preheat the air fryer to 360 F.
2. Take a shallow bowl and combine the cayenne pepper, salt, chili flakes, lemongrass, and garlic powder together.
3. Mix the spices gently.
4. Sprinkle the rib eye steak with the spice mixture.
5. Melt the butter and combine it with cream and olive oil.
6. Churn the mixture.
7. Pour the churned mixture into the air fryer basket tray.
8. Add the rib eye steak.
9. Cook the steak for 13 minutes. Do not stir the steak during the cooking.
10. When the steak is cooked transfer it to a paper towel to soak all the excess Fat.
11. Serve the steak. You can slice the steak if desired.

Nutrition: Calories 708 Fat 59g Carbs 2.3g Protein 40.4g

103. Beef-Chicken Meatball Casserole

Preparation Time: 15 minutes
Cooking Time: 21 minutes
Servings: 7
Ingredients:
- 1 eggplant
- 10 oz. ground chicken
- 8 oz. ground beef
- 1 tsp minced garlic
- 1 tsp ground white pepper
- 1 tomato
- 1 egg
- 1 tbsp. coconut flour
- 8 oz. Parmesan, shredded
- 2 tbsp. butter
- 1/3 cup cream

Directions:
1. Combine the ground chicken and ground beef in a large bowl.
2. Add the minced garlic and ground white pepper.
3. Crack the egg into the bowl with the ground meat mixture and stir it carefully until well combined.
4. Then add the coconut flour and mix.
5. Make small meatballs from the ground meat.
6. Preheat the air fryer to 360 F.
7. Sprinkle the air fryer basket tray with the butter and pour the cream.
8. Peel the eggplant and chop it.
9. Put the meatballs over the cream and sprinkle them with the chopped eggplant.
10. Slice the tomato and place it over the eggplant.
11. Make a layer of shredded cheese over the sliced tomato.
12. Put the casserole in the air fryer and cook it for 21 minutes.
13. Let the casserole cool to room temperature before serving.

Nutrition: Calories 314 Fat 16.8g Carbs 7.5g Protein 33.9g

104. Juicy Pork Chops

Preparation Time: 10 minutes
Cooking Time: 11 minutes
Servings: 3
Ingredients:
- 1 tsp peppercorns
- 1 tsp kosher salt
- 1 tsp minced garlic
- ½ tsp dried rosemary
- 1 tbsp. butter
- 13 oz. pork chops

Directions:
1. Rub the pork chops with the dried rosemary, minced garlic, and kosher salt.
2. Preheat the air fryer to 365 F.

3. Put the butter and peppercorns in the air fryer basket tray. Melt the butter.
4. Place the pork chops in the melted butter.
5. Cook the pork chops for 6 minutes.
6. Turn the pork chops over.
7. Cook the pork chops for 5 minutes more.
8. When the meat is cooked, dry it gently with the paper towel.
9. Serve the juicy pork chops immediately.
Nutrition: Calories 431, Fat 34.4g Carbs 0.9g Protein 27.8

105. Chicken Goulash
Preparation Time: 10 minutes
Cooking Time: 17 minutes
Servings: 6
Ingredients:
- 4 oz. chive stems
- 2 green peppers, chopped
- 1 tsp olive oil
- 14 oz. ground chicken
- 2 tomatoes
- ½ cup chicken stock
- 2 garlic cloves, sliced
- 1 tsp salt
- 1 tsp ground black pepper
- 1 tsp mustard

Directions:
1. Chop chives roughly.
2. Spray the air fryer basket tray with the olive oil.
3. Preheat the air fryer to 365 F.
4. Put the chopped chives in the air fryer basket tray.
5. Add the chopped green pepper and cook the vegetables for 5 minutes.
6. Add the ground chicken.
7. Chop the tomatoes into the small cubes and add them in the air fryer mixture too.
8. Cook the mixture for 6 minutes more.
9. Add the chicken stock, sliced garlic cloves, salt, ground black pepper, and mustard.
10. Mix well to combine.
11. Cook the goulash for 6 minutes more.
Nutrition: Calories 161 Fat 6.1g Carbs 6g Protein 20.3g

106. Chicken & Turkey Meatloaf
Preparation Time: 15 minutes
Cooking Time: 25 minutes
Servings: 12
Ingredients:
- 3 tbsp. butter
- 10 oz. ground turkey
- 7 oz. ground chicken
- 1 teaspoon dried dill
- ½ tsp ground coriander
- 2 tbsp. almond flour
- 1 tbsp. minced garlic
- 3 oz. fresh spinach
- 1 tsp salt
- 1 egg
- ½ tbsp. paprika
- 1 tsp sesame oil

Directions:
1. Put the ground turkey and ground chicken in a large bowl.
2. Sprinkle the meat with dried dill, ground coriander, almond flour, minced garlic, salt, and paprika. Then chop the fresh spinach and add it to the ground poultry mixture.
3. Crack the egg into the meat mixture and mix well until you get a smooth texture. Get the air fryer basket tray with the olive oil.
4. Preheat the air fryer to 350 F.
5. Roll the ground meat mixture gently to make the flat layer.
6. Put the butter in the center of the meat layer. Make the shape of the meatloaf from the ground meat mixture. Use your fingertips for this step. Place the meatloaf in the air fryer basket tray.
7. Cook for 25 minutes. When the meatloaf is cooked allow it to rest before serving.
Nutrition: Calories 142 Fat 9.8 g Carbs 1.7g Protein 13g

107. Turkey Meatballs with Dried Dill
Preparation Time: 15 minutes
Cooking Time: 11 minutes
Servings: 9
Ingredients:
- 1-pound ground turkey
- 1 tsp chili flakes
- ¼ cup chicken stock
- 2 tbsp. dried dill
- 1 egg
- 1 tsp salt
- 1 tsp paprika
- 1 tbsp. coconut flour
- 2 tbsp. heavy cream
- 1 tsp olive oil

Directions:
1. Crack the egg in a bowl and whisk it with a fork. Add the ground turkey and chili flakes. Sprinkle the mixture with dried dill, salt, paprika, coconut flour, and mix it up. Make the meatballs from the ground turkey mixture. Preheat the air fryer to 360 F.
2. Grease the air fryer basket tray with the olive oil. Then put the meatballs inside. Cook the meatballs for 6 minutes – for 3 minutes on each side.
3. Sprinkle the meatballs with the heavy cream. Cook the meatballs for 5 minutes more. Let them rest for 2-3 minutes when the turkey meatballs are cooked.
Nutrition: Calories124 Fat 7.9g Carbs 1.2g Protein 14.8g

108. Chicken Coconut Poppers
Preparation Time: 10 minutes
Cooking Time: 10 minutes
Servings: 6
Ingredients:
- ½ cup coconut flour

- 1 tsp chili flakes
- 1 tsp ground black pepper
- 1 tsp garlic powder
- 11 oz. chicken breast, boneless, skinless
- 1 tsp olive oil

Directions:
1. Cut the chicken breast into medium cubes and put them in a large bowl. Sprinkle the chicken cubes with the chili flakes, ground black pepper, garlic powder and stir them well using your hands.
2. After this, sprinkle the chicken cubes with the almond flour.
3. Shake the bowl with the chicken cubes gently to coat the meat.
4. Preheat the air fryer to 365 F.
5. Grease the air fryer basket tray with the olive oil.
6. Place the chicken cubes inside.
7. Cook the chicken poppers for 10 minutes.
8. Turn the chicken poppers over after 5 minutes of cooking.
9. Allow the cooked chicken poppers to cool before serving.

Nutrition: Calories 123, Fat 4.6g Carbs 6.9g Protein 13.2g

109. Parmesan Beef Slices

Preparation Time: 14 minutes
Cooking Time: 25 minutes
Servings: 4
Ingredients:
- 12 oz. beef brisket
- 1 tsp kosher salt
- 7 oz. Parmesan, sliced
- 5 oz. chive stems
- 1 tsp turmeric
- 1 tsp dried oregano
- 2 tsp butter

Directions:
1. Slice the beef brisket into 4 slices.
2. Sprinkle every beef slice with the turmeric and dried oregano.
3. Grease the air fryer basket tray with the butter.
4. Put the beef slices inside.
5. Dice the chives.
6. Make a layer using the diced chives over the beef slices.
7. Then make a layer using the Parmesan cheese.
8. Preheat the air fryer to 365 F.
9. Cook the beef slices for 25 minutes.

Nutrition: Calories 348 Fat 18g Carbs 5g Protein 42.1g

110. Chili Beef Jerky

Preparation Time: 25 minutes
Cooking Time: 2.5 hours
Servings: 6
Ingredients:
- 14 oz. beef flank steak
- 1 tsp chili pepper
- 3 tbsp. apple cider vinegar
- 1 tsp ground black pepper
- 1 tsp onion powder
- 1 tsp garlic powder
- ¼ tsp liquid smoke

Directions:
1. Slice the beefsteak into the medium strips and then tenderize each piece.
2. Take a bowl and combine the apple cider vinegar, ground black pepper, onion powder, garlic powder, and liquid smoke.
3. Whisk gently with a fork.
4. Then transfer the beef pieces in the mixture and stir well.
5. Leave the meat to marinade for up to 8 hours.
6. Put the marinated beef pieces in the air fryer rack.
7. Cook the beef jerky for 2.5 hours at 150 F.

Nutrition: Calories 129, Fat 4.1g Carbs 1.1g Protein 20.2 g

111. Spinach Beef Heart

Preparation Time: 15 minutes
Cooking Time: 20 minutes
Servings: 4
Ingredients:
- 1-pound beef heart
- 5 oz. chive stems
- ½ cup fresh spinach
- 1 tsp salt
- 1 tsp ground black pepper
- 3 cups chicken stock
- 1 tsp butter

Directions:
1. Remove all the Fat from the beef heart.
2. Dice the chives.
3. Chop the fresh spinach.
4. Combine the diced chives, fresh spinach, and butter together. Stir it.
5. Make a cut in the beef heart and fill it with the spinach-chives mixture.
6. Preheat the air fryer to 400 F.
7. Pour the chicken stock into the air fryer basket tray.
8. Sprinkle the Prepared stuffed beef heart with the salt and ground black pepper.
9. Put the beef heart in the air fryer and cook it for 20 minutes.
10. Remove the cooked heart from the air fryer and slice it.
11. Sprinkle the slices with the remaining liquid from the air fryer.

Nutrition: Calories 216, Fat 6.8g Fiber 0.8g Carbs 3.8g Protein 33.3

112. Paprika Pulled Pork

Preparation Time: 15 minutes
Cooking Time: 20 minutes
Servings: 4
Ingredients:
- 1 tbsp. chili flakes

- 1 tsp ground black pepper
- ½ tsp paprika
- 1 tsp cayenne pepper
- 1/3 cup cream
- 1 tsp kosher salt
- 1-pound pork tenderloin
- 1 tsp ground thyme
- 4 cup chicken stock
- 1 tsp butter

Directions:
1. Pour the chicken stock into the air fryer basket tray.
2. Add the pork steak and sprinkle the mixture with the chili flakes, ground black pepper, paprika, cayenne pepper, and kosher salt.
3. Preheat the air fryer to 370 F and cook the meat for 20 minutes.
4. Strain the liquid and shred the meat with 2 forks.
5. Then add the butter and cream and mix it.
6. Cook the pulled pork for 4 minutes more at 360 F.
7. When the pulled pork is cooked allow to rest briefly.

Nutrition: Calories 198 Fat 6.8g Carbs 2.3, Protein 30.7

113. Paprika Whole Chicken

Preparation Time: 15 minutes
Cooking Time: 75 minutes
Servings: 12
Ingredients:
- 6-pound whole chicken
- 1 tsp kosher salt
- 1 tsp ground black pepper
- 1 tsp ground paprika
- 1 tbsp. minced garlic
- 3 tbsp. butter
- 1 tsp olive oil
- ¼ cup water
- 3 oz. chive stems

Directions:
1. Rub the whole chicken with the kosher salt and ground black pepper inside and outside.
2. Sprinkle it with the ground paprika and minced garlic. Dice the chives.
3. Put the diced chives inside the whole chicken.
4. Then add the butter.
5. Rub the chicken with olive oil.
6. Preheat the air fryer to 360 F and pour water in the air fryer basket.
7. Place the chicken on the rack inside the air fryer.
8. Cook the chicken for 75 minutes.
9. When the chicken is cooked it should have slightly crunchy skin.
10. Cut the cooked chicken into the servings.

Nutrition: Calories 464 Fat 20.1g Carbs 0.9 Protein 65.8

114. Pork Almond Bites

Preparation Time: 10 minutes
Cooking Time: 14 minutes
Servings: 6
Ingredients:
- 1-pound pork tenderloin
- 2 eggs
- 1 tsp butter
- ¼ cup almond flour
- 1 tsp kosher salt
- 1 tsp paprika
- 1 tsp ground coriander
- ½ tsp lemon zest

Directions:
1. Chop the pork tenderloin into the large cubes.
2. Sprinkle the pork cubes with the kosher salt, paprika, ground coriander, and lemon zest.
3. Mix the meat gently.
4. Crack the egg into a bowl and whisk it.
5. Coat the meat cubes with the egg mixture and then the almond flour.
6. Preheat the air fryer to 365 F.
7. Put the butter in the air fryer basket tray and then place the pork bites inside.
8. Cook the pork bites for 14 minutes.
9. Turn the pork bites over after 7 minutes of cooking.
10. When the pork bites are cooked – serve them hot.

Nutrition: Calories 142, Fat 5.4g Carbs 0.6g Protein 21.9g

115. Panda Coconut Chicken

Preparation Time: 20 minutes
Cooking Time: 10 minutes
Servings: 4
Ingredients:
- 15oz. chicken
- 1 panda leaf
- 3 oz. chive stems, diced
- 1 tsp minced garlic
- 1 tsp chili flakes
- 1 tsp stevia
- 1 tsp ground black pepper
- 1 tsp turmeric
- 1 tsp butter
- ¼ cup coconut milk
- 1 tsp chives powder

Directions:
1. Cut the chicken into 4 big cubes.
2. Put the chicken cubes in a large bowl.
3. Sprinkle the chicken with the minced garlic, diced chives, chili flakes, stevia, ground black pepper, chives powder, and turmeric.
4. Mix the meat up using your hands.
5. Cut the panda leaf into 4 parts.
6. Wrap the chicken cubes into the panda leaf.
7. Pour the coconut milk into a bowl with the wrapped chicken and leave it for 10 minutes.
8. Preheat the air fryer to 380 F.

9. Put the panda chicken in the air fryer basket and cook for 10 minutes.
10. When the chicken is cooked – transfer to serving plates and let it chill for at least 2-3 minutes.
Nutrition: Calories 250 Fat 12.6g Carbs 3.1g Protein 29.9g

116. Air Fryer Raspberry Balsamic Smoked Pork Chops
Preparation Time: 15 minutes
Cooking Time: 15 minutes
Servings: 4
Ingredients:
- Bone-in pork chops, smoked - 4 (7½ ounces each)
- 2 large Eggs
- 1 cup bread crumbs
- ¼ cup milk, low Fat
- 1 cup pecans, chopped
- ⅓ Cup balsamic vinegar
- 2 tbsp. Brown Sugar
- 2 tbsp. Raspberry jam
- ¼ cup All-purpose flour
- 1 tbsp. Orange juice concentrate
- Cooking spray – as required

Directions:
1. Set the air fryer at 200 degrees Celsius and pre-heat
2. Slightly coat the air fryer basket with non-stick cooking spray.
3. Combine milk and eggs in a medium bowl.
4. Toss bread crumb and pecans in another medium bowl and keep ready.
5. Lightly coat the pork chops with flour, shrug off excess flour.
6. Dip the pork chop in egg mixture and dredge in bread crumb.
7. Place the dredged chops in the frying basket.
8. Spray non-stick cooking oil over it.
9. Set the timer for 15 minutes and cook until it becomes golden brown.
10. Flip the chops after 8 minutes or intermittently.
11. Spray non-stick oil while flipping.
12. After cooking, remove the food for serving.
13. If you have many pieces to cook, you can do the cooking in batches. Do not place the chops layer above layer.
14. In a saucepan pour raspberry jam, brown sugar, balsamic vinegar, milk and orange juice to make the glaze.
15. Heat on medium temperature and bring to boil
16. Stir continuously and cook for about 8 minutes until it transforms into a thick consistency.
17. Serve hot along with chops.
Nutrition: Calories: 579 Carbohydrates: 36g Fat 36g Protein 32g

117. American Air Fried Cheese Sandwich
Preparation Time: 2 minutes
Cooking Time: 8 minutes
Servings: 1
Ingredients:
- 2 slices sandwich bread
- 2 tsp butter
- 3 slices cheddar cheese

Directions:
1. Keep the cheese between the sandwich bread slices. Butter the bread outside.
2. Put in the air fryer basket. Set the temperature at 190 degrees Celsius and timer to 8 minutes.
3. After 4 minutes, pull out the fryer basket and flip the sandwich and continue cooking further 4 minutes.
4. Serve hot.
Nutrition: Calories: 546 Carbohydrate: 29.1g Fat 37.5g Protein 25g

118. Midnight Nutella Banana Sandwich
Preparation Time: 4 minutes
Cooking Time: 8 minutes
Servings: 2
Ingredients:
- 4 slices white bread
- ¼ cup Nutella chocolate hazelnut spread
- 1 Banana
- Soft butter for spreading

Directions:
1. Set your air fryer at 190 degrees Celsius
2. Spread the butter on one side of the bread slice and keep the buttered side down on flat surface.
3. Now, spread the chocolate hazelnut on the non-buttered side of the bread slice.
4. Cut the banana into half and slice it lengthwise into 3 portions.
5. For making 2 sandwiches, place the bananas on two bread slices and put the remaining bananas on top of the bread slice.
6. Cut the sliced bread into a triangle shape.
7. Put the sliced bread sandwiches into the air fryer basket.
8. Set the timer for 5 minutes and temperature at 190 degrees Celsius.
9. Flip the sandwiches halfway.
10. When both sides become brown, it is ready to serve.
Nutrition: Calories: 341 Carbohydrate: 42.6g Fat 18.4g Protein 4.1g

119. Air Fried Pork Chops with Brussels Sprouts
Preparation Time: 10 minutes
Cooking Time: 25 minutes
Servings: 1
Ingredients:
- 8 ounces' pork chop with bone
- 6 ounces Brussels sprouts quartered
- 1 tsp olive oil
- ½ tsp black pepper, crushed
- 1 tsp mustard

- 1 tsp maple syrup
- ⅛ Tsp kosher salt

Directions:
1. Clean pork chops in running water and pat dry. Oil coats the pork lightly with cooking spray. Sprinkle ¼ teaspoon pepper over it and also sprinkle salt and keep it aside. Now in a medium bowl pour olive oil. Add the remaining pepper, mustard, maple syrup and combine.
2. Put the quartered Brussels sprouts and toss it gently, to coat the mix. Now place the coated pork chop and Brussels sprouts in the air fryer basket. Set the temperature at 200 degrees Celsius and timer to 10 minutes. If you wish to have well-done pork, you can increase the cooking time to the required level.

Nutrition: Calories: 955 Carbohydrate: 21.8g Fat 71.9g Protein 57.7g

120. Air Fryer Fish and Fries

Preparation Time: 15 minutes
Cooking Time: 25 minutes
Servings: 4
Ingredients:
For fish fry:
- ⅓ Cup all-purpose flour
- 1 large egg
- ⅔ cup Cornflakes, crushed
- 1-pound Cod fillets
- ¼ tsp Ground pepper
- 1 tbsp. shredded parmesan cheese
- ⅛ Tsp cayenne pepper
- 2 tbsp. tartar sauce
- 2 tbsp. water
- ¼ tsp Salt

For potato fry:
- 1 pound potatoes
- 2 tbsp. olive oil
- ¼ teaspoon pepper

Directions:
1. Peel, wash and cut the potatoes in lengthwise ½" size and again cut into half. Set the air fryer to 200 degrees Celsius and pre-heat.
2. Toss the cut size potatoes with pepper, salt, and oil in a large bowl. Place the potatoes in the frying basket by not overlapping one another. Fry for 10 minutes or until the potatoes become tender. After 10 minutes, toss the potatoes in the air fryer basket and again fry for another 10 minutes.
3. While the frying is in progress, let us prepare for fish frying. Whisk egg and water in a small bowl. In another medium bowl, combine pepper and flour. Take yet another bowl and toss cheese and cayenne with cornflakes.
4. Dust salt on the fish. Dredge the fish in the flour mixture and let it have an even coating. If any excess coating is there, shake it to remove. Now dip the fish into the egg mixture and after that dredge in the cornflake mixture. By the time the potatoes frying will be over. Remove it and keep warm.
5. Now place the coated fish in the air fryer basket for frying. Set cooking for 8-10 minutes. When the fish turns into light brown, flip it carefully. Once done, transfer the fried potatoes over to fish fillet, so that the potatoes can absorb some heat from fish. Serve along with tartar sauce.

Nutrition: Calories: 312 Carbohydrates: 35g Fat 9g Protein 23g

121. Air Fried Broccoli with Cheese Sauce

Preparation Time: 15 minutes
Cooking Time: 20 Minutes
Servings: 4
Ingredients:
- 6 cups Broccoli florets
- 10 tbsp. Low Fat evaporated milk
- 4 tsp Amarillo paste
- 1½ ounces Fresh Mexican cheese, grated
- Cooking spray – as required
- 6 Low sodium saltine crackers

Directions:
1. Slightly coat the cooking spray on the broccoli florets. Place the broccoli in the air fryer basket.
2. Set the temperature at 190 degrees Celsius and cook for about 8 minutes.
3. Put Mexican chest, milk, and Amarillo paste and saltine crackers in a blender and process it until it becomes smooth. Transfer the cheese sauce into a microwave oven safe bowl and microwave it for 30 seconds.
4. Serve the fried broccoli florets with cheese sauce.

Nutrition: Calories: 108 Carbohydrates: 15g Fat 2g Protein 8g

122. Air Fryer Chicken Sandwich

Preparation Time: 10 minutes
Cooking Time: 16 minutes
Servings: 6
Ingredients:
- Boneless-skinless chicken breast 2
- ½ cup dill Pickle Juice -
- ½ cup milk
- 2 Eggs
- 2 tbsp. potato starch
- 1 cup all-purpose flour
- 2 tbsp. sugar powdered
- 1 tsp paprika
- ½ tsp ground black pepper
- ½ tsp garlic powder
- ¼ tsp Ground celery seed
- 1 tbsp. extra virgin olive oil
- ½ tsp Salt
- ½ cups dill pickle chips
- 6 hamburger buns
- Cooking spray – as required
- ¼ cup mayonnaise -

Directions:
1. Pound the chicken putting in a zip lock bag, so that the chicken thickness become even in all side. The ideal thickness is ½ inch.

2. Cut the chicken into 2-3 pieces. Now put back the chicken pieces into the zip lock bag and pour pickle juice and shake. Keep it in the refrigerator for about 30 minutes to get a better marinade effect.
3. Blend egg and milk in medium bowl. Combine all spices, starch, and flour in another bowl. Using a tong, dip the chicken in the egg mixture. Then dredge in the flour mixture.
4. Remove any excess flour if stuck with the chicken by shaking.
5. Grease the air fryer basket with cooking spray. Place the coated chicken into the air fryer tray and drizzle some cooking spray over it.
6. Set the temperature at 170 degrees Celsius and cook for 6 minutes. After 6 minutes, flip the chicken and spray some cooking oil and continue cooking for 6 more minutes. Now increase the temperature to 200 degrees Celsius and cook for 2 more minutes.
7. Flip the chicken and cook the other side also for 2 minutes at 200 degrees Celsius. Toast the bun and cut open. Place the chicken between the opened buns along with 2 pickle chips and mayonnaise.
Nutrition: Calories: 281 Carbohydrates: 38g Protein 15g Fat 6g

123. Air Fryer Orange Turkey Burgers
Preparation Time: 15 minutes
Cooking Time: 11 minutes
Servings: 4
Ingredients:
- 1-pound ground turkey
- 1 tsp ground mustard seed
- 1 tbsp. grape nuts nuggets
- ¼ tsp Chinese five spice
- 1 diced scallion
- Orange Basting Sauce:
- ½ cup orange marmalade
- 1 tbsp. soy sauce
- 1 tsp fish sauce
- 2 tsp Oyster sauce
- Orange Aioli:
- 1 tbsp. orange juice
- 1 tsp orange zest
- ½ cup mayonnaise
- 1 tsp ground chili paste

Directions:
1. In a small bowl, whisk Orange Aioli ingredients and refrigerate. In another bowl combine basting sauce and keep aside. Set the air fryer at 200 degrees Celsius and pre-heat for about 10 minutes. In a medium bowl combine the burger ingredients and add 1 tablespoon of basting sauce.
2. Shape the mix into 6 patties and create an indentation at the center of the patties. Now slightly grease the surface of air fryer basket with cooking oil and place the patties in the frying basket. Set the temperature at 180 degrees Celsius and cook for 9 minutes. Flip the burgers intermittently every 4 minutes. Baste burger after every 2 minutes.
3. After 9 minutes of cooking, baste the burger and cook a further 3 minutes. Serve hot along with Orange Aioli.
Nutrition: Calories: 443 Carbohydrates: 34.9g Fat 22.5g Protein 32g

124. Cheesy Ravioli Lunch
Preparation Time: 5 minutes
Cooking Time: 15 minutes
Servings: 6
Ingredients:
- 1 package cheese ravioli
- 2 cup Italian breadcrumbs
- ¼ cup Parmesan cheese, grated
- 1 cup buttermilk
- 1 tsp olive oil
- ¼ tsp garlic powder

Directions:
1. Preheat Breville on Air Fry function to 390 F. In a bowl, combine breadcrumbs, Parmesan cheese, garlic, and olive oil.
2. Dip the ravioli in the buttermilk and coat with the breadcrumb mixture.
3. Line a baking sheet with parchment paper and arrange the ravioli on it.
4. Press Start and cook for 5 minutes.
5. Serve with marinara jar sauce.
Nutrition: Calories: 381 Carbohydrates: 18g Protein 25g Fat 5g

125. Carrots & Shallots with Yogurt
Preparation Time: 10 minutes
Cooking Time: 25 minutes
Servings: 4
Ingredients:
- 2 tsp olive oil
- 2 shallots, chopped
- 3 carrots, sliced
- Salt to taste
- ¼ cup yogurt
- 2 garlic cloves, minced
- 3 tbsp. parsley, chopped

Directions:
1. In a bowl, mix sliced carrots, salt, garlic, shallots, parsley, and yogurt. Sprinkle with oil. Place the veggies in the basket and press Start.
2. Cook for 15 minutes on Air Fry function at 370 F.
3. Serve with basil and garlic mayo.
Nutrition: Calories: 251 Carbohydrates: 30g Protein 16g Fat 2g

126. Grandma´s Ratatouille
Preparation Time: 15 minutes
Cooking Time: 30 minutes
Servings: 2
Ingredients:
- 1 tbsp. olive oil
- 3 Roma tomatoes, thinly sliced
- 2 garlic cloves, minced

- 1 zucchini, thinly sliced
- 2 yellow bell peppers, sliced
- 1 tbsp. vinegar
- 2 tbsp. herbs de Provence
- Salt and black pepper to taste

Directions:
1. Preheat Breville on Air Fry function to 390 F. Place all ingredients in a bowl. Season it with salt and pepper and stir to coat. Arrange the vegetable on a baking dish and place in the Breville oven. Cook for 15 minutes, shaking occasionally. Let sit for 5 more minutes after the timer goes off.

Nutrition: Calories: 181 Carbohydrates: 39g Protein 18g Fat 8g

127. Amazing Macadamia Delight
Preparation Time: 10 minutes
Cooking Time: 20 minutes
Servings: 6
Ingredients:
- 3 cups macadamia nuts
- 3 tbsp. liquid smoke
- Salt to taste
- 2 tbsp. molasses

Directions:
1. Preheat Breville on Bake function to 360 F.
2. In a bowl, add salt, liquid, molasses, and cashews and toss to coat.
3. Place the cashews in baking tray and press Start.
4. Cook for 10 minutes, shaking the basket every 5 minutes. Serve.

Nutrition: Calories: 191 Carbohydrates: 18g Protein 35g Fat 3g

128. Veggie Mix Fried Chips
Preparation Time: 25 minutes
Cooking Time: 45 minutes
Servings: 4
Ingredients:
- 1 large eggplant, cut into strips
- 5 potatoes, peeled and cut into strips
- 3 zucchinis cut into strips
- ½ cup cornstarch
- ½ cup olive oil
- Salt to taste

Directions:
1. Preheat Breville on Air Fry function to 390 F. In a bowl, stir cornstarch, ½ cup of water, salt, pepper, olive oil, eggplants, zucchini, and potatoes. Place the veggie mixture in the basket and press Start. Cook for 12 minutes. Serve warm.

Nutrition: Calories: 276 Carbohydrates: 38g Protein 19g Fat 13g

129. Cheese Stuffed Green Peppers with Tomato Sauce
Preparation Time: 15 minutes
Cooking Time: 35 minutes
Servings: 4
Ingredients:
- 2 cans green chili peppers
- 1 cup cheddar cheese, shredded
- 1 cup Monterey Jack cheese, shredded
- 2 tbsp. all-purpose flour
- 2 large eggs, beaten
- ½ cup milk
- 1 cans tomato sauce

Directions:
1. Preheat Breville on Air Fry function to 380 F. Spray the baking dishes with cooking spray. Take half of the chilies and arrange them in the baking dish. Top with half of the cheese and cover with the remaining chilies. In a medium bowl, combine eggs, milk, and flour and pour over the chilies.
2. Press Start and cook for 20 minutes. Remove the chilies and pour the tomato sauce over them; cook for 15 more minutes. Top with the remaining cheese and serve.

Nutrition: Calories: 309 Carbohydrates: 33g Protein 22g Fat 12g

130. Basil White Fish
Preparation Time: 10 minutes
Cooking Time: 20 minutes
Servings: 4
Ingredients:
- 2 tbsp. fresh basil, chopped
- 2 garlic cloves, minced
- 1 tbsp. Parmesan cheese, grated
- Salt and black pepper to taste
- 2 tbsp. pine nuts
- 4 white fish fillets
- 2 tbsp. olive oil

Directions:
1. Preheat Breville on Air Fry function to 350 F. Season the fillets with salt and pepper and place in the basket. Drizzle with some olive oil and press Start. Cook for 12-14 minutes. In a bowl, mix basil, remaining olive oil, pine nuts, garlic, and Parmesan cheese and spread on the fish. Serve.

Nutrition: Calories: 298 Carbohydrates: 31g Protein 34g Fat 8g

131. Cajun Salmon with Lemon
Preparation Time: 5 minutes
Cooking Time: 10 minutes
Servings: 1
Ingredients:
- 1 salmon fillet
- ¼ tsp brown sugar
- Juice of ½ lemons
- 1 tbsp. Cajun seasoning
- 2 lemon wedges
- 1 tbsp. fresh parsley, chopped

Directions:
1. Preheat Breville on Bake function to 350 F.
2. Combine sugar and lemon and coat in the salmon. Sprinkle with the Cajun seasoning as well. Place a parchment paper on a baking tray and press Start.

Cook for 14-16 minutes. Serve with lemon wedges and chopped parsley.
Nutrition: Calories: 221 Carbohydrates: 11g Protein 12g Fat 7g

132. Lemon Salmon
Preparation Time: 10 minutes
Cooking Time: 20 minutes
Servings: 2
Ingredients:
- 2 salmon fillets
- Salt to taste
- Zest of 1 lemon

Directions:
1. Rub the fillets with salt and lemon zest. Place them in the frying basket and spray with cooking spray. Press Start and cook the salmon in the preheated Breville oven for 14 minutes at 360 F on Air Fry function. Serve with steamed asparagus and a drizzle of lemon juice.

Nutrition: Calories: 332 Carbohydrates: 41g Protein 14g Fat 10g

133. Saucy Cod with Green Onions
Preparation Time: 10 minutes
Cooking Time: 20 minutes
Servings: 4
Ingredients:
- 4 cod fillets
- 2 tbsp. fresh cilantro, chopped
- Salt to taste
- 4 green onions, chopped
- 5 slices of ginger, chopped
- 5 tbsp. soy sauce
- 3 tbsp. oil
- 5 rock sugar cubes

Directions:
1. Preheat Breville on Air Fry function to 390 F. Season the cod with salt and coriander and drizzle with some olive oil. Place the fish fillet in the basket and press Start. Cook for 15 minutes.
2. Heat the remaining olive oil in a skillet over medium heat and sauté green onions and ginger for 3 minutes. Add in the remaining ingredients and 1 cup of water. Bring to a boil and cook for 5 minutes until the sauce thickens. Pour the sauce over the fish and serve.

Nutrition: Calories: 266 Carbohydrates: 28g Protein 18g Fat 9g

134. Parmesan Tilapia Fillets
Preparation Time: 5 minutes
Cooking Time: 15 minutes
Servings: 4
Ingredients:
- ¾ cup Parmesan cheese, grated
- 1 tbsp. olive oil
- 1 tsp paprika
- 1 tbsp. fresh parsley, chopped
- ¼ tsp garlic powder
- ¼ tsp salt
- 4 tilapia fillets

Directions:
1. Preheat Breville on Air Fry function to 350 F. In a bowl, mix parsley, Parmesan cheese, garlic, salt, and paprika.
2. Coat in the tilapia fillets and place them in a lined baking sheet.
3. Drizzle with the olive oil press Start.
4. Cook for 8-10 minutes until golden. Serve warm.

Nutrition: Calories: 145 Carbohydrates: 43g Protein 21g Fat 17g

135. Party Cod Nuggets
Preparation Time: 15 minutes
Cooking Time: 25 minutes
Servings: 4
Ingredients:
- 1 ¼ lb. cod fillets, cut into 4 chunks each
- ½ cup flour
- 1 egg
- 1 cup cornflakes
- 1 tbsp. olive oil
- Salt and black pepper to taste

Directions:
1. Place the oil and cornflakes in a food processor and process until crumbed. Season the fish chunks with salt and pepper. In a bowl, beat the egg with 1 tbsp. of water.
2. Dredge the chunks in flour first, then dip in the egg, and finally coat with cornflakes.
3. Arrange on a lined sheet and press Start. Cook on Air Fry function at 350 F for 15 minutes until crispy.
4. Serve.

Nutrition: Calories: 391 Carbohydrates: 56g Protein 11g Fat 2g

136. Lemon Pepper Tilapia Fillets
Preparation Time: 8 minutes
Cooking Time: 15 minutes
Servings: 4
Ingredients:
- 1 lb. tilapia fillets
- 1 tbsp. Italian seasoning
- 2 tbsp. canola oil
- 2 tbsp. lemon pepper
- Salt to taste
- 2-3 butter buds

Directions:
1. Preheat your Breville oven to 400 F on Bake function. Drizzle tilapia fillets with canola oil. In a bowl, mix salt, lemon pepper, butter buds, and Italian seasoning spread on the fish.
2. Place the fillet on a baking tray and press Start. Cook for 10 minutes until tender and crispy. Serve warm.

Nutrition: Calories: 201 Carbohydrates: 28g Protein 17g Fat 13g

137. Citrus Cilantro Catfish

Preparation Time: 10 minutes
Cooking Time: 20 minutes
Servings: 2
Ingredients:
- 2 catfish fillets
- 2 tsp blackening seasoning
- Juice of 1 lime
- 2 tbsp. butter, melted
- 1 garlic clove, mashed
- 2 tbsp. fresh cilantro, chopped

Directions:
1. In a bowl, blend garlic, lime juice, cilantro, and butter. Pour half of the mixture over the fillets and sprinkle with blackening seasoning. Place the fillets in the basket and press Start. Cook for 15 minutes at 360 F on Air Fry function. Serve the fish topped with the remaining sauce.

Nutrition: Calories: 141 Carbohydrates: 32g Protein 10g Fat 7g

138. Salmon & Caper Cakes
Preparation Time: 10 minutes
Cooking Time: 15 minutes
Servings: 2
Ingredients:
- 8 oz. salmon, cooked
- 1 ½ oz. potatoes, mashed
- A handful of capers
- 1 tbsp. fresh parsley, chopped
- Zest of 1 lemon
- 1 ¾ oz. plain flour

Directions:
1. Carefully flake the salmon. In a bowl, mix the salmon, zest, capers, dill, and mashed potatoes. Form small cakes from the mixture and dust them with flour; refrigerate for 60 minutes. Preheat Breville to 350 F. Press Start and cook the cakes for 10 minutes on Air Fry function. Serve chilled.

Nutrition: Calories: 132 Carbohydrates: 28g Protein 25g Fat 15g

139. Lunch Egg Rolls
Preparation Time: 25 Minutes
Cooking Time: 20 minutes
Servings: 4
Ingredients:
- ½ cup mushrooms
- ½ cup carrots
- ½ cup zucchini
- 2 green onions
- 2 tbsp. soy sauce
- 8 egg roll
- 1 egg
- 1 tbsp. Cornstarch

Directions:
1. Mix carrots with soy sauce, zucchini, green onions and mushrooms in a bowl. Stir.
2. Organize egg roll wrappers on a surface. Divide veggie mix on each. Roll well.
3. Mix cornstarch plus egg in a bowl. Whisk well. Brush eggs rolls with this mix.
4. Seal edges. Place all rolls in preheated air fryer. Cook for 15 minutes at 370°F.
5. Arrange them on a platter. Serve.

Nutrition: Calories: 581 Carbohydrates: 12g Protein 16g Fat 22g

140. Veggie Toast
Preparation Time: 25 Minutes
Cooking Time: 15 minutes
Servings: 4
Ingredients:
- 1 red bell pepper
- 1 cup cremini mushrooms
- 2 green Onions
- 1 tbsp. olive oil
- 4 bread slices
- 2 tbsp. butter
- ½ cup goat cheese

Directions:
1. Mix mushrooms and red bell pepper in a bowl squash. Add oil and green onions. Toss. Transfer to air fryer. Cook them for 10 minutes at 350°F. Transfer to a bowl.
2. On bread slices, spread butter. Place them in the air fryer. Cook for 5 minutes at 350°F.
3. Divide veggie mix on the bread slices. Top using crumbled cheese. Serve.

Nutrition: Calories: 432 Carbohydrates: 32g Protein 13g Fat 12g

141. Stuffed Mushrooms
Preparation Time: 30 minutes
Cooking Time: 20 minutes
Servings: 4
Ingredients:
- 4 big Portobello mushroom caps
- 1 tbsp. olive oil
- ¼ cup ricotta cheese
- 5 tbsp. parmesan
- 1 cup spinach
- 1/3 cup bread crumbs
- ¼ tsp. rosemary

Directions:
1. Rub mushrooms caps with the oil. Place them in your air fryer's basket. Cook for 2 minutes at 350°F.
2. Mix half of the parmesan with bread crumbs, rosemary, spinach and ricotta in a bowl. Stir.
3. Stuff mushrooms with this mix.
4. Drizzle with parmesan. Place in your air fryer's basket.
5. Cook for 10 minutes at 350°F.
6. Divide on plates and serve.

Nutrition: Calories: 231 Carbohydrates: 33g Protein 13g Fat 3g

142. Quick Lunch Pizzas
Preparation Time: 17 Minutes

Cooking Time: 15 minutes
Servings: 4
Ingredients:
- 4 pitas
- 1 tablespoon olive oil
- ¾ cup pizza sauce
- 4 ounces jarred mushrooms
- ½ tsp. basil
- 2 green onions
- 2 cup mozzarella
- 1 cup grape tomatoes

Directions:
1. On each pita bread spread pizza sauce.
2. Drizzle basil and green onions.
3. Divide mushrooms top with cheese.
4. Assemble pita pizzas in air fryer.
5. Cook for 7 minutes at 400°F.
6. Top pizza with tomato slices.
7. Divide among plates. Serve.

Nutrition: Calories: 235 Carbohydrates: 32g Protein 12g Fat 9g

143. Lunch Gnocchi
Preparation Time: 10 minutes
Cooking Time: 5 minutes
Servings: 4
Ingredients:
- 1 yellow onion
- 1 tbsp.
- Olive oil
- 3 garlic cloves
- 16 ounces' gnocchi
- ¼ cup parmesan
- 8 oz. Spinach pesto

Directions:
1. Lubricate air fryer's pan with olive oil. Include garlic, onion, and gnocchi. Toss. Place pan in air fryer. Cook for 10 minutes at 400°F.
2. Include pesto. Toss. Cook for 7 minutes at 350°F.
3. Divide among plates. Serve.

Nutrition: Calories: 280 Carbohydrates: 12g Protein 11g Fat 15g

144. Tuna and Zucchini Tortillas
Preparation Time: 10 Minutes
Cooking Time: 6 minutes
Servings: 4
Ingredients:
- 4 corn tortillas
- 4 tbsp. butter
- 6 oz. canned tuna
- 1 cup zucchini
- 1/3 cup mayonnaise
- 2 tbsp. mustard
- 1 cup cheddar cheese

Directions:
1. Spread butter on tortillas. Put in an air fryer's basket. Cook for 3 minutes at 400°F.
2. Mix mustard with mayo, zucchini, and tuna in a bowl. Stir.
3. Mix on each tortilla. Garnish with cheese.
4. Position in your air fryer's basket
5. Cook for 4 minutes at 400°F.
6. Serve.

Nutrition: Calories: 381 Carbohydrates: 28g Protein 19g Fat 18g

145. Squash Fritters
Preparation Time: 10 minutes
Cooking Time: 6 minutes
Servings: 4
Ingredients:
- 3 oz. cream cheese
- 1 egg
- ½ tsp. oregano
- Black pepper and a pinch of salt
- 1 yellow summer squash
- 1/3 cup carrot
- 2/3 cup bread crumbs
- 2 tbsp. olive oil

Directions:
1. Mix cream cheese with pepper, salt, egg, oregano, carrot, bread crumbs and squash in a bowl. Stir.
2. Make medium patties from this mix. Brush them with oil.
3. Arrange squash patties in air fryer. Cook for 7 minutes at 400° F
4. Serve.

Nutrition: Calories: 151 Carbohydrates: 25g Protein 13g Fat 11g

146. Lunch Shrimp Croquettes
Preparation Time: 18 minutes
Cooking Time: 10 minutes
Servings: 4
Ingredients:
- 2/3-pound shrimp
- 1 ½ cups bread crumbs
- 1 egg
- 2 tbsp. lemon juice
- 3 green onions
- ½ tsp. basil
- Salt and black pepper to
- 2 tbsp. olive oil

Directions:
1. Mix egg and half of the bread crumbs with lemon juice in a bowl. Stir.
2. Add basil, green onions, pepper, shrimp and salt. Stir.
3. Mix the rest of the bread crumbs with the oil in a separate bowl. Toss well.
4. Make round balls from the shrimp mix. Dredge in bread crumbs. Put them in a heated air fryer and cook for 8 minutes at 400°F.
5. Serve.

Nutrition: Calories: 431 Carbohydrates: 20g Protein 18g Fat 6g

147. Lunch Special Pancake
Preparation Time: 10 Minutes
Cooking Time: 8 minutes
Servings: 2
Ingredients:
- 1 tbsp. butter
- 3 eggs
- ½ cup flour
- ½ cup milk
- 1 cup of salsa
- 1 cup small shrimp

Directions:
1. Heat the air fryer at 400°F. Include 1 tbsp. butter. Melt it.
2. Mix eggs with milk and in a bowl. Whisk. Pour into the air fryer's pan. Cook for 12 minutes at 350°F. Transfer to a plate.
3. Mix salsa with shrimp in a bowl. Stir.
4. Serve.

Nutrition: Calories: 97 Carbohydrates: 8g Protein 6g Fat 3g

148. Scallops and Dill
Preparation Time: 15 Minutes
Cooking Time: 10 minutes
Servings: 4
Ingredients:
- 1 lb. sea scallops
- 1 tbsp. lemon juice
- 1 tsp. dill
- 2 tsp. olive oil
- Black pepper and salt

Directions:
1. Mix scallops with oil, dill, pepper, lemon juice and salt in the air fryer. Close. Cook for 5 minutes at 360°F.
2. Dispose uncovered ones. Divide dill sauce and scallops on plates.
3. Serve.

Nutrition: Calories: 254 Carbohydrates: 5g Protein 11g Fat 2g

149. Chicken Sandwiches
Preparation Time: 20 minutes
Cooking Time: 10 minutes
Servings: 4
Ingredients:
- 2 chicken breasts, boneless, skinless
- 1 red onion
- 1 red bell pepper
- ½ cup Italian seasoning
- ½ tsp. thyme
- 2 cups butter lettuce
- 4 pita pockets
- 1 cup cherry tomatoes
- 1 tablespoon olive oil

Directions:
1. Mix chicken with bell pepper, onion, oil, and Italian seasoning. Toss. Cook for 10 minutes at 380°F.
2. Place chicken mixture into a bowl. Include butter lettuce, cherry tomatoes, and thyme. Toss. Stuff pita pockets with this mix. Serve.

Nutrition: Calories: 167 Carbohydrates: 16g Protein 16g Fat 1g

150. Hot Bacon Sandwiches
Preparation Time: 10 Minutes
Cooking Time: 8 minutes
Servings: 4
Ingredients:
- 1/3 cup barbeque sauce
- 2 tbsp. Honey
- 8 bacon slices
- 1 red bell pepper
- 1 yellow bell pepper
- 3 pita pockets
- 1¼ cup butter lettuce leaves
- 2 tomatoes

Directions:
1. Mix barbeque with honey with sauce in a bowl. Whisk.
2. Brush all bell peppers and bacon with this mix. Put them in the air fryer. Cook at 350°F for 4 minutes.
3. Stuff pita pockets with lettuce, bacon mix and tomatoes spread the rest of the barbeque sauce and serve for lunch.

Nutrition: Calories: 354 Carbohydrates: 27g Protein 25g Fat 20g

151. Tasty Air Fried Cod
Preparation Time: 22 minutes
Cooking Time: 15 minutes
Servings: 4
Ingredients:
- 7 oz. 2 cod fish
- Sesame oil
- Salt and black pepper
- 1 cup water
- 1 tsp. dark soy sauce
- 4 tbsp. light soy sauce
- 1 tbsp. sugar
- 3 tbsp. olive oil
- 4 ginger slices
- 3 spring onions
- 2 tbsp. coriander

Directions:
1. Season fish with pepper, salt, sprinkle sesame oil, rub well and allow for 10 minutes.
2. Add fish to air fryer. Cook at 356°F for 12 minutes.
3. Heat a pot with the water over medium heat. Add sugar and light and dark soy sauce. Allow to simmer. Take off heat.
4. Heat pan with the olive oil over medium heat. Add green onions and ginger. Cook for a few minutes. Take off heat.
5. Divide fish on plates. Top with ginger and green onions. Drizzle soy sauce mix. Sprinkle coriander and serve.

Nutrition: Calories: 182 Carbohydrates: 23g Protein 22g Fat 21g

152. Delicious Catfish
Preparation Time: 10 minutes
Cooking Time: 20 minutes
Servings: 4
Ingredients:
- 4 catfish fillets
- Black pepper and Salt
- A pinch of sweet paprika
- 1 tbsp. parsley
- 1 tbsp. lemon juice
- 1 tbsp. olive oil

Directions:
1. Season catfish fillets with salt, paprika, pepper, drizzle oil, rub well. Then put in air fryer basket and cook at 400°F for 20 minutes. Flip the fish after 10 minutes of time.
2. Share fish on plates. Sprinkle parsley and drizzle some lemon juice over it, serve.

Nutrition: Calories: 225 Carbohydrates: 10g Protein 13g Fat 18g

153. Cod Fillets with Fennel and Grapes Salad
Preparation Time: 5 minutes
Cooking Time: 20 minutes
Servings: 2
Ingredients:
- 2 black cod fillets
- 1 tbsp. olive oil
- Black pepper and Salt
- 1 fennel bulb
- 1 cup grapes
- ½ cup pecans

Directions:
1. Sprinkle half of the oil over fish fillets, season with pepper and salt, rub well, place fillets in air fryer basket. Then cook for 10 minutes' time at 400°F and put in the plate.
2. Mix pecans with grapes, fennel, the rest of the oil, salt, and pepper, toss to coat, in a bowl. Add to pan that fits air fryer. Cook at 400° F for 5 minutes.
3. Share cod on plates, add grapes and fennel mix on the side then serve.

Nutrition: Calories: 185 Carbohydrates: 20g Protein 13g Fat 9g

APPETIZERS AND SIDES

154. Parmesan Zucchini Rounds
Preparation Time: 25 minutes
Cooking Time: 20 minutes
Servings: 4
Ingredients:
- 4 zucchinis; sliced
- 1 ½ cups parmesan; grated
- ¼ cup parsley; chopped.
- 1 egg whisked
- 1 egg white; whisked
- ½ tsp. garlic powder
- Cooking spray

Directions:
1. Take a bowl and mix the egg with egg whites, parmesan, parsley and garlic powder and whisk.
2. Dredge each zucchini slice in this mix, place them all in your air fryer's basket, grease them with cooking spray and cook at 370°F for 20 minutes
3. Divide between plates and serve as a side dish.
Nutrition: Calories: 183 Fat 6g Fiber 2g Carbs: 3g Protein 8g

155. Green Bean Casserole
Preparation Time: 25 minutes
Cooking Time: 20 minutes
Servings: 4
Ingredients:
- 1 lb. fresh green beans, edges trimmed
- ½ oz. pork rinds, finely ground
- 1 oz. full-Fat cream cheese
- ½ cup heavy whipping cream
- ¼ cup diced yellow onion
- ½ cup chopped white mushrooms
- ½ cup chicken broth
- 4 tbsp. unsalted butter.
- ¼ tsp. xanthan gum

Directions:
1. In a medium saucepan over medium heat, melt the butter. Sauté onion and mushrooms until smooth and fragrant. Do it for about 3-5 minutes.
2. Add thick cream, cream cheese, and stock to skillet. Whisk until smooth. Bring to a boil and then simmer. Pour the blonde chewing gum into the pan and remove from the heat
3. Cut the green beans into 2-inch pieces and place them in a 4-cup round skillet. Pour sauce mixture over them and stir until covered. Fill the plate with ground pork rind. Place in the fryer basket
4. Set the temperature to 320 degrees F and set the timer for 15 minutes. The top will be green and gold beans when fully cooked. Serve hot.
Nutrition: Calories: 267 Protein 3.6g Fat 23.4g Carbs: 9.7g

156. Zucchini Spaghetti
Preparation Time: 20 minutes
Cooking Time: 15 minutes
Servings: 4
Ingredients:
- 1 lb. zucchinis cut with a spiralizer
- 1 cup parmesan; grated
- ¼ cup parsley; chopped.
- ¼ cup olive oil
- 6 garlic cloves; minced
- ½ tsp. red pepper flakes
- Salt
- Black pepper

Directions:
1. In a pan that fits your air fryer, mix all the ingredients, toss, introduce in the fryer and cook at 370°F for 15 minutes Divide between plates and serve as a side dish.
Nutrition: Calories: 200 Fat 6gCarbs: 4g Protein 5g

157. Cabbage and Radishes Mix
Preparation Time: 20 minutes
Cooking Time: 15 minutes
Servings: 4
Ingredients:
- 6 cups green cabbage; shredded
- ½ cup celery leaves; chopped.
- ¼ cup green onions; chopped.
- 6 radishes; sliced
- 3 tbsp. olive oil
- 2 tbsp. balsamic vinegar
- ½ tsp. hot paprika
- 1 tsp. lemon juice

Directions:
1. In your skillet, combine all ingredients and pour well.
2. Place skillet in deep fryer and cook at 380 ° F for 15 minutes. Divide between dishes and serve as a dish.
Nutrition: Calories: 130 Fat 4g Carbs: 4g Protein 7g

158. Jicama Fries
Preparation Time: 30 minutes
Cooking Time: 20 minutes
Servings: 4
Ingredients:
- 1 small jicama; peeled.
- ¼ tsp. onion powder
- ¾ tsp. chili powder
- ¼ tsp. ground black pepper
- ¼ tsp garlic powder

Directions:
1. Cut jicama into matchstick-sized pieces.
2. Place pieces into a small bowl and sprinkle with remaining ingredients. Place the fries into the air fryer basket
3. Adjust the temperature to 350 Degrees F and set the timer for 20 minutes. Toss the basket two or three times during cooking. Serve warm.
Nutrition: Calories: 37 Protein 0.8g Fat 0.1g Carbs: 8.7g

159. Kale Chips
Preparation Time: 10 minutes
Cooking Time: 5 minutes
Servings: 4
Ingredients:
- 4 cups stemmed kale
- ½ tsp. salt
- 2 tsp. avocado oil

Directions:
1. Take a large bowl, toss kale in avocado oil and sprinkle with salt. Place into the air fryer basket.
2. Adjust the temperature to 400 Degrees F and set the timer for 5 minutes. Kale will be crispy when done. Serve immediately.

Nutrition: Calories: 25 Protein 0.5g Fat 2.2g Carbs: 1.1g

160. Coriander Artichokes
Preparation Time: 20 minutes
Cooking Time: 15 minutes
Servings: 4
Ingredients:
- 12 oz. artichoke hearts
- 1 tbsp. lemon juice
- 1 tsp. coriander, ground
- ½ tsp. cumin seeds
- ½ tsp. olive oil
- Salt and black pepper

Directions:
1. In a pan that fits your air fryer, mix all the ingredients, toss, introduce the pan in the fryer and cook at 370°F for 15 minutes Divide the mix between plates and serve as a side dish.

Nutrition: Calories: 200 Fat 7g Carbs: 5g Protein 8g

161. Spinach and Artichokes Sauté
Preparation Time: 20 minutes
Cooking Time: 15 minutes
Servings: 4
Ingredients:
- 10 oz. artichoke hearts; halved
- 2 cups baby spinach
- 3 garlic cloves
- ¼ cup veggie stock
- 2 tsp. lime juice
- Salt and black pepper

Directions:
1. In a pan that fits your air fryer, mix all the ingredients, toss, introduce in the fryer and cook at 370°F for 15 minutes Divide between plates and serve as a side dish.

Nutrition: Calories: 209 Fat 6g Carbs: 4g Protein 8g

162. Green Beans
Preparation Time: 5 minutes
Cooking Time: 20 minutes
Servings: 4
Ingredients:
- 6 cups green beans; trimmed
- 1 tbsp. hot paprika
- 2 tbsp. olive oil
- A pinch of salt and black pepper

Directions:
1. Take a bowl and mix the beans with the other ingredients, toss them, put them in the fryer basket, and cook at 370 ° F for 20 minutes.
2. Divide between dishes and serve as a garnish.

Nutrition: Calories: 120 Fat 5g Carbs: 4g Protein 2g

163. Balsamic Cabbage
Preparation Time: 10 minutes
Cooking Time: 15 minutes
Servings: 4
Ingredients:
- 6 cups red cabbage; shredded
- 4 garlic cloves; minced
- 1 tbsp. olive oil
- 1 tbsp. balsamic vinegar
- Salt and black pepper

Directions:
1. In a frying pan that fits the deep fryer, combine all ingredients, mix, place skillet in deep fryer, and cook at 380 ° F for 15 minutes. Divide between dishes and serve as a garnish.

Nutrition: Calories: 151 Fat 2g Carbs: 5g Protein 5g

164. Herbed Radish Sauté
Preparation Time: 5 minutes
Cooking Time: 15 minutes
Servings: 4
Ingredients:
- 2 bunches red radishes; halved
- 2 tbsp. parsley; chopped.
- 2 tbsp. balsamic vinegar
- 1 tbsp. olive oil
- Salt and black pepper

Directions:
1. Take a bowl and mix the radishes with the remaining ingredients except the parsley, toss and put them in your air fryer's basket.
2. Cook at 400°F for 15 minutes, divide between plates, sprinkle the parsley on top and serve as a side dish

Nutrition: Calories: 180 Fat 4g Carbs: 3g Protein 5g

165. Roasted Tomatoes
Preparation Time: 5 minutes
Cooking Time: 15 minutes
Servings: 4
Ingredients:
- 4 tomatoes; halved
- ½ cup parmesan; grated
- 1 tbsp. basil; chopped.
- ½ tsp. onion powder
- ½ tsp. oregano; dried
- ½ tsp. smoked paprika
- ½ tsp. garlic powder
- Cooking spray

Directions:
1. Get a bowl and add up all the ingredients except the cooking spray and the parmesan.

2. Arrange the tomatoes in your air fryer's pan sprinkle the parmesan on top and grease with cooking spray
3. Cook at 370°F for 15 minutes, divide between plates and serve.
Nutrition: Calories: 200 Fat 7g Carbs: 4g Protein 6g

166. Kale and Walnuts
Preparation Time: 5 minutes
Cooking Time: 15 minutes
Servings: 4
Ingredients:
- 3 garlic cloves
- 10 cups kale; roughly chopped
- 1/3 cup parmesan; grated
- ½ cup almond milk
- ¼ cup walnuts; chopped.
- 1 tbsp. butter; melted
- ¼ tsp. nutmeg, ground
- Salt and black pepper

Directions:
1. In a pan that fits the air fryer, combine all the ingredients, toss, introduce the pan in the machine and cook at 360°F for 15 minutes
2. Divide between plates and serve.
Nutrition: Calories: 160 Fat 7g Carbs: 4g Protein 5g

167. Bok Choy and Butter Sauce
Preparation Time: 5 minutes
Cooking Time: 15 minutes
Servings: 4
Ingredients:
- 2 bok choy heads; trimmed and cut into strips
- 1 tbsp. butter; melted
- 2 tbsp. chicken stock
- 1 tsp. lemon juice
- 1 tbsp. olive oil
- A pinch of salt and black pepper

Directions:
1. In a pan that fits your air fryer, mix all the ingredients, toss, introduce the pan in the air fryer and cook at 380°F for 15 minutes. Divide between plates and serve as a side dish
Nutrition: Calories: 141 Fat 3g Carbs: 4g Protein 3g

168. Turmeric Mushroom
Preparation Time: 5 minutes
Cooking Time: 15 minutes
Servings: 4
Ingredients:
- 1 lb. brown mushrooms
- 4 garlic cloves; minced
- ¼ tsp. cinnamon powder
- 1 tsp. olive oil
- ½ tsp. turmeric powder
- Salt and black pepper to taste

Directions:
1. In a bowl, combine all the ingredients and toss.
2. Put the mushrooms in your air fryer's basket and cook at 370°F for 15 minutes
3. Divide the mix between plates and serve as a side dish.
Nutrition: Calories: 208 Fat 7g Carbs: 5g Protein 7g

169. Broccoli Gratin
Preparation Time: 10 minutes
Cooking Time: 30 minutes
Servings: 6
Ingredients:
- 2 cups broccoli florets
- 1 teaspoon salt
- 1 teaspoon chili flakes
- 3 eggs, whisked
- 2 oz. Swiss cheese, grated
- 1 onion, diced
- 1 cup heavy cream

Directions:
1. Whisk together chili flakes, salt, eggs, and heavy cream.
2. Add the diced onion in the mixture and stir gently.
3. After this, place broccoli florets into the non-sticky gratin mold.
4. Sprinkle the vegetables with Swiss cheese and heavy cream mixture.
5. Cover the gratin with foil and secure the edges.
6. Cook gratin for 30 minutes in the preheated to the 360F oven.
7. When the time is over, discard the foil and check if the broccoli is tender.
8. Chill the gratin little and transfer on the serving plates.
Nutrition: Calories 154 Fat 12.3g Carbs 5g Protein 6.8g

170. Coleslaw
Preparation Time: 10 minutes
Cooking Time: 2 minutes
Servings: 2
Ingredients:
- 1 cup white cabbage
- 1 tablespoon mayonnaise
- ½ teaspoon ground black pepper
- ½ teaspoon salt

Directions:
1. Shred the white cabbage and place it in the big salad bowl.
2. Sprinkle it with ground black pepper and salt.
3. Add mayonnaise and mix up coleslaw very carefully.
Nutrition: Calories 39 Fat 2.5g Carbs 4.1g Protein 0.6g

171. Roasted Zucchini and Pumpkin Cubes
Preparation Time: 10 minutes
Cooking Time: 20 minutes
Servings: 3
Ingredients:
- 1 cup zucchini, chopped
- ¼ cup pumpkin, chopped
- ¼ tsp thyme
- ½ tsp ground coriander

- ½ tsp ground cloves
- 1 tbsp. olive oil
- ½ tsp butter
- 1 tsp dried dill

Directions:
1. Toss butter in the skillet and melt it.
2. Add olive oil, zucchini, and pumpkin.
3. Start to roast vegetables over the medium heat for 5 minutes.
4. Then sprinkle them with thyme, ground coriander, ground cloves, and dried dill.
5. Mix up well and close the lid.
6. Cook the vegetables on the low heat for 15 minutes.

Nutrition: Calories 66 Fat 5.5g Carbs 3.4g Protein 0.8g

172. Chile Casserole
Preparation Time: 15 minutes
Cooking Time: 15 minutes
Servings: 4
Ingredients:
- 1 cup chili peppers, green, raw
- 1 teaspoon olive oil
- 3 oz. Cheddar cheese, shredded
- 1 teaspoon butter
- 2 eggs, whisked
- ¼ cup heavy cream
- ½ teaspoon salt

Directions:
1. Preheat the grill well and place chili peppers on it.
2. Grill the chili peppers for 5 minutes. Stir them from time to time.
3. Then chill the peppers little and peel them. Remove the seeds.
4. Place the peppers in the casserole tray.
5. Add butter and sprinkle with salt.
6. In the separated bowl, mix up together heavy cream, whisked eggs, and cheese.
7. Pour the liquid over the chili peppers and transfer casserole in the [reheated to the 365F oven.
8. Cook casserole for 10 minutes.

Nutrition: Calories 169 Fat 14.2g Carbs 2.4g Protein 8.6g

173. Pickled Jalapeno
Preparation Time: 10 minutes
Cooking Time: 10 minutes
Servings: 6
Ingredients:
- 6 jalapeno peppers
- ¼ cup apple cider vinegar
- 1/3 cup water
- ¼ teaspoon peppercorns
- 1 garlic clove, peeled
- ½ teaspoon ground coriander

Directions:
1. Pour apple cider vinegar in the saucepan.
2. Add water, peppercorns, and bring the liquid to boil.
3. Wash the jalapeno peppers and slice them.
4. Put the sliced jalapenos in the glass jar.
5. Add ground cinnamon and garlic clove.
6. After this, add boiled apple cider vinegar liquid and close the lid.
7. Marinate the jalapenos as a minimum for 1 hour.

Nutrition: Calories 9 Fat 0.2g Carbs 1.4g Protein 0.2g

174. Sautéed Tomato Cabbage
Preparation Time: 10 minutes
Cooking Time: 35 minutes
Servings: 4
Ingredients:
- 1 tbsp. tomato paste
- 1 bell pepper, chopped
- ½ oz. celery, grated
- 2 cups white cabbage, shredded
- 1 tbsp. butter
- 1 tbsp. dried oregano
- 1/3 cup water
- ¼ cup coconut cream
- 1 tsp salt

Directions:
1. Mix up together tomato paste, coconut cream, and water. Pour the liquid in the saucepan.
2. Add bell pepper, grated celery, white cabbage, butter, and dried oregano.
3. Sprinkle the mixture with salt and mix up gently.
4. Close the lid and sauté cabbage for 35 minutes over the medium-low heat.

Nutrition: Calories 86g Fat 6.7g Fiber 2.3g Carbs 6.7g Protein 1.4g

175. Tender Radicchio
Preparation Time: 10 minutes
Cooking Time: 8 minutes
Servings: 4
Ingredients:
- 8 oz. radicchio
- 1 teaspoon canola oil
- ½ teaspoon apple cider vinegar
- ¼ cup heavy cream
- 1 teaspoon minced garlic
- 1 teaspoon dried dill

Directions:
1. Slice the radicchio into 4 slices. Line the baking dish with parchment and put sliced radicchio on it.
2. Sprinkle the vegetables with canola oil, apple cider vinegar, and dried dill. Bake radicchio in the preheated to the 360F oven for 8 minutes. Meanwhile, whisk together heavy cream with minced garlic. Transfer the cooked radicchio on the serving plates and sprinkle with minced heavy cream mixture.

Nutrition: Calories 43 Fat 4 Fiber 0.2 Carbs 1.5 Protein 0.5

176. Green Salad with Walnuts

Preparation Time: 10 minutes
Cooking Time: 0 minutes
Servings: 2
Ingredients:
- 1 cup arugula
- 2 tbsp. walnuts, chopped
- 1 tbsp. avocado oil
- ½ tsp sesame seeds
- 1 tsp lemon juice
- ½ tsp lemon zest, grated
- 1 tomato, chopped

Directions:
1. Chop arugula roughly and put in the salad bowl.
2. Add walnuts, sesame seeds, and chopped tomato.
3. Make the dressing: mix up together avocado oil, sesame seeds, lemon juice, and grated lemon zest.
4. Pour the dressing over salad and shake it gently.

Nutrition: Calories 71 Fat 6g Carbs 3.1g Protein 2.7g

177. Jicama Slaw

Preparation Time: 10 minutes
Cooking Time: 0 minutes
Servings: 4
Ingredients:
- 1 cup jicama, julienned
- 1 bell pepper, julienned
- 1 onion, sliced
- 1 tablespoon fresh cilantro, chopped
- ½ carrots, julienned
- 2 tablespoons olive oil
- 1 tsp apple cider vinegar
- ½ tsp cayenne pepper
- ½ tsp salt
- 1/3 cup red cabbage, shredded
- ¼ tsp liquid stevia

Directions:
1. In the mixing bowl, combine together jicama, bell pepper, sliced onion, fresh cilantro, carrot, olive oil, apple cider vinegar, and liquid stevia. Mix up the salad mixture.
2. Then sprinkle slaw with cayenne pepper, salt, and red cabbage.
3. Mix up the cooked slaw one more time and transfer on the serving plates.

Nutrition: Calories 98 Fat 7.2g Fiber 2.9g Carbs 8.7g Protein 1g

178. Peanut Slaw

Preparation Time: 10 minutes
Cooking Time: 2 minutes
Servings: 4
Ingredients:
- 1 cup white cabbage
- 1 tsp peanut butter
- 1 tsp lemon juice
- 1 tbsp. peanuts, chopped
- ½ tsp ground black pepper
- 1 tbsp. canola oil
- 1 oz. scallions, chopped
- 1 tsp sriracha
- ¼ cup fresh parsley, chopped

Directions:
1. Shred the white cabbage and transfer in the mixing bowl.
2. Add peanuts, chopped fresh parsley, and scallions.
3. Then make the slaw dressing: whisk together peanut butter, lemon juice, ground black pepper, and canola oil.
4. Pour the dressing over the white cabbage mixture.
5. Add sriracha and chopped parsley. Shake the slaw gently and transfer on the serving plates.

Nutrition: Calories 62 Fat 5.4g Fiber 1.1g Carbs 2.9g Protein 1.4g

179. White Mushroom Sauté

Preparation Time: 15 minutes
Cooking Time: 25 minutes
Servings: 6
Ingredients:
- 10 oz. white mushrooms, chopped
- 1 carrot, chopped
- 1 onion, chopped
- ½ cup of water
- 3 tbsp. coconut cream
- 1 tsp salt
- ½ teaspoon turmeric
- 1 tsp chili flakes
- 1 tsp coconut oil
- ½ tsp Italian seasoning

Directions:
1. In the saucepan, combine together white mushrooms, chopped carrot, onion, and mix up gently.
2. Sprinkle the vegetables with coconut cream, salt, turmeric, chili flakes, and coconut oil.
3. Add Italian seasoning and mix up well.
4. Cook the mixture over the high heat for 5 minutes.
5. Stir the vegetables constantly.
6. Then add water and close the lid, sauté the meal in medium heat for 20 minutes.
7. Then let sauté rest for 10 minutes before serving.

Nutrition: Calories 47 Fat 2.9g Fiber 1.3g Carbs 4.9g Protein 1.9g

180. Caesar Salad

Preparation Time: 15 minutes
Cooking Time: 0 minutes
Servings: 5
Ingredients:
- 1 tbsp. capers
- 2 cups lettuce, chopped
- 1 tsp walnuts, chopped
- 1 tsp mustard

- 2 tsp canola oil
- 1 tsp lime juice
- ½ tsp white pepper
- 1 avocado, peeled, chopped

Directions:
1. Place walnuts, mustard, canola oil, lime juice, white pepper, and avocado in the blender.
2. Blend the mixture until smooth.
3. After this, transfer the avocado smooth mixture in the salad bowl.
4. Add chopped lettuce.
5. Sprinkle the salad with capers. Don't stir the salad before serving.

Nutrition: Calories 142 Fat 14g Fiber 3.1g Carbs 4.6g Protein 1.2

181. Cranberry Relish
Preparation Time: 5 minutes
Cooking Time: 2 minutes
Servings: 6
Ingredients:
- 1 cup cranberries
- 1 orange, peeled, chopped
- 1 tablespoon Erythritol
- 3 tablespoons lemon juice

Directions:
1. Place cranberries and chopped orange in the blender.
2. Add Erythritol and lemon juice. Pulse the ingredients for 1 minute.
3. Transfer the relish in the serving plate. The side dish tastes the best with meat meals.

Nutrition: Calories 26 Fat 0.1 Fiber 1.4 Carbs 5.4 Protein 0.4

182. Vegetable Tots
Preparation Time: 15 minutes
Cooking Time: 12 minutes
Servings: 8
Ingredients:
- 2 cups cauliflower
- 1 cup broccoli
- 4 eggs
- 1/3 cup almond flour
- 3 oz. Parmesan, grated
- 1 teaspoon ground coriander
- ½ teaspoon ground thyme
- 1 teaspoon olive oil

Directions:
1. Grate the broccoli and cauliflower.
2. Transfer the grated vegetables in the cheesecloth and squeeze the liquid.
3. Then put vegetables in the mixing bowl.
4. Beat the eggs in the mixture and add grated cheese.
5. Then add almond flour, ground coriander, ground thyme, and mix it up.
6. Line the baking tray with baking paper and brush with 1 teaspoon of olive oil.
7. Make the medium size tots from the vegetable mixture and put them in the baking tray.
8. Bake the vegetable tots for 12 minutes at 365F.
9. Chill the meal to the room temperature before serving.

Nutrition: Calories 88 Fat 5.7g Fiber 1.1g Carbs 2.9g Protein 7.3g

183. Kale Chips
Preparation Time: 10 minutes
Cooking Time: 5 minutes
Servings: 4
Ingredients:
- 4 cups stemmed kale
- ½ tsp. salt
- 2 tsp. avocado oil

Directions:
1. Take a large bowl, toss kale in avocado oil and sprinkle with salt. Place into the air fryer basket.
2. Adjust the temperature to 400 Degrees F and set the timer for 5 minutes. Kale will be crispy when done. Serve immediately.

Nutrition: Calories: 25 Protein 5g Fiber 4g Fat 2g Carbs: 1g

184. Air Fried Pickles
Preparation Time: 15 minutes
Cooking Time: 5 minutes
Servings: 4
Ingredients:
- ⅓ cup blanched finely ground almond flour.
- 1 cup sliced pickles
- 1 large egg
- 1 tbsp. coconut flour
- ¼ tsp garlic powder
- 1 tsp. chili powder

Directions:
1. Whisk coconut flour, almond flour, chili powder and garlic powder together in a medium bowl. Whisk egg in a small bowl Pat each pickle with a paper towel and dip into the egg. Then dredge in the flour mixture. Place pickles into the air fryer basket
2. Adjust the temperature to 400 Degrees F and set the timer for 5 minutes. Flip the pickles halfway through the cooking time.

Nutrition: Calories: 85 Protein 3g Fiber 3g Fat 1g Carbs: 6g

185. Air Fried Green Tomatoes
Preparation Time: 17 minutes
Cooking Time: 7 minutes
Servings: 4
Ingredients:
- 2 medium green tomatoes
- ⅓ cup grated Parmesan cheese.
- ¼ cup blanched finely ground almond flour.
- 1 large egg

Directions:

1. Slice tomatoes into ½-inch-thick slices. Take a medium bowl, whisk the egg. Take a large bowl, mix the almond flour and Parmesan.
2. Dip each tomato slice into the egg, and then dredge in the almond flour mixture. Place the slices into the air fryer basket Adjust the temperature to 400 Degrees F and set the timer for 7 minutes. Flip the slices halfway through the cooking time. Serve immediately
Nutrition Calories: 106 Protein 2g Fiber 4g Fat 7g Carbs: 9g

186. Chives Radishes
Preparation Time: 20 minutes
Cooking Time: 15 minutes
Servings: 4
Ingredients:
- 20 radishes; halved
- 2 tbsp. olive oil
- 1 tbsp. garlic; minced
- 1 tsp. chives; chopped.
- Salt and black pepper to taste

Directions:
1. Insert skillet into machine and cook at 370 ° F for 15 minutes. Divide between dishes and serve as a garnish.
Nutrition: Calories: 160 Fat 2g Fiber 3g Carbs: 4g Protein 6g

187. Kale and Pine Nuts
Preparation Time: 20 minutes
Cooking Time: 15 minutes
Servings: 4
Ingredients:
- 10 cups kale; torn
- 1/3 cup pine nuts
- 2 tbsp. lemon zest; grated
- 1 tbsp. lemon juice
- 2 tbsp. olive oil
- Salt and black pepper to taste

Directions:
1. In a pan that fits the air fryer, combine all the ingredients, toss, introduce the pan in the machine and cook at 380°F for 15 minutes Divide between plates and serve as a side dish.
Nutrition: Calories: 121 Fat 9g Fiber 2g Carbs: 4g Protein 5g

188. Cabbage and Radishes Mix
Preparation Time: 20 minutes
Cooking Time: 15 minutes
Servings: 4
Ingredients:
- 6 cups green cabbage; shredded
- ½ cup celery leaves; chopped.
- ¼ cup green onions; chopped.
- 6 radishes; sliced
- 3 tbsp. olive oil
- 2 tbsp. balsamic vinegar
- ½ tsp. hot paprika
- 1 tsp. lemon juice

Directions:
1. In your air fryer's pan, combine all the ingredients and toss well. Introduce the pan in the fryer and cook at 380°F for 15 minutes. Divide between plates and serve as a side dish
Nutrition: Calories: 130 Fat 4g Fiber 3g Carbs: 4g Protein 7g

189. Turmeric Mushroom
Preparation Time: 20 minutes
Cooking Time: 15 minutes
Servings: 4
Ingredients:
- 1 lb. brown mushrooms
- 4 garlic cloves; minced
- ¼ tsp. cinnamon powder
- 1 tsp. olive oil
- ½ tsp. turmeric powder
- Salt and black pepper to taste

Directions:
1. In a bowl, combine all the ingredients and toss.
2. Put the mushrooms in your air fryer's basket and cook at 370°F for 15 minutes
3. Divide the mix between plates and serve as a side dish.
Nutrition: Calories: 208 Fat 7g Fiber 3g Carbs: 5g Protein 7g

190. Cheesy Garlic Biscuits
Preparation Time: 17 minutes
Cooking Time: 12 minutes
Servings: 4
Ingredients:
- 1 large egg,
- 1 scallion, sliced
- ¼ cup unsalted butter; melted and divided
- ½ cup shredded sharp Cheddar cheese.
- ⅓ cup coconut flour
- ½ tsp. baking powder
- ½ tsp. garlic powder

Directions:
1. Take a large bowl, mix coconut flour, baking powder and garlic powder.
2. Stir in half of the melted butter, egg, Cheddar cheese and scallions. Pour the mixture into a 6-inch round baking pan. Place into the air fryer basket
3. Adjust the temperature to 320 Degrees F and set the timer for 12 minutes
4. To serve, remove from pan. Allow it to gently cool. divide into four pieces and pour remaining melted butter into it.
Nutrition: Calories: 218 Protein 2g Fiber 4g Fat 19g Carbs: 8g

191. Green Bean Casserole
Preparation Time: 25 minutes
Cooking Time: 20 minutes
Servings: 4
Ingredients:
- 1 lb. fresh green beans, edges trimmed

- ½ oz. pork rinds, finely ground
- 1 oz. full-Fat cream cheese
- ½ cup heavy whipping cream
- ¼ cup diced yellow onion
- ½ cup chopped white mushrooms
- ½ cup chicken broth
- 4 tbsp. unsalted butter.
- ¼ tsp. xanthan gum

Directions:
1. Melt the butter in a pan over medium heat. Sauté onion and mushrooms until smooth and fragrant, cook for about 3-5 minutes.
2. Add thick cream, cream cheese, and stock to skillet. Whisk until smooth. Bring to a boil and then simmer. Pour the blonde chewing gum into the pan and remove from the heat
3. Cut the green beans into 2-inch pieces and place them in a 4-cup round skillet. Pour sauce mixture over them and stir until covered. Fill the plate with ground pork rind. Place in the fryer basket
4. Set the temperature to 320 degrees F and set the timer for 15 minutes. The top will be green and gold beans when fully cooked. Serve hot.

Nutrition: Calories: 267 Protein 6g Fiber 2g Fat 24g Carbs: 7g

192. Roasted Garlic

Preparation Time: 25 minutes
Cooking Time: 20 minutes
Servings: 12
Ingredients:
- 1 medium head garlic
- 2 tsp. avocado oil

Directions:
1. Remove any hanging excess peel from the garlic but leave the cloves covered. Cut off ¼ of the head of garlic, exposing the tips of the cloves
2. Drizzle with avocado oil. Place the garlic head into a small sheet of aluminum foil, completely enclosing it. Place it into the air fryer basket. Adjust the temperature to 400 Degrees F and set the timer for 20 minutes. If your garlic head is a bit smaller, check it after 15 minutes.
3. To serve, cloves should pop out and easily be spread or sliced. You may also freeze individual cloves on a baking sheet, then store together in a freezer-safe storage bag once frozen.

Nutrition: Calories: 11 Protein 2g Fiber 1g Fat 7g Carbs: 0g

193. Coriander Artichokes

Preparation Time: 20 minutes
Cooking Time: 15 minutes
Servings: 4
Ingredients:
- 12 oz. artichoke hearts
- 1 tbsp. lemon juice
- 1 tsp. coriander, ground
- ½ tsp. cumin seeds
- ½ tsp. olive oil
- Salt and black pepper to taste

Directions:
1. In a pan that fits your air fryer, mix all the ingredients, toss, introduce the pan in the fryer and cook at 370°F for 15 minutes
2. Divide the mix between plates and serve as a side dish.

Nutrition: Calories: 200 Fat 7g Fiber 2g Carbs: 5g Protein 8g

194. Herbed Radish Sauté

Preparation Time: 20 minutes
Cooking Time: 15 minutes
Servings: 4
Ingredients:
- 2 bunches red radishes; halved
- 2 tbsp. parsley; chopped.
- 2 tbsp. balsamic vinegar
- 1 tbsp. olive oil
- Salt and black pepper to taste

Directions:
1. Take a bowl and mix the radishes with the remaining ingredients except the parsley, toss and put them in your air fryer's basket. Cook at 400°F for 15 minutes, divide between plates, sprinkle the parsley on top and serve as a side dish.

Nutrition: Calories: 180 Fat 4g Fiber 2g Carbs: 3g Protein 5g

195. Mexican Style Cauliflower Bake

Preparation Time: 25 minutes
Cooking Time: 20-30 minutes
Servings: 4
Ingredients:
- 2 cups cauliflower florets; roughly chopped
- 1 red chili pepper; chopped.
- 2 tomatoes; cubed
- 1 avocado, peeled, pitted and sliced
- 4 garlic cloves; minced
- 1 tbsp. Coriander; chopped.
- 1 tbsp. Lime juice
- 1 tbsp. Olive oil
- 1 tsp. Cumin powder
- ½ tsp. Chili powder
- Salt and black pepper to taste

Directions:
1. In a pan that fits the air fryer, combine the cauliflower with the other ingredients except the coriander, avocado and lime juice, toss, introduce the pan in the machine and cook at 380°f for 20 minutes. Divide between plates, top each serving with coriander, avocado and lime juice and serve as a side dish.

Nutrition: Calories: 187 Fat 8g Fiber 2g Carbs: 5g Protein 7g

196. Curry Cabbage

Preparation Time: 25 minutes
Cooking Time: 20-30 minutes
Servings: 4
Ingredients:

- 30 oz. Green cabbage; shredded
- 3 tbsp. Coconut oil; melted
- 1 tbsp. Red curry paste
- A pinch of salt and black pepper

Directions:
1. In a pan that fits the air fryer, combine the cabbage with the rest of the ingredients, toss, introduce the pan in the machine and cook at 380°f for 20 minutes
2. Divide between plates and serve as a side dish.

Nutrition: Calories: 180 Fat 14g Fiber 4g Carbs: 6g Protein 8g

197. Brussels Sprouts

Preparation Time: 15 minutes
Cooking Time: 20-30 minutes
Servings: 4
Ingredients:
- 1 lb. Brussels sprouts
- 1 tbsp. Unsalted butter; melted.
- 1 tbsp. Coconut oil

Directions:
1. Remove all the loose leaves from the Brussels sprouts and cut them in half. Drizzle the cabbage with coconut oil and place it in the freezer basket. Set the temperature to 400 degrees' f and set the timer for 10 minutes. You may want to gently stir half the cooking time, depending on how they begin to brown when fully cooked; they should be smooth with darker caramelized spots. Remove from the pan and sprinkle with melted butter. Serve immediately.

Nutrition: Calories: 90 Protein 2.9g Fiber 3.2g Fat 6.1g Carbs: 7.5g

198. Kale and Walnuts

Preparation Time: 20 Minutes
Cooking Time: 20-30 minutes
Servings: 4
Ingredients:
- 3 garlic cloves
- 10 cups kale; roughly chopped
- 1/3 cup parmesan; grated
- ½ cup almond milk s
- ¼ cup walnuts; chopped.
- 1 tbsp. Butter; melted
- ¼ tsp. Nutmeg, ground
- Salt and black pepper to taste

Directions:
1. In a pan that fits the air fryer, combine all the ingredients, toss, place the pan inside the machine and allow boiling at 360°f for 15 minutes. Divide between plates and serve.

Nutrition: Calories: 160 Fat 7g Fiber 2g Carbs: 4g Protein 5g

199. Pesto Zucchini Pasta

Preparation Time: 20 minutes
Cooking Time: 20-30 minutes
Servings: 4
Ingredients:
- 4 oz. Mozzarella; shredded
- 2 cups zucchinis cut with a spiralizer
- ½ cup coconut cream
- ¼ cup basil pesto
- 1 tbsp. Olive oil
- Salt and black pepper to taste

Directions:
1. In a pan that fits your air fryer, mix the zucchini noodles with the pesto and the rest of the ingredients, toss, introduce the pan in the fryer and cook at 370°f for 15 minutes Divide between plates and serve as a side dish.

Nutrition: Calories: 200 Fat 8g Fiber 2g Carbs: 4g Protein 10g

200. Kale and Cauliflower Mash

Preparation Time: 25 minutes
Cooking Time: 20-30 minutes
Servings: 4
Ingredients:
- 1 cauliflower head, florets separated
- 4 garlic cloves; minced
- 3 cups kale; chopped.
- 2 scallions; chopped.
- 1/3 cup coconut cream
- 1 tbsp. Parsley; chopped.
- 4 tsp. Butter; melted
- A pinch of salt and black pepper

Directions:
1. In a pan that fits the air fryer, combine the cauliflower with the butter, garlic, scallions, salt, pepper and the cream, toss, introduce the pan in the machine and cook at 380°f for 20 minutes
2. Mash the mix well, add the remaining ingredients, whisk, divide between plates and serve. Enjoy!

Nutrition: Calories: 198 Fat 9g Fiber 2g Carbs: 6g Protein 8g

201. Zucchini Gratin

Preparation Time: 30 minutes
Cooking Time: 20-30 minutes
Servings: 4
Ingredients:
- 4 cups zucchinis; sliced
- 1 ½ cups mozzarella; shredded
- ½ cup coconut cream
- ½ tbsp. Parsley; chopped.
- 2 tbsp. Butter; melted
- ½ tsp. Garlic powder

Directions:
1. In a baking pan that fits the air fryer, mix all the ingredients except the mozzarella and the parsley and toss.
2. Sprinkle the mozzarella and parsley, introduce in the air fryer and cook at 370°f for 25 minutes.
3. Divide between plates and serve as a side dish.
4. Enjoy!

Nutrition: Calories: 220 Fat 14g Fiber 2g Carbs: 5g Protein 9g

202. Spiced Cauliflower
Preparation Time: 20 minutes
Cooking Time: 20-30 minutes
Servings: 4
Ingredients:
- 1 cauliflower head, florets separated
- 1 tbsp. Olive oil
- 1 tbsp. Butter; melted
- ¼ tsp. Cinnamon powder
- ¼ tsp. Cloves, ground
- ¼ tsp. Turmeric powder
- ½ tsp. Cumin, ground
- A pinch of salt and black pepper

Directions:
1. Take a bowl and mix cauliflower florets with the rest of the ingredients and toss.
2. Put the cauliflower in your air fryer's basket and cook at 390°f for 15 minutes.
3. Divide between plates and serve as a side dish.
4. Enjoy!

Nutrition: Calories: 182Fat 8gFiber 2gCarbs: 4gProtein 8g

203. Roasted Tomatoes
Preparation Time: 20 minutes
Cooking Time: 20-30 minutes
Servings: 4
Ingredients:
- 4 tomatoes; halved
- ½ cup parmesan; grated
- 1 tbsp. Basil; chopped.
- ½ tsp. Onion powder
- ½ tsp. Oregano; dried
- ½ tsp. Smoked paprika
- ½ tsp. Garlic powder
- Cooking spray

Directions:
1. Take a bowl and mix all the ingredients except the cooking spray and the parmesan.
2. Arrange the tomatoes in your air fryer's pan.
3. Sprinkle the parmesan on top and grease with cooking spray.
4. Cook at 370°f for 15 minutes, divide between plates and

Nutrition: Calories: 200Fat 7gfiber 2gCarbs: 4gprotein 6g

204. Cauliflower and Artichokes
Preparation Time: 25 minutes
Cooking Time: 20-30 minutes
Servings: 4
Ingredients:
- 2 garlic cloves; minced
- ½ cup chicken stock
- 1 cup cauliflower florets
- 15 oz. Canned artichoke hearts; chopped.
- 1 ½ tbsp. Parsley; chopped.
- 1 tbsp. Olive oil
- 1 tbsp. Parmesan; grated
- Salt and black pepper to taste

Directions:
1. In a pan that fits your air fryer, mix all the ingredients except the parmesan and toss.
2. Sprinkle the parmesan on top, introduce the pan in the air fryer and cook at 380°f for 20 minutes
3. Divide between plates and serve as a side dish.

Nutrition: Calories: 195Fat 6gFiber 2gCarbs: 4gProtein 8g

205. Zucchini Noodles and Sauce
Preparation Time: 20 minutes
Cooking Time: 20-30 minutes
Servings: 4
Ingredients:
- 4 zucchinis cut with a spiralizer
- 1 ½ cups tomatoes, crushed
- 4 garlic cloves; minced
- ¼ cup green onions; chopped.
- 1 tbsp. Olive oil
- 1 tbsp. Basil; chopped.
- Salt and black pepper to taste

Directions:
1. In a pan that fits your air fryer, mix zucchini noodles with the other ingredients, toss, introduce in the fryer and cook at 380°f for 15 minutes. Divide between plates and serve as a side dish

Nutrition: Calories: 194Fat 7gFiber 2gCarbs: 4gProtein 9g

206. Broccoli Mash
Preparation Time: 25 minutes
Cooking Time: 20-30 minutes
Servings: 4
Ingredients:
- 20 oz. Broccoli florets
- 3 oz. Butter; melted
- 1 garlic clove; minced
- 4 tbsp. Basil; chopped.
- A drizzle of olive oil
- A pinch of salt and black pepper

Directions:
1. Take a bowl and mix the broccoli with the oil, salt and pepper, toss and transfer to your air fryer's basket. Cook at 380°f for 20 minutes, cool the broccoli down and put it in a blender. Add the rest of the ingredients, pulse, divide the mash between plates and serve as a side dish.

Nutrition: Calories: 200 Fat 14g Fiber 3gCarbs: 6gProtein 7g

207. Cream Cheese Zucchini
Preparation Time: 20 minutes
Cooking Time: 20-30 minutes
Servings: 4
Ingredients:
- 1 green onion; sliced
- 1 cup cream cheese, soft
- 1 tbsp. Butter; melted
- 2 tbsp. Basil1 lb. Zucchinis; cut into wedges

- ; chopped.
- 1 tsp. Garlic powder
- A pinch of salt and black pepper

Directions:
1. In a pan that fits your air fryer, mix the zucchinis with all the other ingredients, toss, introduce in the air fryer and cook at 370°f for 15 minutes
2. Divide between plates and serve as a side dish.

Nutrition: Calories: 129 Fat 6g Fiber 2g Carbs: 5g Protein 8g

208. Parmesan Zucchini Rounds
Preparation Time: 25 minutes
Cooking Time: 20-30 minutes
Servings: 4
Ingredients:
- 4 zucchinis; sliced
- 1 ½ cups parmesan; grated
- ¼ cup parsley; chopped.
- 1 egg whisked
- 1 egg white; whisked
- ½ tsp. Garlic powder
- Cooking spray

Directions:
1. Take a bowl and mix the egg with egg whites, parmesan, parsley and garlic powder and whisk.
2. Dredge each zucchini slice in this mix, place them all in your air fryer's basket, grease them with cooking spray and cook at 370°f for 20 minutes
3. Divide between plates and serve as a side dish.

Nutrition: Calories: 183 Fat 6g Fiber 2g Carbs: 3g Protein 8g

209. Zucchini Spaghetti
Preparation Time: 20 minutes
Cooking Time: 20-30 minutes
Servings: 4
Ingredients:
- 1 lb. Zucchinis, cut with a spiralizer
- 1 cup parmesan; grated
- ¼ cup parsley; chopped.
- ¼ cup olive oil
- 6 garlic cloves; minced
- ½ tsp. Red pepper flakes
- Salt and black pepper

Directions:
1. In a pan that fits your air fryer, mix all the ingredients, toss, introduce in the fryer and cook at 370°f for 15 minutes
2. Divide between plates and serve as a side dish.

Nutrition: Calories: 200 Fiber 3g Carbs: 4g Protein 5g

210. Pac Cheri Cramoisy Alla Sorrentino
Preparation Time: 5 minutes
Cooking Time: 30 minutes
Servings: 4
Ingredients:
- Paccheri 320 G
- 300 ml tomato sauce (or peeled)
- 200 g fresh provola
- 2-3 fresh basil leaves
- 1 clove of garlic
- Olive oil to taste
- Fine salt to taste

Directions:
1. To prepare the Paccheri Alla prepare the sauce.
2. Brown the garlic in the oil in a pan.
3. Add the tomato puree.
4. Cook over a low heat for about twenty minutes.
5. Salt to your liking and add the basil.
6. Cook the paccheri in plenty of salted water.
7. Cut the provola into pieces.
8. Drain the paccheri and put them in a large pot or pan.
9. Season the paccheri with the sauce and add the provola.
10. Stir over low heat so that the provola is melted.
11. Serve the creamy paccheri with parmesan, if you like.

Nutrition: Calories: 213; Fat 1g Protein 14g Sugar 20g

211. Fast Mashed Speck and Stracchino without Yeast
Preparation Time: 10 minutes
Cooking Time: 20 minutes
Ingredients:
- 250 g flour
- 2 tablespoons olive oil
- 130 ml water
- 1 pinch of salt
- 120 g speck (or salami, ham)
- 150 g Stracchino (or Crescenzago, Charterhouse)
- Oregano or rosemary to taste (for the surface)

Directions:
1. To prepare the fast flattened speck and stracchino, put the flour in the mixer bowl or on the work surface.
2. Add the oil and water little by little.
3. Finally, add the salt.
4. Knead until a soft and non-sticky dough is obtained.
5. If it is a little soft, add a little flour.
6. Form a loaf and divide it into 2 equal parts.
7. With a rolling pin or with your hands roll it out forming a fairly thin, round or rectangular sheet depending on how you prefer it.
8. Add the slices of speck and the stracchino with a spoon.
9. Cover with another sheet of thin dough.
10. Brush the surface with a little oil and oregano.
11. Bake in the oven at 180 degrees for about 20 minutes until golden brown.
12. Let it cool before serving the fast flattened speck and stracchino cheese.
13. It is also excellent cold or just heated in the microwave or in an oven.

Nutrition: Calories: 563; Fat 21g Protein 24g Sugar 22g

212. Baked Potatoes and Fennels

Preparation Time: 15 minutes
Cooking Time: 30 minutes
Servings: 4
Ingredients:
- 500 g Potatoes
- 3 fennels
- 120g of Breadcrumbs
- 20 g Parmesan
- Aromatic herbs (rosemary, oregano, sage, thyme ...) to taste
- Olive oil to taste
- Fine salt to taste

Directions:
1. Peel the potatoes and rinse them thoroughly under running water. Cut them into pieces that are not too large.
2. Clean the fennel by removing the stems and the tuft, also the external part if necessary. The beard (the green tuft) you can also keep it and, after washing it, use it as an aromatic herb.
3. Cut the fennel into thin slices and rinse them under running water.
4. In a bowl put the breadcrumbs, parmesan, aromatic herbs of your choice, fine salt and add 2-3 tablespoons of olive oil.
5. Stir with a spoon so that the oil evenly seasons all the breadcrumbs. If necessary, add more.
6. Combine both the potatoes and the fennel in the bowl with the breadcrumbs, mixing with your hands so that they all bread perfectly.
7. Line a dripping pan with parchment paper and spread potatoes and fennel over the entire surface so that they do not overlap.
8. Sprinkle the rest of the breadcrumbs, which surely remain on the bottom of the bowl.
9. Add another drizzle of olive oil.
10. Cooking Potatoes and Fennels Free in the Oven:
11. Preheat the oven to 200 ° in static mode, then bake potatoes and fennel first in the bottom shelf for 15 minutes and then in the top shelf for another 15 minutes.
12. If you cook them in the microwave with the crisp or combined fringe, just cook them at 200 °.
13. No need to stir while cooking.

Nutrition: Calories: 103; Fat 9g Protein 12g Sugar 13g

213. Baked Fennels

Preparation Time: 10 minutes
Cooking Time: 20 minutes
Servings: 2 people
Ingredients:
- 2 fennels
- 2 tablespoons olive oil
- Fine salt to taste
- Aromatic herbs to taste

Directions:
1. Clean the fennel: remove the stems up to the base and also the green herbs. You can also use the herbs to season the fennel before cooking. They are also perfect for flavoring other side dishes or soups and minestrone.
2. If necessary, also remove the outer white leaves if they are not perfect or if they are the hardest. Also cut the base of the core.
3. Cut the fennel into thin slices, you will have to get really thin slices. In this way they will cook in a short time and will be tender and soft.
4. Put the fennel in a colander and rinse them thoroughly under running water. Drain them and pat them dry with a clean cloth.
5. Put the fennel in a large bowl. Season with olive oil (you can use the quantity you prefer, depending on your taste). Add the salt, pepper and aromatic herbs you prefer.
6. Mix well so that all the ingredients are mixed. You can also flavor with well-washed herbs.
7. Cooking of Fennels
8. Cover the dripping pan with parchment paper, spread the fennel so that they do not overlap and cook all at the same temperature and at the same time.
9. Bake the first 10 minutes on the lower shelf and the last 10-15 minutes on the top shelf in a preheated static oven at 200 °. In this way, you won't even need to mix them.

Nutrition: Calories: 478; Fat 6g Protein 26g Sugar 9g

214. Baked Crisp Fennels

Preparation Time: 5 minutes
Cooking Time: 20 minutes
Servings: 4 people
Ingredients:
- 3 fennels
- 80 g Breadcrumbs (approx.)
- 20 g Parmesan
- 2 tablespoons olive oil
- Aromatic herbs (thyme, sage, oregano, parsley) to taste
- Fine salt to taste

Directions:
1. How to Make Free Fennels in the Oven:
2. To prepare the fennel au gratin in the oven without béchamel, clean the fennel by removing the external parts and the tufts.
3. Cut them thinly with a knife, the slices must be a few millimeters thick.
4. rinse thoroughly under running water and dab them with a clean cloth to remove excess water.
5. Put the fennel in a large bowl. Add the breadcrumbs, Parmesan and the herbs you prefer.
6. Also add the oil, adjusting the quantity according to your preference
7. Stir so that the breading is uniform.
8. Spread the fennel on parchment paper, without overlapping them.
9. Sprinkle the fennel with the breading that will surely remain on the bottom of the bowl.
10. How to Cook Free Fennels in the Oven:

11. Bake in a static oven at 200 ° for about 20 minutes, preferably 10 minutes on the bottom shelf and 10-15 minutes on the top shelf with grill function.
Nutrition: Calories: 363 Fat 17g Protein 54g Sugar 29g

215. Free Fennel Ham and Mozzarella
Preparation Time: 10 minutes
Cooking Time: 20 minutes
Servings: 2 people
Ingredients
- 2 fennels
- 50 g Cooked ham
- 125 g Mozzarella
- 30 g grated Parmesan
- to taste Olive oil
- salt and pepper to taste

Directions:
1. To prepare the Fennels, Ham and Mozzarella, clean the fennel by removing the external parts, if necessary, and the tuft.
2. Cut the fennel into thin slices.
3. Rinse them under running water.
4. Boil them in boiling water for 5-6 minutes, they must be quite soft.
5. Drain.
6. Brush the bottom of a baking dish with a little olive oil. Lay the fennel into a layer.
7. Season with salt and pepper (if you don't like pepper, omit it).
8. Spread the grated Parmesan.
9. Then add the chopped cooked ham and mozzarella.
10. Form layers until the ingredients are finished.
11. Bake in the oven at 200 ° for about 15 minutes.
12. Cooking is short as the fennel is already blanched.
13. The last few minutes use the grill function so that the crust is formed on the surface.
Nutrition: Calories: 198; Fat 7g Protein 13g Sugar 1g

216. Meat Rolls with Bacon and Camorra
Preparation Time: 10 minutes
Cooking Time: 10 minutes
Servings: 2 people
Ingredients:
- The quantities are for preparing rolls with bacon and scamorza cheese for 2 people: double or halve the doses according to how many people will taste them.
- 8 loin slices (or pork ham, chicken breast or turkey)
- 8 slices of fresh bacon (long or round)
- 100 g smoked scamorza (or other cheese)
- 30 g butter (or olive oil)
- 8 fresh sage leaves
- Salt to taste

Directions:
1. To prepare meat rolls with bacon and scamorza cheese, I recommend using thin slices of meat in case you want to make them thin, use the meat tenderizer. In this way the meat will be very tender even after cooking.
2. How to Make Bacon and Scamorza Wraps?
3. Place the slices of bacon on a clean cutting board, distant from each other. Beat the meat with the meat mallet if you need to make it as thin as possible. Then, lay each slice of meat on a slice of bacon.
4. At the center of each slice add a rectangle of scamorza cheese, obtained from slices at least 1 centimeter thick.
5. Roll the slices from one end, taking care to tighten them well to prevent the filling from coming out when cooking.
6. At this point you can close the rolls with a kitchen string or a toothpick or even, you can cook them directly, taking care to turn them gently in a pan.
7. Cooking Meat Rolls in a Pan
8. Put the butter and sage leaves in a non-stick pan. At low heat, melt it, without frying.
9. Place the stuffed meat rolls and brown them for a few minutes with a lid: in this way the steam created will make the meat very tender even inside. Lift the lid and turn the rolls gently, then remove it and continue cooking. Add salt to taste. The meat rolls must be browned on all sides; you will see the golden bacon externally.
Nutrition: Calories: 209; Fat 1g Protein 64g Sugar 20g

217. Pineapple with Honey and Coconut
Preparation Time: 10 minutes
Cooking Time: 10-30 minutes
Servings: 4
Ingredients:
- ½ small, fresh pineapples
- 1 tbsp. honey
- ½ tbsp. lemon juice
- 1 tablespoon of ground coconut
- ¼ l ice cream or mango sorbet
- Baking paper

Directions:
1. Preheat the Air fryer to 200 ° C. Line the bottom of the basket with baking paper. Leave 1 cm on the edge. Cut the pineapple lengthwise into eight pieces and remove the peel with the "eyes". Also remove the woody middle trunk.
2. Mix the honey with the lemon juice in a bowl. Brush the pineapple pieces with the honey and add to the basket. Sprinkle the coconut over it.
3. Push the basket into the Air fryer and set the timer to 12 minutes. The pineapple with the coconut should be hot and golden brown.
4. TIP: Spicy pineapple; -Stir a finely chopped red chili pepper or 1 teaspoon of red chili paste with 1 tablespoon of finely chopped, fresh coriander into the honey mixture. Prepare the pineapple pieces according to the recipe. These savory pineapple pieces go well with Asian dishes, but are also delicious as a dessert. Serve the pineapple as a dessert with coconut ice cream.
Nutrition: Calories435 Protein 9gFat 16gCarbohydrates61g

218. Ratatouille

Preparation Time: 8 minutes
Cooking Time: 15 minutes
Servings: 4
Ingredients:
- 200 g zucchini and / or eggplant
- 1 yellow pepper
- 2 tomatoes
- 1 onion, peeled
- 1 clove of garlic, crushed
- 2 teaspoons of dried herbs from Pair fryers
- Freshly ground black pepper
- 1 tablespoon of olive oil

Directions:
1. Preheat the Air fryer to 200 ° C.
2. Cut the zucchini, aborigine, bell pepper, tomatoes and onion into 2 cm cubes.
3. Mix the vegetables in a bowl with the garlic, the herbs of fryers and ½ teaspoon of salt. Season it with pepper. Also stir in the olive oil.
4. Place the bowl in the basket and slide the basket into the Air fryer. Set the timer to 15 minutes and cook the ratatouille. Stir the vegetables once while cooking. Serve the ratatouille with roasted meat such as a steak or schnitzel.

Nutrition: Calories421 Protein 10g Fat 24g Carbohydrates 42g

219. Potatoes with Paprika Powder and Greek Yogurt

Preparation Time: 10 minutes
Cooking Time: 20 minutes
Servings: 4
Ingredients:
- 800 g waxy potatoes
- 2 tablespoons of olive oil
- 1 tbsp. hot paprika powder
- Freshly ground black pepper
- 150 ml Greek yogurt

Directions:
1. Preheat the Air fryer to 180 ° C. Peel the potatoes and cut them into 3 cm cubes. Soak them in water for at least 30 minutes. Then drain thoroughly and dry with kitchen paper.
2. Mix 1 tablespoon of olive oil with the paprika powder in a medium bowl and season them with pepper. Turn the potato cubes in the spicy oil.
3. Place the potato sticks in the cooking basket and push the basket into the Air fryer. Set the timer to 20 minutes and bake the potato sticks until they are golden brown and done every now and then.
4. Mix the Greek yogurt in a small bowl with the remaining spoon of olive oil and season with salt and pepper. Sprinkle with paprika powder. Serve the yogurt as a dip with the potatoes.

Nutrition: Calories503 Protein 12g Fat10g Carbohydrates 82g

220. Pork Satay with Peanut Sauce

Preparation Time: 35 minutes
Cooking Time: 10 m
Servings: 4
Ingredients:
- 2 cloves of garlic, crushed
- 2 cm fresh ginger root, grated, or 1 tsp ginger powder
- 2 tsp chili paste or hot pepper sauce
- 2 - 3 tbsp. sweet soy sauce
- 2 tablespoons vegetable oil
- 400 g lean pork chop, in 3 cm cubes
- 1 shallot, finely chopped
- 1 tsp ground coriander
- 200 ml coconut milk
- 100 g unsalted peanuts, ground

Directions:
1. Mix half of the garlic in a bowl with the ginger, 1 teaspoon of hot pepper sauce, 1 tablespoon of soy sauce and 1 tablespoon of oil. Mix the meat with the mixture and marinate for 15 minutes.
2. Preheat the Air fryer to 200 ° C.
3. Place the marinated meat in the basket and slide the basket into the Air fryer. Set the timer to 12 minutes and roast the meat until it is brown and cooked. Turn once when roasting.
4. In the meantime, prepare the peanut sauce: Put 1 tablespoon of oil in a saucepan and briefly fry the shallot with the remaining garlic. Add the coriander and continue to roast a little.
5. Mix the coconut milk and the peanuts with 1 teaspoon of hot pepper sauce, 1 tablespoon of soy sauce and the shallot mixture and cook on a low flame for 5 minutes stirring. If the sauce becomes too thick, add a little water. Season it with soy sauce and hot pepper sauce.

Nutrition: Calories534 Protein 12g Fat 27g Carbohydrates58g

221. Spicy Roulades

Preparation Time: 15 minutes
Cooking Time: 40 minutes
Servings: 4
Ingredients:
- 1 turkey breast fillet, 500 g
- 1 clove of garlic, crushed
- ½ tsp chili powder
- 1 tsp cinnamon
- 1½ tsp ground cumin
- 1 tsp freshly ground black pepper
- 2 tablespoons of olive oil
- 1 small red onion, finely chopped
- 3 tbsp. flat-leaf parsley, finely chopped
- Roulades thread

Directions:
1. Place the meat on a chopping board with the narrow end facing you and cut horizontally from 1/3 of the top edge over the entire length from top to bottom. Leave 2 cm distance to the edge. Unfold this part and cut open again from this end. You now have a long piece of meat.

2. Mix the garlic in a bowl with the chili powder, cinnamon, cumin, pepper and 1 teaspoon of salt. Add the olive oil. Put 1 tablespoon of this mixture in another small bowl. Mix the onion and the parsley with the mixture in the large bowl.
3. Preheat the air fryer to 180 ° C.
4. Put the rolled meat in the basket and slide the basket into the air fryer. Set the timer to 40 minutes and fry the rolled meat until it is brown and cooked. Cover the rolled meat with aluminum foil and let it rest for 5 minutes. Then cut the meat into thin slices. Make it delicious with French fries and braised cherry tomatoes.
Nutrition: Calories 421 Protein 10gFat 24gCarbohydrates 42g

222. Spicy Chicken Legs with Grilled Marinade
Preparation Time: 25 minutes
Cooking Time: 20 minutes
Servings: 4
Ingredients:
- 1 clove of garlic, crushed
- ½ tbsp. mustard
- 2 tsp brown Sugar
- 1 tsp chili powder
- Freshly ground black pepper
- 1 tablespoon of olive oil
- 4 chicken legs

Directions:
1. Preheat the Air fryer to 200 ° C.
2. Mix the garlic with the mustard, brown sugar, chili powder, a pinch of salt and freshly ground pepper. Mix with the oil.
3. Rub the chicken legs completely with the marinade and marinate for 20 minutes.
4. Then reduce the temperature to 150 ° C and fry the chicken legs for another 10 minutes until cooked.
Nutrition: Calories168 Protein 4g Fat7gCarbohydrates21g

223. Thick French Fries - Spicy
Preparation Time: 10 minutes
Cooking Time: 20 minutes
Servings: 4
Ingredients:
- 800 g waxy potatoes
- 2 small, dried chili peppers or 1 heaped teaspoon of freshly ground, dried chili flakes
- ½ tbsp. freshly ground black pepper
- ½ tbsp. curry powder
- 1 tablespoon of olive oil

Directions:
1. Preheat the Air fryer to 180 ° C.
2. Wash the potatoes under running water. Cut lengthways into 1½ cm fries.
3. Soak the fries in water for at least 30 minutes. Then drain thoroughly and dry with kitchen paper.
4. Finely crush the chili peppers (in a mortar) and mix in a bowl with the olive oil, pepper and, if you like, with curry powder. Turn the fries in this mixture.
5. Place half of the fries in the basket and slide the basket into the Air fryer. Set the timer to 20 minutes to bake the chips until golden brown. Bake the remaining sausages in the same way.
Nutrition: Calories393 Protein 17g Fat21gCarbohydrates 30g

224. Minced Beef Steak with Ham
Preparation Time: 10 minutes
Cooking Time: 8 minutes
Servings: 4
Ingredients:
- 400 g minced beef
- 5 cm from the white part of a leek, very finely chopped
- 50 g of cooked ham in fine strips
- 3 tbsp. breadcrumbs
- Freshly ground pepper
- Nutmeg

Directions:
1. Preheat the air fryer to 200 ° C. Mix the minced beef with the leek, the ham.
2. the breadcrumbs, a little salt and pepper and the nutmeg. Knead well so that a uniform mass is created.
3. Divide the minced beef into four servings and shape into smooth minced steaks with wet hands.
4. Put the minced steaks in the basket and slide the basket into the air fryer. Set the timer to 8 minutes and fry the minced steaks until they are brown. Inside they can still be pink.
5. Serve the beef steaks with boiled potatoes and cauliflower or broccoli.
Nutrition: Calories503 Protein 13g Fat 22gCarbohydrates 62g

225. Saltimbocca - Veal Rolls with Sage
Preparation Time: 15 minutes
Cooking Time: 15 minutes
Servings: 4
Ingredients:
- 400 ml broth
- 200 ml dry white wine
- 4 veal chops
- Freshly ground pepper
- 8 fresh sage leaves
- 4 slices of raw ham
- 25 g butter

Directions:
1. Preheat the air fryer to 200 ° C. Cook the broth and the wine in a large pan on a medium flame until the liquid is reduced to a third of the original amount.
2. Sprinkle the chops with salt and pepper and cover with the sage leaves. Roll up the chops closely and wrap a slice of ham around each chop.
3. Brush the whole chops thinly with butter and add to the basket. Push the basket into the air fryer and set the timer to 10 minutes. Fry the veal rolls until they are nice and brown. Reduce the temperature to 150 ° C

and set the timer to 5 minutes. Fry the rolls until they're done.
4. Mix the remaining butter with the reduced broth and season the gravy with salt and pepper.
5. Cut the veal rolls into thin slices and serve with the gravy. Make it delicious with green beans.
Nutrition: Calories299 Protein 26gFat11gCarbohydrates 20g

226. Salmon Quiche
Preparation Time: 15 minutes
Cooking Time: 20 minutes
Servings: 2
Ingredients:
- 150 g salmon fillet, cut into small cubes
- ½ tbsp. lemon juice
- Freshly ground black pepper
- 100 g of flour
- 50 g cold butter, diced
- 2 eggs + 1 egg yolk
- 3 tbsp. whipped cream
- ½ tbsp. (tarragon) mustard
- 1 spring onion, cut into 1 cm pieces
- Small, flat quiche dish, approx. 15 cm in diameter, greased

Directions:
1. Preheat the Air fryer to 180 ° C. Mix the salmon pieces with the lemon juice and season with salt and pepper. Let the salmon rest.
2. Mix the flour in a bowl with the butter, the egg yolk and ½ to 1 tablespoon of cold water and knead into a smooth ball.
3. Roll out the dough on a floured work surface into a round shape of 18 cm in diameter.
4. Beat the eggs lightly with the whipped cream and mustard and season with salt and pepper. Pour the mixture into the quiche pan and place the salmon pieces on top. Spread the spring onions evenly over the contents of the quiche pan.
5. Place the quiche pan in the cooking basket and push the basket into the Air fryer. Set the timer to 20 minutes and bake the gratin until browned and cooked.
Nutrition: Calories280 Protein 10gFat16gCarbohydrates 22g

227. Cinnamon Maple Chickpeas
Preparation Time: 10 minutes
Cooking Time: 12 minutes
Servings: 4
Ingredients:
- 14 oz. can chickpeas, rinsed, drained and pat dry
- 1 tsp ground cinnamon
- 1 tbsp. brown sugar
- 1 tbsp. maple syrup
- 1 tbsp. olive oil
- Pepper
- Salt

Directions:
1. Place the dehydrating tray in a multi-level air fryer basket and place basket in the instant pot.
2. Spread chickpeas on dehydrating tray.
3. Seal pot with air fryer lid and select air fry mode then set the temperature to 375 F and timer for 12 minutes. Stir halfway through.
4. In a mixing bowl, mix together cinnamon, brown sugar, maple syrup, oil, pepper, and salt. Add chickpeas and toss well to coat.
5. Serve and enjoy.
Nutrition: Calories 171 Fat 4.7 g Carbohydrates 28.5 g Protein 4.9 g

228. Parmesan Carrot Fries
Preparation Time: 10 minutes
Cooking Time: 15 minutes
Servings: 4
Ingredients:
- 4 carrots, peeled and cut into fries
- 2 tbsp. parmesan cheese, grated
- 1 1/2 tbsp. garlic, minced
- 2 tbsp. olive oil
- Pepper
- Salt

Directions:
1. Add carrots and remaining ingredients into the mixing bowl and toss well.
2. Spray instant pot multi-level air fryer basket with cooking spray.
3. Add carrots fries into the air fryer basket and place basket into the instant pot.
4. Seal pot with air fryer lid and select air fry mode then set the temperature to 350 F and timer for 15 minutes. Stir halfway through.
5. Serve and enjoy.
Nutrition: Calories 99 Fat 7.6 g Carbohydrates 7.2 g Protein 1.6 g

229. Tater Tots
Preparation Time: 10 minutes
Cooking Time: 10 minutes
Servings: 2
Ingredients:
- 16 oz. frozen tater tots
- 1 tbsp. olive oil
- Salt

Directions:
1. Drizzle tater tots with olive oil and season with salt.
2. Spray instant pot multi-level air fryer basket with cooking spray.
3. Add tater tots into the air fryer basket and place basket into the instant pot.
4. Seal pot with air fryer lid and select air fry mode then set the temperature to 400 F and timer for 10 minutes. Stir halfway through.
5. Serve and enjoy.
Nutrition: Calories 492 Fat 28.6 g Carbohydrates 54 g Protein 5.4 g

230. Chili Lime Chickpeas
Preparation Time: 10 minutes
Cooking Time: 12 minutes
Servings: 4
Ingredients:
- 14 oz. can chickpeas, rinsed, drained and pat dry
- 1 tbsp. lime juice
- 1/4 tsp red pepper
- 1/2 tsp chili powder
- 1 tbsp. olive oil
- Pepper
- Salt

Directions:
1. Add chickpeas, red pepper, chili powder, oil, pepper, and salt into the mixing bowl and toss well.
2. Place the dehydrating tray in a multi-level air fryer basket and place basket in the instant pot.
3. Spread chickpeas on dehydrating tray.
4. Seal pot with air fryer lid and select air fry mode then set the temperature to 375 F and timer for 12 minutes. Stir halfway through.
5. Drizzle lemon juice over chickpeas and serve.

Nutrition: Calories 154 Fat 4.7 g Carbohydrates 24.1 g Protein 5.1 g

231. Salted Peanuts
Preparation Time: 10 minutes
Cooking Time: 10 minutes
Servings: 4
Ingredients:
- 1 cup peanuts
- 2 tbsp. olive oil
- Salt

Directions:
1. In a bowl, toss peanuts, oil, and salt.
2. Place the dehydrating tray in a multi-level air fryer basket and place basket in the instant pot.
3. Spread peanuts on dehydrating tray.
4. Seal pot with air fryer lid and select air fry mode then set the temperature to 320 F and timer for 10 minutes. Stir halfway through.
5. Serve and enjoy.

Nutrition: Calories 267 Fat 25 g Carbohydrates 5.9 g Sugar 1.5 g Protein 9.4 g

232. Potato Wedges
Preparation Time: 10 minutes
Cooking Time: 24 minutes
Servings: 2
Ingredients:
- 1/2 lb. potatoes, cut into wedges
- 1 tbsp. olive oil
- Pepper
- Salt

Directions:
1. In a bowl, toss potato wedges with oil, pepper, and salt. Spray instant pot multi-level air fryer basket with cooking spray.
2. Potato wedges into the air fryer basket and place basket into the instant pot.
3. Seal pot with air fryer lid and select air fry mode then set the temperature to 390 F and timer for 24 minutes. Stir halfway through.
4. Serve and enjoy.

Nutrition: Calories 138 Fat 7.1 g Carbohydrates 17.9 g Protein 1.9 g

233. Ranch Chickpeas
Preparation Time: 10 minutes
Cooking Time: 12 minutes
Servings: 4
Ingredients:
- 14 oz. can chickpeas, rinsed, drained and pat dry
- 1 1/2 tsp ranch seasoning mix
- Pepper
- Salt

Directions:
1. Add chickpeas, ranch seasoning, pepper, and salt into the mixing bowl and toss well.
2. Place the dehydrating tray in a multi-level air fryer basket and place basket in the instant pot.
3. Spread chickpeas on dehydrating tray.
4. Seal pot with air fryer lid and select air fry mode then set the temperature to 375 F and timer for 12 minutes. Stir halfway through.
5. Serve and enjoy.

Nutrition: Calories 120 Fat 1.1 g Carbohydrates 22.5 g Protein 4.9 g

234. Radish Chips
Preparation Time: 10 minutes
Cooking Time: 12 minutes
Servings: 2
Ingredients:
- 1/2 lb. radishes, sliced thinly
- 1/2 tsp red pepper flakes, crushed
- 1/2 tbsp. olive oil
- 1/2 tbsp. lime juice
- Pepper
- Salt

Directions:
1. Add radish slices and remaining ingredients into the mixing bowl and toss well. Spray instant pot multi-level air fryer basket with cooking spray.
2. Add radish slices into the air fryer basket and place basket into the instant pot.
3. Seal pot with air fryer lid and select air fry mode then set the temperature to 380 F and timer for 12 minutes. Stir halfway through.
4. Serve and enjoy.

Nutrition: Calories 52 Fat 3.7 g Carbohydrates 5.1 g Protein 0.9 g

235. Beef Olive Balls
Preparation Time: 10 minutes
Cooking Time: 14 minutes
Servings: 4

Ingredients:
- 1 lb. ground beef
- 1 tbsp. oregano, chopped
- 1 tbsp. breadcrumbs
- 1 tbsp. chives, chopped
- 1 cup olives, pitted and chopped
- Pepper
- Salt

Directions:
1. Add all ingredients into the mixing bowl and mix until well combined.
2. Place the dehydrating tray in a multi-level air fryer basket and place basket in the instant pot.
3. Make small balls from meat mixture and place on dehydrating tray.
4. Seal pot with air fryer lid and select air fry mode then set the temperature to 400 F and timer for 14 minutes. Turn meatballs halfway through.
5. Serve and enjoy.

Nutrition: Calories 260 Fat 10.9 g Carbohydrates 4.1 g Protein 35.1 g

236. Easy Salmon Bites

Preparation Time: 10 minutes
Cooking Time: 12 minutes
Servings: 4
Ingredients:
- 1 lb. salmon fillets, boneless and cut into chunks
- 2 tsp olive oil
- 1/4 tsp cayenne
- 1/2 tsp chili powder
- 1 tsp dried dill
- Pepper
- Salt

Directions:
1. Add salmon and remaining ingredients into the large bowl and toss well. Spray instant pot multi-level air fryer basket with cooking spray.
2. Add salmon chunks into the air fryer basket and place basket into the instant pot. Seal pot with air fryer lid and select air fry mode then set the temperature to 350 F and timer for 12 minutes. Turn salmon chunks halfway through.
3. Serve and enjoy.

Nutrition: Calories 172 Fat 9.4 g Carbohydrates 0.4 g Sugar 0 g Protein 22.1 g 50 mg

237. Air Fried Cauliflower Bites

Preparation Time: 10 minutes
Cooking Time: 14 minutes
Servings: 4
Ingredients:
- 1 lb. cauliflower florets
- 1 1/2 tsp garlic powder
- 1 tbsp. olive oil
- 1 tsp ground coriander
- 1 tsp dried rosemary
- Pepper
- Salt

Directions:
1. Add cauliflower florets into the large bowl. Add remaining ingredients and toss well. Spray instant pot multi-level air fryer basket with cooking spray.
2. Add cauliflower florets into the air fryer basket and place basket into the instant pot.
3. Seal pot with air fryer lid and select air fry mode then set the temperature to 400 F and timer for 14 minutes. Stir halfway through.
4. Serve and enjoy.

Nutrition: Calories 63 Fat 3.7 g Carbohydrates 7 g Protein 2.4 g

238. Air Fried Simple Tofu Bites

Preparation Time: 10 minutes
Cooking Time: 20 minutes
Servings: 4
Ingredients:
- 10 oz. tofu, cut into cubes
- 1 1/2 tbsp. dried rosemary
- 1 tsp vinegar
- 2 tsp olive oil
- Pepper
- Salt

Directions:
1. Add tofu and remaining ingredients into the large bowl and toss well.
2. Spray instant pot multi-level air fryer basket with cooking spray.
3. Add tofu cubes into the air fryer basket and place basket into the instant pot.
4. Seal pot with air fryer lid and select air fry mode then set the temperature to 350 F and timer for 20 minutes. Stir halfway through.
5. Serve and enjoy.

Nutrition: Calories 74 Fat 5.5 g Carbohydrates 2 g Protein 5.9 g

239. Roasted Almonds

Preparation Time: 10 minutes
Cooking Time: 5 minutes
Servings: 4
Ingredients:
- 1/4 tsp cayenne
- Salt
- 1 cup almonds
- Pepper
- 1 tsp olive oil

Directions:
1. In a bowl, toss almonds with cayenne, oil, pepper, and salt.
2. Spray instant pot multi-level air fryer basket with cooking spray.
3. Add almonds into the air fryer basket and place basket into the instant pot.
4. Seal pot with air fryer lid and select air fry mode then set the temperature to 350 F and timer for 5 minutes. Stir after 3 minutes.
5. Serve and enjoy.

Nutrition: Calories 148 Fat 13.1 g Carbohydrates 5.2 g Protein 5 g

240. Healthy Eggplant Chips
Preparation Time: 10 minutes
Cooking Time: 30 minutes
Servings: 2
Ingredients:
- 1 eggplant, sliced 1/4-inch thick
- 2 tbsp. rosemary, chopped
- 1/2 cup parmesan cheese, grated
- Pepper
- Salt

Directions:
1. Add eggplant slices, cheese, rosemary, pepper, and salt into the mixing bowl and toss well. Place the dehydrating tray in a multi-level air fryer basket and place basket in the instant pot.
2. Arrange eggplant slices on the dehydrating tray.
3. Seal pot with air fryer lid and select air fry mode then set the temperature to 400 F and timer for 30 minutes. Turn eggplant slices halfway through.
4. Serve and enjoy.

Nutrition: Calories 141 Fat 5.7 g Carbohydrates 16.4 g

241. Crispy Roasted Cashews
Preparation Time: 10 minutes
Cooking Time: 6 minutes
Servings: 3
Ingredients:
- 1 cup cashews
- 1/4 tsp onion powder
- 1/4 tsp garlic powder
- 1/2 tsp nutritional yeast
- 1 tbsp. rice flour
- 1 tbsp. olive oil
- Pepper
- Salt

Directions:
1. Add cashews and remaining ingredients into the large bowl and toss well. Place the dehydrating tray in a multi-level air fryer basket and place basket in the instant pot.
2. Spread cashews on dehydrating tray.
3. Seal pot with air fryer lid and select air fry mode then set the temperature to 350 F and timer for 6 minutes. Stir halfway through.
4. Serve and enjoy.

Nutrition: Calories 318 Fat 25.9 g Carbohydrates 18.2 g Protein 7.5 g

242. Grilled Pineapple with Cinnamon
Preparation Time: 5 minutes
Cooking Time: 20 minutes
Servings: 2
Ingredients:
- 4 pineapple slices
- 2 tablespoons Truvia
- 1 teaspoon cinnamon

Directions:
1. Add the cinnamon and Truvia into a Ziploc bag and shake well. Add the pineapple slices to it and shake and coat. Leave to marinate in the fridge for 20-minutes. Preheat your air fryer for 5-minutes at 360°Fahrenheit. Place the pineapple pieces on the air fryer rack and grill them for 10-minutes. Flip and grill them for additional 10-minutes.

Nutrition: Calories 276 Fat 5.3g Carbs 4.2g Protein 4.6g

243. Bell Peppers with Potato Stuffing
Preparation Time: 5 minutes
Cooking Time: 20 minutes
Servings: 4
Ingredients:
- 4 green bell peppers, top cut and deseeded
- 4 potatoes, boiled, peeled and mashed
- 2 onions, finely chopped
- 1 teaspoon lemon juice
- 2 tablespoons coriander leaves, chopped
- 2 green chilies, finely chopped
- Olive oil as needed
- Salt to taste
- ¼ teaspoon Garam Masala
- ½ teaspoon chili powder
- ¼ teaspoon turmeric powder
- 1 teaspoon cumin seeds

Directions:
1. Heat the oil in a pan and sauté the onion, chilies and cumin seeds. Add the rest of the ingredients except the bell peppers and mix well. Preheat your air fryer to 390°Fahrenheit for 10-minutes. Brush your bell peppers with olive oil, inside and out and stuff each pepper with potato mixture. Place in air fryer basket and grill for 10-minutes. Check and grill for an additional 5-minutes.

Nutrition: Calories 282 Total Fat 9.2g Carbs 7.1g Protein 4.2g

SEAFOOD

244. Coconut Shrimp
Preparation Time: 5 minutes
Cooking Time: 10 minutes
Servings: 3
Ingredients:
- 1 cup almond flour
- 1 cup panko breadcrumbs
- 1 tbsp. coconut flour
- 1 cup unsweetened, dried coconut
- 1 egg white
- 12 raw large shrimp

Directions:
1. Put shrimp on paper towels to drain.
2. Mix coconut and panko breadcrumbs together. Then mix in coconut flour and almond flour in a different bowl. Set to the side.
3. Dip the shrimp into flour mixture, then into egg white, and then into coconut mixture.
4. Place into air fryer basket. Repeat with remaining shrimp.
5. Cook 10 minutes at 350 degrees. Turn halfway through cooking process.

Nutrition: Calories: 213 Fat 8g Protein 15g Sugar 3g

245. Air Fryer Salmon
Preparation Time: 5 minutes
Cooking Time: 10 minutes
Servings: 2
Ingredients:
- ½ tsp. salt
- ½ tsp. garlic powder
- ½ tsp. smoked paprika
- Salmon

Directions:
1. Mix spices together and sprinkle onto salmon.
2. Place seasoned salmon into air fryer.
3. Cook 8-10 minutes at 400 degrees.

Nutrition: Calories: 185 Fat 11g Protein 21g Sugar 0g

246. Healthy Fish and Chips
Preparation Time: 15 minutes
Cooking Time: 15 minutes
Servings: 3
Ingredients:
- Old Bay seasoning
- ½ cup panko breadcrumbs
- 1 egg
- 2 tbsp. almond flour
- 2 4-6-ounce tilapia fillets
- Frozen crinkle cut fries

Directions:
1. Add almond flour to one bowl, beat egg in another bowl, and add panko breadcrumbs to the third bowl, mixed with Old Bay seasoning.
2. Dredge tilapia in flour, then egg, and then breadcrumbs.
3. Place coated fish in air fryer along with fries.
4. Cook 15 minutes at 390 degrees.

Nutrition: Calories: 219 Carbs: 18 Fat 5g Protein 25g Sugar 1g

247. 3-Ingredient Air Fryer Calf
Preparation Time: 15 minutes
Cooking Time: 13 minutes
Servings: 4
Ingredients:
- 1 tbsp. chopped parsley
- 1 tbsp. olive oil
- ¼ cups seasoned fish fry
- 4 catfish fillets

Directions:
1. Ensure your air fryer is preheated to 400 degrees.
2. Rinse off catfish fillets and pat dry.
3. Add fish fry seasoning to Ziploc baggie, then catfish. Shake bag and ensure fish gets well coated.
4. Spray each fillet with olive oil.
5. Add fillets to air fryer basket. Cook 10 minutes. Then flip and cook another 2-3 minutes.

Nutrition: Calories: 208 Carbs: 8 Fat 5g Protein 17g Sugar 0.5g

248. Bang Bang Panko Breaded Fried Shrimp
Preparation Time: 15 minutes
Cooking Time: 8 minutes
Servings: 4
Ingredients:
- 1 tsp. paprika
- Montreal chicken seasoning
- ¾ cup panko bread crumbs
- ½ cup almond flour
- 1 egg white
- 1-pound raw shrimp (peeled and deveined)
- Bang Bang Sauce:
- ¼ cup sweet chili sauce
- 2 tbsp. sriracha sauce
- 1/3 cup plain Greek yogurt

Directions:
1. Ensure your air fryer is preheated to 400 degrees.
2. Season all shrimp with seasonings. Add flour to one bowl, egg white in another, and breadcrumbs to a third.
3. Dip seasoned shrimp in flour, then egg whites, and then breadcrumbs. Spray coated shrimp with olive oil and add to air fryer basket.
4. Cook 4 minutes, flip, and cook an additional 4 minutes. To make the sauce, mix together all sauce ingredients until smooth.

Nutrition: Calories: 212 Carbs: 12 Fat 1g Protein 37g Sugar 0.5g

249. Louisiana Shrimp Po Boy
Preparation Time: 15 minutes

Cooking Time: 10 minutes
Servings: 4
Ingredients:
- 1 tsp. creole seasoning
- 8 slices of tomato
- Lettuce leaves
- ¼ C. buttermilk
- ½ C. Louisiana Fish Fry
- 1-pound deveined shrimp
- Remoulade sauce:
- 1 chopped green onion
- 1 tsp. hot sauce
- 1 tsp. Dijon mustard
- ½ tsp. creole seasoning
- 1 tsp. Worcestershire sauce
- Juice of ½ a lemon
- ½ cup vegan mayo

Directions:
1. Combine all the sauce ingredients until well combined. Bake when cooking shrimp. Mix the spices and season the shrimp.
2. Add buttermilk to a bowl. Dip each shrimp into milk and place in a Ziploc bag. Chill half an hour to marinate.
3. Add fish fry to a bowl. Take shrimp from marinating bag and dip into fish fry, and then add to air fryer. Ensure your air fryer is preheated to 400 degrees.
4. Spray shrimp with olive oil. Cook 5 minutes, flip and then cook another 5 minutes.
5. Assemble "Keto" Po Boy by adding sauce to lettuce leaves, along with shrimp and tomato.

Nutrition: Calories: 337 Carbs: 55 Fat 12g Protein 24g Sugar 2g

250. Air Fryer Salmon Patties

Preparation Time: 15 minutes
Cooking Time: 7 minutes
Servings: 4
Ingredients:
- 1 tbsp. olive oil
- 1 tbsp. ghee
- ¼ tsp. salt
- 1/8 tsp. pepper
- 1 egg
- 1 C. almond flour
- 1 cans wild Alaskan pink salmon

Directions:
1. Drain can of salmon into a bowl and keeps liquid. Discard skin and bones.
2. Add salt, pepper, and egg to salmon, mixing well with hands to incorporate. Make patties.
3. Dredge in flour and remaining egg. If it seems dry, spoon reserved salmon liquid from the can onto patties.
4. Add patties to air fryer. Cook 7 minutes at 378 degrees till golden, making sure to flip once during cooking process.

Nutrition: Calories: 437 Carbs: 55 Fat 12g Protein 24g Sugar 2g

251. Fried Calamari

Preparation Time: 15 minutes
Cooking Time: 15 minutes
Servings: 8
Ingredients:
- ½ tsp. salt
- ½ tsp. Old Bay seasoning
- 1/3 cup plain cornmeal
- ½ cup semolina flour
- ½ cup almond flour
- 5-6 cup olive oil
- 1 ½ pounds baby squid

Directions:
1. Rinse squid in cold water and slice tentacles, keeping just ¼-inch of the hood in one piece.
2. Combine 1-2 pinches of pepper, salt, Old Bay seasoning, cornmeal, and both flours together. Dredge squid pieces into flour mixture and place into air fryer. Spray liberally with olive oil.
3. Cook 15 minutes at 345 degrees till coating turns a golden brown.

Nutrition: Calories: 211 Fat 6g Protein 21g Sugar 1g

252. Panko-Crusted Tilapia

Preparation Time: 5 minutes
Cooking Time: 11 minutes
Servings: 3
Ingredients:
- 2 tsp. Italian seasoning
- 2 tsp. lemon pepper
- 1/3 cup panko breadcrumbs
- 1/3 cup egg whites
- 1/3 cup almond flour
- 3 tilapia fillets
- Olive oil

Directions:
1. Place panko, egg whites, and flour into separate bowls. Mix lemon pepper and Italian seasoning in with breadcrumbs. Pat tilapia fillets dry. Dredge in flour, then egg, then breadcrumb mixture. Add to air fryer basket and spray lightly with olive oil. Cook 10-11 minutes at 400 degrees, making sure to flip halfway through cooking.

Nutrition: Calories: 256 Fat 9g Protein 39g Sugar 5g

253. Salmon Croquettes

Preparation Time: 15 minutes
Cooking Time: 10 minutes
Servings: 8
Ingredients:
- Panko breadcrumbs
- Almond flour
- 2 egg whites
- 2 tbsp. chopped chives
- 2 tbsp. minced garlic cloves
- ½ C. chopped onion
- 2/3 C. grated carrots
- 1 pound chopped salmon fillet

Directions:

1. Mix together all ingredients minus breadcrumbs, flour, and egg whites.
2. Shape mixture into balls. Then coat them in flour, then egg, and then breadcrumbs. Drizzle with olive oil.
3. Add coated salmon balls to air fryer and cook 6 minutes at 350 degrees. Shake and cook an additional 4 minutes until golden in color.

Nutrition: Calories: 503 Carbs: 61g Fat 9g Protein 5g Sugar 4g

254. Air Fryer Fish Tacos
Preparation Time: 5 minutes
Cooking Time: 15 minutes
Servings: 4
Ingredients:
- 1-pound cod
- 1 tbsp. cumin
- ½ tbsp. chili powder
- 1 ½ cup of almond flour
- 1 ½ cup of coconut flour
- 10 ounces' Mexican beer
- 2 eggs

Directions:
1. Whisk beer and eggs together.
2. Whisk flours, pepper, salt, cumin, and chili powder together. Slice cod into large pieces and coat in egg mixture then flour mixture.
3. Spray bottom of your air fryer basket with olive oil and add coated codpieces.
4. Cook 15 minutes at 375 degrees.
5. Serve on lettuce leaves topped with homemade salsa!

Nutrition: Calories: 178 Fat 10g Protein 19g Sugar 1g

255. Bacon Wrapped Scallops
Preparation Time: 10 minutes
Cooking Time: 6 minutes
Servings: 4
Ingredients:
- 1 tsp. paprika
- 1 tsp. lemon pepper
- 5 slices of center-cut bacon
- 20 raw sea scallops

Directions:
1. Rinse and drain scallops, placing on paper towels to soak up excess moisture.
2. Cut slices of bacon into 4 pieces.
3. Wrap each scallop with a piece of bacon, using toothpicks to secure. Sprinkle wrapped scallops with paprika and lemon pepper.
4. Spray air fryer basket with olive oil and add scallops.
5. Cook 5-6 minutes at 400 degrees, making sure to flip halfway through.

Nutrition: Calories: 389 Fat 17g Protein 21g Sugar 1g

256. Parmesan Shrimp
Preparation Time: 10 minutes
Cooking Time: 10 minutes
Servings: 6
Ingredients:
- 2 tbsp. olive oil
- 1 tsp. onion powder
- 1 tsp. basil
- ½ tsp. oregano
- 1 tsp. pepper
- 2/3 cup grated parmesan cheese
- 4 minced garlic cloves
- 2 pounds of jumbo cooked shrimp (peeled/deveined)

Directions:
1. Mix all seasonings together and gently toss shrimp with mixture.
2. Spray olive oil into air fryer basket and add seasoned shrimp.
3. Cook 8-10 minutes at 350 degrees.
4. Squeeze lemon juice over shrimp right before devouring!

Nutrition: Calories: 351 Fat 11g Protein 19g Sugar 1g

257. Honey Glazed Salmon
Preparation Time: 5 minutes
Cooking Time: 13 minutes
Servings: 2
Ingredients:
- 1 tsp. water
- 3 tsp. rice wine vinegar
- 6 tbsp. low-sodium soy sauce
- 6 tbsp. raw honey
- 2 salmon fillets

Directions:
1. Combine water, vinegar, honey, and soy sauce together. Pour half of this mixture into a bowl.
2. Place salmon in one bowl of marinade and let chill 2 hours.
3. Ensure your air fryer is preheated to 356 degrees and add salmon.
4. Cook 8 minutes, flipping halfway through. Baste salmon with some of the remaining marinade mixture and cook another 5 minutes.
5. To make a sauce to serve salmon with, pour remaining marinade mixture into a saucepan, heating till simmering. Let simmer 2 minutes. Serve drizzled over salmon!

Nutrition: Calories: 390 Fat 8g Protein 16g Sugar 5g

258. Crispy Air Fried Sushi Roll
Preparation Time: 15 minutes
Cooking Time: 10 minutes
Servings: 12
Ingredients:
- Kale Salad:
- 1 tbsp. sesame seeds
- ¾ tsp. soy sauce
- ¼ tsp. ginger
- 1/8 tsp. garlic powder
- ¾ tsp. toasted sesame oil
- ½ tsp. rice vinegar

- 1 ½ cup chopped kale
- Sushi Rolls:
- ½ of a sliced avocado
- 3 sheets of sushi nor
- 1 batch cauliflower rice
- Sriracha Mayo:
- Sriracha sauce
- ¼ cup vegan mayo
- Coating:
- ½ cup panko breadcrumbs

Directions:
1. Combine all of kale salad ingredients together, tossing well. Set to the side.
2. Lay out a sheet of nor and spread a handful of rice on. Then place 2-3 tbsp. of kale salad over rice, followed by avocado. Roll up sushi. To make mayo, whisk mayo ingredients together until smooth.
3. Add breadcrumbs to a bowl. Coat sushi rolls in crumbs till coated and add to air fryer.
4. Cook rolls 10 minutes at 390 degrees, shaking gently at 5 minutes.
5. Slice each roll into 6-8 pieces and enjoy!

Nutrition: Calories: 267 Fat 13g Protein 6g Sugar 3g

259. Crab Legs

Preparation Time: 5 minutes
Cooking Time: 20 minutes
Servings: 3
Ingredients:
- 3 lb. crab legs
- ¼ cup salted butter, melted and divided
- ½ lemon, juiced
- ¼ tsp. garlic powder

Directions:
1. In a bowl, toss the crab legs and two tablespoons of the melted butter together. Place the crab legs in the basket of the fryer. Cook at 400°F for fifteen minutes, giving the basket a good shake halfway through.
2. Combine the remaining butter with the lemon juice and garlic powder. Crack open the cooked crab legs and remove the meat. Serve with the butter dip on the side and enjoy!

Nutrition: Calories: 392 Fat 10g Protein 18g Sugar 8g

260. Crusty Pesto Salmon

Preparation Time: 5 minutes
Cooking Time: 15 minutes
Servings: 2
Ingredients:
- ¼ cup s, roughly chopped
- ¼ cup pesto
- 2 x 4-oz. salmon fillets
- 2 tbsp. unsalted butter, melted

Directions:
1. Mix the s and pesto together.
2. Place the salmon fillets in a round baking dish, roughly six inches in diameter.
3. Brush the fillets with butter, followed by the pesto mixture, ensuring to coat both the top and bottom. Put the baking dish inside the fryer.
4. Cook for twelve minutes at 390°F.
5. When it flakes easily when prodded with a fork, Then the salmon is ready. Serve warm.

Nutrition: Fat 11g Protein 20g Sugar 9g

261. Buttery Cod

Preparation Time: 10 minutes
Cooking Time: 12 minutes
Servings: 2
Ingredients:
- 2 x 4-oz. cod fillets
- 2 tbsp. salted butter, melted
- 1 tsp. Old Bay seasoning
- ½ medium lemon, sliced

Directions:
1. Place the cod fillets in a pan.
2. Brush with melted butter, season with Old Bay and finish with some lemon wedges.
3. Wrap the fish in aluminum foil and put it in your deep fryer.
4. Cook for eight minutes at 350 ° F.
5. Cod is ready when peeled easily. Serve hot.

Nutrition: Calories: 394 Fat 5g Protein 12g Sugar 4g

262. Sesame Tuna Steak

Preparation Time: 5 minutes
Cooking Time: 12 minutes
Servings: 2
Ingredients:
- 1 tbsp. coconut oil, melted
- 2 x 6-oz. tuna steaks
- ½ tsp. garlic powder
- 2 tsp. black sesame seeds
- 2 tsp. white sesame seeds

Directions:
1. Apply the coconut oil to the tuna steaks with a brunch, then season with garlic powder.
2. Combine the black and white sesame seeds. Embed them in the tuna steaks, covering the fish all over. Place the tuna into your air fryer.
3. Cook for eight minutes at 400°F, turning the fish halfway through.
4. The tuna steaks are ready when they have reached a temperature of 145°F. Serve straightaway.

Nutrition: Calories: 160 Fat 6g Protein 26g Sugar 7g

263. Lemon Garlic Shrimp

Preparation Time: 10 minutes
Cooking Time: 15 minutes
Servings: 2
Ingredients:
- 1 medium lemon
- ½ lb. medium shrimp, shelled and deveined
- ½ tsp. Old Bay seasoning
- 2 tbsp. unsalted butter, melted
- ½ tsp. minced garlic

Directions:

1. Grate the rind of the lemon into a bowl. Cut the lemon in half and juice it over the same bowl. Toss in the shrimp, Old Bay, and butter, mixing everything to make sure the shrimp is completely covered.
2. Transfer to a round baking dish roughly six inches wide, then place this dish in your fryer.
3. Cook at 400°F for six minutes. The shrimp is cooked when it turns a bright pink color.
4. Serve hot, drizzling any leftover sauce over the shrimp.

Nutrition: Calories: 490 Fat 9g Protein 12g Sugar 11g

264. Foil Packet Salmon

Preparation Time: 5 minutes
Cooking Time: 15 minutes
Servings: 2
Ingredients:
- 2 x 4-oz. skinless salmon fillets
- 2 tbsp. unsalted butter, melted
- ½ tsp. garlic powder
- 1 medium lemon
- ½ tsp. dried dill

Directions:
1. Take a sheet of aluminum foil and cut into two squares measuring roughly 5" x 5". Lay each fillet at the center of each piece. Brush both fillets with a tablespoon of bullet and season with a quarter-teaspoon of garlic powder. Halve the lemon and grate the skin of one half over the fish. Cut four half-slices of lemon, using two to top each fillet. Season each fillet with a quarter-teaspoon of dill.
2. Fold the tops and sides of the aluminum foil over the fish to create a kind of packet. Place each one in the fryer. Cook for twelve minutes at 400°F. The salmon is ready when it flakes easily. Serve hot.

Nutrition: Calories: 240 Fat 13g Protein 21g Sugar 9g

265. Foil Packet Lobster Tail

Preparation Time: 5 minutes
Cooking Time: 15 minutes
Servings: 2
Ingredients:
- 2 x 6-oz. lobster tail halves
- 2 tbsp. salted butter, melted
- ½ medium lemon, juiced
- ½ tsp. Old Bay seasoning
- 1 tsp. dried parsley

Directions:
1. Lay each lobster on a sheet of aluminum foil. Pour a light drizzle of melted butter and lemon juice over each one, and season with Old Bay.
2. Fold down the sides and ends of the foil to seal the lobster. Place each one in the fryer.
3. Cook at 375°F for twelve minutes.
4. Just before serving, top the lobster with dried parsley.

Nutrition: Calories: 510 Fat 18g Protein 26g Sugar 12g

266. Avocado Shrimp

Preparation Time: 10 minutes
Cooking Time: 20 minutes
Servings: 2
Ingredients:
- ½ cup onion, chopped
- 2 lb. shrimp
- 1 tbsp. seasoned salt
- 1 avocado
- ½ cup pecans, chopped

Directions:
1. Pre-heat the fryer at 400°F.
2. Put the chopped onion in the basket of the fryer and sprits with some cooking spray. Leave to cook for five minutes. Add the shrimp and set the timer for a further five minutes. Sprinkle with some seasoned salt. Allow to cook for an additional five minutes.
3. During these last five minutes, halve your avocado and remove the pit. Cube each half, then scoop out the flesh. Take care when removing the shrimp from the fryer. Place it on a dish and top with the avocado and the chopped pecans.

Nutrition: Calories: 195 Fat 14g Protein 36g Sugar 10g

267. Lemon Butter Scallops

Preparation Time: 15 minutes
Cooking Time: 30 minutes
Servings: 1
Ingredients:
- 1 lemon
- 1 lb. scallops
- ½ cup butter
- ¼ cup parsley, chopped

Directions:
1. Juice the lemon into a Ziploc bag.
2. Wash your scallops, dry them, and season to taste. Put them in the bag with the lemon juice. Refrigerate for an hour.
3. Remove the bag from the refrigerator and leave for about twenty minutes until it returns to room temperature. Transfer the scallops into a foil pan that is small enough to be placed inside the fryer.
4. Pre-heat the fryer at 400°F and put the rack inside.
5. Place the foil pan on the rack and cook for five minutes.
6. In the meantime, melt the butter in a saucepan over a medium heat. Zest the lemon over the saucepan, and then add in the chopped parsley. Mix well.
7. Take care when removing the pan from the fryer. Transfer the contents to a plate and drizzle with the lemon-butter mixture. Serve hot.

Nutrition: Calories: 420 Fat 12g Protein 23g Sugar 13g

268. Cheesy Lemon Halibut

Preparation Time: 10 minutes
Cooking Time: 20 minutes
Servings: 2
Ingredients:
- 1 lb. halibut fillet
- ½ cup butter
- 2 ½ tbsp. mayonnaises

- 2 ½ tbsp. lemon juices
- ¾ cup parmesan cheese, grated

Directions:
1. Pre-heat your fryer at 375°F.
2. Sprits the halibut fillets with cooking spray and season as desired. Put the halibut in the fryer and cook for twelve minutes. In the meantime, combine the butter, mayonnaise, and lemon juice in a bowl with a hand mixer. Ensure a creamy texture is achieved. Stir in the grated parmesan. When the halibut is ready, open the drawer and spread the butter over the fish with a butter knife. leave to cook for another two minutes, then serve hot.

Nutrition: Calories: 432 Fat 18g Protein 14g Sugar 12g

269. Spicy Mackerel
Preparation Time: 10 minutes
Cooking Time: 20 minutes
Servings: 2
Ingredients:
- 2 mackerel fillets
- 2 tbsp. red chili flakes
- 2 tsp. garlic, minced
- 1 tsp. lemon juice

Directions:
1. Season the mackerel fillets with the red pepper flakes, minced garlic, and a drizzle of lemon juice. Allow to sit for five minutes.
2. Preheat your fryer at 350°F.
3. Cook the mackerel for five minutes, before opening the drawer, flipping the fillets. Allow to cook on the other side for another five minutes.
4. Plate the fillets, making sure to spoon any remaining juice over them before serving.

Nutrition: Calories: 240 Fat 4g Protein 16g Sugar 3g

270. Thyme Scallops
Preparation Time: 5 minutes
Cooking Time: 12 minutes
Servings: 1
Ingredients:
- 1 lb. scallops
- Salt and pepper
- ½ tbsp. butter
- ½ cup thyme, chopped

Directions:
1. Wash the scallops and dry them completely. Season with pepper and salt, then set aside while you prepare the pan.
2. Grease a foil pan in several spots with the butter and cover the bottom with the thyme. Place the scallops on top.
3. Pre-heat the fryer at 400°F and set the rack inside.
4. Place the foil pan on the rack and allow cooking for seven minutes.
5. Take care when removing the pan from the fryer and transfer the scallops to a serving dish. Spoon any remaining butter in the pan over the fish and enjoy.

Nutrition: Calories: 291 Fat 9g Protein 17g Sugar 5g

271. Crispy Calamari
Preparation Time: 5 minutes
Cooking Time: 15 minutes
Servings: 4
Ingredients:
- 1 lb. fresh squid
- Salt and pepper
- 2 cups flour
- 1 cup water
- 2 cloves garlic, minced
- ½ cup mayonnaise

Directions:
1. Remove the skin from the squid and discard any ink. Slice the squid into rings and season with some salt and pepper.
2. Put the flour and water in separate bowls. Dip the squid firstly in the flour, then into the water, then into the flour again, ensuring that it is entirely covered with flour.
3. Pre-heat the fryer at 400°F. Put the squid inside and cook for six minutes.
4. In the meantime, prepare the aioli by combining the garlic with the mayonnaise in a bowl.
5. Once the squid is ready, plate up and serve with the aioli.

Nutrition: Calories: 247 Fat 3g Protein 18g Sugar 3g

272. Filipino Bistek
Preparation Time: 5 minutes
Cooking Time: 10 minutes
Servings: 4
Ingredients:
- 2 milkfish bellies, deboned and sliced into 4 portions
- ¾ tsp. salt
- ¼ tsp. ground black pepper
- ¼ tsp. cumin powder
- 2 tbsp. calamansi juice
- 2 lemongrasses, trimmed and cut crosswise into small pieces
- ½ cup tamari sauce
- 2 tbsp. fish sauce
- 2 tbsp. sugar
- 1 tsp. garlic powder
- ½ cup chicken broth
- 2 tbsp. olive oil

Directions:
1. Dry the fish using some paper towels.
2. Put the fish in a large bowl and coat with the rest of the ingredients. Allow to marinate for 3 hours in the refrigerator.
3. Cook the fish steaks on an Air Fryer grill basket at 340°F for 5 minutes.
4. Turn the steaks over. Allow to grill for an additional 4 minutes. Cook until medium brown.
5. Serve with steamed white rice.

Nutrition: Calories: 259 Fat 3g Protein 10g Sugar 2g

273. Saltine Fish Fillets

Preparation Time: 10 minutes
Cooking Time: 15 minutes
Servings: 4
Ingredients:
- 1 cup crushed saltines
- ¼ cup extra-virgin olive oil
- 1 tsp. garlic powder
- ½ tsp. shallot powder
- 1 egg, well whisked
- 4 white fish fillets
- Salt and ground black pepper to taste
- Fresh Italian parsley to serve

Directions:
1. In a shallow bowl, combine the crushed saltines and olive oil.
2. In a separate bowl, mix together the garlic powder, shallot powder, and the beaten egg.
3. Sprinkle a good amount of salt and pepper over the fish, before dipping each fillet into the egg mixture.
4. Coat the fillets with the crumb mixture.
5. Airs fry the fish at 370°F for 10 - 12 minutes.
6. Serve with fresh parsley.

Nutrition: Calories: 502 Fat 4g Protein 11g Sugar 9g

274. Air Fried Cod with Basil Vinaigrette
Preparation Time: 5 minutes
Cooking Time: 15 minutes
Servings: 4
Ingredients:
- ¼ cup olive oil
- 4 cod fillets
- A bunch of basil, torn
- Juice from 1 lemon, freshly squeezed
- Salt and pepper to taste

Directions:
1. Preheat the fryer for 5 minutes. Season the cod fillets with salt and pepper.
2. Place in the fryer and cook for 15 minutes at 3500F. Meanwhile, mix the remaining ingredients in a bowl and mix to combine. Serve the fried cod with the basil vinaigrette.

Nutrition: Calories 235 Carbohydrates 1.9g Protein 14.3g Fat 18.9g

275. Almond Flour Coated Crispy Shrimps
Preparation Time: 5 minutes
Cooking Time: 10 minutes
Servings: 4
Ingredients:
- ½ cup almond flour
- 1 tablespoon yellow mustard
- 1-pound raw shrimps, peeled and deveined
- 3 tablespoons olive oil
- Salt and pepper to taste

Directions:
1. Put all the ingredients in a Ziploc bag and shake well.
2. Put in the fryer and cook for 10 minutes at 4000F.

Nutrition: Calories 206 Carbohydrates 1.3g Protein 23.5g Fat 11.9g

276. Another Crispy Coconut Shrimp Recipe
Preparation Time: 5 minutes
Cooking Time: 20 minutes
Servings: 4
Ingredients:
- ½ cup flour
- ½ stick cold butter, cut into cubes
- ½ tablespoon lemon juice
- 1 egg yolk, beaten
- 1 green onion, chopped
- 1-pound salmon fillets cut into small cubes
- 3 tablespoons whipping cream
- 4 eggs, beaten
- Salt and pepper to taste

Directions:
1. Preheat fryer to 3900F.
2. Seasonal salmon fillets with lemon juice, salt and pepper.
3. In another bowl, combine the flour and butter. Gradually add cold water to form a dough. Knead the dough on a flat surface to form a sheet.
4. Place the dough on the baking dish and press firmly on the dish.
5. Beat the eggs and egg yolk and season with salt and pepper to taste.
6. Place the salmon cubes on the pan lined with dough and pour the egg over.
7. Cook for 15 to 20 minutes.
8. Garnish with green onions once cooked.

Nutrition: Calories 483 Carbs: 5.2g Protein 45.2g Fat 31.2g

277. Apple Slaw Topped Alaskan Cod Filet
Preparation Time: 5 minutes
Cooking Time: 15 minutes
Servings: 3
Ingredients:
- ¼ cup mayonnaise
- ½ red onion, diced
- 1 ½ pounds frozen Alaskan cod
- 1 box whole wheat panko bread crumbs
- 1 granny smith apple, julienned
- 1 tbsp. vegetable oil
- 1 tsp paprika
- 2 cups Napa cabbage, shredded
- Salt and pepper to taste

Directions:
1. Preheat the air fryer to 3900F. Place the grill pan accessory in the air fryer.
2. Brush the fish with oil and dredge in the breadcrumbs. Place the fish on the grill pan and cook for 15 minutes. Make sure to flip the fish halfway through the cooking time. Meanwhile, prepare the slaw by mixing the remaining Ingredients in a bowl. Serve the fish with the slaw.

Nutrition: Calories 316 Carbs: 13.5g Protein 37.8g Fat 12.2g

278. Baked Cod Fillet Recipe from Thailand
Preparation Time: 5 minutes
Cooking Time: 20 minutes
Servings: 4
Ingredients:
- ¼ cup coconut milk, freshly squeezed
- 1 tbsp. lime juice, freshly squeezed
- 1-pound cod fillet, cut into bite-sized pieces
- Salt and pepper to taste

Directions:
1. Preheat the air fryer for 5 minutes.
2. Place all ingredients in a baking dish that will fit in the air fryer.
3. Place in the air fryer.
4. Cook for 20 minutes at 3250F.

Nutrition: Calories 844Carbohydrates 2.3g Protein 21.6gFat 83.1g

279. Baked Scallops with Garlic Aioli
Preparation Time: 5 minutes
Cooking Time: 10 minutes
Servings: 4
Ingredients:
- 1 cup bread crumbs
- 1/4 cup chopped parsley
- 16 sea scallops, rinsed and drained
- 2 shallots, chopped
- 3 pinches ground nutmeg
- 4 tbsp. olive oil
- 5 cloves garlic, minced
- 5 tbsp. butter, melted
- Salt and pepper to taste

Directions:
1. Lightly grease baking pan of air fryer with cooking spray.
2. Mix in shallots, garlic, melted butter, and scallops. Season it with pepper, salt, and nutmeg.
3. In a small bowl, whisk well olive oil and bread crumbs. Sprinkle over scallops.
4. Cook on 390oF until tops are lightly browned for 10 minutes.
5. Serve and enjoy with a sprinkle of parsley.

Nutrition: Calories 452Carbs: 29.8gProtein 15.2gFat 30.2g

280. Basil 'n Lime-Chili Clams
Preparation Time: 5 minutes
Cooking Time: 15 minutes
Servings: 3
Ingredients:
- ½ cup basil leaves
- ½ cup tomatoes, chopped
- 1 tbsp. fresh lime juice
- 25 littleneck clams
- 4 cloves of garlic, minced
- 6 tbsp. unsalted butter
- Salt and pepper to taste

Directions:
1. Preheat the air fryer to 3900F.
2. Place the grill pan accessory in the air fryer.
3. On a large foil, place all ingredients. Fold over the foil and close by crimping the edges.
4. Place on the grill pan and cook for 15 minutes.
5. Serve with bread.

Nutrition: Calories 16 Carbs: 4.1gProtein 1.7gFat 15.5g

281. Bass Filet in Coconut Sauce
Preparation Time: 5 minutes
Cooking Time: 15 minutes
Servings: 4
Ingredients:
- ¼ cup coconut milk
- ½ pound bass fillet
- 1 tbsp. olive oil
- 2 tbsp. jalapeno, chopped
- 2 tbsp. lime juice, freshly squeezed
- 3 tbsp. parsley, chopped
- Salt and pepper to taste

Directions:
1. Preheat the air fryer for 5 minutes
2. Season the bass with salt and pepper to taste
3. Brush the surface with olive oil.
4. Place in the air fryer and cook for 15 minutes at 3500F.
5. Meanwhile, place in a saucepan, the coconut milk, lime juice, jalapeno and parsley. Heat it with medium flame.
6. Serve the fish with the coconut sauce.

Nutrition: Calories 139Carbohydrates: 2.7gProtein 8.7gFat 10.3

282. Beer Battered Cod Filet
Preparation Time: 5 minutes
Cooking Time: 15 minutes
Servings: 2
Ingredients:
- ½ cup all-purpose flour
- ¾ tsp baking powder
- 1 ¼ cup lager beer
- 2 cod fillets
- 2 eggs, beaten
- Salt and pepper to taste

Directions:
1. Preheat the air fryer to 3900F.
2. Pat the fish fillets dry then set aside.
3. In a bowl, combine the rest of the Ingredients to create a batter.
4. Dip the fillets on the batter and place on the double layer rack.
5. Cook for 15 minutes.

Nutrition: Calories 229Carbs: 33.2gProtein 31.1gFat 10.2g

283. Buttered Baked Cod with Wine
Preparation Time: 5 minutes
Cooking Time: 12 minutes
Servings: 2
Ingredients:
- 1 tbsp. butter

- 1 tbsp. butter
- 2 tbsp. dry white wine
- 1/2 pound thick-cut cod loin
- 1-1/2 tsp chopped fresh parsley
- 1-1/2 tsp chopped green onion
- 1/2 lemon, cut into wedges
- 1/4 sleeve buttery round crackers (such as Ritz®), crushed
- 1/4 lemon, juiced

Directions:
1. In a small bowl, melt butter in microwave. Whisk in crackers. Lightly grease baking pan of air fryer with remaining butter. And melt for 2 minutes at 390oF. In a small bowl, whisk well lemon juice, white wine, parsley, and green onion. Coat cod filets in melted butter. Pour dressing. Top with butter-cracker mixture.
2. Cook for 10 minutes at 390oF.
3. Serve and enjoy.

Nutrition: Calories 266Carbs: 9.3gProtein 20.9gFat 16.1g

284. Buttered Garlic-Oregano on Clams

Preparation Time: 5 minutes
Cooking Time: 5 minutes
Servings: 4
Ingredients:
- ¼ cup parmesan cheese, grated
- ¼ cup parsley, chopped
- 1 cup breadcrumbs
- 1 tsp dried oregano
- 2 dozen clams, shucked
- 3 cloves of garlic, minced
- 4 tbsp. butter, melted

Directions:
1. In a medium bowl, mix the crumbs, parmesan cheese, parsley, oregano, and garlic. Add the melted butter. Preheat fryer to 3900F.
2. Place the baking dish accessory in the air fryer and place the clams.
3. Sprinkle the crumb mixture over the clams.
4. Cook for 5 minutes.

Nutrition: Calories 160Carbs: 6.3gProtein 2.9gFat 13.6g

285. Butterflied Prawns with Garlic-Sriracha

Preparation Time: 5 minutes
Cooking Time: 15 minutes
Servings: 2
Ingredients:
- 1 tbsp. lime juice
- 1 tbsp. sriracha
- 1-pound large prawns, shells removed and cut lengthwise or butterflied
- 1tsp fish sauce
- 2 tbsp. melted butter
- 2 tbsp. minced garlic
- Salt and pepper to taste

Directions:
1. Preheat the air fryer to 3900F.
2. Place the grill pan accessory in the air fryer.
3. Season the prawns with the rest of the ingredients.
4. Place on the grill pan and cook for 15 minutes. Make sure to flip the prawns halfway through the cooking time.

Nutrition: Calories 443Carbs: 9.7 g Protein 62.8gFat 16.9g

286. Cajun Seasoned Salmon Filet

Preparation Time: 5 minutes
Cooking Time: 15 minutes
Servings: 1
Ingredients:
- 1 salmon fillet
- 1 tsp juice from lemon, freshly squeezed
- 3 tbsp. extra virgin olive oil
- A dash of Cajun seasoning mix
- Salt and pepper to taste

Directions:
1. Preheat the air fryer for 5 minutes.
2. Place all ingredients in a bowl and toss to coat.
3. Place the fish fillet in the air fryer basket.
4. Bake for 15 minutes at 3250F.
5. Once cooked drizzle with olive oil

Nutrition: Calories 523Carbohydrates: 4.6gProtein 47.9gFat 34.8g

287. Cajun Spiced Lemon-Shrimp Kebabs

Preparation Time: 5 minutes
Cooking Time: 10 minutes
Servings: 2
Ingredients:
- 1 tsp cayenne
- 1 tsp garlic powder
- 1 tsp kosher salt
- 1 tsp onion powder
- 1 tsp oregano
- 1 tsp paprika
- 12 pieces XL shrimp
- 2 lemons, sliced thinly crosswise
- 2 tbsp. olive oil

Directions:
1. In a bowl, mix all Ingredients except for sliced lemons. Marinate for 10 minutes.
2. Thread 3 shrimps per steel skewer.
3. Place in skewer rack.
4. Cook for 5 minutes at 390oF.
5. Serve and enjoy with freshly squeezed lemon.

Nutrition: Calories 232Carbs: 7.9gProtein 15.9gFat 15.1g

288. Cajun Spiced Veggie-Shrimp Bake

Preparation Time: 5 minutes
Cooking Time: 20 minutes
Servings: 4
Ingredients:
- 1 Bag of Frozen Mixed Vegetables
- 1 Tbsp. Gluten Free Cajun Seasoning
- Olive Oil Spray
- Season with salt and pepper

- Small Shrimp Peeled & Deveined (Regular Size Bag about 50-80 Small Shrimp)

Directions:
1. Lightly grease baking pan of air fryer with cooking spray. Add all Ingredients and toss well to coat. Season it with pepper and salt, generously. For 10 minutes, cook it on 330oF. Halfway through cooking time, stir. Cook for 10 minutes at 330oF.
2. Serve and enjoy.

Nutrition: Calories 78Carbs: 13.2gProtein 2.8gFat 1.5g

289. Sweet Cod Fillets

Preparation Time: 10 minutes
Cooking Time: 15 minutes
Servings: 4
Ingredients:
- 4 cod fillets, boneless
- Salt and black pepper to taste
- 1 cup water
- 4 tbsp. light soy sauce
- 1 tbsp. sugar
- 3 tbsp. olive oil + a drizzle
- 4 ginger slices
- 3 spring onions, chopped
- 2 tbsp. coriander, chopped

Directions:
1. Season the fish with salt and also pepper and then pour a little oil on it and grate it well. Place the fish in your deep fryer and cook at 360 degrees F for 12 minutes. Put the water in a saucepan and heat over medium heat. Add soy sauce and sugar, stir, simmer, and remove from heat.
2. Heat up a pan with the olive oil over medium heat; add the ginger and green onions, stir, cook for 2-3 minutes, and remove from the heat. Divide the fish between plates and top with ginger, coriander, and green onions.
3. Drizzle the soy sauce mixture all over, serve, and enjoy!

Nutrition: Calories 270gFat 12gFiber 8gCarbs 16gProtein 14g

290. Pecan Cod

Preparation Time: 10 minutes
Cooking Time: 15 minutes
Servings: 2
Ingredients:
- 2 black cod fillets, boneless
- 1 tbsp. olive oil
- Salt and black pepper to taste
- 2 leeks, sliced
- ½ cup pecans, chopped

Directions:
1. In a bowl, mix the cod with the oil, salt, pepper, and the leeks; toss / coat well.
2. Transfer the cod to your air fryer and cook at 360 degrees F for 15 minutes.
3. Divide the fish and leeks between plates, sprinkle the pecans on top, and serve immediately.

Nutrition: Calories 280g Fat 4g Fiber 2g Carbs 12g Protein 15g

291. Balsamic Cod

Preparation Time: 5 minutes
Cooking Time: 12 minutes
Servings: 2
Ingredients:
- 2 cod fillets, boneless
- 2 tbsp. lemon juice
- Salt and black pepper to taste
- ½ tsp garlic powder
- ⅓ Cup water
- ⅓ Cup balsamic vinegar
- 3 shallots, chopped
- 2 tbsp. olive oil

Directions:
1. In a bowl, toss the cod with the salt, pepper, lemon juice, garlic powder, water, vinegar, and oil; coat well. Transfer the fish to your fryer's basket and cook at 360 degrees F for 12 minutes, flipping them halfway. Divide the fish between plates, sprinkle the shallots on top, and serve.

Nutrition: Calories 27g Fat 12gFiber 10gCarbs 16gProtein 20g

292. Garlic Salmon Fillets

Preparation Time: 5 minutes
Cooking Time: 8 minutes
Servings: 2
Ingredients:
- 2 salmon fillets, boneless
- Salt and black pepper to taste
- 3 red chili peppers, chopped
- 2 tbsp. lemon juice
- 2 tbsp. olive oil
- 2 tbsp. garlic, minced

Directions:
1. In a bowl, combine the ingredients, toss, and coat fish well.
2. Transfer everything to your air fryer and cook at 365 degrees F for 8 minutes, flipping the fish halfway.
3. Divide between plates and serve right away.

Nutrition: Calories 280g Fat 4g Fiber 8gCarbs 15gProtein 20g

293. Shrimp and Veggie Mix

Preparation Time: 10 minutes
Cooking Time: 20 minutes
Servings: 4
Ingredients:
- ½ cup red onion, chopped
- 1 cup red bell pepper, chopped
- 1 cup celery, chopped
- 1-pound shrimp, peeled and deveined
- 1 tsp Worcestershire sauce
- Salt and black pepper to taste
- 1 tbsp. butter, melted
- 1 tsp sweet paprika

Directions:

1. Add up all the ingredients to a bowl and mix thoroughly.
2. Transfer everything to your air fryer and cook 320 degrees F for 20 minutes, shaking halfway.
3. Divide between plates and serve.
Nutrition: Calories 220gFat 14gCarbs 17gProtein 20g

294. White Fish with Peas and Basil
Preparation Time: 10 minutes
Cooking Time: 12 minutes
Servings: 4
Ingredients:
- 4 white fish fillets, boneless
- 2 tbsp. cilantro, chopped
- 2 cups peas, cooked and drained
- 4 tbsp. veggie stock
- ½ tsp basil, dried
- ½ tsp sweet paprika
- 2 garlic cloves, minced
- Salt and pepper to taste

Directions:
1. In a bowl, mix the fish with all ingredients except the peas; toss to coat the fish well.
2. Transfer everything to your air fryer and cook at 360 degrees F for 12 minutes.
3. Add the peas, toss, and divide everything between plates.
4. Serve and enjoy.
Nutrition: Calories 241gFat 8gFiber 12gCarbs 15gProtein 18g

295. Cod and Chives
Preparation Time: 5 minutes
Cooking Time: 12 minutes
Servings: 4
Ingredients:
- 4 cod fillets, boneless
- Salt and black pepper to taste
- 3 tsp lime zest
- 2 tsp lime juice
- 3 tbsp. chives, chopped
- 6 tbsp. butter, melted
- 2 tbsp. olive oil

Directions:
1. Season the fish with pepper and salt, rub it with oil, and then put it in the fryer. Cook at 360 degrees F for 10 minutes, turning once.
2. Heat a frying pan with the butter over medium heat and then add the chives, salt, pepper, lime juice and the zest, beat lightly. cook for 1-2 minutes. Separate the fish between the dishes, chop the lime sauce and serve immediately.
Nutrition: Calories 280gFat 12g Fiber 9gCarbs 17gProtein 15g

296. Paprika Salmon Fillets
Preparation Time: 5 minutes
Cooking Time: 12 minutes
Servings: 4
Ingredients:
- 4 salmon fillets, boneless
- 1 tbsp. olive oil
- Salt and black pepper to taste
- 1 tsp cumin, ground
- 1 tsp sweet paprika
- ½ tsp chili powder
- 1 tsp garlic powder
- Juice of 1 lime

Directions:
1. In a bowl, mix the salmon with the other ingredients, rub / coat well, and transfer to your air fryer. Cook at 350 degrees F for 6 minutes on each side.
2. Divide the fish between plates and serve right away with a side salad.
Nutrition: Calories 280g Fat 14g Fiber 4g Carbs 18g Protein 20g

297. Thyme Tuna
Preparation Time: 10 minutes
Cooking Time: 8 minutes
Servings: 4
Ingredients:
- ½ cup cilantro, chopped
- ⅓ Cup olive oil
- 1 small red onion, chopped
- 3 tbsp. balsamic vinegar
- 2 tbsp. parsley, chopped
- 2 tbsp. basil, chopped
- 1 jalapeno pepper, chopped
- 4 sushi tuna steaks
- Salt and black pepper to taste
- 1 tsp red pepper flakes
- 1 tsp thyme, chopped
- 3 garlic cloves, minced

Directions:
1. Place all ingredients except the fish into a bowl and stir well.
2. Add the fish and toss, coating it well.
3. Transfer everything to your air fryer and cook at 360 degrees F for 4 minutes on each side.
4. Divide the fish between plates and serve.
Nutrition: Calories 306gFat 8g Fiber 1g Carbs 14g Protein 16g

298. Buttery Shrimp
Preparation Time: 5 minutes
Cooking Time: 10 minutes
Servings: 2
Ingredients:
- 1 tbsp. butter, melted
- A drizzle of olive oil
- 1-pound shrimp, peeled and deveined
- ¼ cup heavy cream
- 8 ounces' mushrooms, roughly sliced
- A pinch of red pepper flakes
- Salt and black pepper to taste
- 2 garlic cloves, minced
- ½ cup beef stock
- 1 tbsp. parsley, chopped

- 1 tbsp. chives, chopped

Directions:
1. Season shrimp with salt and pepper and grease with oil.
2. Place the shrimp in your deep fryer, cook at 360 degrees F for 7 minutes and separate the dishes.
3. Heat a pan with butter over medium heat, add the mushrooms, stir and cook for 3-4 minutes.
4. Add all remaining ingredients; stir and then cook for a few minutes more.
5. Drizzle the butter / garlic mixture over the shrimp and serve.

Nutrition: Calories 305g Fat 13gFiber 4gCarbs 14g Protein 11g

299. Maple Salmon
Preparation Time: 5 minutes
Cooking Time: 10 minutes
Servings: 2
Ingredients:
- 2 salmon fillets, boneless
- Salt and black pepper to taste
- 2 tbsp. mustard
- 1 tbsp. olive oil
- 1 tbsp. maple syrup

Directions:
1. In a bowl, mix the mustard with the oil and the maple syrup; whisk well and brush the salmon with this mix.
2. Place the salmon in your air fryer and cook it at 370 degrees F for 5 minutes on each side.
3. Serve immediately with a side salad.

Nutrition: Calories 290g Fat 7g Fiber 14g Carbs 18g Protein 17g

300. Balsamic Orange Salmon
Preparation Time: 5 minutes
Cooking Time: 15 minutes
Servings: 4
Ingredients:
- 4 salmon fillets, boneless and cubed
- 2 lemons, sliced
- ¼ cup balsamic vinegar
- ¼ cup orange juice
- A pinch of salt and black pepper

Directions:
1. In a pan that fits your air fryer, mix all ingredients except the fish; whisk.
2. Heat the mixture up over medium-high heat for 5 minutes and add the salmon.
3. Toss gently, and place the pan in the air fryer and cook at 360 degrees F for 10 minutes.
4. Divide between plates and serve right away with a side salad.

Nutrition: Calories 227g Fat 9gFiber 12g Carbs 14g Protein 11g

301. Crunchy Pistachio Cod
Preparation Time: 10 minutes
Cooking Time: 10 minutes
Servings: 4
Ingredients:
- 1 cup pistachios, chopped
- 4 cod fillets, boneless
- ¼ cup lime juice
- 2 tbsp. honey
- 1 tsp parsley, chopped
- Salt and black pepper to taste
- 1 tbsp. mustard

Directions:
1. Place all the ingredients except the fish into a bowl; whisk.
2. Spread the mixture over the fish fillets, put them in your air fryer, and cook at 350 degrees F for 10 minutes.
3. Divide the fish between plates and serve immediately with a side salad.

Nutrition: Calories 270g Fat 17gFiber 12gCarbs 20g Protein 12g

302. Roasted Parsley Cod
Preparation Time: 10 minutes
Cooking Time: 10 minutes
Servings: 4
Ingredients:
- 3 tbsp. parsley, chopped
- 4 medium cod filets, boneless
- ¼ cup butter, melted
- 2 garlic cloves, minced
- 2 tbsp. lemon juice
- 1 shallot, chopped
- Salt and black pepper to taste

Directions:
1. In a bowl, mix all ingredients except the fish; whisk well.
2. Spread this mixture over the cod fillets.
3. Put them in your air fryer and cook at 390 degrees F for 10 minutes.
4. Divide the fish between plates and serve.

Nutrition: Calories 280g Fat 4g Fiber 7gCarbs 12g Protein 15g

303. Salmon with Almonds
Preparation Time: 10 minutes
Cooking Time: 20 minutes
Servings: 4
Ingredients:
- 2 red onions, chopped
- 2 tbsp. olive oil
- 2 small fennel bulbs, trimmed and sliced
- ¼ cup almonds, toasted and sliced
- Salt and black pepper to taste
- 4 salmon fillets, boneless
- 5 tsp fennel seeds, toasted

Directions:
1. Season the fish with salt and pepper, grease it with 1 tablespoon of the oil, and place in your air fryer's basket.

2. Cook at 350 degrees F for 5-6 minutes on each side and divide between plates.
3. Heat up a pan with the remaining tablespoon of oil over medium-high heat; add the onions, stir, and sauté for 2 minutes.
4. Add the fennel bulbs and seeds, almonds, salt, and pepper, and cook for 2-3 minutes more.
5. Spread the mixture over the fish and serve right away; enjoy!
Nutrition: Calories 284g Fat 7gFiber 10gCarbs 17gProtein 16g

304. Crispy Paprika Fish Fillets
Preparation Time: 5 Minutes
Cooking Time: 15 Minutes
Servings: 4
Ingredients:
- 1/2 cup seasoned breadcrumbs
- 1 tbsp. balsamic vinegar
- 1/2 tsp seasoned salt
- 1 tsp paprika
- 1/2 tsp ground black pepper
- 1 tsp celery seed
- Fish fillets, halved
- 1 egg, beaten

Directions:
1. Prepare the ingredients. Add the breadcrumbs, vinegar, salt, paprika, ground black pepper, and celery seeds to your food processor. Do the process for about 30 seconds?
2. Coat the fish fillets with the beaten egg then, coat them with the breadcrumbs mixture.
3. Cook at 350 degrees F for about 15 minutes.
Nutrition: Calories 143g Fat 14g Fiber 17g Carbs 12g Protein 10g

305. Air Fryer Salmon
Preparation Time: 5 Minutes
Cooking Time: 10 Minutes
Servings: 2
Ingredients:
- ½ tsp. salt
- ½ tsp. garlic powder
- ½ tsp. smoked paprika
- Salmon

Directions:
1. Prepare the ingredients. Mix spices and sprinkle onto salmon.
2. Place seasoned salmon into the air fryer oven.
3. Set temperature to 400°F, and set time to 10 minutes.
Nutrition: Calories: 185g Fat 11g Protein 21g Sugar 0g

306. Sweet and Savory Breaded Shrimp
Preparation Time: 5 Minutes
Cooking Time: 20 Minutes
Servings: 2
Ingredient:
- ½ pound of fresh shrimp, peeled from their shells and rinsed
- Raw eggs
- ½ cup of breadcrumbs (we like panko, but any brand or home recipe will do)
- ½ white onion, peeled and rinsed and finely chopped
- 1 tsp of ginger-garlic paste
- ½ tsp of turmeric powder
- ½ tsp of red chili powder
- ½ tsp of cumin powder
- ½ tsp of black pepper powder
- ½ tsp of dry mango powder
- Pinch of salt

Directions:
1. Prepare the ingredients. Cover the pan with aluminum foil, leaving the edges uncovered to allow air to circulate through the basket. Preheat oven to 350 degrees.
2. In a large bowl, beat the eggs until fluffy and combine thoroughly with the yolks and whites. Dip all the shrimp in the egg mixture, dipping them completely. In a separate mixing bowl, combine the breadcrumbs with all the dry ingredients until well blended.
3. One by one, cover the egg covered shrimp in the mixed dry ingredients so that they are completely covered and place on the lid with the fryer. Set the air-fryer timer to 20 minutes.
4. Halfway through the cooking time, shake the handle of the air-fryer so that the breaded shrimp jostles inside and fry-coverage is even.
5. After 20 minutes, when the fryer shuts off, the shrimp will be perfectly cooked and their breaded crust golden-brown and delicious! Using tongs, remove from the air fryer oven and set on a serving dish to cool.
Nutrition: Calories: 135gFat 14g Protein 22g Sugar 0g

307. Quick Paella
Preparation Time: 7 Minutes
Cooking Time: 15 Minutes
Servings: 4
Ingredients:
- 1 (10-ounce) package frozen cooked rice, thawed
- 1 (6-ounce) jar artichoke hearts, drained and chopped
- ¼ cup vegetable broth
- ½ tsp turmeric
- ½ tsp dried thyme
- 1 cup frozen cooked small shrimp
- ½ cup frozen baby peas
- 1 tomato, diced

Directions:
1. Prepare the ingredients. In a 6-by-6-by-2-inch pan, combine the rice, artichoke hearts, vegetable broth, turmeric, and thyme, and stir gently.
2. Place in the air fryer oven and bake for 8 to 9 minutes or until the rice is hot.
3. Remove from the air fryer oven and gently stir in the shrimp, peas, and tomato.

4. Cook for 5 to 8 minutes or until the shrimp and peas are hot and the paella is bubbling.
Nutrition: Calories: 345g Fat 1g Protein 18g Fiber 4g

308. Coconut Shrimp
Preparation Time: 15 Minutes
Cooking Time: 5 Minutes
Servings: 4
Ingredients:
- 1 (8-ounce) can crushed pineapple
- ½ cup sour cream
- ¼ cup pineapple preserves
- Egg whites
- ⅔ Cup of cornstarch
- ⅔ Cup sweetened coconut
- 1 cup panko bread crumbs
- 1-pound uncooked large shrimp, thawed if frozen, deveined and shelled
- Olive oil for misting

Directions:
1. Prepare the materials. Drain the crushed pineapple well, retaining the juice. In a small bowl, combine pineapple, sour cream, and mix well. Set aside. In a shallow bowl, beat the egg whites with 2 tablespoons of pineapple juice. Place the cornstarch on a plate. Combine the coconut crumbs and bread on another plate. Dip the shrimp in the cornstarch, shake and then dip in the egg white mixture and finally in the coconut mixture. Place the shrimp in a wire rack / deep fryer and sprinkle with oil.
2. Fry in the air for 5 to 7 minutes or until the shrimp are crisp and golden.
Nutrition: Calories: 524g Fat 14g Protein 33g Fiber 4g

309. Cilantro-Lime Fried Shrimp
Preparation Time: 10 Minutes
Cooking Time: 10 Minutes
Servings: 4
Ingredients:
- 1-pound raw shrimp, peeled and deveined with tails on or off (see Prep tip)
- ½ cup chopped fresh cilantro
- Juice of 1 lime
- 1 egg
- ½ cup all-purpose flour
- ¾ cup bread crumbs
- Salt
- Pepper
- Cooking oil
- ½ cup cocktail sauce (optional)

Directions:
1. Prepare the ingredients. Place the shrimp in a plastic bag and add the cilantro and lime juice. Seal the bag. Shake to combine. Marinate in the refrigerator for 30 minutes.
2. In a small bowl, beat the egg. In another small bowl, place the flour. Place the bread crumbs in a third small bowl, and season with salt and pepper to taste.
3. Spray the air fryer rack/basket with cooking oil.
4. Remove the shrimp from the plastic bag. Dip each in the flour, then the egg, and then the bread crumbs.
5. Place the shrimp in the air fryer oven. It is okay to stack them. Spray the shrimp with cooking oil. Cook for 4 minutes.
6. Open the air fryer oven and flip the shrimp. I recommend flipping individually instead of shaking to keep the breading intact. Cook for an additional 4 minutes, or until crisp.
7. Cool before serving. Serve with cocktail sauce if desired.
Nutrition: Calories: 254g Fat 4g Protein 29g Fiber 1g

310. Lemony Tuna
Preparation Time: 10 Minutes
Cooking Time: 10 Minutes
Servings: 4
Ingredients:
- (6-ounce) cans water packed plain tuna
- 1 tsp Dijon mustard
- ½ cup breadcrumbs
- 1 tablespoon fresh lime juice
- 1 tbsp. fresh parsley, chopped
- 1 egg
- Chef man of hot sauce
- Canola oil
- Freshly ground black pepper and Salt, to taste

Directions:
1. Prepare the ingredients. Drain most of the liquid from the canned tuna. In a bowl, add the fish, mustard, crumbs, citrus juice, parsley, and hot sauce and mix till well combined. Add a little canola oil if it seems too dry. Add egg, salt and stir to combine. Make the patties from tuna mixture. Refrigerate the tuna patties for about 2 hours.
2. Preheat the air fryer oven to 355 degrees F. Cook for about 10-12 minutes.
Nutrition: Calories: 509g Fat 12g Protein 32g Fiber 5g

311. Grilled Soy Salmon Fillets
Preparation Time: 5 Minutes
Cooking Time: 8 Minutes
Servings: 4
Ingredients:
- Salmon fillets
- 1/4 tsp ground black pepper
- 1/2 tsp cayenne pepper
- 1/2 tsp salt
- 1 tsp onion powder
- 1 tbsp. fresh lemon juice
- 1/2 cup soy sauce
- 1/2 cup water
- 1 tbsp. honey
- 2 tbsp. extra-virgin olive oil

Directions:
1. Prepare the ingredients. Firstly, pat the salmon fillets dry using kitchen towels. Season the salmon with black pepper, cayenne pepper, salt, and onion powder.

2. To make the marinade, combine together the lemon juice, soy sauce, water, honey, and olive oil. Marinate the salmon for at minimum of 2 hours in your refrigerator.
3. Arrange the fish fillets on a grill basket in your air fryer oven. Bake at 330 degrees for 8 to 9 minutes, or until salmon fillets are easily flaked with a fork. Work with batches and serve warm.
Nutrition: Calories: 432g Fat 15g Protein 23g Fiber 6g

312. Old Bay Crab Cakes
Preparation Time: 10 Minutes
Cooking Time: 20 Minutes
Servings: 4
Ingredients:
- Slices dried bread, crusts removed
- Small amount of milk
- 1 tbsp. mayonnaise
- 1 tbsp. Worcestershire sauce
- 1 tbsp. baking powder
- 1 tbsp. parsley flakes
- 1 tsp Old Bay® Seasoning
- 1/4 tsp salt
- 1 egg
- 1-pound lump crabmeat

Directions:
1. Prepare the ingredients. Crush your bread over a large bowl until it is broken down into small pieces. Add milk and stir until bread crumbs are moistened. Mix in mayo and Worcestershire sauce. Add remaining ingredients and mix well. Shape into 4 patties
2. Cook at 360 degrees for 20 minutes, flip half way through.
Nutrition: Calories: 165g Carbs: 5.8g Fat 4.5g Protein 24g Fiber 0g

313. Scallops and Spring Veggies
Preparation Time: 10 Minutes
Cooking Time: 8 Minutes
Servings: 4
Ingredient:
- ½ pound asparagus ends trimmed, cut into 2-inch pieces
- 1 cup sugars snap peas
- 1-pound Sea scallops
- 1 tablespoon lemon juice
- 1 tsp olive oil
- ½ teaspoon dried thyme
- Pinch salt
- Freshly ground black pepper

Directions:
1. Prepare the materials. Place the asparagus and sugar peas on the oven rack / rack. Place the rack on the oven middle rack of the fryer.
2. Cook 2 to 3 minutes or until vegetables begin to soften.
3. In the meantime, check the combs to see if there is a small muscle attached to one side, pull it out and discard it.
4. In a medium bowl, mix the scallops with lemon juice, olive oil, thyme, salt, and pepper. Place it in the oven / basket on top of the vegetables. Place the rack on the oven middle rack of the fryer.
5. Steam 5 to 7 minutes. Until the scallops are firm and the vegetables are soft. Serve immediately.
Nutrition: Calories: 162g Carbs: 10g Fat 4g Protein 22g Fiber 3g

314. Fried Calamari
Preparation Time: 8 Minutes
Cooking Time: 7 Minutes
Servings: 6-8
Ingredients:
- ½ tsp. salt
- ½ tsp. Old Bay seasoning
- 1/3 cup plain cornmeal
- ½ cup semolina flour
- ½cup. almond flour
- 5-6 cup olive oil
- 1 ½ pounds baby squid

Directions:
1. Prepare the ingredients. Rinse squid in cold water and slice tentacles, keeping just ¼-inch of the hood in one piece. Combine 1-2 pinches of pepper, salt, Old Bay seasoning, cornmeal, and both flours together. Dredge squid pieces into flour mixture and place into the air fryer oven. Spray liberally with olive oil. Cook 15 minutes at 345 degrees till coating turns a golden brown.
Nutrition: Calories: 211g Carbs: 55g Fat 6g Protein 21g Sugar 1g

315. Soy and Ginger Shrimp
Preparation Time: 8 Minutes
Cooking Time: 10 Minutes
Servings: 4
Ingredients:
- 2 tbsp. olive oil
- 2 tbsp. scallions, finely chopped
- 2 cloves garlic, chopped
- 1 tsp fresh ginger, grated
- 1 tbsp. dry white wine
- 1 tbsp. balsamic vinegar
- 1/4 cup soy sauce
- 1 tbsp. sugar
- 1-pound shrimp
- Salt and ground black pepper, to taste

Directions:
1. Prepare the ingredients. To make the marinade, warm the oil in a saucepan; cook all ingredients, except the shrimp, salt, and black pepper. Now, let it cool. Marinate the shrimp, covered, at least an hour, in the refrigerator. After that, bake the shrimp at 350 degrees F for 8 to 10 minutes (depending on the size), turning once or twice. Season prepared shrimp with salt and black pepper and serve right away.
Nutrition: Calories: 500g Fat 3g Protein 20g Fiber 7g

316. Halibut and Sun Dried Tomatoes Mix

Preparation Time: 10 minutes
Cooking Time: 10 minutes
Servings: 2
Ingredients:
- 2 medium halibut fillets
- 2 garlic cloves
- 2 tbsp. olive oil
- Salt and black pepper
- 6 sun dried tomatoes
- 2 small red onions
- 1 fennel bulb
- 9 black olives
- 4 rosemary springs
- ½ tsp. red pepper flakes

Directions:
1. Season fish with pepper, salt, rub with oil and garlic then put in heat proof dish and transfer to air fryer. Add sun dried tomatoes, onion slices, fennel, rosemary and sprinkle pepper flakes, olives. Add air fryer and cook at 380°F for 10 minutes. Divide veggies and fish on plates then serve.

Nutrition: Calories: 400g Fat 11g Protein 12g Fiber 9g

317. Black Cod and Plum Sauce
Preparation Time: 10 minutes
Cooking Time: 15 minutes
Servings: 2
Ingredients:
- 1 egg white
- ½ cup red quinoa
- 2 tsp. whole wheat flour
- 4 tsp. lemon juice
- ½ tsp. smoked paprika
- 1 tsp. olive oil
- 2 medium black cod fillets
- 1 red plum
- 2 tsp. raw honey
- ¼ tsp. black peppercorns
- 2 tsp. parsley
- ¼ cup water

Directions:
1. Mix 1 tsp. lemon juice, egg white, ¼ teaspoon paprika, flour and whisk well. Place quinoa in bowl then mix with 1/3 of egg white mix. Put the fish in bowl with the rest of egg white mix then toss to coat. Put fish into quinoa mix, allow to coat well and leave it aside for 10 minutes.
2. Heat pan with 1 tsp. oil over medium heat, add honey and plum, peppercorns, stir allow to simmer then cook for 1 minute. Add the remaining lemon juice, paprika and water. Stir very well and simmer for 5 minutes. Add parsley and stir, take the sauce off heat.
3. Put fish in air fryer and cook at 380°F for 10 minutes Place fish on plates and sprinkle plum sauce on top then serve.

Nutrition: Calories: 434g Fat 13g Protein 22g Fiber 17g

318. Fish and Couscous
Preparation Time: 10 minutes
Cooking Time: 15 minutes
Servings: 4
Ingredients:
- 2 red onions
- Cooking spray
- 2 small fennel bulbs
- ¼ cup almonds
- Salt and black pepper
- 2 and ½ lb. sea bass
- 5 tsp. fennel seeds
- ¾ cup whole wheat couscous

Directions:
1. Season fish with salt and pepper, drizzle with cooking spray, place in fryer, and cook at 350 °F for 10 minutes.
2. Drizzle the pan with cooking oil and heat over medium heat. Put the fennel seeds in a pan, stir and toast for 1 minute. Add pepper, salt, onion, fennel bulbs, couscous, and almonds, mix, and then cook for 2-3 minutes. Divide into plates. Place the fish next to the couscous mixture and serve.

Nutrition: Calories: 321g Fat 11g Protein 23g Fiber 12g

319. Chinese Cod
Preparation Time: 10 minutes
Cooking Time: 10 minutes
Servings: 2
Ingredients:
- 2 medium cod fillets
- 1 tsp. peanuts
- 2 tsp. garlic powder
- 1 tbsp. light soy sauce
- ½ tsp. ginger

Directions:
1. Place fish fillets in heat proof dish, add soy sauce and ginger, garlic powder, toss well, put in air fryer and cook at 350°F for 10 minutes. Divide fish and sprinkle peanuts on top then serve.

Nutrition: Calories: 209g Fat 5g Protein 24g Fiber 8g

320. Cod with Pearl Onions
Preparation Time: 10 minutes
Cooking Time: 15 minutes
Servings: 2
Ingredients:
- 14 oz. pearl onions
- 2 medium cod fillets
- 1 tbsp. parsley
- 1 tsp. thyme
- Black pepper
- 8 oz. mushrooms

Directions:
1. Place fish in heat proof dish add onions, mushrooms, parsley, black pepper and thyme, toss well, put in air fryer and cook at 350°F and cook for 15 minutes.
2. Divide on plates then serve.

Nutrition: Calories: 123g Fat 12g Protein 28g Fiber 14g

321. Hawaiian Salmon

Preparation Time: 10 minutes
Cooking Time: 10 minutes
Servings: 2
Ingredients:
- 20 oz. canned pineapple pieces and juice
- ½ tsp. ginger
- 2 tsp. garlic powder
- 1 tsp. onion powder
- 1 tsp. balsamic vinegar
- 2 medium salmon fillets
- Salt and black pepper

Directions:
1. Season salmon with onion powder, salt and black pepper, garlic powder, rub. Add to heat proof dish and then add pineapple chunks and ginger and toss them gently.
2. Drizzle the vinegar all over, put in your air fryer and cook at 350 degrees F for 10 minutes.
3. Divide everything on plates and serve.

Nutrition: Calories: 456g Fat 9g Protein 30g Fiber 27g

322. Salmon and Avocado Salad
Preparation Time: 10 minutes
Cooking Time: 20 minutes
Servings: 4
Ingredients:
- 2 medium salmon fillets
- ¼ cup melted butter
- 4 oz. mushrooms
- Sea salt and black pepper
- 12 cherry tomatoes
- 2 tbsp. olive oil
- 8 oz. lettuce leaves
- 1 avocado
- 1 jalapeno pepper
- 5 cilantro springs
- 2 tbsp. white wine vinegar
- 1 oz. feta cheese

Directions:
1. Place salmon on lined baking sheet, brush using 2 tbsp. melted butter, season with pepper and salt and broil it for 15 minutes over medium heat and keep it warm.
2. Hence, heat pan with remaining butter over medium heat. Add mushrooms and stir. Cook for a couple of minutes.
3. Place tomatoes in bowl. Add salt, 1 tbsp. olive oil and pepper then toss to coat.
4. Mix salmon with mushrooms, avocado, lettuce, jalapeno, tomatoes and cilantro in salad bowl.
5. Add remaining oil, pepper, vinegar, salt and sprinkle cheese on top then serve.

Nutrition: Calories: 545g Fat 15g Protein 29g Fiber 8g

323. Salmon and Greek Yogurt Sauce
Preparation Time: 10 minutes
Cooking Time: 20 minutes
Servings: 2
Ingredients:
- 2 medium salmon fillets
- 1 tbsp. basil
- 6 lemon slices
- Sea salt and black
- 1 cup Greek yogurt
- 2 tsp. curry powder
- A pinch of cayenne pepper
- 1 garlic clove
- ½ tsp. cilantro
- ½ tsp. mint

Directions:
1. Put salmon fillet on parchment paper make three (3) splits each then stuff with basil. Season it with pepper and salt. Top every fillets with three (3) lemon slices, fold parchment, seal edges, place in oven at 400°F and bake for 20 minutes. Mix in bowl, yogurt with cayenne pepper, salt, curry, garlic, cilantro and mint and whisk well. Place fish to plates, sprinkle yogurt sauce on top then serve.

Nutrition: Calories: 578g Fat 17g Protein 40g Fiber 26g

324. Spanish Salmon
Preparation Time: 10 minutes
Cooking Time: 15 minutes
Servings: 6
Ingredients:
- 2 cups bread croutons
- 3 red onions
- ¾ cup green olives
- 3 red bell peppers
- ½ tsp. smoked paprika
- Salt and black pepper
- 5 tbsp. olive oil
- 6 medium salmon fillets
- 2 tbsp. parsley

Directions:
1. Mix bread croutons with onion wedges, olives, bell pepper ones, salt, paprika, pepper and 3 tablespoons olive oil in heat proof dish and toss well, place in air fryer then cook at 356°F for 7 minutes.
2. Polish salmon with remaining oil put over veggies and cook at 360°F for 8 minutes.
3. Divide fish and veggie mix then sprinkle parsley on top and serve.

Nutrition: Calories: 300g Fat 19g Protein 21g Fiber 13g

325. Marinated Salmon
Preparation Time: 10 minutes
Cooking Time: 25 minutes
Servings: 6
Ingredients:
- 1 whole salmon
- 1 tbsp. dill
- 1 tbsp. tarragon
- 1 tbsp. garlic
- Juice from 2 lemons
- 1 lemon
- A pinch of salt and black pepper

Directions:

1. Mix fish with salt, lemon juice and pepper, toss and keep in fridge for an hour. Stuff it with lemon slices and garlic, place in air fryer and cook at 320°F for 25 minutes. Divide it on plates. Serve with tasty coleslaw on the side.
Nutrition: Calories: 200g Fat 6g Protein 21.3g Fiber 7.8g

326. Delicious Red Snapper
Preparation Time: 10 minutes
Cooking Time: 35 minutes
Servings: 4
Ingredients:
- 1 big red snapper
- Salt and black pepper
- 3 garlic cloves
- 1 jalapeno
- ¼ lb. okra
- 1 tbsp. butter
- 2 tbsp. olive oil
- 1 red bell pepper
- 2 tbsp. white wine
- 2 tbsp. parsley

Directions:
1. Mix jalapeno, garlic with wine and stir it well then rub snapper with it.
2. Season fish with pepper and salt then leave aside for 30 minutes.
3. Heat pan with 1 tbsp. butter over medium heat, add okra and bell pepper, stir then cook for 5 minutes.
4. Stuff red snapper belly with mix. Add parsley and polish with olive oil.
5. Put in preheated air fryer. Cook at 400 °F for 15 minutes.
6. Divide on plates and serve.

Nutrition: Calories: 340g Fat 13.7g Protein 20.3g Fiber 8g

327. Snapper Fillets and Veggies
Preparation Time: 10 minutes
Cooking Time: 14 minutes
Servings: 2
Ingredients:
- 2 red snapper fillets
- 1 tbsp. olive oil
- ½ cup red bell pepper
- ½ cup green bell pepper
- ½ cup leeks
- Salt and black pepper
- 1 tsp. tarragon
- A splash of white wine

Directions:
1. In heat proof dish, mix fish fillets with salt, oil, pepper, green bell pepper, leeks, red bell pepper, tarragon and wine, toss everything well. Introduce in preheated air fryer at 350°F and cook for 14 minutes.
2. Divide fish and veggies on plates then serve warm.

Nutrition: Calories: 150g Fat 3.7g Protein 24.7g Fiber 18g

328. Air Fried Branzino
Preparation Time: 10 minutes
Cooking Time: 10 minutes
Servings: 4
Ingredients:
- Zest from 1 lemon
- Zest from 1 orange
- Juice from ½ lemons
- Juice from ½ orange
- Salt and black pepper
- 4 medium branzino fillets
- ½ cup parsley
- 2 tbsp. olive oil
- A pinch of red pepper flakes

Directions:
1. Using large bowl, mix orange zest, fish fillets with lemon zest, lemon juice, salt, orange juice, pepper, oil and pepper flakes, toss it well. Transfer fillets to preheated air fryer at 350°F and bake for 10 minutes. Divide fish on plates. Sprinkle with parsley then serve immediately.

Nutrition: Calories: 210g Fat 14.7g Protein 29.9g Fiber 2.7g

329. Lemon Sole and Swiss Chard
Preparation Time: 10 minutes
Cooking Time: 14 minutes
Servings: 4
Ingredients:
- 1 tsp. lemon zest
- 4 white bread slices
- ¼ cup walnuts
- ¼ cup parmesan
- 4 tbsp. olive oil
- 4 sole fillets
- Salt and black pepper
- 4 tbsp. butter
- ¼ cup lemon juice
- 3 tbsp. capers
- 2 garlic cloves
- 2 bunches Swiss chard

Directions:
1. Mix bread with walnuts, cheese and lemon zest and pulse well. Add half olive oil, pulse well again allow for now. Heat pan with butter over medium heat. Add lemon juice, pepper and capers, salt, stir it well. Put fish then toss it.
2. Transfer to your preheated air fryer top with bread mix made earlier and cook at 350°F for 14 minutes. Again heat different pan with remaining oil, and add garlic, salt and pepper, Swiss chard, stir it gently. Cook for 2 minutes and take off heat.
3. Divide fish on plates and serve with sautéed chard on the side.

Nutrition: Calories: 455g Fat 6.7g Protein 23,4g Fiber 32g

330. Salmon and Blackberry Glaze
Preparation Time: 10 minutes

Cooking Time: 33 minutes
Servings: 4
Ingredients:
- 1 cup water
- 1-inch ginger piece
- Juice from ½ lemon
- 12 oz. blackberries
- 1 tbsp. olive oil
- ¼ cup sugar
- 4 medium salmon fillets
- Salt and black pepper

Directions:
1. Heat the pot with water over high heat. Add ginger, blackberries and lemon juice and stir. Boil then cook for 4-5 minutes, take off heat, strain and pour into pan mix with sugar.
2. Stir the mix, simmer over low heat then cook for 20 minutes.
3. Allow blackberry sauce to cool. Brush salmon and season with pepper and salt, sprinkle olive oil over then rub fish well. Place fish in preheated air fryer at 350°F and cook for 10 minutes.
4. Divide on plates, sprinkle some blackberry sauce over and serve.

Nutrition: Calories: 156gFat 5.3g Protein 33.2g Fiber 16.8g

331. Persian Mushrooms

Preparation Time: 10 minutes
Cooking Time: 20 minutes
Servings: 3
Ingredients:
- 6 Portobello large mushrooms
- 3-ounces of softened butter
- 1 cup parmesan cheese, grated
- A pinch of black pepper
- A pinch of sea salt
- 1 tablespoon parsley, fresh, chopped
- 2 cloves of garlic
- 2 large shallots

Directions:
1. Preheat your air fryer to 390°Fahrenheit. Clean the mushrooms and remove the stems. Slice the shallots and garlic cloves. Now, place the mushroom stems, garlic, shallots, parsley and softened butter into a blender. Arrange the caps of the mushrooms in the air fryer basket. Stuff the caps with the mixture and sprinkle tops with parmesan cheese. Cook for 20-minutes. Serve warm and enjoy!

Nutrition: Calories: 278, Total Fat 9.8g, Carbs: 7.2g, Protein 4.3g

POULTRY

332. Chicken Tears
Preparation Time: 15 minutes
Cooking Time: 25 minutes
Servings: 4
Ingredients:
- 2 chicken breasts
- Flour
- Salt
- Ground pepper
- Extra virgin olive oil
- Lemon juice
- Garlic powder

Directions:
1. Place the tears in the basket of the air fryer and paint with extra virgin olive oil. Select 180 degrees, 20 minutes.
2. Move from time to time, so that the tears are made on Cut the chicken breasts into tears. Season and put some lemon juice and garlic powder. Let flirt well. Go through flour and shake.
3. all their faces.

Nutrition: Calories: 197g Fat 8g Carbohydrates: 16g Protein 14g Sugar 0mg Cholesterol: 0mg

333. Breaded Chicken with Seed Chips
Preparation Time: 10 minutes
Cooking Time: 40 minutes
Servings: 4
Ingredients:
- 12 chicken breast fillets
- Salt
- 2 eggs
- 1 small bag of seed chips
- Breadcrumbs
- Extra virgin olive oil

Directions:
1. Put the salt to chicken fillets. Crush the seed chips and when we have them fine, bind with the breadcrumbs.
2. Beat the two eggs. Pass the chicken breast fillets through the beaten egg and then through the seed chips that you have tied with the breadcrumbs.
3. When you have them all breaded, paint with a brush of extra virgin olive oil. Place the fillets in the basket of the air fryer without being piled up. Select 170 degrees, 20 minutes.
4. Take out and put another batch, repeat temperature and time. So, until you use up all the steaks.

Nutrition: Calories: 242g Fat 13g Carbohydrates: 13.5g Protein 18g Sugar 0g Cholesterol: 42mg

334. Salted Biscuit Pie Turkey Chops
Preparation Time: 5 minutes
Cooking Time: 20 minutes
Servings: 4
Ingredients:
- 8 large turkey chops
- 300 grams of crackers
- 2 eggs
- Extra virgin olive oil
- Salt
- Ground pepper

Directions:
1. Put the turkey chops on the worktable, and salt and pepper. Beat the eggs in a bowl.
2. Crush the cookies in the Thermos mix with a few turbo strokes until they are made grit, or you can crush them with the blender. Put the cookies in a bowl. Pass the chops through the beaten egg and then passed them through the crushed cookies. Press well so that the empanada is perfect.
3. Paint the empanada with a silicone brush and extra virgin olive oil. Put the chops in the basket of the air fryer, not all will enter. They will be done in batches.
4. Select 200 degrees, 15 minutes. When you have all the chops made, serve.

Nutrition: Calories: 126g Fat 6g Carbohydrates 0g Protein 18g Sugar 0g

335. Lemon Chicken with Basil
Preparation Time: 10 minutes
Cooking Time: 1 hour
Servings: 4
Ingredients:
- 1kg chopped chicken
- 1 or 2 lemons
- Basil, salt, and ground pepper
- Extra virgin olive oil

Directions:
1. Put the chicken in a bowl with a jet of extra virgin olive oil. Put salt, pepper, and basil. Bind well and let stand for at least 30 minutes stirring occasionally. Put the pieces of chicken in the air fryer basket and take the air fryer
2. Select 30 minutes. Occasionally remove. Take out and put another batch.
3. Do the same operation.

Nutrition: Calories: 126g Fat 6g Carbohydrates 0g Protein 18g Sugar 0g

336. Fried Chicken Tamari and Mustard
Preparation Time: 15 minutes
Cooking Time: 1 hour 20 minutes
Servings: 4
Ingredients:
- 1kg of very small chopped chicken
- Tamari Sauce
- Original mustard
- Ground pepper
- 1 lemon
- Flour
- Extra virgin olive oil

Directions:
1. Put the chicken in a bowl, you can put the chicken with or without the skin, to everyone's taste.

2. Add a generous stream of tamari, one or two tablespoons of mustard, a little ground pepper and a splash of lemon juice.
3. Link everything very well and let macerate an hour. Pass the chicken pieces for flour and place in the air fryer basket. Put 20 minutes at 200 degrees. At half time, move the chicken from the basket.
4. Do not crush the chicken, it is preferable to make two or three batches of chicken to pile up and do not fry the pieces well.
Nutrition: Calories: 100g Fat 6g Carbohydrates 0g Protein 18g Sugar 0g

337. Breaded Chicken Fillets
Preparation Time: 10 minutes
Cooking Time: 25 minutes
Servings: 4
Ingredients:
- 3 small chicken breasts or 2 large chicken breasts
- Salt
- Ground pepper
- 3 garlic cloves
- 1 lemon
- Beaten eggs
- Breadcrumbs
- Extra virgin olive oil

Directions:
1. Cut the breasts into fillets.
2. Put in a bowl and add the lemon juice, chopped garlic cloves and pepper. Flirt well and leave 10 minutes. Beat the eggs and put breadcrumbs on another plate. Pass the chicken breast fillets through the beaten egg and the breadcrumbs.
3. When you have them all breaded, start to fry. Paint the breaded breasts with a silicone brush and extra virgin olive oil. Place a batch of fillets in the basket of the air fryer and select 10 minutes 180 degrees.
4. Turn around and leave another 5 minutes at 180 degrees.
Nutrition: Calories: 120g Fat 6g Carbohydrates 0g Protein 18g Sugar 0g

338. Dry Rub Chicken Wings
Preparation Time: 5 minutes
Cooking Time: 30 minutes
Servings: 4
Ingredients:
- 9g garlic powder
- 1 cube of chicken broth, reduced sodium
- 5g of salt
- 3g black pepper
- 1g smoked paprika
- 1g cayenne pepper
- 3g Old Bay seasoning, sodium free
- 3g onion powder
- 1g dried oregano
- 453g chicken wings
- Nonstick Spray Oil
- Ranch sauce, to serve

Directions:
1. Preheat the air fryer. Set the temperature to 180 °C. add all necessary ingredients in an open bowl and mix.
2. Season the chicken wings with half the seasoning mixture and sprinkle abundantly with oil spray. Place the chicken wings in the preheated air fryer.
3. Select Chicken, set the timer to 30 minutes. Shake the baskets halfway through cooking.
4. Move the chicken wings to an open bowl and sprinkle them with the other half of the seasonings until they are well covered. Serve with ranch sauce
Nutrition: Calories: 120g Fat 6g Carbohydrates 0g Protein 18g Sugar 0g

339. Chicken Soup
Preparation Time: 20 minutes
Cooking Time: 1 hour 20 minutes
Servings: 6
Ingredients:
- 4 lbs. Chicken, cut into pieces
- 5 carrots, sliced thick
- 8 cups of water
- 2 celery stalks, sliced 1 inch thick
- 2 large onions, sliced

Directions:
1. In a large pot add chicken, water, and salt. Bring to boil. Add celery and onion in the pot and stir well.
2. Turn heat to medium-low and simmer for 30 minutes. Add carrots and cover pot with a lid and simmer for 40 minutes.
3. Remove Chicken from the pot and remove bones and cut Chicken into bite-size pieces. Return chicken into the pot and stir well.
4. Serve and enjoy.
Nutrition: Calories: 89g Fat 6.33g Carbohydrates: 0g Protein 7.56g Sugar 0g Cholesterol: 0mg

340. Ginger Chili Broccoli
Preparation Time: 15 minutes
Cooking Time: 25 minutes
Servings: 5
Ingredients:
- 8 cups broccoli florets
- 1/2 cup olive oil
- 2 fresh lime juices
- 2 tbsp. fresh ginger, grated
- 2 tsp chili pepper, chopped

Directions:
1. Add broccoli florets into the steamer and steam for 8 minutes. Meanwhile, for dressing in a small bowl, combine lime juice, oil, ginger, and chili pepper.
2. Add steamed broccoli in a large bowl then pour dressing over broccoli. Toss well.
Nutrition: Calories 239g Fat 20.8 g, Carbohydrates 13.7 g, Sugar 3 g, Protein 4.5 g, Cholesterol 0 mg

341. Chicken Wings with Garlic Parmesan
Preparation Time: 5 minutes

Cooking Time: 25 minutes
Servings: 3
Ingredients:
- 25g cornstarch
- 20g grated Parmesan cheese
- 9g garlic powder
- Salt and pepper to taste
- 680g chicken wings
- Nonstick Spray Oil

Directions:
1. Select Preheat, set the temperature to 200 °C and press Start / Pause. Combine corn starch, Parmesan, garlic powder, salt, and pepper in a bowl.
2. Mix the chicken wings in the seasoning and dip until well coated. Spray the baskets and the air fryer with oil spray and add the wings, sprinkling the tops of the wings as well.
3. Select Chicken and press Start/Pause. Be sure to shake the baskets in the middle of cooking.
4. Sprinkle with what's left of the Parmesan mix and serve.

Nutrition: Calories: 204g Fat 15g Carbohydrates: 1g Protein s: 12g Sugar 0g Cholesterol: 63mg

342. Jerk Style Chicken Wings

Preparation Time: 5 minutes
Cooking Time: 25 minutes
Servings: 3
Ingredients:
- 1g ground thyme
- 1g dried rosemary
- 2g allspice
- 4g ground ginger
- 3 g garlic powder
- 2g onion powder
- 1g of cinnamon
- 2g of paprika
- 2g chili powder
- 1g nutmeg
- Salt to taste
- 30 ml of vegetable oil
- 0.5 - 1 kg of chicken wings
- 1 lime, juice

Directions:
1. Select Preheat, set the temperature to 200°C and press Start/Pause.
2. Add up all spices and oil in a medium bowl to create a marinade. Mix the chicken wings in the marinade until they are well covered.
3. Place the chicken wings in the preheated air fryer. Select Chicken and press Start/Pause. Be sure to shake the baskets in the middle of cooking. Squeeze fresh lemon juice over the wings and serve.

Nutrition: Calories: 240g Fat 15g Carbohydrate: 5g Protein 19g Sugars: 4g Cholesterol: 60mg

343. Tasty Chicken Tenders

Preparation Time: 10 minutes
Cooking Time: 25 minutes
Servings: 4
Ingredients:
- 1 ½ lbs. chicken tenders
- 1 tbsp. extra virgin olive oil
- 1 tsp. rotisserie chicken seasoning
- 2 tbsp. BBQ sauce

Directions:
1. Add all ingredients except oil in a zip-lock bag.
2. Seal bag and place in the refrigerator for 2-3 hours.
3. Heat the oil in a pan.
4. Cook marinated chicken tenders in a pan until lightly brown and cooked.

Nutrition: Calories 365g Fat 16.1 g, Carbohydrates 2.8 g Sugar 2 g Protein 49.2 g, Cholesterol 151 mg

344. Chicken Skewers with Yogurt

Preparation Time: 4hours 10 minutes
Cooking Time: 10 minutes
Servings: 4
Ingredients:
- 123g of plain whole milk Greek yogurt
- 20 ml of olive oil
- 2g of paprika
- 1g cumin
- 1g crushed red pepper
- 1 lemon, juice and zest of the peel
- 5g of salt
- 1g freshly ground black pepper
- 4 cloves garlic, minced
- 454g chicken thighs, boneless, skinless, cut into 38 mm pieces
- 2 wooden skewers cut in half
- Nonstick Spray Oil

Directions:
1. Combine the yogurt, olive oil, paprika, cumin, red pepper, lemon juice, lemon zest, salt, pepper, and garlic in a big bowl.
2. Marinade the chicken and refrigerate for at least 4 hours.
3. Select Preheat and press Start / Pause.
4. Cut the marinated chicken legs into 38mm pieces and spread them on skewers.
5. Place the skewers in the air fryer.
6. Cook at 200 ° C for 10 minutes.

Nutrition: Calories: 113g Fat 3.4g Carbohydrates: 0g Protein 20.6g

345. Fried Lemon Chicken

Preparation Time: 5 minutes
Cooking Time: 20 minutes
Servings: 6
Ingredients:
- 6 chicken thighs
- 2 tbsp. olive oil
- 2 tbsp. lemon juice
- 1 tbsp. Italian herbal seasoning mix
- 1 tsp. Celtic sea salt
- 1 tsp. ground fresh pepper
- 1 lemon, thinly slice

Directions:
1. Add all ingredients, except sliced lemon, to bowl or bag, stir to cover chicken. Let marinate for 30 minutes overnight.
2. Remove the chicken and let the excess oil drip (it does not need to dry out, just do not drip with tons of excess oil). Arrange the chicken thighs and the lemon slices in the fryer basket, being careful not to push the chicken thighs too close to each other.
3. Set the fryer to 200 degrees and cook for 10 minutes. Remove the basket from the fryer and turn the chicken thighs to the other side.
4. Cook again at 200 for another 10 minutes.
Nutrition: Calories: 215g Fat 13g Carbohydrates: 1g Protein 2g Sugar 1g Cholesterol: 130mg

346. Chicken's Liver
Preparation Time: 10 minutes
Cooking Time: 30 minutes
Servings: 4
Ingredients:
- 500g of chicken livers
- 2 or 3 carrots
- 1 green pepper
- 1 red pepper
- 1 onion
- 4 tomatoes
- Salt
- Ground pepper
- 1 glass of white wine
- ½ glass of water
- Extra virgin olive oil

Directions:
1. Peel the carrots, cut them into slices and add them to the bowl of the air fryer with a tablespoon of extra virgin olive oil 5 minutes. After 5 minutes, add the peppers and onion in julienne. Select 5 minutes. After that time, add the tomatoes in wedges and select 5 more minutes.
2. Add now the chicken liver clean and chopped. Season, add the wine and water.
3. Select 10 minutes.
4. Check that the liver is tender.
Nutrition: Calories: 76g Fat 13g Carbohydrates: 1g Protein 2g Sugar 1g Cholesterol: 130mg

347. Chicken Parmigiana with Fresh Rosemary
Preparation Time: 5 minutes
Cooking Time: 15 minutes
Servings: 4
Ingredients:
- 1 lb. chicken breasts, halved
- 1 cup seasoned breadcrumbs
- ½ cup Parmesan cheese, grated
- Salt and black pepper to taste
- 2 eggs
- 2 sprigs rosemary, chopped

Directions:
1. Preheat air fryer to 380 F. Spray the air fryer basket with cooking spray.
2. Put the chicken halves on a clean flat surface and cover with Clingfilm.
3. Gently pound them to become thinner using a rolling pin. break the eggs in a bowl and season with black pepper. In another bowl, add and mix up the crumbs with Parmesan cheese.
4. Dip the chicken in the eggs, then in the breadcrumbs. Spray with cooking spray and Air Fry in the fryer for 6 minutes. Flip and cook for 6 more minutes.
5. Sprinkle with rosemary and serve.
Nutrition: Calories: 344g Carbohydrates: 30g Fiber 4g Protein 14g

348. Chicken Pinchos with Salsa Verde
Preparation Time: 10 minutes
Cooking Time: 25 minutes
Servings: 3
Ingredients:
- 2 chicken breasts cut in large cubes
- Salt to taste
- 1 tbsp. chili powder
- ¼ cup maple syrup
- ½ cup soy sauce
- 2 red peppers cut into sticks
- 1 green pepper, cut into sticks
- 7 mushrooms, halved
- 2 tbsp. sesame seeds
- Salsa Verde:
- 1 garlic clove
- 2 tbsp. olive oil
- Zest and juice from 1 lime
- ¼ cup fresh parsley, chopped
- A bunch of skewers

Directions:
1. In a bowl, mix chili powder, salt, maple syrup, soy sauce, sesame seeds and toss in the chicken to coat. Start stacking up the ingredients, alternately, on skewers: red pepper, green pepper, a chicken cube, and a mushroom half, until the skewer is fully loaded. Repeat the process for all the ingredients.
2. Preheat air fryer to 330 F. Brush the pinchos with soy sauce mixture and place them into the frying basket. Grease with cooking spray and cook for 20 minutes, flipping once halfway through.
3. Blend all salsa Verde ingredients in a food processor until you obtain a chunky paste; season with salt. Serve pinchos with salsa Verde.
Nutrition: Calories: 324g Carbohydrates: 20g Fiber 8g Protein 24g

349. Paprika Chicken Breasts
Preparation Time: 5 minutes
Cooking Time: 20 minutes
Servings: 4
Ingredients:
- 4 chicken breasts
- Salt and black pepper to taste

- ¼ tsp garlic powder
- 1 tbsp. paprika
- 2 tbsp. butter, melted
- 2 tbsp. fresh thyme, chopped

Directions:
1. Preheat air fryer to 360 F. Grease the frying basket with cooking spray. Rub the chicken with salt, black pepper, garlic powder, and paprika. Brush with butter.
2. Place in the air fryer and Air Fry for 15 minutes, flipping once halfway through cooking. Let cool slightly, then slice, and sprinkle with thyme to serve.

Nutrition: Calories: 244; Carbohydrates: 10g Fiber 14g Protein 19g

350. Spinach Loaded Chicken Breasts
Preparation Time: 5 minutes
Cooking Time: 10 minutes
Servings: 4
Ingredients:
- 1 cup spinach, chopped
- 4 tbsp. cottage cheese
- 2 chicken breasts
- Juice of ½ limes
- 2 tbsp. Italian seasoning
- 2 tbsp. olive oil

Directions:
1. Preheat air fryer to 390 F and grease the basket with cooking spray. Mix spinach and cottage cheese in a bowl. Halve the breasts with a knife and flatten them with a meat mallet. Season it with Italian seasoning. Divide the spinach/cheese mixture between the chicken pieces.
2. Roll up to form cylinders and use toothpicks to secure them. Brush with olive oil and place them in the frying basket. Bake for 7-8 minutes, flip, and cook for 6 minutes. Serve warm.

Nutrition: Calories: 144g Carbohydrates: 10g Fiber 12g Protein 34g

351. Texas BBQ Chicken Thighs
Preparation Time: 5 minutes
Cooking Time: 25 minutes
Servings: 4
Ingredients:
- 8 chicken thighs
- Salt and black pepper to taste
- 2 tsp Texas BBQ Jerky seasoning
- 1 tbsp. olive oil
- 2 tbsp. fresh cilantro, chopped

Directions:
1. Preheat air fryer to 380 F. Grease the frying basket with cooking spray.
2. Drizzles the chicken with olive oil, season with salt and black pepper, and sprinkle with BBQ seasoning. Place in the fryer and Bake for 15 minutes in total, flipping once. Top with fresh cilantro to serve.

Nutrition: Calories: 234g Carbohydrates: 11g Fiber 16g Protein 17g

352. French-Style Chicken Thighs
Preparation Time: 5 minutes
Cooking Time: 15 minutes
Servings: 4
Ingredients:
- 1 tbsp. herbes de Provence
- 1-pound bone-in, skinless chicken thighs
- Salt and black pepper to taste
- 2 garlic cloves, minced
- ½ cup honey
- ¼ cup Dijon mustard
- 2 tbsp. butter
- 2 tbsp. dill, chopped

Directions:
1. Preheat air fryer to 390 F. Spray the air fryer basket with cooking spray.
2. In a bowl, mix herbes de Provence, salt, and black pepper. Rub the chicken with this mixture. Transfer to the greased air fryer basket and Bake for 15 minutes, flipping once halfway through.
3. Heat the butter in a pan over. Stir in honey, mustard, and garlic; cook until reduced to a thick consistency, about 3 minutes. Serve the chicken drizzled with the honey-mustard sauce.

Nutrition: Calories: 200g Carbohydrates: 15g Fiber 18g Protein 12g

353. Sweet Chili & Ginger Chicken Wings
Preparation Time: 5 minutes
Cooking Time: 15 minutes
Servings: 4
Ingredients:
- 1-pound chicken wings
- 1 tsp ginger root powder
- 1 tbsp. tamarind powder
- ¼ cup sweet chili sauce

Directions:
1. Preheat air fryer to 390 F. Rub the chicken wings with tamarind and ginger root powders. Spray with cooking spray and place in the air fryer basket. Cook for 6 minutes.
2. Slide-out the basket and cover with sweet chili sauce; cook for 8 more minutes. Serve warm.

Nutrition: Calories: 244 Carbohydrates: 22g Fiber 33g Protein 37g

354. Spice-Rubbed Jerk Chicken Wings
Preparation Time: 5 minutes
Cooking Time: 20 minutes
Servings: 4
Ingredients:
- 2 lb. chicken wings
- 2 tbsp. olive oil
- 3 cloves garlic, minced
- 1 tbsp. chili powder
- ½ tbsp. cinnamon powder
- ½ tsp allspice
- 1 habanero pepper, seeded
- 1 tbsp. soy sauce

- ½ tbsp. lemon pepper
- ¼ cup red wine vinegar
- 3 tbsp. lime juice
- ½ tbsp. grated ginger
- ½ tbsp. fresh thyme, chopped
- ⅓ tbsp. sugar
- ½ tbsp. salt

Directions:
1. In a bowl, add olive oil, soy sauce, garlic, habanero pepper, allspice, cinnamon powder, chili powder, lemon pepper, salt, sugar, thyme, ginger, lime juice, and red wine vinegar; mix well. Add the chicken wings to the mixture and toss to coat. Cover and refrigerate for 1 hour.
2. Preheat air fryer to 380 F. Remove the chicken from the fridge, drain all the liquid, and pat dry with paper towels. Working simultaneously, place the wings in the air fryer oven for 16 minutes in total. Shake once halfway through. Serve with a blue cheese dip or ranch dressing.

Nutrition: Calories: 320 Carbohydrates: 20g Fiber 14g Protein 34g

355. Juicy Chicken with Bell Peppers
Preparation Time: 15 minutes
Cooking Time: 25 minutes
Servings: 2
Ingredients:
- 2 chicken fillets, cubed
- Salt and black pepper to taste
- 1 cup flour
- 2 eggs
- ½ cup apple cider vinegar
- ½ tbsp. ginger paste
- ½ tbsp. garlic paste
- 1 red bell pepper, cut into strips
- 1 tbsp. sugar
- 1 red chili, minced
- 2 tbsp. tomato puree
- 1 green bell pepper, cut into strips
- 1 tbsp. paprika
- 4 tbsp. water

Directions:
1. In a bowl, add olive oil, soy sauce, garlic, habanero pepper, allspice, cinnamon powder, chili powder, lemon, salt, sugar, thyme, ginger, lime juice, and red wine vinegar. Mix well. Add the chicken wings to the mixture and mix with the layer. Cover and refrigerate for 1 hour.
2. Preheat fryer to 380 F. Remove chicken from refrigerator, drain all liquid, and pat dry. Working in batches, cook the wings in the fryer for a total of 16 minutes. Shake the waist. Remove to a serving platter and serve with a little blue cheese or ranch sauce.

Nutrition: Calories: 434; Carbohydrates: 19g Fiber 9g Protein 44g

356. Quinoa Chicken Nuggets
Preparation Time: 5 minutes
Cooking Time: 10 minutes
Servings: 2
Ingredients:
- 2 chicken breasts cut into bite-size chunks
- ½ cup cooked quinoa, cooled
- ½ cup flour
- 1 egg
- ½ tsp cayenne pepper
- Salt and black pepper to taste

Directions:
1. In a bowl, beat the egg with salt and black pepper. Spread flour on a plate and mix with cayenne pepper. Coat the chicken in flour, then in the egg, shake off and place in the quinoa. Press firmly so quinoa sticks on the chicken pieces. Spray with cooking spray and Air Fry the nuggets in the greased frying basket for 14-16 minutes on 360 F, turning once halfway through. Serve hot.

Nutrition: Calories: 104; Carbohydrates: 22g Fiber 23g Protein 35g

357. Tarragon & Garlic Roasted Chicken
Preparation Time: 15 minutes
Cooking Time: 40 minutes
Servings: 4
Ingredients:
- 1 chicken (around 3 lb.), rinsed, pat-dried
- 1 sprig fresh tarragon
- 2 tbsp. butter, melted
- Salt and black pepper to taste
- 1 lemon, cut into wedges
- 1 garlic bulb

Directions:
1. Preheat air fryer to 380 F. Grease the air fryer basket with cooking spray.
2. Brush the chicken with melted butter and season with salt and pepper. Put tarragon, garlic, and lemon into the cavity of the chicken and place in the air fryer basket. Bake for 40 minutes. Then, cover with foil and let rest for 10 minutes, then carve, slice, and serve with fresh salad or baked potatoes.

Nutrition: Calories: 424 Carbohydrates: 27g Fiber 28g Protein 20g

358. Comfort Chicken Drumsticks
Preparation Time: 10 minutes
Cooking Time: 10 minutes
Servings: 4
Ingredients:
- 1-pound chicken drumsticks
- 1 tsp garlic powder
- 1 tsp cayenne pepper
- ½ cup flour
- ¼ cup milk
- ¼ tbsp. lemon juice
- Salt and black pepper to taste

Directions:
1. Preheat air fryer to 390 F. Spray the air fryer basket with cooking spray.

2. In a small bowl, mix garlic powder, cayenne pepper, salt, and black pepper. Rub the chicken drumsticks with the mixture. In a separate bowl, combine milk with lemon juice. Pour the flour on a plate.
3. Dunk the chicken in the milk mixture, and then roll in the flour to coat. Place the chicken in the frying basket and spray it with cooking spray. Air Fry for 14 minutes, flipping once. Serve warm.
Nutrition: Calories: 214; Carbohydrates: 15g Fiber 16g Protein 28g

359. Greek-Style Chicken Tacos
Preparation Time: 5 minutes
Cooking Time: 20 minutes
Servings: 4
Ingredients:
- 2 chicken breasts cut into strips
- 1 tbsp. taco seasoning
- Salt and black pepper to taste
- 1 cup flour
- 1 egg, beaten
- ½ cup breadcrumbs
- 4 taco shells
- 2 cups white cabbage, shredded
- 3 tbsp. Greek yogurt dressing

Directions:
1. Preheat air fryer to 380 F. Spray the air fryer basket with cooking spray. Season the chicken with taco seasoning, salt, and black pepper.
2. In 3 separate bowls, add breadcrumbs to one bowl, flour to another and beaten egg to a third bowl. roll the chicken in the flour, then the egg and then the toast. Spray with cooking spray and transfer to the frying basket. Air Fry for 12 minutes, flipping once halfway through. Fill the taco shells with chicken strips, cabbage, and yogurt dressing to serve.
Nutrition: Calories: 194 Carbohydrates: 10g Fiber 32g Protein 44g

360. Cheesy Chicken Thighs with Parmesan Crust
Preparation Time: 15 minutes
Cooking Time: 10 minutes
Servings: 4
Ingredients:
- ½ cup Italian breadcrumbs
- 2 tbsp. Parmesan cheese, grated
- 1 tbsp. butter, melted
- 4 chicken thighs
- ½ cup marinara sauce
- ½ cup Monterrey jack cheese, shredded

Directions:
1. Preheat air fryer to 380 F. In a bowl, mix the crumbs with Parmesan cheese. Brush the thighs with butter. Dip each thigh into the crumb mixture. Arrange them on the greased air fryer basket.
2. Air Fry for 6-7 minutes at 380 F, flip, top with marinara sauce and shredded Monterrey Jack cheese and continue to cook for another 4-5 minutes. Serve immediately.

Nutrition: Calories: 287 Carbohydrates: 33g Fiber 20g Protein 39g

361. Pretzel Crusted Chicken with Spicy Mustard Sauce
Preparation Time: 10 minutes
Cooking Time: 14 minutes
Servings: 6
Ingredients:
- 2 eggs
- 1 ½ pound chicken breasts, boneless, skinless, cut into bite-sized chunks
- 1/2 cup crushed pretzels
- 1 tsp shallot powder
- 1 tsp paprika
- ground black pepper and Sea salt, to taste
- 1/2 cup vegetable broth
- 1 tbsp. cornstarch
- 3 tbsp. Worcestershire sauce
- 3 tbsp. tomato paste
- 1 tbsp. apple cider vinegar
- 2 tbsp. olive oil
- 2 garlic cloves, chopped
- 1 jalapeno pepper, minced
- 1 tsp yellow mustard

Directions:
1. Firstly, heat the oven to 390 degrees F.
2. In a mixing dish, whisk the eggs until frothy; toss the chicken chunks into the whisked eggs and coat well.
3. In another dish, combine the crushed pretzels with shallot powder, paprika, salt and pepper. Then, lay the chicken chunks in the pretzel mixture; turn it over until well coated.
4. Place the chicken pieces in the air fryer basket. Cook the chicken for 12 minutes, shaking the basket halfway through.
5. Meanwhile, whisk the vegetable broth with cornstarch, Worcestershire sauce, tomato paste, and apple cider vinegar.
6. Preheat a cast-iron skillet over medium flame. Heat the olive oil and sauté the garlic with jalapeno pepper for 30 to 40 seconds, stirring frequently.
7. Add the cornstarch mixture and let it simmer until the sauce has thickened a little. Now, add the air-fried chicken and mustard; let it simmer for 2 minute more or until heated through.
8. Serve immediately and enjoy!
Nutrition: Calories; 14.6g Fat; 22.3g Carbs; 21.1g Protein ; 2.3g Sugars: 332

362. Chinese-Style Sticky Turkey Thighs
Preparation Time: 10 minutes
Cooking Time: 35 minutes
Servings: 6
Ingredients:
- 1 tbsp. sesame oil
- 2 pounds' turkey thighs
- 1 tsp Chinese Five-spice powder

- 1 tsp pink Himalayan salt
- 1/4 tsp Sichuan pepper
- 6 tbsp. honey
- 1 tbsp. Chinese rice vinegar
- 2 tbsp. soy sauce
- 1 tbsp. sweet chili sauce
- 1 tbsp. mustard

Directions:
1. Preheat the fryer to 360 degrees F.
2. Brush sesame oil on all turkey thighs. Sprinkle with spices.
3. Cook for 23 minutes, turning once or twice. Be sure to work in batches to ensure even cooking. Meanwhile, combine the remaining ingredients in a preheated wok (or similar skillet) over a moderately high temperature. Cook and stir until sauce is reduced by about a third.
4. Add the fried turkey thighs to the wok. Gently mix in the layer with the sauce. Enjoy!

Nutrition: Calories; 10.1g Fat; 19g Carbs; 27.7g Protein 17.9g Sugars 279:

363. Easy Hot Chicken Drumsticks

Preparation Time: 10 minutes
Cooking Time: 30 minutes
Servings: 6
Ingredients:
- 6 chicken drumsticks
- Sauce:
- 6 ounces' hot sauce
- 3 tbsp. olive oil
- 3 tbsp. tamari sauce
- 1 tsp dried thyme
- 1/2 tsp dried oregano

Directions:
1. Sprit the sides and bottom of the cooking basket with a nonstick cooking spray.
2. Cook the chicken drumsticks at 380 degrees F for 35 minutes, flipping them over halfway through.
3. Meanwhile, heat the hot sauce, olive oil, tamari sauce, thyme, and oregano it in a pan over medium-low heat; reserve.
4. Drizzle the sauce over the prepared chicken drumsticks; toss to coat well and serve. Bon appétit!

Nutrition: Calories; 18.7g Fat; 2.6g Carbs; 24.1g Protein ; 1.4g Sugars: 280

364. Crunchy Munch Chicken Tenders with Peanuts

Preparation Time: 10 minutes
Cooking Time: 25 minutes
Servings: 4
Ingredients:
- 1 ½ lb. of chicken tenderloin
- 2 tbsp. peanut oil
- 1/2 cup tortilla chips, crushed
- Ground black pepper and salt to taste
- 1/2 tsp garlic powder
- 1 tsp red pepper flakes
- 2 tbsp. peanuts, roasted and roughly chopped

Directions:
1. Brush the chicken tenderloins with peanut oil on all sides.
2. In a mixing bowl, thoroughly combine the crushed chips, salt, black pepper, garlic powder, and red pepper flakes.
3. Dredge the chicken in the breading, shaking off any residual coating.
4. Lay the chicken tenderloins into the cooking basket.
5. Cook it for 12 to 13 minutes or until it is no longer pink in the center. Work in batches; an instant-read thermometer should read at least 165 degrees F.
6. Serve garnished with roasted peanuts. Bon appétit!

Nutrition: Calories 343 Fat 16.4g Carbs 10.6g Protein 36.8g Sugars 1g

365. Tarragon Turkey Tenderloins with Baby Potatoes

Preparation Time: 10 minutes
Cooking Time: 40 minutes
Servings: 6
Ingredients:
- 2 pounds' turkey tenderloins
- 2 tsp olive oil
- Salt and ground black pepper, to taste
- 1 tsp smoked paprika
- 2 tbsp. dry white wine
- 1 tbsp. fresh tarragon leaves, chopped
- 1-pound baby potatoes, rubbed

Directions:
1. Brush the turkey tenderloins with olive oil. Season it with black pepper, salt, and paprika.
2. Afterwards, add the white wine and tarragon.
3. Cook the turkey tenderloins at 350 degrees F for 30 minutes, flipping them over halfway through. Let them rest for 5 to 9 minutes before slicing and serving.
4. Sprit the sides and bottom of the cooking basket with the remaining 1 teaspoon of olive oil after that.
5. Then, heat your oven to 400 degrees F; cook the baby potatoes for 15 minutes. Serve with the turkey and enjoy!

Nutrition: Calories; 7.4g Fat; 14.2g Carbs; 45.7g Protein ; 1.1g

366. Mediterranean Chicken Breasts with Roasted Tomatoes

Preparation Time: 10 minutes
Cooking Time: 1 hour
Servings: 8
Ingredients:
- 2 tsp olive oil, melted
- 3 pounds' chicken breasts, bone-in
- 1/2 tsp black pepper, freshly ground
- 1/2 tsp salt
- 1 tsp cayenne pepper

- 2 tbsp. fresh parsley, minced
- 1 tsp fresh basil, minced
- 1 tsp fresh rosemary, minced
- 4 medium-sized Roma tomatoes, halved

Directions:
1. Firstly, preheat the oven to 370 degrees F. Brush the cooking basket with 1 teaspoon of olive oil.
2. Sprinkle the chicken breasts with all seasonings listed above.
3. Cook it for 25 minutes or until chicken breasts are slightly browned. Work in batches.
4. Arrange the tomatoes in the cooking basket and brush them with the remaining teaspoon of olive oil. Season it with sea salt.
5. Cook the tomatoes at 350 degrees F for 10 minutes, shaking halfway through the cooking time. Serve with chicken breasts.
6. Bon appétit!

Nutrition: Calories; 17.1g Fat; 2.7g Carbs; 36g Protein ; 1.7g

367. Thai Red Duck with Candy Onion

Preparation Time: 10 minutes
Cooking Time: 25 minutes
Servings: 4
Ingredients:
- 1 ½ pounds duck breasts, skin removed
- 1 tsp kosher salt
- 1/2 tsp cayenne pepper
- 1/3 tsp black pepper
- 1/2 tsp smoked paprika
- 1 tbsp. Thai red curry paste
- 1 cup candy onions, halved
- 1/4 small pack coriander, chopped

Directions:
1. Place the duck breasts between 2 sheets of foil, then, use a rolling pin to bash the duck until they are 1-inch thick.
2. Preheat your Air Fryer to 395 degrees F.
3. Rub the duck breasts with salt, cayenne pepper, black pepper, paprika, and red curry paste. Place the duck breast in the cooking basket.
4. Cook for 11 to 12 minutes. Top with candy onions and cook for another 10 to 11 minutes. Serve garnished with coriander and enjoy!

Nutrition: Calories 18.7g Fat 4g Carbs 42.3g Protein 1.3g

368. Rustic Chicken Legs with Turnip Chips

Preparation Time: 10 minutes
Cooking Time: 20 minutes
Servings: 3
Ingredients:
- 1-pound chicken legs
- 1 tsp Himalayan salt
- 1 tsp paprika
- 1/2 tsp ground black pepper
- 1 tsp butter, melted
- 1 turnip, trimmed and sliced

Directions:
1. Sprit the sides and bottom of the cooking basket with a nonstick cooking spray. Season the chicken legs with salt, paprika, and ground black pepper. Cook at 370 degrees F for 10 minutes. Increase the temperature to 380 degrees F.
2. Drizzle turnip slices with melted butter and transfer them to the cooking basket with the chicken. Cook the turnips and chicken for 15 minutes more, flipping them halfway through the cooking time.
3. As for the chicken, an instant-read thermometer should read at least 165 degrees F. Serve and enjoy!

Nutrition: Calories; 7.8g Fat; 3.4g Carbs; 29.5g Protein ; 1.6g

369. Easy Ritzy Chicken Nuggets

Preparation Time: 10 minutes
Cooking Time: 20 minutes
Servings: 4
Ingredients:
- 1 ½ pounds chicken tenderloin cut into small pieces
- 1/2 tsp garlic salt
- 1/2 tsp cayenne pepper
- 1/4 tsp black pepper, freshly cracked
- 4 tbsp. olive oil
- 1/3 cup saltines (e.g. Ritz crackers), crushed
- 4 tbsp. Parmesan cheese, freshly grated

Directions:
1. Firstly, heat the oven to 390 degrees F.
2. Season each piece of the chicken with garlic salt, cayenne pepper, and black pepper.
3. In a mixing bowl, thoroughly combine the olive oil with crushed saltines. Dip each piece of chicken in the cracker mixture.
4. Finally, roll the chicken pieces over the Parmesan cheese. Cook for 8 minutes, working in batches.
5. Later, if you want to warm the chicken nuggets add them to the basket and cook for 1 minute more. Serve with French fries, if desired.

Nutrition: Calories; 20.1g Fat; 5.3g Carbs; 36.6g Protein ; 0.2g

370. Asian Chicken Filets with Cheese

Preparation Time: 10 minutes
Cooking Time: 50 minutes
Servings: 2
Ingredients:
- 4 rashers smoked bacon
- 2 chicken filets
- 1/2 taps coarse sea salt
- 1/4 tap black pepper, preferably freshly ground
- 1 tap garlic, minced
- 1 (2-inch) piece ginger, peeled and minced
- 1 taps black mustard seeds
- 1 taps mild curry powder
- 1/2 cup coconut milk
- 1/3 cup tortilla chips, crushed

- 1/2 cup Pecorino cheese, grated

Directions:
1. Firstly, preheat the oven to 400 degrees F. add the smoked bacon and cook in the preheated Air Fryer for 5 to 7 minutes. Then reserve. In a mixing bowl, place the chicken fillets, salt, black pepper, garlic, ginger, mustard seeds, curry powder, and milk. Let it marinate in your refrigerator about 30 minutes.
2. In another bowl, mix the crushed chips and grated Pecorino Romano cheese. Dredge the chicken fillets through the chips mixture and transfer them to the cooking basket. Reduce the temperature to 380 degrees F and cook the chicken for 6 minutes.
3. Flip and cook for an extra 6 minutes. Repeat the procedure for all the remaining ingredients. Serve with reserved bacon. Enjoy!

Nutrition: Calories; 19.6g Fat; 12.1g Carbs; 36.2g Protein ; 3.4g

371. Paprika Chicken Legs with Brussels Sprouts

Preparation Time: 10 minutes
Cooking Time: 30 minutes
Servings: 2
Ingredients:
- 2 chicken legs
- 1/2 tsp paprika
- 1/2 tsp kosher salt
- 1/2 tsp black pepper
- 1 pound Brussels sprouts
- 1 tsp dill, fresh or dried

Directions:
1. Firstly, preheat the oven to 370 degrees F.
2. Now, season your chicken with paprika, salt, and pepper. Transfer the chicken legs to the cooking basket. Cook for 10 minutes.
3. Flip the chicken legs and cook an additional 10 minutes. Then reserve.
4. Add the Brussels sprouts to the cooking basket sprinkle with dill. Cook at 380 degrees F for 15 minutes, shaking the basket halfway through.
5. Serve with the reserved chicken legs. Bon appétit!

Nutrition: Calories; 20.1g Fat; 5.3g Carbs; 36.6g Protein ; 0.2g

372. Asian Spicy Turkey

Preparation Time: 10 minutes
Cooking Time: 25 minutes
Servings: 6
Ingredients:
- 1 tbsp. sesame oil
- 2 pounds' turkey thighs
- 1 tsp Chinese Five-spice powder
- 1 tsp pink Himalayan salt
- 1/4 teaspoon Sichuan pepper
- 1 tbsp. Chinese rice vinegar
- 2 tbsp. soy sauce
- 1 tbsp. chili sauce
- 1 tbsp. mustard

Directions:
1. Firstly, heat your oven to 360 degrees F. Brush the sesame oil all over the turkey thighs. Season them with spices. Cook for 23 minutes, turning over once or twice. Make sure to work in batches to ensure even cooking
2. Combine the remaining ingredients in a wok (or similar type pan) that is preheated over medium-high heat. Cook and stir until the sauce reduces by about a third. Add the fried turkey thighs to the wok; gently stir to coat with the sauce. Allow to cool before slicing and serving. Enjoy!

Nutrition: Calories; 16.2g Fat; 2.4g Carbs; 29g Protein ; 1.4g Sugars; 2.2g

373. Spicy Chicken Drumsticks with Herbs

Preparation Time: 10 minutes
Cooking Time: 30 minutes
Servings: 6
Ingredients:
- 6 chicken drumsticks
- Sauce:
- 6 ounces' hot sauce
- 3 tbsp. olive oil
- 3 tbsp. tamari sauce
- 1 tsp dried thyme
- 1/2 tsp dried oregano

Directions:
1. Sprit the sides and bottom of the cooking basket with a nonstick cooking spray. Cook the chicken drumsticks at 380 degrees F for 35 minutes, flipping them over halfway through.
2. Heat the hot sauce, olive oil, tamari sauce, thyme, and oregano in a pan over medium-low heat. Then reserve. Drizzle the sauce over the prepared chicken drumsticks; toss to coat well and serve. Bon appétit!

Nutrition: Calories; 18.7g Fat; 2.6g Carbs; 24.1g Protein ; 1.4g Sugars; 0.5g

374. Classic Chicken with Peanuts

Preparation Time: 10 minutes
Cooking Time: 15 minutes
Servings: 4
Ingredients:
- 1 ½ pounds of chicken tenderloin
- 2 tbsp. peanut oil
- 1/2 cup parmesan cheese, grated
- ground black pepper and Sea salt and to taste
- 1/2 tsp garlic powder
- 1 tsp red pepper flakes
- 2 tbsp. peanuts, roasted and roughly chopped

Directions:
1. Firstly, preheat the oven to 360 degrees F.
2. Brush the chicken tenderloins with peanut oil on all sides.
3. In a mixing bowl, thoroughly combine grated parmesan cheese, salt, black pepper, garlic powder, and red pepper flakes. Dredge the chicken in the breading, shaking off any residual coating.

4. Lay the chicken tenderloins into the cooking basket. Cook it for 12 to 13 minutes or until it is no longer pink in the center. Work in batches; an instant-read thermometer should read at least 165 degrees F. Serve garnished with roasted peanuts. Bon appétit!
Nutrition: Calories; 17.4g Fat; 6.3g Carbs; 40g Protein ; 1.4g Sugars; 0.7g

375. Turkey with Paprika and Tarragon
Preparation Time: 10 minutes
Cooking Time: 30 minutes
Servings: 6
Ingredients:
- 2 pounds' turkey tenderloins
- 2 tbsp. olive oil
- Salt and ground black pepper, to taste
- 1 tsp smoked paprika
- 2 tbsp. dry white wine
- 1 tbsp. fresh tarragon leaves, chopped

Directions:
1. Brush the turkey tenderloins with olive oil. add salt, black pepper, and paprika.
2. Afterwards, add the white wine and tarragon.
3. Cook the turkey tenderloins at 350 degrees F for 30 minutes, flipping them over halfway through. Let them rest for 5 to 9 minutes before slicing and serving. Enjoy!

Nutrition: Calories; 7.5g Fat; 1.2g Carbs; 34.7g Protein ; 0.5g Sugars; 0.3g

376. Italian-Style Chicken with Roma Tomatoes
Preparation Time: 15 minutes
Cooking Time: 30 minutes
Servings: 8
Ingredients:
- 2 tsp olive oil, melted
- 3 pounds' chicken breasts, bone-in
- 1/2 tsp black pepper, freshly ground
- 1/2 tsp salt
- 1 tsp cayenne pepper
- 2 tbsp. fresh parsley, minced
- 1 tsp fresh basil, minced
- 1 tsp fresh rosemary, minced
- 4 medium-sized Roma tomatoes, halved

Directions:
1. Firstly, preheat the oven to 370 degrees F. Brush the cooking basket with 1 teaspoon of olive oil. Sprinkle the chicken breasts with all seasonings listed above.
2. Cook it for 25 minutes or until chicken breasts are slightly browned. Work in batches. Arrange the tomatoes in the cooking basket and brush them with the remaining teaspoon of olive oil. Season it with sea salt. Cook the tomatoes at 350 degrees F for 10 minutes, shaking halfway through the cooking time. Serve with chicken breasts. Bon appétit!

Nutrition: Calories; 17.1g Fat; 2.7g Carbs; 36g Protein ; 1.7g Sugars; 0.9g

377. Duck Breasts with Candy Onion and Coriander
Preparation Time: 10 minutes
Cooking Time: 25 minutes
Servings: 4
Ingredients:
- 1 ½ pounds duck breasts, skin removed
- 1 tsp kosher salt
- 1/2 tsp cayenne pepper
- 1/3 tsp black pepper
- 1/2 tsp smoked paprika
- 1 tbsp. Thai red curry paste
- 1 cup candy onions, halved
- 1/4 small pack coriander, chopped

Directions:
1. Place the duck breasts between 2 sheets of foil; then, use a rolling pin to bash the duck until they are 1-inch thick. Preheat your Air Fryer to 395 degrees F.
2. Rub the duck breasts with salt, cayenne pepper, black pepper, paprika, and red curry paste. Place the duck breast in the cooking basket. Cook for 11 to 12 minutes. Top with candy onions and cook for another 10 to 11 minutes. Serve garnished with coriander and enjoy!

Nutrition: Calories; 362 Fat; 4g Carbs; 42.3g Protein ; 1.3g Sugars; 2.5g

378. Turkey Burgers with Crispy Bacon
Preparation Time: 10 minutes
Cooking Time: 30 minutes
Servings: 4
Ingredients:
- 2 tbsp. vermouth
- 2 strips Canadian bacon, sliced
- 1-pound ground turkey
- 1/2 shallot, minced
- 2 garlic cloves, minced
- 2 tablespoons fish sauce
- ground black pepper and Sea salt and to taste
- 1 tsp red pepper flakes
- 4 tbsp. tomato ketchup
- 4 tbsp. mayonnaise
- 4 (1-ounce) slices Cheddar cheese
- 4 lettuce leaves

Directions:
1. Start preheating the fryer to 400 degrees F. Brush the Canadian bacon with vermouth.
2. Cook for 3 minutes. Flip the bacon and cook for an additional 3 minutes.
3. Then mix the ground turkey, onion, garlic, fish sauce, salt, black pepper, and red pepper well. Form the meat mixture into 4 hamburger patties.
4. Bake in the preheated air fryer at 370 degrees F for 9 minutes. Flip over and cook for extra 10 minutes.
5. Serve the turkey burger with tomato sauce, mayonnaise, bacon, cheese, and lettuce. serve immediately.

Nutrition: Calories; 16.4g Fat; 7.4g Carbs; 30.9g Protein ; 4.4g Sugars; 0.6g

379. Turkey Tenderloins with Gravy
Preparation Time: 10 minutes
Cooking Time: 20 minutes
Servings: 4
Ingredients:
- 1-pound turkey tenderloins
- 1 tbsp. Dijon-style mustard
- 1 tbsp. olive oil
- ground black pepper and Sea salt and to taste
- 1 tsp Italian seasoning mix
- 1 cup turkey stock
- 1/2 tsp xanthan gum
- 4 tbsp. tomato ketchup
- 4 tbsp. mayonnaise
- 4 pickles, sliced

Directions:
1. Rub the turkey tenderloins with the mustard and olive oil. Season it with salt, black pepper, and Italian seasoning mix.
2. Cook the turkey tenderloins at 350 degrees F for 30 minutes, flipping them over halfway through. Let them rest for 5 to 7 minutes before slicing. For the gravy, in a saucepan, place the drippings from the roasted turkey. Add in turkey stock and bring to a boil.
3. Stir in xanthan gum and whisk to combine. Let simmer another 5 to 10 minutes until starting to thicken. Gravy will thicken more as it cools.
4. Serve turkey tenderloins with gravy, tomato ketchup, mayonnaise, and pickles. Serve and enjoy!

Nutrition: Calories 276 Fat; 5.2g Carbs; 26.9g Protein ; 2.3g Sugars; 1.9g

380. Old-Fashioned Turkey Chili
Preparation Time: 10 minutes
Cooking Time: 40 minutes
Servings: 4
Ingredients:
- 1/2 medium-sized leek, chopped
- 1/2 red onion, chopped
- 2 garlic cloves, minced
- 1 jalapeno pepper, seeded and minced
- 1 bell pepper, seeded and chopped
- 2 tbsp. olive oil
- 1-pound ground turkey, 85% lean 15% Fat
- 2 cups tomato puree
- 2 cups chicken stock
- 1/2 teaspoon black peppercorns
- Salt, to taste
- 1 tsp chili powder
- 1 tsp mustard seeds
- 1 tsp ground cumin

Directions:
1. Start by preheating your Air Fryer to 365 degrees F.
2. Place the leeks, onion, garlic and peppers in a baking pan; drizzle olive oil evenly over the top. Cook for 4 to 6 minutes. Add the ground turkey. Cook for 6 minutes more or until the meat is no longer pink. Now, add the tomato puree, 1 cup of chicken stock, black peppercorns, salt, chili powder, mustard seeds, and cumin to the baking pan. Cook for 24 minutes, stirring every 7 to 10 minutes.
3. Bon appétit!

Nutrition: Calories; 271 Fat; 7.6g Carbs; 25.7g Protein ; 3.6g Sugars; 1.4g

381. Rustic Chicken Drumettes with Chives
Preparation Time: 10 minutes
Cooking Time: 22 minutes
Servings: 3
Ingredients:
- 1/3 cup almond meal
- 1/2 tsp ground white pepper
- 1 tsp seasoning salt
- 1 tsp garlic paste
- 1 tsp rosemary
- 1 whole egg + 1 egg white
- 6 chicken drumettes
- 1 heaping tablespoon fresh chives, chopped

Directions:
1. Start by preheating your Air Fryer to 390 degrees.
2. Mix the almond meal with white pepper, salt, garlic paste, and rosemary in a small-sized bowl.
3. In another bowl, beat the eggs until frothy.
4. Dip the chicken into the flour mixture, then into the beaten eggs; coat with the flour mixture one more time. Cook the chicken drumettes for 22 minutes. Serve warm, garnished with chives.

Nutrition: Calories; 319 Fat; 2.4g Carbs; 49.5g Protein ; 0.5g Sugars; 1.4g

382. Chicken Sausage in Dijon Sauce
Preparation Time: 10 minutes
Cooking Time: 13 minutes
Servings: 4
Ingredients:
- 4 chicken sausages
- 1/4 cup mayonnaise
- 2 tbsp. Dijon mustard
- 1 tbsp. balsamic vinegar
- 1/2 tsp dried rosemary

Directions:
1. Arrange the sausages on the grill pan and transfer it to the preheated Air Fryer.
2. Grill the sausages at 350 degrees F for approximately 13 minutes. Turn them halfway through cooking. Meanwhile, prepare the sauce by mixing the remaining ingredients with a wire whisk. Serve the warm sausages with chilled Dijon sauce. Enjoy!

Nutrition: Calories; 575 Fat; 2.5g Carbs; 22.4g Protein ; 0.8g Sugars; 0.5g

383. Parsley & Lemon Turkey Risotto
Preparation Time: 40 minutes
Cooking Time: 12 minutes
Servings: 4
Ingredients
- 2 boneless turkey breasts, cut into strips

- 2 lemons, juiced
- 1 tbsp. dried oregano
- 2 garlic cloves, minced
- 1 ½ tbsp. olive oil
- 1 onion, diced
- 2 cups chicken broth
- 1 cup Arborio rice, rinsed
- Salt and black pepper to taste
- ¼ cup chopped fresh parsley
- 8 lemon slices

Directions:
1. In a Ziploc bag, mix turkey, oregano, salt, garlic juice and zest of two lemons. Marinate for 10 minutes.
2. Warm the oil on sauté. Add onion and cook for 3 minutes; add rice and chicken broth and season with pepper and salt. Empty the Ziploc having the chicken and marinade into pot. Seal the lid and cook on High Pressure for 12 minutes. Release the Pressure quickly. Garnish with lemon slices and parsley to serve.

Nutrition: Calories: 376 Fat; 4.5g Carbs; 32.4g Protein; 4.8g Sugars; 5.5g

384. Chicken with Vegetables & Coconut Milk Stew

Preparation Time: 20 minutes
Cooking Time: 20 minutes
Servings: 4
Ingredients:
- 2 cups fire-roasted tomatoes, diced
- 1 lb. chicken breast, boneless and skinless, chopped
- 1 tbsp. fresh basil, chopped
- 2 cups coconut milk
- 1 cup chicken broth
- Salt and black pepper to taste
- 2 tbsp. tomato paste
- 2 celery stalks, chopped
- 2 carrots, chopped
- 2 tbsp. coconut oil
- 1 onion, finely chopped
- 3 garlic cloves, crushed
- ½ cup button mushrooms, sliced

Directions:
1. Grease the inner pot with oil. Add celery, onion, and carrots and cook on Sauté for 7 minutes, stirring constantly. Add tomato paste, basil, garlic, and mushrooms. Continue to cook for 10 more minutes. Add the rest of the ingredients, seal the lid. Cook on Poultry for 15 minutes on High. Do a quickly release.

Nutrition: Calories; 275 Fat; 2.2g Carbs; 22.3g Protein; 24.g Sugars; 23g

385. Grilled Chicken Drumsticks with Summer Salad

Preparation Time: 20 minutes
Cooking Time: 20 minutes
Servings: 4
Ingredients
- 4 chicken drumsticks
- 3 cups chicken broth
- 1 tomato, roughly chopped
- 2 oz. lettuce, torn
- 1 cup Kalamata olives
- 1 cucumber, chopped
- 3 tbsp. olive oil
- 1 tbsp. Dijon mustard
- ¼ cup white wine
- 1 tsp lemon juice
- 1 tbsp. Italian seasoning mix
- 1 tsp salt

Directions:
1. In a bowl, mix mustard, 2 tbsp. olive oil, Italian mix, wine, and salt. Stir and brush the meat. Wrap in aluminum foil and refrigerate for 30 minutes.
2. Place the tomato, lettuce, cucumber, and Kalamata olive in a serving bowl. Season with salt, black pepper and add in the remaining olive oil. Stir and set aside.
3. Remove the drumsticks from the fridge and transfer to the pot. Pour in the broth and seal the lid. Cook on Poultry mode for 15 minutes on High Pressure.
4. Do a quickly release and remove the drumsticks? Preheat a non-stick grill pan over high heat. Brown the drumsticks for 6-7 minutes, turning once. Serve with the salad.

Nutrition: Calories; 135 Fat; 5g Carbs; 4g Protein; 8g Sugars; 5g

386. Tuscan Vegetable Chicken Stew

Preparation Time: 10 minutes
Cooking Time: 35 minutes
Servings: 4
Ingredients:
- 1 whole chicken, 3 lb.
- 14 oz. mixed broccoli and cauliflower florets
- 1 onion, peeled, chopped
- 1 potato, peeled and chopped
- 3 carrots, chopped
- 1 tomato, peeled and chopped
- A handful of yellow wax beans, whole
- A handful of fresh parsley, chopped
- ¼ cup extra virgin olive oil
- Salt and black pepper to taste

Directions:
1. Grease the bottom of the pot with 3 tbsp. of olive oil. Stir-fry the onion, for 3-4 minutes, on Sauté mode. Add the carrots and Sauté for 5 more minutes.
2. Add the remaining oil, vegetables, salt, black pepper, and top with chicken. Add 1 cup of water and seal the lid. Cook on High Pressure for 30 minutes. Release the Pressure naturally, for about 10 minutes.

Nutrition: Calories 342 Fat 23g Carbs 7.5g Protein 27.4g Sugars 32.8g Fiber 4.5g

387. Hot Chicken with Garlic & Mushrooms

Preparation Time: 15 minutes
Cooking Time: 30 minutes
Servings: 3

Ingredients:
- 1 lb. chicken breasts, skinless, boneless, cut into pieces
- 1 cup button mushrooms, chopped
- 2 cups chicken broth
- 2 tbsp. flour
- 1 tsp cayenne pepper, ground
- Salt and black pepper to taste
- 1 tbsp. olive oil
- 2 garlic cloves, chopped

Directions:
1. Grease the inner pot with oil. Add garlic and chicken, season with salt, and stir-fry for 3 minutes. Add mushrooms and Pour the chicken broth. Seal the lid. Cook on High Pressure for 8 minutes.
2. Release the steam naturally, for 10 minutes and stir in flour, cayenne, and black pepper. Cook for 5 minutes, on Sauté mode. Serve warm.

Nutrition: Calories; 208 Fat; 6.5g Carbs; 32.4g Protein ; 34.8g Sugars; 5.5g

388. Sage Chicken in Orange Gravy
Preparation Time: 10 minutes
Cooking Time: 35 minutes
Servings: 8
Ingredients:
- 1 Whole Chicken about 3.5 lb.
- ¼ cup oil
- 2 tbsp. fresh sage, minced
- 2 tbsp. lemon zest
- 1 tsp garlic powder
- ¼ tsp red pepper flakes
- 3 cups chicken broth
- 1 cup red wine
- 5 tbsp. butter
- 1 cup orange juice
- 1 tsp Sugar
- ½ cup flour
- Salt and black pepper to taste

Directions:
1. Mix oil, tarragon, lemon zest, garlic, salt, black pepper, and red pepper. Rub the mixture onto chicken. Melt butter on Sauté. Brown the chicken for 3-4 minutes Pour in broth and wine. Seal the lid and cook on Poultry for 30 minutes on High. Do a quickly release and remove the chicken?
2. In a bowl, mix the orange juice, 1 cup of cooking liquid, flour, and sugar. Cook for 5 minutes on Sauté mode until sauce has thickened. Scatter the sauce over the chicken and serve.

Nutrition: Calories; 570 Fat; 25g Carbs; 24g Protein ; 8g Sugars; 15g

389. Awesome Spicy Turkey Casserole with Tomatoes
Preparation Time: 15 minutes
Cooking Time: 20 minutes
Servings: 5
Ingredients:
- 1 tbsp. olive oil
- ½ sweet onion, diced
- 3 cloves garlic, minced
- 1 jalapeño pepper, minced
- 1-pound turkey breast, cubed
- 2 (14-ouncecans fire-roasted tomatoes
- 1 ½ cups of water
- 1 cup salsa
- 2 bell peppers cut into thick strips
- 2 tsp chili powder
- 1 tsp ground cumin
- Salt to taste
- 5 tbsp. fresh oregano, chopped

Directions:
1. Warm the oil on sauté. Add in garlic, onion and jalapeño and cook for 5 minutes, until fragrant. Stir turkey into the pot; cook for 5-6 minutes until browned.
2. Add in salsa, tomatoes, bell peppers, and water. Season it with salt, cumin, and chili powder. Seal the lid, Press Soup, and cook for 10 minutes on High. Release the pressure quickly. Top with oregano and serve.

Nutrition: Calories; 325 Fat; 13g Carbs; 14g Protein ; 18g Sugars; 15g

390. Easy Italian Chicken Stew with Potatoes
Preparation Time: 10 minutes
Cooking Time: 10 minutes
Servings: 4
Ingredients:
- 2 lb. chicken wings
- 2 potatoes, peeled, cut into chunks
- 2 fire-roasted tomatoes, peeled, chopped
- 1 carrot, peeled, cut into chunks
- 2 garlic cloves, chopped
- 2 tbsp. olive oil
- 1 tsp smoked paprika, ground
- 4 cups chicken broth
- 2 tbsp. fresh parsley, chopped
- Salt and black pepper to taste
- 1 cup spinach, chopped

Directions:
1. Rub the chicken with salt, pepper, and paprika, and place in the pot. Add in all remaining ingredients and seal the lid. Cook on High Pressure for 8 minutes.
2. When ready, do a quickly release. Serve hot.

Nutrition: Calories; 123 Fat; 34g Carbs; 28g Protein ; 3g Sugars; 6g

391. Quick Swiss Chard & Chicken Stew
Preparation Time: 15 minutes
Cooking Time: 15 minutes
Servings: 4
Ingredients:
- 2 lb. chicken breasts, boneless, skinless, cut into pieces
- 2 lb. Swiss chard, chopped
- 2 cups chicken broth
- 2 tbsp. butter, unsalted
- 2 tbsp. olive oil

- Salt and black pepper to taste

Directions:
1. Add the chicken, oil and broth to the pot. Season with salt and black pepper, seal the lid and cook on Manual for 13 minutes on High. Does a quickly release, add Swiss chard and butter? Cook on Sauté for 5 minutes. Serve warm.

Nutrition: Calories; 209 Fat; 20g Carbs; 33g Protein ; 0.5g Sugars; 0.2g

392. Delicious Turkey Burgers

Preparation Time: 5 minutes
Cooking Time: 20 minutes
Servings: 4
Ingredients:
- 1 lb. ground turkey
- 2 eggs
- 1 cup flour
- 1 onion, finely chopped
- 2 tsp dried dill, chopped
- Salt and black pepper to taste
- 1 cup sour cream

Directions:
1. In a bowl, add all ingredients and mix well with hands. Form the patties with the previously prepared mixture. Line parchment paper over a baking dish and arrange the patties. Pour 1 cup of water in the pot.
2. Lay the trivet and place the baking dish on top. Seal the lid. Cook on Pressure Cook mode for 15 minutes on High. Release the pressure naturally, for 10 minutes. Serve with lettuce and tomatoes.

Nutrition: Calories; 506 Fat; 35g Carbs; 44g Protein ; 0.9g Sugars; 0.2g

393. Easy Primavera Chicken Stew

Preparation Time: 15 minutes
Cooking Time: 40 minutes
Servings: 4
Ingredients:
- 4 green onions, chopped
- 3 garlic cloves, peeled and crushed
- 3 new potatoes, peeled and chopped
- 8 baby carrots, chopped
- 4 oz. can tomato sauce
- 1 tsp salt
- 8 oz. chicken breast, cut into bite-sized pieces
- 2 cups chicken broth
- 2 tbsp. olive oil

Directions:
1. Place the veggies in the instant pot and pour enough water to cover. Seal the lid and cook on Manual/Pressure Cook for 15 minutes on High. Do a quickly release. Remove the vegetables along with the liquid.
2. Heat oil on Sauté and stir-fry the vegetables for 5 minutes. Add the remaining ingredients and seal the lid. Set on Poultry and cook for 15 minutes on High. Do a natural release, for 10 minutes and serve hot.

Nutrition: Calories; 178 Fat; 45g Carbs; 2.4g Protein ; 1g Sugars; 2g

394. Dijon Mustard Chicken Breast

Preparation Time: 15 minutes
Cooking Time: 20 minutes
Servings: 2
Ingredients:
- 1 lb. chicken breasts, boneless and skinless
- ¼ cup apple cider vinegar
- 1 tsp garlic powder
- 2 tbsp. Dijon mustard
- Salt and black pepper to taste
- 2 tbsp. olive oil
- 2 cups chicken stock

Directions:
1. Season the chicken with garlic, salt, and black pepper. Place in the instant pot and pour in the stock. Seal the lid and cook on Poultry mode for 20 minutes on High. Do a quickly release and remove the meat along with the stock.
2. In a bowl, mix olive oil, mustard, and apple cider vinegar. Pour into the pot and press Sauté. Place the chicken in this mixture and cook for 10 minutes, turning once. When done, remove from the pot and drizzle with the sauce.

Nutrition: Calories; 342 Fat; 17g Carbs; 43.4g Protein ; 8.4g Sugars; 5.4g

395. Bell Pepper & Chicken Stew

Preparation Time: 15 minutes
Cooking Time: 20 minutes
Servings: 4
Ingredients:
- 1 lb. chicken breasts, boneless, skinless, cut into pieces
- 2 potatoes, peeled, chopped
- 5 green bell peppers, chopped, seeds removed
- 2 carrots, chopped
- 2 ½ cups chicken broth
- 1 tomato, roughly chopped
- A handful of freshly chopped parsley
- 3 tbsp. extra virgin olive oil
- 1 tsp cayenne pepper
- 1 tsp salt

Directions:
1. Warm the oil on Sauté, and stir-fry bell peppers and carrots, for 3 minutes. Add potatoes, tomato, and parsley. Sprinkle with cayenne, and salt, and stir well.
2. Top with the chicken, pour in broth and seal the lid. Cook on High Pressure for 13 minutes. When ready, do a quick Pressure release, and serve hot.

Nutrition: Calories; 501 Fat; 17g Carbs; 12g Protein ; 1g Sugars; 3g

396. Weekend Turkey with Vegetables

Preparation Time: 20 minutes
Cooking Time: 25 minutes
Servings: 4

Ingredients:
- 1 lb. turkey breast, chopped
- 1 tsp red pepper flakes
- 2 cups canned tomatoes, diced
- 3 cups chicken broth
- 1 tsp honey
- 2 cups zucchini, cubed
- 3 garlic cloves, chopped
- 1 cup onions, finely chopped
- 2 tbsp. tomato paste
- 1 cup baby carrots, chopped
- Salt and black pepper to taste
- 2 tbsp. olive oil

Directions:
1. Mix all ingredients in your instant pot. Seal the lid and cook on Meat/Stew mode for 25 minutes on High Pressure. When ready, do a quickly release and open the lid. Serve immediately.

Nutrition: Calories; 404 Fat; 10g Carbs; 32.1g Protein ; 4g Sugars; 9g

397. Cranberry Turkey with Hazelnuts
Preparation Time: 15 minutes
Cooking Time: 25 minutes
Servings: 5
Ingredients:
- 1 lb. turkey breast, boneless, skinless, cut into thick slices
- 3 tbsp. butter, softened
- 2 cups fresh cranberries
- 1 cup toasted hazelnuts, chopped
- 1 cup red wine
- 1 tbsp. fresh rosemary, chopped
- 2 tbsp. olive oil
- 2 tbsp. orange zest
- Salt and black pepper to taste

Directions:
1. Rub the turkey with oil and sprinkle with orange zest, salt, pepper, and rosemary. Melt butter in pot, and brown turkey breast for 5-6 minutes, on Sauté mode. Pour in wine, cranberries and 1 cup of water. Seal the lid. Cook on High Pressure for 25 minutes. Do a quickly release. Serve with chopped hazelnuts.

Nutrition: Calories; 175 Fat; 15g Carbs; 44g Protein ; 2.8g Sugars; 7.5g

398. Pork Tenders with Bell Peppers
Preparation Time: 5 Minutes
Cooking Time: 15 Minutes
Servings: 4
Ingredients:
- 11 Oz. Pork Tenderloin
- 1 Bell Pepper, in thin strips
- 1 Red Onion, sliced
- Tsp. Provencal Herbs
- Black Pepper to taste
- 1 Tbsp. Olive Oil
- 1/2 Tbsp. Mustard
- Round Oven Dish

Directions:
1. Preheat the air fryer to 390 degrees.
2. In the oven dish, mix the bell pepper strips with the onion, herbs, and some salt and pepper to taste. Add half a tablespoon of olive oil to the mixture
3. Cut the pork tenderloin into four pieces and rub with salt, pepper and mustard. Thinly coat the pieces with remaining olive oil and place them upright in the oven dish on top of the pepper mixture
4. Place the bowl into the air fryer. Set the timer to 15 minutes and roast the meat and the vegetables
5. Turn the meat and mix the peppers halfway through.
6. Serve with a fresh salad.

Nutrition: Calories: 123 Fat 21g Protein 32g Sugar 5g

399. Dijon Garlic Pork Tenderloin
Preparation Time: 5 Minutes
Cooking Time: 10 Minutes
Servings: 6
Ingredients:
- 1cup breadcrumbs
- Pinch of cayenne pepper
- Crushed garlic cloves
- 2 tbsp. ground ginger
- 2 tbsp. Dijon mustard
- 2 tbsp. raw honey
- Tbsp. water
- 2 tsp. salt
- 1-pound pork tenderloin, sliced into 1-inch rounds

Directions:
1. With pepper and salt, season all sides of tenderloin.
2. Combine cayenne pepper, garlic, ginger, mustard, honey, and water until smooth.
3. Dip pork rounds into honey mixture and then into breadcrumbs, ensuring they all get coated well.
4. Place coated pork rounds into your air fryer.
5. Set temperature to 400°F, and set time to 10 minutes. Cook 10 minutes at 400 degrees. Flip and then cook an additional 5 minutes until golden in color.

Nutrition: Calories: 423 Fat 18g Protein 31g Sugar 3g

400. Pork Neck with Salad
Preparation Time: 10 Minutes
Cooking Time: 12 Minutes
Servings: 2
Ingredients:
For Pork:
- 1 tbsp. soy sauce
- 1 tbsp. fish sauce
- ½ tbsp. oyster sauce
- ½ pound pork neck

For Salad:
- 1 ripe tomato, sliced tickly
- 8-10 Thai shallots, sliced
- 1 scallion, chopped
- 1 bunch fresh basil leaves
- 1 bunch fresh cilantro leaves

For fish sauce
- 2 tbsp. olive oil
- 1 tsp apple cider vinegar
- 1 tbsp. palm sugar
- 2 bird eye chili

- 1 tbsp. garlic, minced

Directions:
1. For pork in a bowl, mix together all ingredients except pork.
2. Add pork neck and coat with marinade evenly. Refrigerate for about 2-3 hours.
3. Preheat the air fryer to 340 degrees F.
4. Place the pork neck onto a grill pan. Cook for about 12 minutes.
5. Meanwhile in a large salad bowl, mix together all salad ingredients.
6. In a bowl, add all dressing ingredients and beat till well combined.
7. Remove pork neck from Air fryer and cut into desired slices.
8. Place pork slices over salad.

Nutrition: Calories: 542 Fat 35g Protein 19g Sugar 2g

401. Cajun Pork Steaks
Preparation Time: 5 Minutes
Cooking Time: 20 Minutes
Servings: 6
Ingredients:
- 4-6 pork steaks
- BBQ sauce:
- Cajun seasoning
- 1 tbsp. vinegar
- 1 tsp. low-sodium soy sauce
- ½ cup brown Sugar
- ½ cup vegan ketchup

Directions:
1. Ensure your air fryer is preheated to 290 degrees.
2. Sprinkle pork steaks with Cajun seasoning.
3. Combine remaining ingredients and brush onto steaks. Add coated steaks to air fryer.
4. Set temperature to 290°F, and set time to 20 minutes. Cook 15-20 minutes till just browned.

Nutrition: Calories: 209 Fat 11g Protein 28g Sugar 2g

402. Wonton Taco Cups
Preparation Time: 5 Minutes
Cooking Time: 10 Minutes
Servings: 8
Ingredients:
- 1/2-pound ground pork, browned and drained
- 1/2-pound ground beef, browned and drained
- 1 envelope taco seasoning
- 1 (10-ounce) can tomatoes with chilies, diced and drained
- 1 bell pepper, seeded and chopped
- 32 wonton wrappers
- 1 cup Cheddar cheese, shredded

Directions:
1. Combine the pork, beef, taco seasoning, diced tomatoes, and bell pepper; mix well.
2. Line all the muffin cups with wonton wrappers. Sprit it with nonstick cooking oil. Divide the beef filling among wrappers; top with the shredded cheese.
3. Bake it at 370 degrees F for about 10 minutes or until heated through.

Nutrition: Calories 322 Fat 15g Protein 14g Sugar 3g

403. Cajun Sweet-Sour Grilled Pork
Preparation Time: 5 Minutes
Cooking Time: 12 Minutes
Servings: 3
Ingredients:
- ¼ cup brown Sugar
- 1/4 cup cider vinegar
- 1-lb pork loin, sliced into 1-inch cubes
- Tbsp. Cajun seasoning
- Tbsp. brown Sugar

Directions:
1. In a shallow dish, mix well pork loin, 3 tablespoons brown sugar, and Cajun seasoning. Toss well to coat. Marinate in the ref for 3 hours.
2. In a medium bowl mix well, brown sugar and vinegar for basting.
3. Thread pork pieces in skewers. Baste with sauce and place on skewer rack in air fryer.
4. For 12 minutes, cook it on 360°F. Halfway through cooking time, turnover skewers and baste with sauce. If needed, cook in batches.
5. Serve and enjoy.

Nutrition: Calories: 428 Fat 16.7g Protein 39g Sugar 2g

404. Chinese Braised Pork Belly
Preparation Time: 5 Minutes
Cooking Time: 20 Minutes
Servings: 8
Ingredients:
- 1 lb. Pork Belly, sliced
- 1 Tbsp. Oyster Sauce
- 1 Tbsp. Sugar
- Red Fermented Bean Curds
- 1 Tbsp. Red Fermented Bean Curd Paste
- 1 Tbsp. Cooking Wine
- 1/2 Tbsp. Soy Sauce
- 1 Tsp Sesame Oil
- 1 Cup All Purpose Flour

Directions:
1. Preheat the air fryer to 390 degrees.
2. In a small bowl, mix all ingredients together and rub the pork thoroughly with this mixture
3. Set aside to marinate for at least 30 minutes or preferably overnight for the flavors to permeate the meat
4. Coat each marinated pork belly slice in flour and place in the Chef man air fryer tray
5. Cook for 15 to 20 minutes until crispy and tender.

Nutrition: Calories 214 Fat 8g Protein 12g Sugar 7g

405. Air Fryer Sweet and Sour Pork
Preparation Time: 10 Minutes
Cooking Time: 12 Minutes
Servings: 6
Ingredients:
- Tbsp. olive oil
- 1/16 tsp. Chinese Five Spice
- ¼ tsp. pepper
- ½ tsp. sea salt
- 1 tsp. pure sesame oil
- Eggs
- 1 cup almond flour

- Pounds pork, sliced into chunks
- Sweet and Sour Sauce:
- ¼ tsp. sea salt
- ½ tsp. garlic powder
- 1 tbsp. low-sodium soy sauce
- ½ cup rice vinegar
- 1 tbsp. tomato paste
- 1/8 tsp. water
- ½ cup sweetener of choice

Directions:
1. To make the dipping sauce, whisk all sauce ingredients together over medium heat, stirring 5 minutes. Simmer uncovered 5 minutes' till thickened.
2. Meanwhile, combine almond flour, five spice, pepper, and salt.
3. In another bowl, mix eggs with sesame oil.
4. Dredge the pork in flour mixture and then in egg mixture. Shake any excess off before adding to air fryer basket.
5. Set temperature to 340°F, and set time to 12 minutes.
6. Serve with sweet and sour dipping sauce!

Nutrition: Calories: 371 Fat 17g Protein 27g Sugar 1g

406. Pork Loin with Potatoes

Preparation Time: 10 Minutes
Cooking Time: 25 Minutes
Servings: 2
Ingredients:
- Pounds pork loin
- 1 tsp fresh parsley, chopped
- 2 large red potatoes, chopped
- ½ tsp garlic powder
- ½ tsp red pepper flakes, crushed
- Salt and freshly ground black pepper, to taste

Directions:
1. In a large bowl, add all ingredients except glaze and toss to coat well. Preheat the Air fryer to 325 degrees F. Place the loin in the air fryer basket.
2. Arrange the potatoes around pork loin.
3. Cook for about 25 minutes.

Nutrition: Calories: 189 Fat 1g Protein 11g Sugar 8g

407. Fried Pork Scotch Egg

Preparation Time: 10 Minutes
Cooking Time: 25 Minutes
Servings: 2
Ingredients:
- Soft-boiled eggs, peeled
- 8 ounces of raw minced pork, or sausage outside the casings
- 2 tsp of ground rosemary
- 2 tsp of garlic powder
- Pinch of salt and pepper
- 2 raw eggs
- 1 cup of breadcrumbs (Panko, but other brands are fine, or home-made bread crumbs work too)

Directions:
1. Cover the basket of the air fryer with a lining of tin foil, leaving the edges uncovered to allow air to circulate through the basket. Preheat the air fryer to 350 degrees.
2. In a mixing bowl, combine the raw pork with the rosemary, garlic powder, salt and pepper. This will probably be easiest to do with your masher or bare hands (though make sure to wash thoroughly after handling raw meat!); combine until all the spices are evenly spread throughout the meat.
3. Divide the meat mixture into three equal portions in the mixing bowl, and form each into balls with your hands.
4. Lay a sheet of wrap on the countertop, and flatten one of the balls of meat on top of it, to form a wide, flat meat-circle.
5. Place one of the peeled soft-boiled eggs in the center of the meat-circle and then, using the ends of the plastic wrap, pull the meat-circle so that it is fully covering and surrounding the soft-boiled egg.
6. Tighten and shape the plastic wrap covering the meat so that if forms a ball, and make sure not to squeeze too hard lest you squish the soft-boiled egg at the center of the ball! Set aside.
7. Repeat steps 5-7 with the other two soft-boiled eggs and portions of meat-mixture.
8. In a separate mixing bowl, beat the two raw eggs until fluffy and until the yolks and whites are fully combined.
9. One by one, remove the plastic wrap and dunk the pork-covered balls into the raw egg, and then roll them in the bread crumbs, covering fully and generously.
10. Place each of the bread-crumb covered meat-wrapped balls onto the foil-lined surface of the air fryer. Three of them should fit nicely, without touching.
11. Set the air fryer timer to 25 minutes.
12. About halfway through the cooking time, shake the handle of the air-fryer vigorously, so that the scotch eggs inside roll around and ensure full coverage.
13. After 25 minutes, the air fryer will shut off and the scotch eggs should be perfect – the meat fully cooked the egg-yolks still runny on the inside, and the outsides crispy and golden-brown. Using tongs, place them on serving plates, slice in half, and enjoy

Nutrition: Calories: 560 Fat 5g Protein 24g Sugar 2g

MEAT

408. Spicy Pork Tenderloin with Broccoli
Preparation Time: 20 minutes
Cooking Time: 35 minutes
Servings: 4
Ingredients:
- 1 package (1½ pound) pork tenderloin, trimmed
- 1 tsp ground mustard
- ¼ tsp garlic powder
- 2 tbsp. brown sugar
- 1 tbsp. smoked paprika
- ¼ tsp cayenne pepper (optional)
- 1 tbsp. olive oil
- 4 cups broccoli, chop into florets
- 1 tbsp. olive oil
- Salt and black pepper, to taste

Directions:
1. In a bowl, put in the ground mustard, garlic powder, brown sugar, paprika, cayenne pepper, salt, and pepper, stir to mix well. Then reserve.
2. Place the pork tenderloin on a clean working surface. Rub the tenderloin with olive oil on both sides, and then dredge it in the mustard mixture to coat well. Let it sit for 5 minutes.
3. Gently arrange the tenderloin in the air fryer basket, and cook in the preheated instant pot at 400°F for 10 minutes or until cooked through. Flip the tenderloin when the lid indicates 'TURN FOOD' halfway through the cooking.
4. In the meantime, in a microwave-safe bowl, put in the broccoli and microwave on high for 3 minutes or until soft, then remove the broccoli from the microwave to a large dish, drizzle with olive oil and sprinkle with salt and pepper, toss to coat well. then reserve.
5. Remove the tenderloin from the basket to a clean working surface. Allow to cool for 10 minutes.
6. Meanwhile, transfer the broccoli to the air fryer basket and cook in the preheated instant pot at 400°F for 10 minutes. Give the basket a shake when the lid indicates 'TURN FOOD' halfway through the cooking.
7. Remove the cooked broccoli from the basket to a large dish. Slice the cooled tenderloin and serve with broccoli.

Nutrition: Calories: 270, Total Fat 11.1 g, Cholesterol: 74 mg, Sodium: 710 mg, Carbohydrates: 14 g, Protein 29.5 g

409. Mexican Hot Meatloaf
Preparation Time: 15 minutes
Cooking Time: 35minutes
Servings: 4
Ingredients:
- ½ pound ground veal
- ½ pound ground pork
- 2 tsp gluten-free chipotle sauce
- ¼ cup cilantro, chopped
- ¼ cup gluten-free bread crumbs
- 1 large egg, beaten
- 2 medium spring onions, diced
- Sriracha salt and ground black pepper, to taste
- ½ cup ketchup
- 1 tsp blackstrap molasses
- 1 tsp olive oil
- Cooking spray

Directions:
1. In a bowl, mix the chipotle chili sauce, ketchup, molasses, and olive oil. Reserve it under room temperature.
2. Combine the veal and pork in a clean working surface.
3. Make a well in the middle of the meat mixture, and then put in the cilantro, bread crumbs, beaten egg, spring onion, sriracha salt, and black pepper. Combine all of them well with your hands.
4. Shape the mixture into a loaf. Grease your hands with cooking spray to avoid a sticky situation. Arrange the meatloaf in a 6×6×2-inch baking pan.
5. Arrange the baking pan in the air fryer basket. Put the air fryer lid on and cook in the preheated instant pot at 400°f for 25 minutes.
6. Remove the baking pan from the basket and pour the ketchup mixture on top of the meatloaf to cover generously.
7. Arrange the baking pan back to basket and bake for another 7 minutes or until an instant-read thermometer register at least 160°f.
8. Let the meatloaf stand in the basket for 5 minutes, then remove the meatloaf from the basket and cool for 5 minutes. Slice to serve.

Nutrition: Calories: 272 Fat 14.4 g Cholesterol 123 mgSodium 536 mgCarbohydrates 13.3g Protein 22.1g

410. Garlicky Pork Belly with New Potatoes
Preparation Time: 10 minutes
Cooking Time: 30minutes
Servings: 4
Ingredients:
- 1 ½ pounds pork belly, cut into 4 pieces, rinsed and drained
- 1 pound new potatoes, peeled, scrubbed, and halved
- 1/2 tsp turmeric powder
- 1 tsp smoked paprika
- 2 tbsp. oyster sauce
- 2 tbsp. green onions, chopped
- 4 garlic cloves, sliced
- Kosher salt and black pepper, to taste
- Cooking spray

Directions:
1. Lay the pork belly on a cutting board; sprinkle with turmeric powder, smoked paprika, salt, and pepper to season. Let sit it for 10 minutes.

2. Generously top the pork belly with oyster sauce. Arrange the belly in the air fryer basket, and then sprit the belly with cooking spray on both sides.
3. Put the air fryer lid on and cook in preheated instant pot at 380°F for 20 minutes. Flip the belly when it shows 'TURN FOOD' on the lid screen halfway through the cooking.
4. Remove the belly from the basket, and reserve. Put the new potatoes, green onions and sliced garlic in the basket.
5. Put the lid on and cook at 380°F for 15 minutes or until the new potatoes are brown and crispy on the edges and cooked through in the center. Shake the basket periodically.
6. Remove them from the basket and serve with pork belly in a large dish.
Nutrition: Calories: 546 Fat 30.3g Carbs: 20.7g Protein 45.2g Sugars: 1.3g

411. Spanish Pork Kabobs (Pinchos Moreno's)
Preparation Time: 35 minutes
Cooking Time: 2 hours
Servings: 4
Ingredients:
- 2 pounds' center cut pork loin chop, cut into bite-sized pieces
- 1/4 cup dry red wine
- 1/2 tsp ground turmeric
- 1/2 tsp ground coriander
- 1 tsp oregano
- 1 tsp ground cumin
- 2 garlic cloves, minced
- 2 tsp sweet Spanish paprika
- 2 tbsp. extra virgin olive oil
- Sea salt and freshly ground black pepper, to taste
- 1 lemon, 1/2 juiced 1/2 wedges
- 4 skewers soak for 30 minutes

Directions:
1. Place the pork loin chops in a large bowl; pour the red wine on top; sprinkle with turmeric, coriander, oregano, cumin, minced garlic, Spanish paprika, salt, and pepper, toss to coat evenly, then drizzle with olive oil. Wrap the bowl with plastic and refrigerate to marinate for 2 hours.
2. To make the kabobs, run the skewers through each marinated loin chop lengthwise, and then arrange them in the air fryer basket.
3. Put the air fryer lid on and cook in batches in the preheated instant pot at 360°F for 15 to 17 minutes. Shake the basket at least three times during the cooking.
4. Remove the kabobs from the basket to a serving dish, top with lemon juice, and garnished with lemon wedges to serve.
Nutrition: Calories: 433 Fat 24g Carbs: 3.5g Protein 49.5g Sugars: 0.5g

412. Simple Greek Pork Sirloin with Tzatziki
Preparation Time: 5 minutes
Cooking Time: 20 minutes
Servings: 4
Ingredients:
- Greek Pork:
- 2 pounds' pork sirloin roast
- 1/2 tsp celery seeds
- 1/2 tsp mustard seeds
- 1/2 tsp ground ginger
- 1 tsp fennel seeds
- 1 tsp smoked paprika
- 1 tsp turmeric powder
- 1 tsp ancho chili powder
- 2 cloves garlic, finely chopped
- Salt and black pepper, to taste
- 2 tablespoons olive oil
- Tzatziki:
- 1/2 cucumber, finely chopped and squeezed
- 1 garlic clove, minced
- 1 cup full-Fat Greek yogurt
- 1 tsp fresh dill, minced
- 1 tsp balsamic vinegar
- 1 tbsp. extra-virgin olive oil
- Salt, to taste

Directions:
1. In a large bowl, mix the celery seeds, mustard seeds, ground ginger, fennel seeds, paprika, turmeric powder, Ancho chili powder, chopped garlic, salt, and pepper. Toss the sirloin in the mixture to coat well, and then drizzle the olive oil on both sides of the sirloin.
2. Arrange the sirloin in the air fryer basket. Place the air fryer lid on and cook in the preheated instant pot at 360°F for 20 minutes. Flip the sirloin when it shows 'TURN FOOD' on the lid screen during the cooking.
3. In the meantime, combine all the tzatziki ingredients in a separate bowl. Leave the tzatziki in the fridge to marinate until ready to serve.
4. Remove the sirloin from the basket to a large serving dish. Slice to serve, with tzatziki on the side.
Nutrition: Calories: 561, Fat 30.2g, Carbs: 4.6g, Protein 64.5g, Sugars: 1.8g

413. Beef Sausage and Veggie Sandwiches
Preparation Time: 5 minutes
Cooking Time: 30minutes
Servings: 4
Ingredients:
- 4 hot dog buns, halved
- 4 beef sausages
- 4 bell peppers, deseeded and cut into 1-inch pieces
- 1 onion, chopped
- 2 medium-sized tomatoes cut into slices
- 2 tbsp. canola oil
- 1 tbsp. mustard

Directions:
1. Arrange the bell peppers in the air fryer basket. Brush them with 1 tablespoon of canola oil on

both sides. Put the air fryer lid on and cook in preheated instant pot at 380°F for 5 minutes.

2. Afterwards, give the basket a toss, and put the onion and tomatoes in the basket and cook at 350°F for 5 minutes more or until the onions are translucent and peppers are wilted. Remove them from the basket and set aside. Place the beef sausages in the basket. Brush the remaining 1 tablespoon of canola oil all over the sausages.

3. Place the lid on and cook at 380°F for 15 minutes. Turn the sausages over when it shows 'TURN FOOD' on the lid screen halfway through the cooking.

4. Remove the sausages from the basket to a clean working surface. Assemble each sausage into the hot dog buns. Spread the cooked vegetables and mustard on the top of the buns. Serve warm.

Nutrition: Calories: 626 Fat 41.8g Carbs: 41.4g Protein 22.3g Sugars: 9.4g

414. Cheese and Sausage Pepper Pocket

Preparation Time: 20 minutes
Cooking Time: 1 hour
Servings: 12
Ingredients:
- 8 ounces' bulk Italian sausage
- 1 (16 ounce) package miniature multi-colored sweet peppers
- 1 (8 ounce) package cream cheese, softened
- 1/2 cup shredded Cheddar cheese
- 2 tbsp. crumbled blue cheese (optional)
- 2 tbsp. olive oil, divided
- 1 tbsp. finely chopped fresh chives
- 1 clove garlic, minced
- 1/4 tsp ground black pepper
- 2 tbsp. panko bread crumbs

Directions:
1. Stir fry sausage in the hot pan over medium heat for five to seven minutes or until browned and golden on edges. Set aside. Cut a slit on each sweet pepper lengthwise to create a pocket. Brush the peppers' skin with 1 tablespoon olive oil and arrange the in the basket.

2. Put the air fry lid on and cook in the preheated instant pot at 356ºF for 3 minutes. Flip the batter when it shows 'TURN FOOD' on the lid screen halfway through the cooking or until soft and brown for 3 minutes. Remove the peppers to a platter and let it cool down.

3. Meanwhile, in a bowl, stir in sausage, Cheddar cheese, cream cheese, blue cheese, garlic, chives, and black pepper and combine well. In a medium bowl, add the remaining 1 tablespoon olive oil with bread crumbs and mix well.

4. Use a spoon to stuff the cheese mixture into each pepper pocket and top with the bread crumb mixture. Place the stuffed pepper pockets in the basket and put the air fry lid on. Air fry about 4 to 5 minutes, until filling is cooked and the bread crumbs are crispy.

Nutrition: Calories 101 Fat 8.6g Carbohydrates 2.6g Protein ; 3.6g Cholesterol 20mg Sodium 159mg

415. Sizzling Beef Steak Fajitas

Preparation Time: 5 minutes
Cooking Time: 20 minutes
Servings: 4
Ingredients:
- 1-pound beef steak, cut into strips
- 1 red bell pepper, cut into strips
- 1 green bell pepper, cut into strips
- 2 tablespoons taco or fajita seasoning
- ½ red onions cut into strips
- 2 tbsp. extra-virgin olive oil
- Salt and pepper to taste
- Cooking spray

Directions:
1. In a large bowl, mix together the beef steak, bell peppers, taco seasoning, onion, olive oil, salt and pepper. Toss well to coat the beef evenly.

2. Arrange the beef mixture in the air fryer basket and sprits with cooking spray.

3. Put the air fryer lid on and cook the beef in the preheated instant pot at 380°F for 5 minutes. Flip the beef once when it shows 'TURN FOOD' on the air fryer lid screen during cooking time. Cook for an additional 4 to 5 minutes.

4. Transfer the cooked beef mixture to a platter. Serve with the parsley, if desired.

Nutrition: Calories: 491 Total Fat 16g Saturated Fat 4g Cholesterol: 50mg Sodium: 389mg Carbohydrates: 52g Fiber 4g Protein 33g

416. Pork Belly

Preparation Time: 20 minutes
Cooking Time: 40 minutes
Servings: 4
Ingredients:
- 1-pound pork belly, pastured
- 6 cloves of garlic, peeled
- 1 tsp ground black pepper
- 1 tsp salt
- 2 tbsp. soy sauce
- 2 bay leaves
- 3 cups of water

Directions:
1. Cut the pork belly evenly into three pieces, place them in an instant pot, and add remaining ingredients.

2. Switch on the instant pot, then shut it with lid and cook the pork belly for 15 minutes at high pressure.

3. When done, let the pressure release naturally for 10 minutes and then do quick pressure release.

4. Rake out the pork by tongs and let it drain and dry for 10 minutes.

5. Then switch on the air fryer, insert fryer basket, grease it with olive oil, then shut with its lid, set the fryer at 400 degrees F and preheat for 5 minutes.

6. While the air fryer preheats, cut each piece of the pork into two long slices.

7. Open the fryer, add pork slices in it, close with its lid and cook for 15 minutes until nicely golden and crispy, flipping the pork halfway through the frying.
8. When air fryer beeps, open its lid, transfer pork slices onto a serving plate and serve.

Nutrition: Calories: 594 Carbs: 2g Fat 60g Protein 11g Fiber 0g

417. Sirloin Steak

Preparation Time: 5 minutes
Cooking Time: 15 minutes
Servings: 6
Ingredients:
- 2 sirloin steaks, grass-fed
- 1 tbsp. olive oil
- 2 tbsp. steak seasoning

Directions:
1. Switch on the air fryer, insert fryer basket, grease it with olive oil, then shut with its lid, set the fryer at 392 degrees F and preheat for 5 minutes.
2. Meanwhile, pat dries the steaks, then brush with oil and then season well with steak seasoning until coated on both sides.
3. Open the fryer, add steaks in it, close with its lid and cook for 10 minutes until nicely golden and crispy, flipping the steaks halfway through the frying.
4. When air fryer beeps, open its lid, transfer steaks onto a serving plate and serve.

Nutrition: Calories: 253.6 Carbs: 0.2g Fat 18.1g Protein 21.1g Fiber 0.1g

418. Vietnamese Grilled Pork

Preparation Time: 1 hour and 5 minutes
Cooking Time: 15 minutes
Servings: 6
Ingredients:
- 1-pound sliced pork shoulder, pastured, Fat trimmed
- 2 tbsp. chopped parsley
- 1/4 cup crushed roasted peanuts
- For the Marinade:
- 1/4 cup minced white onions
- 1 tbsp. minced garlic
- 1 tbsp. lemongrass paste
- 1 tbsp. erythritol sweetener
- 1/2 tsp ground black pepper
- 1 tbsp. fish sauce
- 2 tsp soy sauce
- 2 tbsp. olive oil

Directions:
1. Place all the ingredients for the marinade in a bowl, stir well until combined and add it into a large plastic bag.
2. Cut the pork into ½-inch slices, cut each slice into 1-inches pieces, then add them into the plastic bag containing marinade, seal the bag, turn it upside down to coat the pork pieces with the marinade and marinate for a minimum of 1 hour.
3. Then switch on the air fryer, insert fryer basket, grease it with olive oil, then shut with its lid, set the fryer at 400 degrees F and preheat for 5 minutes.
4. Open the fryer, add marinated pork in it in a single layer, close with its lid and cook for 10 minutes until nicely golden and cooked, flipping the pork halfway through the frying.
5. When air fryer beeps, open its lid, transfer pork onto a serving plate, and keep warm.
6. Air fryer the remaining pork pieces in the same manner and then serve.

Nutrition: Calories: 231 Carbs: 4g Fat 16g Protein 16g Fiber 1g

419. Meatloaf

Preparation Time: 5 minutes
Cooking Time: 20 minutes
Servings: 4
Ingredients:
- 1-pound ground beef, grass-fed
- 1 tbsp. minced garlic
- 1 cup white onion, peeled and diced
- 1 tbsp. minced ginger
- 1/4 cup chopped cilantro
- 2 tsp garam masala
- 1 tsp cayenne pepper
- 1 tsp salt
- 1/2 tsp ground cinnamon
- 1 tsp turmeric powder
- 1/8 tsp ground cardamom
- 2 eggs, pastured

Directions:
1. Switch on the air fryer, insert fryer basket, then shut with its lid, set the fryer at 360 degrees F and preheat for 5 minutes.
2. Meanwhile, place all the ingredients in a bowl, stir until well mixed, then take an 8-inches round pan, grease it with oil, add the beef mixture in it and spread it evenly.
3. Open the fryer, place the pan in it, close with its lid and cook for 15 minutes until the top is nicely golden and meatloaf is thoroughly cooked.
4. When air fryer beeps, open its lid, take out the pan, then drain the excess Fat and take out the meatloaf. Cut the meatloaf into four pieces and serve.

Nutrition: Calories: 260 Carbs: 6g Fat 16g Protein 26g Fiber 1g

420. Herbed Lamb Chops

Preparation Time: 1 hour and 10 minutes
Cooking Time: 13 minutes
Servings: 6
Ingredients:
- 1-pound lamb chops, pastured
- For the Marinate:
- 2 tbsp. lemon juice
- 1 tsp dried rosemary
- 1 tsp salt
- 1 tsp dried thyme
- 1 tsp coriander

- 1 tsp dried oregano
- 2 tbsp. olive oil

Directions:
1. Prepare the marinade and for this, place all its ingredients in a bowl and whisk until combined.
2. Pour the marinade in a large plastic bag, add lamb chops in it, seal the bag, then turn it upside down to coat lamb chops with the marinade and let it marinate in the refrigerator for a minimum of 1 hour.
3. Then switch on the air fryer, insert fryer basket, grease it with olive oil, then shut with its lid, set the fryer at 390 degrees F and preheat for 5 minutes.
4. Meanwhile,
5. Open the fryer, add marinated lamb chops in it, close with its lid and cook for 8 minutes until nicely golden and cooked, turning the lamb chops halfway through the frying.
6. When air fryer beeps, open its lid, transfer lamb chops onto a serving plate and serve.

Nutrition: Calories: 177.4 Carbs: 1.7g Fat 8gProtein 23.4g Fiber 0.5g

421. Spicy Lamb Sirloin Steak

Preparation Time: 40 minutes
Cooking Time: 20 minutes
Servings: 4
Ingredients:

- 1-pound lamb sirloin steaks, pastured, boneless
- For the Marinade:
- ½ of white onion, peeled
- 1 teaspoon ground fennel
- 5 cloves of garlic, peeled
- 4 slices of ginger
- 1 tsp salt
- 1/2 tsp ground cardamom
- 1 tsp garam masala
- 1 tsp ground cinnamon
- 1 tsp cayenne pepper

Directions:
1. Place all the ingredients for the marinade in a food processor and then pulse until well blended.
2. Make cuts in the lamb chops by using a knife, then place them in a large bowl and add prepared marinade in it.
3. Mix well until lamb chops are coated with the marinade and let them marinate in the refrigerator for a minimum of 30 minutes.
4. Then switch on the air fryer, insert fryer basket, grease it with olive oil, then shut with its lid, set the fryer at 330 degrees F and preheat for 5 minutes.
5. Open the fryer; add lamb chops in it, close with its lid and cook for 15 minutes until nicely golden and cooked, flipping the steaks halfway through the frying.
6. When air fryer beeps, open its lid, transfer lamb steaks onto a serving plate and serve.

Nutrition: Calories: 182 Carbs: 3gFat 7gProtein 24g Fiber 1g

422. Pork Chops

Preparation Time: 5 minutes
Cooking Time: 15 minutes
Servings: 5
Ingredients:

- 4 slices of almond bread
- 5 pork chops, bone-in, pastured
- 3.5 ounces' coconut flour
- 1 tsp salt
- 3 tbsp. parsley
- ½ tsp ground black pepper
- 1 tbsp. pork seasoning
- 2 tbsp. olive oil
- 1/3 cup apple juice, unsweetened
- 1 egg, pastured

Directions:
1. Switch on the air fryer, insert fryer basket, grease it with olive oil, then shut with its lid, set the fryer at 350 degrees F and preheat for 5 minutes.
2. Meanwhile, place bread slices in a food processor and pulse until mixture resembles crumbs.
3. Tip the bread crumbs in a shallow dish, add parsley, ½ teaspoon salt, ¼ teaspoon ground black pepper and stir until mixed.
4. Place flour in another shallow dish, add remaining salt and black pepper, along with pork seasoning and stir until mixed.
5. Crack the egg in a bowl, pour in apple juice and whisk until combined.
6. Working on one pork chop at a time, first coat it into the flour mixture, then dip into egg and then evenly coat with breadcrumbs mixture.
7. Open the fryer; add coated pork chops in it in a single layer, close with its lid and cook for 10 minutes until nicely golden and cooked, flipping the pork chops halfway through the frying.
8. When air fryer beeps, open its lid, transfer pork chops onto a serving plate and serve.

Nutrition: Calories: 441 Carbs: 28.6g Fat 22.3g Protein 30.6g Fiber 0.6g

423. Steak

Preparation Time: 10 minutes
Cooking Time: 18 minutes
Servings: 2
Ingredients:

- 2 steaks, grass-fed, each about 6 ounces and ¾ inch thick
- 1 tbsp. butter, unsalted
- ¾ tsp ground black pepper
- 1/2 tsp garlic powder
- ¾ tsp salt
- 1 tsp olive oil

Directions:
1. Switch on the air fryer, insert fryer basket, grease it with olive oil, then shut with its lid, set the fryer at 400 degrees F and preheat for 5 minutes. Meanwhile, coat the steaks with oil and then season with black pepper, garlic, and salt.

2. Open the fryer, add steaks in it, close with its lid and cook 10 to 18 minutes at until nicely golden and steaks are cooked to desired doneness, flipping the steaks halfway through the frying. When air fryer beeps, open its lid and transfer steaks to a cutting board.

3. Take two large pieces of aluminum foil, place a steak on each piece, top steak with ½ tablespoon butter, then cover with foil and let it rest for 5 minutes. Serve straight away.

Nutrition: Calories: 82 Carbs: 0g Fat 5g Protein 8.7g Fiber 0g

424. Meatloaf Slider Wraps

Preparation Time: 15 minutes
Cooking Time: 10 minutes
Servings: 6
Ingredients:
- 1-pound ground beef, grass-fed
- ½ cup almond flour
- ¼ cup coconut flour
- ½ tbsp. minced garlic
- ¼ cup chopped white onion
- 1 tsp Italian seasoning
- ½ tsp sea salt
- ½ tsp dried tarragon
- ½ tsp ground black pepper
- 1 tbsp. Worcestershire sauce
- ¼ cup ketchup
- 2 eggs, pastured, beaten

Directions:
1. Place all the ingredients in a bowl, stir well, then shape the mixture into 2-inch diameter and 1-inch thick patties and refrigerate them for 10 minutes. Meanwhile, switch on the air fryer, insert fryer basket, grease it with olive oil, then shut with its lid, set the fryer at 360 degrees F and preheat for 10 minutes. Open the fryer, add patties in it in a single layer, close with its lid and cook for 10 minutes until nicely golden and cooked, flipping the patties halfway through the frying.

2. When air fryer beeps, open its lid and transfer patties to a plate. Wrap each patty in lettuce and serve.

Nutrition: Calories: 228 Carbs: 6g Fat 16g Protein 13g Fiber 2g

425. Homemade Beef Liver Soufflé

Preparation Time: 10 minutes
Cooking Time: 30 minutes
Servings: 4
Ingredients:
- ½ lb. of beef liver
- 3 eggs
- 3 oz. buns
- 1 cup warm milk
- Salt and black pepper to taste

Directions:
1. Cut the liver in slices and put it in the fridge for 15 minutes.
2. Divide the buns into pieces and soak them in milk for 10 minutes. Put the liver in a blender, and add the yolks, the bread mixture, and the spices. Grind the components and stuff in the ramekins. Line the ramekins in the Air Fryer's basket; cook for 20 minutes at 350 F.

Nutrition: Calories: 400 Fat 15g Protein 23g Sugar 26g

426. Rib Eye Steak with Avocado Sauce

Preparation Time: 15 minutes
Cooking Time: 25 minutes
Servings: 4
Ingredients:
- 1 ½ lb. rib eye steak
- 2 tsp olive oil
- 1 tbsp. chipotle chili pepper
- Salt and black pepper to taste
- 1 avocado, diced
- Juice from ½ limes

Directions:
1. Place the steak on a chopping board. Pour the olive oil over and sprinkle with the chipotle pepper, salt, and black pepper. Use your hands to rub the spices on the meat. Leave it to sit and marinate for 10 minutes.
2. Preheat the Air Fryer to 400 F.
3. Pull out the fryer basket and place the meat inside. Slide it back into the Air Fryer and cook for 14 minutes. Turn the steak and continue cooking for 6 minutes. Remove the steak, cover with foil, and let it sit for 5 minutes before slicing.
4. Meanwhile, prepare the avocado salsa by mashing the avocado with potato mash. Add in the lime juice and mix until smooth. Taste, adjust the seasoning, slice and serve with salsa.

Nutrition: Calories: 328 Fat 19g Protein 28g Sugar 20g

427. Hot Flank Steaks with Roasted Peanuts

Preparation Time: 5 minutes
Cooking Time: 10 minutes
Servings: 3 to 4
Ingredients:
- 2 lb. flank steaks, cut in long strips
- 2 tbsp. fish sauce
- 2 tbsp. soy sauce
- 2 tbsp. sugar
- 2 tbsp. ground garlic
- 2 tbsp. ground ginger
- 2 tsp hot sauce
- 1 cup chopped cilantro, divided into two
- ½ cup roasted peanuts, chopped

Directions:
1. Preheat the Air Fryer to 400 F. In a zipper bag, add the beef, fish sauce, swerve sweetener, garlic, soy sauce, ginger, half of the cilantro, and hot sauce. Zip the bag and massage the **Ingredients:** with your hands to mix well.
2. Open the bag, remove the beef, shake off the excess marinade and place the beef strips in the fryer basket in a single layer; avoid overlapping. Close the Air Fryer and cook for 5 minutes. Turn the beef and cook further for 5 minutes. Dish the cooked meat in a serving platter, garnish with the peanuts and the remaining cilantro.

Nutrition: Calories: 602 Fat 32g Protein 40g Sugar 20g

428. Authentic Wiener Beef Schnitzel
Preparation Time: 5 minutes
Cooking Time: 10 minutes
Servings: 4
Ingredients:
- 4 beef schnitzel cutlets
- ½ cup flour
- 2 eggs, beaten
- Salt and black pepper
- 1 cup breadcrumbs

Directions:
1. Coat the cutlets in flour and shake off any excess. Dip the coated cutlets into the beaten egg. Sprinkle with salt and black pepper. Then dip into the crumbs and to coat well. Spray them generously with oil and cook for 10 minutes at 360 F, turning once halfway through.

Nutrition: Calories: 432 Fat 2g Protein 22g Sugar 17g

429. Dreamy Beef Steak with Rice, Broccoli and Green Beans
Preparation Time: 10 minutes
Cooking Time: 30 minutes
Servings: 2
Ingredients:
- Beef:
- 1 lb. beef steak,
- Salt and black pepper to taste to season
- Fried Rice:
- 2 ½ cups rice
- 1 ½ tbsp. soy sauce
- 2 tsp sesame oil
- 2 tsp minced ginger
- 2 tsp vinegar
- 1 clove garlic, minced
- ¼ cup chopped broccoli
- ¼ cup green beans

Directions:
1. Put the beef on a chopping board and use a knife to cut it in 2-inch strips. Add the beef to a bowl, sprinkle with pepper and salt, and mix it with a spoon. Let it sit for 10 minutes. Preheat the Air Fryer to 400 F. Add the beef to the fryer basket, and cook for 5 minutes. Turn the beef strips with kitchen tongs and cook further for 3 minutes.
2. Once ready, remove the beef to a safe-oven dish that fits in the fryer's basket. Add the rice, broccoli, green beans, garlic, ginger, sesame oil, vinegar and soy sauce. Mix evenly using a spoon.
3. Place the dish in the fryer basket, close, and cook at 370 F for 10 minutes. Open the Air Fryer, mix the rice well, and cook for 4 minutes; season with salt and pepper. Dish the rice into serving bowls and serve with hot sauce.

Nutrition: Calories: 132 Fat 5g Protein 19g Sugar 16g

430. Mustard Pork Chops with Lemon Zest
Preparation Time: 5 minutes
Cooking Time: 20 minutes
Servings: 3
Ingredients:
- 3 lean pork chops
- Salt and black pepper to taste to season
- 2 eggs, cracked into a bowl
- 1 tbsp. water
- 1 cup breadcrumbs
- ½ tsp garlic powder
- 3 tsp paprika
- 1 ½ tsp of oregano
- ½ tsp cayenne pepper
- ¼ tsp dry mustard
- 1 lemon, zest

Directions:
1. Put the pork chops on a chopping board and use a knife to trim off any excess Fat. Add the water to the eggs and whisk; set aside. In another bowl, add the breadcrumbs, salt, pepper, garlic powder, paprika, oregano, cayenne pepper, lemon zest, and dry mustard. Use a fork to mix evenly.
2. Preheat the Air Fryer to 380 F and grease the basket with cooking spray. In the egg mixture, dip each pork chop and then in the breadcrumb mixture. Place the breaded chops in the fryer. Don't spray with cooking spray. The Fat in the chops will be enough oil to cook them. Close the Air Fryer and cook for 12 minutes.
3. Flip to other side and cook for another 5 minutes.
4. Once ready, place the chops on a chopping board to rest for 3 minutes before slicing and serving. Serve with a side of vegetable fries.

Nutrition: Calories: 308 Fat 13.4g Protein 45g Sugar 6.4g

431. Herbed Beef Roast
Preparation Time: 10 minutes
Cooking Time: 50 minutes
Servings: 2
Ingredients:
- 2 tsp olive oil
- 1 lb. beef Roast
- ½ tsp dried rosemary
- ½ tsp dried thyme
- ½ tsp dried oregano
- Salt and black pepper to taste

Directions:
1. Preheat the Air Fryer to 400 F. Drizzle oil over the beef, and sprinkle with salt, pepper, and herbs. Rub onto the meat with hands. Cook for 45 minutes for medium-rare and 50 minutes for well-done.
2. Check halfway through, and flip to ensure they cook evenly. Wrap the beef in foil for 10 minutes after cooking to allow the juices to reabsorb into the meat. Slice the beef and serve with a side of steamed asparagus.

Nutrition: Calories: 321 Fat 12g Protein 49g Sugar 5g

432. Roast Pork Belly with Cumin
Preparation Time: 30 minutes

Cooking Time: 1 hour 20 minutes
Servings: 8
Ingredients:
- 1 ½ lb. pork belly
- 1 ½ tsp garlic powder
- 1 ½ tsp coriander powder
- ⅓ tsp salt
- 1 ½ tsp black pepper
- 1 ½ dried thyme
- 1 ½ tsp of dried oregano
- 1 ½ tsp cumin powder
- 3 cups water
- 1 lemon, halved

Directions:
1. Leave the pork to air fry for 3 hours. In a small bowl, add the garlic powder, coriander powder, ½ tsp of salt, black pepper, thyme, oregano, and cumin powder. After the pork is well dried, poke holes all around it using a fork. Smear the oregano rub thoroughly on all sides with your hands and squeeze the lemon juice all over it.
2. Leave to sit for 5 minutes. Put the pork in the center of the fryer basket and cook for 30 minutes. Turn the pork with the help of two spatulas, increase the temperature to 350 F and continue cooking for 25 minutes. Once ready, remove it and place it in on a chopping board to sit for 4 minutes before slicing. Serve the pork slices with a side of sautéed asparagus and hot sauce.

Nutrition: Calories: 321 Fat 11g Protein 30g Sugar 9g

433. Ginger Rack Rib Steak
Preparation Time: 5 minutes
Cooking Time: 35 minutes
Servings: 2
Ingredients:
- 1 rack rib steak
- Salt to season
- 1 tsp white pepper
- 1 tsp garlic powder
- ½ tsp red pepper flakes
- 1 tsp ginger powder
- 1 cup hot sauce

Directions:
1. Preheat the Air Fryer to 360 F. Place the rib rack on a flat surface and pat dry using a paper towel. Season the ribs with salt, garlic, ginger, white pepper, and red pepper flakes.
2. Place the ribs in the fryer's basket and cook for 15 minutes. Turn the ribs with kitchen tongs and cook further for 15 minutes. Remove the ribs onto a chopping board and let sit for 3 minutes before slicing. Plate and drizzle hot sauce over and serve.

Nutrition: Calories: 222 Fat 11g Protein 34g Sugar 11g

434. Sunday Night Garlic Beef Schnitzel
Preparation Time: 10 minutes
Cooking Time: 12 minutes
Servings: 1
Ingredients:
- 2 tbsp. olive oil
- 1 thin beef cutlet
- 1 egg, beaten
- 2 oz. breadcrumbs
- 1 tsp paprika
- ¼ tsp garlic powder
- Salt and black pepper to taste

Directions:
1. Preheat the air fryer to 350 F. Combine olive oil, breadcrumbs, paprika, garlic powder, and salt, in a bowl. Dip the beef in with the egg first, and then coat it with the breadcrumb mixture completely. Line a baking dish with parchment paper and place the breaded meat on it. Cook for 12 minutes. Serve and enjoy.

Nutrition: Calories: 134 Fat 19g Protein 20g Sugar 4g

435. Meatballs with Parsley and Thyme
Preparation Time: 10 minutes
Cooking Time: 25 minutes
Servings: 6
Ingredients:
- 1 small onion, chopped
- ¾ pound grounded beef
- 1 tbsp. fresh parsley, chopped
- ½ tbsp. fresh thyme leaves, chopped
- 1 whole egg, beaten
- 3 tbsp. breadcrumbs
- Salt and black pepper to taste
- Tomato sauce for coating

Directions:
1. Preheat your Air Fryer to 390 F. In a mixing bowl, mix all the **Ingredients:** except tomato sauce. Roll the mixture into 10-12 balls. Place the balls in your air fryer's cooking basket, and cook for 8 minutes. Add tomato sauce to the balls to coat and cook for 5 minutes at 300 F. Gently stir and enjoy!

Nutrition: Calories: 155 Fat 14g Protein 25g Sugar 16g

436. Garlic Lamb Chops with Thyme
Preparation Time: 8 minutes
Cooking Time: 22 minutes
Servings: 4
Ingredients:
- 4 lamb chops
- 1 garlic clove, peeled
- 1 tbsp. plus
- 2 tsp olive oil
- ½ tbsp. oregano
- ½ tbsp. thyme
- ½ tsp salt
- ¼ tsp black pepper

Directions:
1. Preheat the air fryer to 390 F. Coat the garlic clove with 1 tsp. of olive oil and place it in the air fryer for 10 minutes. Meanwhile, mix the herbs and seasonings with the remaining olive oil.
2. Using a towel or a mitten, squeeze the hot roasted garlic clove into the herb mixture and stir to

combine. Coat the lamb chops with the mixture well, and place in the air fryer. Cook for 8 to 12 minutes.
Nutrition: Calories: 402 Fat 12g Protein 35g Sugar 13g

437. Bacon-Wrapped Stuffed Pork Tenderloin
Preparation Time: 20 minutes
Cooking Time: 20 minutes
Servings: 4
Ingredients:
- 16 bacon slices
- 16 oz. pork tenderloin
- Salt and black pepper to taste to season
- 1 cup spinach
- 3 oz. cream cheese
- 1 small onion, sliced
- 1 tbsp. olive oil
- 1 clove garlic, minced
- ½ tsp dried thyme
- ½ tsp dried rosemary

Directions:
1. Place the tenderloin on a chopping board, cover it with a plastic wrap and pound it using a kitchen hammer to 2-inches flat and square piece. Trim the uneven sides with a knife to have a perfect square. Set aside on a flat plate. On the same chopping board, place and weave the bacon slices into a square of the size of the pork.
2. Place the pork on the bacon weave and set aside. Put a skillet over medium heat on a stovetop, add olive oil, onions, and garlic; sauté until transparent. Add the spinach, ½ tsp rosemary, ½ tsp thyme, a bit of salt, and pepper. Stir with a spoon and allow the spinach to wilt. Stir in the cream cheese, until the mixture is even. Turn off.
3. Preheat the Air Fryer to 360 F. Spoon and spread the spinach mixture onto the pork loin. Roll up the bacon and pork over the spinach stuffing. Secure the ends with as many toothpicks as necessary. Season it with more salt and pepper. Place it in the fryer basket and cook for 15 minutes. Flip to other side and cook for another 5 minutes. Once ready, remove to a clean chopping board. Let sit it for 4 minutes before slicing. Serve with steamed veggies.
Nutrition: Calories: 366 Fat 10g Protein 32g Sugar 7g

438. Basil Meatloaf with Parmesan
Preparation Time: 20 minutes
Cooking Time: 50 minutes
Servings: 5
Ingredients:
- 1 cup tomato basil sauce, divided in 2
- 1 ½ lb. ground beef
- 1 ¼ cup diced onion
- 2 tbsp. minced garlic
- 2 tbsp. minced ginger
- ½ cup breadcrumbs
- ½ cup grated Parmesan cheese
- Salt and black pepper to taste to season
- 2 tsp cayenne pepper
- ½ tsp dried basil
- ⅓ Cup of chopped parsley
- 2 egg whites

Directions:
1. Preheat the Air Fryer to 360 F. In a bowl, add the beef, half of the tomato sauce, onion, garlic, ginger, breadcrumbs, cheese, salt, pepper, cayenne pepper, dried basil, parsley, and egg whites; mix well.
2. Grease an 8 or 10-inch pan with cooking spray and scoop the meat mixture into it. Shape the meat into the pan while pressing firmly. Brush the remaining tomato sauce onto meat. Place the pan in the fryer basket and close the Air Fryer; cook for 25 minutes. After 15 minutes, open the fryer, and use a meat thermometer to ensure the meat has reached 160 F internally. If not, cook further for 5 minutes. Remove the pan; drain any excess liquid and Fat. Let meatloaf cool for 20 minutes before slicing. Serve with a side of sautéed green beans.
Nutrition: Calories: 387 Fat 20g Protein 26g Sugar 8g

439. Cheesy Ground Beef and Mac Taco Casserole
Preparation Time: 10 Minutes
Cooking Time: 25 Minutes
Servings: 5
Ingredients:
- 1-ounce shredded Cheddar cheese
- 1-ounce shredded Monterey Jack cheese
- 2 tbsp. chopped green onions
- 1/2 (10.75 ounce) can condensed tomato soup
- 1/2-pound lean ground beef
- 1/2 cup crushed tortilla chips
- 1/4-pound macaroni, cooked according to manufacturer's **Directions:**
- 1/4 cup chopped onion
- 1/4 cup sour cream (optional)
- 1/2 (1.25 ounce) package taco seasoning mix
- 1/2 (14.5 ounce) can diced tomatoes

Directions:
1. Lightly grease baking pan of air fryer with cooking spray. Add onion and ground beef. For 10 minutes, cook it on 360°F. Halfway through cooking time, stir and crumble ground beef.
2. Add taco seasoning, diced tomatoes, and tomato soup. Mix well. Mix in pasta.
3. Sprinkle crushed tortilla chips. Sprinkle cheese.
4. Cook for 15 minutes at 390°F until tops are lightly browned and cheese is melted.
5. Serve and enjoy.
Nutrition: Calories: 329 Fat 17g Protein 15.6g

440. Beefy Steak Topped with Chimichurri Sauce
Preparation Time: 5 Minutes
Cooking Time: 60 Minutes
Servings: 6
Ingredients:

- 1 cup commercial chimichurri
- 3 pounds' steak
- Salt and pepper to taste

Directions:
1. Place all ingredients in a Ziploc bag and marinate in the fridge for 2 hours.
2. Preheat the air fryer to 390°F.
3. Place the grill pan accessory in the air fryer.
4. Grill the skirt steak for 20 minutes per batch.
5. Flip the steak every 10 minutes for even grilling.

Nutrition: Calories: 507 Fat 27g Protein 63 G

441. Beef Ribeye Steak

Preparation Time: 5 Minutes
Cooking Time: 20 Minutes
Servings: 4
Ingredients:
- 4 (8-ounce) ribeye steaks
- 1 tbsp. McCormick Grill Mates Montreal Steak Seasoning
- Salt
- Pepper

Directions:
1. Season the steaks with the steak seasoning and salt and pepper to taste. Place the 2 steaks in the air fryer. You can use an accessory grill pan, a layer rack, or the air fryer basket.
2. Cook for 4 minutes. Open the air fryer and flip the steaks.
3. Cook for an additional 4 to 5 minutes. Check for doneness to determine how much additional cook time is need. Remove the cooked steaks from the air fryer, and then repeat for the remaining 2 steaks. Cool before serving.

Nutrition: Calories: 293 Fat 22g Protein 23g Fiber 0g

442. Air Fryer Roast Beef

Preparation Time: 5 Minutes
Cooking Time: 45 Minutes
Servings: 6
Ingredients:
- Roast beef
- 1 tbsp. olive oil
- Seasonings of choice

Directions:
1. Ensure your air fryer is preheated to 160 degrees.
2. Place roast in bowl and toss with olive oil and desired seasonings. Put seasoned roast into air fryer.
3. Set temperature to 160°F, and set time to 30 minutes and cook 30 minutes.
4. Turn roast when the timer sounds and cook another 15 minutes.

Nutrition: Calories: 267 Fat 8g Protein 21g Sugar 1g

443. Beef Korma

Preparation Time: 10 Minutes
Cooking Time: 20 Minutes
Servings: 6
Ingredients:
- ½ cup yogurt
- 1 tbsp. curry powder
- 1 tbsp. olive oil
- 1 onion, chopped
- 2 cloves garlic, minced
- 1 tomato, diced
- ½ cup frozen baby peas, thawed

Directions:
1. In a medium bowl, combine the steak, yogurt, and curry powder. Stir and set aside.
2. In a 6-inch metal bowl, combine the olive oil, onion, and garlic.
3. Cook for 3 to 4 minutes or until crisp and tender.
4. Add the steak along with the yogurt and the diced tomato. Cook for 12 to 13 minutes or until steak is almost tender. Stir in the peas and cook for 2 to 3 minutes or until hot.

Nutrition: Calories: 289 Fat 11g Protein 38g Fiber 2g

444. Cumin-Paprika Rubbed Beef Brisket

Preparation Time: 5 Minutes
Cooking Time: 2 Hours
Servings: 12
Ingredients:
- ¼ tsp cayenne pepper
- 1 ½ tbsp. paprika
- 1 tsp garlic powder
- 1 tsp ground cumin
- 1 teaspoon onion powder
- 2 tsp dry mustard
- 2 tsp ground black pepper
- 2 tsp salt
- 5 pounds' brisket roast
- 5 tbsp. olive oil

Directions:
1. Place all ingredients in a Ziploc bag and allow marinating in the fridge for at least 2 hours.
2. Preheat the air fryer for 5 minutes.
3. Place the meat in a baking dish that will fit in the air fryer.
4. Place in the air fryer and cook for 2 hours at 350°F.

Nutrition: Calories: 269 Fat 12.8g Protein 35.6g Fiber 2g

445. Chili-Espresso Marinated Steak

Preparation Time: 5 Minutes
Cooking Time: 50 Minutes
Servings: 3
Ingredients:
- ½ tsp garlic powder
- 1 ½ pounds beef flank steak
- 1 tsp instant espresso powder
- 2 tbsp. olive oil
- 2 tsp chili powder
- Salt and pepper to taste

Directions:

1. Preheat the air fryer to 390°F.
2. Place the grill pan accessory in the air fryer.
3. Make the dry rub by mixing the chili powder, salt, pepper, espresso powder, and garlic powder.
4. Rub all over the steak and brush with oil.
5. Place on the grill pan and cook for 40 minutes.
6. Halfway through the cooking time, flip the beef to cook evenly.

Nutrition: Calories: 249 Fat 17g Protein 20g Fiber 2g

446. Crispy Mongolian Beef
Preparation Time: 5 Minutes
Cooking Time: 10 Minutes
Servings: 6
Ingredients:
- Olive oil
- ½ cup almond flour
- 2 pounds' beef tenderloin or beef chuck, sliced into strips
- Sauce:
- ½ cup chopped green onion
- 1 tsp. red chili flakes
- 1 tsp. almond flour
- ½ cup brown Sugar
- 1 tsp. hoisin sauce
- ½ cup water
- ½ cup rice vinegar
- ½ cup low-sodium soy sauce
- 1 tbsp. chopped garlic
- 1 tbsp. finely chopped ginger
- 2 tbsp. olive oil

Directions:
1. Toss strips of beef in almond flour, ensuring they are coated well. Add to the air fryer.
2. Set temperature to 300°F, and set time to 10 minutes, and cook 10 minutes.
3. Meanwhile, add all sauce ingredients to the pan and bring to a boil. Mix well.
4. Add beef strips to the sauce and cook 2 minutes.
5. Serve over cauliflower rice!

Nutrition: Calories: 290 Fat 14g Protein 22g Sugar 1g

447. Beef & Lemon Schnitzel for One
Preparation Time: 5 Minutes
Cooking Time: 12 Minutes
Servings: 1
Ingredients:
- 2 Tbsp. Oil
- 2–3 oz. Breadcrumbs
- 1 Whisked Egg in a Saucer/Soup Plate
- 1 Beef Schnitzel
- 1 Freshly Picked Lemon

Directions:
1. Mix the oil and breadcrumbs together until loose and crumbly. Dip the meat into the egg, then into the crumbs. Make sure that it is evenly covered.
2. Gently place in the air fryer basket, and cook at 350° F (preheat if needed) until done. The timing will depend on the thickness of the schnitzel, but for a relatively thin one, it should take roughly 12 min. Serve with a lemon half and a garden salad.

Nutrition: Calories 493 Fat 28g Protein 32g Fiber 0g

448. Crispy Beef Schnitzel
Preparation Time: 5 Minutes
Cooking Time: 12 Minutes
Servings: 1
Ingredients:
- 1 beef schnitzel
- Salt and ground black pepper, to taste
- 2 tablespoons olive oil
- 1/3 cup breadcrumbs
- 1 egg, whisked

Directions:
1. Season the schnitzel with salt and black pepper. In a mixing bowl, combine the oil and breadcrumbs. In another shallow bowl, beat the egg until frothy.
2. Dip the schnitzel in the egg then, dip it in the oil mixture. Pour into the Oven rack/basket. Place the Rack on the middle-shelf of the air fryer. Set temperature to 350°F, and set time to 12 minutes.
3. Enjoy!

Nutrition: Calories 383 Fat 12g Protein 43g Fiber 0g

449. Simple Steak
Preparation Time: 6minutes
Cooking Time: 14 Minutes
Servings: 2
Ingredients:
- ½ pound quality cuts steak
- Salt and freshly ground black pepper, to taste

Directions:
1. Preheat the air fryer to 390 degrees F.
2. Rub the steak with salt and pepper evenly.
3. Place the steak in the air fryer basket and cook for about 14 minutes crispy.

Nutrition: Calories 198 Fat 7g Protein 43g Fiber 0g

450. Garlic-Cumin and Orange Juice Marinated Steak
Preparation Time: 6 Minutes
Cooking Time: 60 Minutes
Servings: 4
Ingredients:
- ¼ cup orange juice
- 1 teaspoon ground cumin
- 2 pounds' skirt steak, trimmed from excess Fat
- 2 tablespoons lime juice
- 2 tablespoons olive oil
- 4 cloves of garlic, minced
- Salt and pepper to taste

Directions:
1. Place all ingredients in a mixing bowl and allow the marinate in the fridge for at least 2 hours
2. Preheat the air fryer to 390°F.
3. Place the grill pan accessory in the air fryer.
4. Grill for 15 minutes per batch and flip the beef every 8 minutes for even grilling.

5. Meanwhile, pour the marinade on a saucepan and allow to simmer for 10 minutes or until the sauce thickens.
6. Slice the beef and pour over the sauce.
Nutrition: Calories 568 Fat 34.7g Protein 59.1g Sugar 1g

451. Beef Taco Fried Egg Rolls
Preparation Time: 10 Minutes
Cooking Time: 12 Minutes
Servings: 8
Ingredients:
- 1 tsp. cilantro
- 2 chopped garlic cloves
- 1 tbsp. olive oil
- 1 C. shredded Mexican cheese
- ½ packet taco seasoning
- ½ can cilantro lime rotel
- ½ chopped onion
- 16 egg roll wrappers
- 1-pound lean ground beef

Directions:
1. Ensure that your air fryer is preheated to 400 degrees.
2. Add onions and garlic to a skillet, cooking till fragrant. Then add taco seasoning, pepper, salt, and beef, cooking till beef is broke up into tiny pieces and cooked thoroughly.
3. Add rotel and stir well.
4. Pour into the Oven rack/basket. Place the Rack on the middle-shelf of the air fryer. Set temperature to 400°F, and set time to 8 minutes. Cook 8 minutes, flip, and cook another 4 minutes.
5. Served it sprinkled with cilantro.
Nutrition: Calories: 348 Fat 11g Protein 24g Sugar 1g

452. Beef with Beans
Preparation Time: 10 Minutes
Cooking Time: 13 Minutes
Servings: 4
Ingredients:
- 12 Oz. lean steak
- 1 Onion, sliced
- 1 Can Chopped Tomatoes
- 3/4 Cup Beef Stock
- 4 Tsp Fresh Thyme, chopped
- 1 Can Red Kidney Beans
- Salt and Pepper to taste

Directions:
1. Preheat the air fryer oven to 390 degrees.
2. Set temperature to 390°F, and set time to 13 minutes, Cook for 3 minutes. Add the meat and continue cooking for 5 minutes.
3. Add the tomatoes and their juice, beef stock, thyme and the beans and cook for an additional 5 minutes
4. Season it with black pepper to taste.
Nutrition: Calories: 178 Fat 14g Protein 9g Fiber 0g

453. Flavors Herb Lamb Chops
Preparation Time: 10 minutes
Cooking Time: 7 minutes
Servings: 4
Ingredients:
- 1 lb. lamb chops
- 1 tsp oregano
- 1 tsp thyme
- 1 tsp rosemary
- 2 tbsp. fresh lemon juice
- 2 tbsp. olive oil
- 1 tsp coriander
- 1 tsp salt

Directions:
1. Insert wire rack in rack position 4. Select air fry, set temperature 400 F, timer for 7 minutes. Press start to preheat the oven.
2. Add all ingredients except lamb chops into the zip-lock bag.
3. Add lamb chops to the bag. Seal bag and shake well and place it in the refrigerator overnight.
4. Place marinated lamb chops into the air fryer basket and cook for 7 minutes.
5. Serve and enjoy.
Nutrition: Calories 276 Fat 15.5 g Carbohydrates 0.8 g Sugar 0.2 g Protein 32 g Cholesterol 102 mg

454. Simple & Quick Lamb Chops
Preparation Time: 10 minutes
Cooking Time: 5 minutes
Servings: 2
Ingredients:
- 2 lamb chops
- 1/2 tbsp. fresh oregano, chopped
- 1 tbsp. olive oil
- 1 garlic clove, minced
- Pepper
- Salt

Directions:
1. Insert wire rack in rack position 4. Select air fry, set temperature 400 F, timer for 5 minutes. Press start to preheat the oven.
2. Mix together garlic, olive oil, oregano, pepper, and salt and rub over lamb chops.
3. Place lamb chops into the air fryer basket and cook for 5 minutes.
4. Serve and enjoy.
Nutrition: Calories 674 Fat 31.1 g Carbohydrates 1.3 g Sugar 0.1 g Protein 92.1 g Cholesterol 294 mg

455. Breaded Pork Chops
Preparation Time: 10 minutes
Cooking Time: 20 minutes
Servings: 4
Ingredients:
- 4 pork chops, boneless
- 2 eggs, lightly beaten
- 1 cup almond meal
- 1/4 cup parmesan cheese, grated
- 1 tbsp. onion powder
- 1 tbsp. garlic powder

- 1/4 tbsp. black pepper
- 1/2 tsp sea salt

Directions:
1. Insert wire rack in rack position 4. Select air fry, set temperature 350 F, timer for 20 minutes. Press start to preheat the oven.
2. In a bowl, mix together almond meal, parmesan cheese, onion powder, garlic powder, pepper, and salt.
3. Whisk eggs in a shallow dish.
4. Dip pork chops into the egg then coat with almond meal mixture and place into the air fryer basket.
5. Cook pork chops for 20 minutes.
6. Serve and enjoy.

Nutrition: Calories 457 Fat 35.2 g Carbohydrates 8.7 g Sugar 2.3 g Protein 28.2 g Cholesterol 155 mg

456. Cheese Garlic Pork Chops

Preparation Time: 10 minutes
Cooking Time: 20 minutes
Servings: 8
Ingredients:
- 8 pork chops, boneless
- 3/4 cup parmesan cheese
- 2 tbsp. butter, melted
- 2 tbsp. coconut oil
- 1 tsp thyme
- 1 tbsp. parsley
- 6 garlic cloves, minced
- 1/4 tsp pepper
- 1/2 tsp sea salt

Directions:
1. Insert wire rack in rack position 4. Select air fry, set temperature 400 F, timer for 20 minutes. Press start to preheat the oven.
2. In a bowl, mix together butter, spices, parmesan cheese, and coconut oil.
3. Brush butter mixture on top of pork chops and place it into the air fryer basket and cook for 20 minutes.
4. Serve and enjoy.

Nutrition: Calories 342 Fat 28 g Carbohydrates 1.2 g Sugar 0 g Protein 20.9 g Cholesterol 82 mg

457. Creole Pork Chops

Preparation Time: 10 minutes
Cooking Time: 12 minutes
Servings: 6
Ingredients:
- 1 1/2 lbs. pork chops, boneless
- 1 tsp garlic powder
- 1/4 cup parmesan cheese, grated
- 1/3 cup almond flour
- 1 tsp paprika
- 1 tsp Creole seasoning

Directions:
1. Insert wire rack in rack position 4. Select air fry, set temperature 360 F, timer for 12 minutes. Press start to preheat the oven.
2. Add all ingredients except pork chops into the zip-lock bag.
3. Add pork chops into the bag. Seal bag and shake well.
4. Remove pork chops from the zip-lock bag and place it into the air fryer basket and cook for 12 minutes.
5. Serve and enjoy.

Nutrition: Calories 415 Fat 32 g Carbohydrates 2 g Sugar 0.2 g Protein 28.2 g Cholesterol 100 mg

458. Tender Pork Chops

Preparation Time: 10 minutes
Cooking Time: 13 minutes
Servings: 4
Ingredients:
- 4 pork chops, boneless
- 1/2 tsp celery seeds
- 1/2 tsp parsley
- 1/2 tsp granulated onion
- 1/2 tsp granulated garlic
- 2 tsp olive oil
- 1/2 tsp salt

Directions:
1. Insert wire rack in rack position 4. Select air fry, set temperature 350 F, timer for 13 minutes. Press start to preheat the oven.
2. In a small bowl, mix together with seasonings and sprinkle onto the pork chops.
3. Place pork chops into the air fryer basket and cook for 13 minutes.
4. Serve and enjoy.

Nutrition: Calories 278 Fat 22.3 g Carbohydrates 0.4 g Sugar 0.1 g Protein 18.1 g Cholesterol 69 mg

459. Simple Dash Seasoned Pork Chops

Preparation Time: 10 minutes
Cooking Time: 20 minutes
Servings: 2
Ingredients:
- 2 pork chops, boneless
- 1 tbsp. dash seasoning

Directions:
1. Insert wire rack in rack position 4. Select air fry, set temperature 360 F, timer for 20 minutes. Press start to preheat the oven.
2. Rub seasoning all over the pork chops.
3. Place seasoned pork chops into the air fryer basket and cook for 20 minutes.
4. Serve and enjoy.

Nutrition: Calories 256 Fat 19.9 g Carbohydrates 0 g Sugar 0 g Protein 18 g Cholesterol 69 mg

460. Jerk Pork Butt

Preparation Time: 10 minutes
Cooking Time: 20 minutes
Servings: 4
Ingredients:
- 1 1/2 lbs. pork butt, cut into pieces
- 1/4 cup jerk paste

Directions:

1. Insert wire rack in rack position 4. Select air fry, set temperature 390 F, timer for 20 minutes. Press start to preheat the oven.
2. Add meat and jerk paste into the bowl and coat well. Place in refrigerator overnight.
3. Place marinated meat into the air fryer basket and cook for 20 minutes.
4. Serve and enjoy.
Nutrition: Calories 339 Fat 12.1 g Carbohydrates 0.8 g Sugar 0.6 g Protein 53 g Cholesterol 156 mg

461. Asian Lamb
Preparation Time: 10 minutes
Cooking Time: 10 minutes
Servings: 4
Ingredients:
- 1 lb. lamb, cut into 2-inch pieces
- 1 tbsp. soy sauce
- 2 tbsp. vegetable oil
- 1/2 tsp cayenne
- 1 1/2 tbsp. ground cumin
- 2 red chili peppers, chopped
- 1 tbsp. garlic, minced
- 1 tsp salt

Directions:
1. Insert wire rack in rack position 4. Select air fry, set temperature 360 F, timer for 10 minutes. Press start to preheat the oven.
2. Mix together cumin and cayenne in a small bowl. Rub meat with cumin mixture and place in a large bowl.
3. Add oil, soy sauce, garlic, chili peppers, and salt over the meat. Coat well and place it in the refrigerator overnight.
4. Add marinated meat to the air fryer basket and cook for 10 minutes.
5. Serve and enjoy.
Nutrition: Calories 286 Fat 15.7 g Carbohydrates 2.3 g Sugar 0.3 g Protein 32.7 g Cholesterol 102 mg

462. Beef Stew
Preparation Time: 10 minutes
Cooking Time: 5 hours
Servings: 8
Ingredients:
- 3 lbs. beef stew meat, trimmed
- 1/2 cup Thai red curry paste
- 1/3 cup tomato paste
- 13 oz. can coconut milk
- 2 tsp ginger, minced
- 2 garlic cloves, minced
- 1 medium onion, sliced
- 2 tbsp. extra virgin olive oil
- 2 cups carrots, julienned
- 2 cups broccoli florets
- 2 tsp fresh lime juice
- 2 tbsp. fish sauce
- 2 tsp sea salt

Directions:
1. Insert wire rack in rack position 8. Select slow cook, Set HIGH for 5 hours. Press start to preheat the oven.
2. Heat the 1 tbsp. oil in a pan over medium-high heat. Add meat and brown the meat on all sides.
3. Transfer brown meat into the Dutch oven.
4. Add remaining oil in a pan and sauté ginger, garlic, and onion over medium-high heat for 5 minutes. Add coconut milk and stir well.
5. Transfer pan mixture into the Dutch oven.
6. Add remaining ingredients except for carrots and broccoli into the Dutch oven.
7. Cover the Dutch oven and cook on high for 5 hours.
8. Add carrots and broccoli during the last 30 minutes of cooking.
9. Serve and enjoy.
Nutrition: Calories 537 Fat 28.6 g Carbohydrates 13 g Protein 54.4 g Cholesterol 152 mg

463. Mushroom Beef Stew
Preparation Time: 10 minutes
Cooking Time: 8 hours
Servings: 6
Ingredients:
- 3 lbs. stewing steak, cut into pieces
- 4 cups mushrooms, quartered
- 1 tbsp. Worcestershire sauce
- 2 tbsp. tomato paste
- 1 1/4 cup beef stock
- 2 tbsp. parsley, chopped
- 1 tbsp. thyme leaves
- 1 bay leaf
- 3 medium carrots, peeled and cut into chunks
- Pepper
- Salt

Directions:
1. Insert wire rack in rack position 8. Select slow cook, Set LOW for 8 hours. Press start to preheat the oven.
2. Add beef, thyme, bay leaf, carrots, and mushrooms to the Dutch oven.
3. Whisk together beef stock, Worcestershire sauce, and tomato paste and pour into the Dutch oven. Season it beef mixture with pepper and salt. Stir well.
4. Cover and cook on low for 8 hours.
5. Garnish with parsley and serve.
Nutrition: Calories 399 Fat 15.3 g Carbohydrates 6.4 g Protein 57.5 g Cholesterol 0 mg

464. Spicy Pepper Beef
Preparation Time: 10 minutes
Cooking Time: 4 hours
Servings: 6
Ingredients:
- 2 lbs. beef chuck, sliced
- 1 cup beef broth
- 1/2 medium onion, sliced
- 2 cups bell pepper, chopped
- 1 tbsp. sriracha sauce

- 1/3 cup parsley, chopped
- 2 tsp garlic powder
- 1 tsp black pepper
- 2 tsp salt

Directions:
1. Insert wire rack in rack position 8. Select slow cook, Set HIGH for 4 hours. Press start to preheat the oven.
2. Place meat into the Dutch oven.
3. Top the meat with sliced onion and bell pepper. Season it with garlic powder, pepper, and salt.
4. Mix together sriracha and broth and pour over meat mixture.
5. Cover and cook on high for 4 hours.
6. Garnish with chopped parsley and serve.

Nutrition: Calories 325 Fat 11.5 g Carbohydrates 5.3 g Protein 47.5 g Cholesterol 137 mg

465. Slow Cooked Beef Brisket

Preparation Time: 10 minutes
Cooking Time: 7 hours
Servings: 6
Ingredients:
- 3 lbs. beef brisket
- 1 tbsp. chili powder
- 4 garlic cloves, chopped
- 1/2 onion, chopped
- 1 tsp cumin
- 3 tbsp. chili sauce
- 1/4 cup beef broth
- 1 1/2 tsp liquid smoke
- 1 tbsp. Worcestershire sauce
- 1/2 tsp black pepper

Directions:
1. Insert wire rack in rack position 8. Select slow cook, Set LOW for 7 hours. Press start to preheat the oven.
2. Mix together chili powder, pepper, cumin, Worcestershire sauce, and garlic and rub over brisket.
3. Place the beef brisket into the Dutch oven. Mix together broth, chili sauce, onion, and liquid smoke and pour over brisket.
4. Cover and cook on low for 7 hours.
5. Remove brisket from Dutch oven and cut into slices.
6. Serve and enjoy.

Nutrition: Calories 439 Fat 14.5 g Carbohydrates 3.1 g Protein 69.5 g Cholesterol 203 mg

466. Slow Cooked Pork Chops

Preparation Time: 10 minutes
Cooking Time: 6 hours
Servings: 4
Ingredients:
- 4 pork chops
- 1 1/2 cups chicken broth
- 2 tbsp. butter, melted
- 3 garlic cloves, minced
- 1 medium onion, chopped
- 3/4 tsp poultry seasoning
- 1/2 tsp salt

Directions:
1. Insert wire rack in rack position 8. Select slow cook, Set LOW for 6 hours. Press start to preheat the oven. In a large bowl, mix together butter, broth, and poultry seasoning and salt.
2. Pour bowl mixture into the Dutch oven. Add pork chops, onion, and garlic into the Dutch oven.
3. Cover and cook on low for 6 hours. Serve and enjoy.

Nutrition: Calories 337 Fat 26.2 g Carbohydrates 3.8 g Protein 20.3 g Cholesterol 84 mg

VEGETABLE RECIPES

467. Sweet Potato Casserole
Preparation Time: 15 minutes
Cooking Time: 30 minutes
Servings: 4
Ingredients:
- 2 c. sweet potatoes
- ¼ c. melted butter
- 1½ tbsp. milk
- ¼ c. honey
- Vanilla
- 1 large egg
- ¼ c. brown Sugar
- ¼ c. wheat flour
- 2 tbsp. butter
- ½ c. chopped pecans
- Cooking spray

Directions:
1. Spray baking sheet with cooking spray.
2. In a large mixing bowl, combine milk, honey, sweet potatoes, vanilla, melted butter, and egg. Mix well.
3. In another mixing bowl, combine brown sugar and flour. Cut in 3 tablespoons butter till crumbly. Add pecans and mix well.
4. Sprinkle the mixture over sweet potatoes.
5. Place on 1-inch rack and cook for 25-30 minutes at 350°C (High) or until golden brown.
6. Serve Immediately.

Nutrition: Calories: 310 Total Fat 13g Carbs: 49g Protein 3g

468. Delicious Roasted Garlic Mushrooms
Preparation Time: 10 minutes
Cooking Time: 25 minutes
Servings: 2
Ingredients:
- 8 oz. package crimini or button mushrooms
- 2 garlic cloves, minced
- 2 tbsp. olive oil
- 1 tbsp. chopped thyme
- Salt and black pepper to taste

Directions:
1. In a medium mixing bowl combine the olive oil, garlic and fresh thyme together. Whisk till well combined. Add pepper and salt to taste.
2. Pour the marinade on the mushrooms and mix well until the mushrooms are properly coated.
3. Place marinated mushrooms directly onto the lined pan.
4. Roast on the 'HI' setting for about 20 to 25 minutes.
5. Serve hot. Enjoy!

Nutrition: Calories: 260 Total Fat 18g Carbs: 44g Protein 6g

469. Roasted Cauliflower, Olives and Chickpeas
Preparation Time: 15 minutes
Cooking Time: 24 minutes
Servings: 3
Ingredients:
- 3 c. cauliflower florets
- 4 chopped garlic cloves
- ½ c. Spanish green olives
- 15 oz. chickpeas, rinsed and drained
- ¼ tsp crushed red pepper
- 1 ½ tbsp. olive oil
- 1 ½ tbsp. of parsley
- Salt to taste

Directions:
1. Place the cauliflower florets, garlic, Spanish green olives, chickpeas, crushed red pepper, parsley and salt in a large bowl.
2. Pour oil over the ingredients, and then let it stand for about 2 to 3 minutes.
3. Toss until all the ingredients are well coated in the olive oil.
4. Place the olive oil coated ingredients at the bottom of a lined pan in a single even layer. Cook on 'HI' setting for about 22 to 24 minutes.
5. Serve hot with your preferred condiment on the side.

Nutrition: Calories: 176 Fat 10.1g Protein 4.2g Carbs: 17.6g

470. Fruit and Vegetable Skewers
Preparation Time: 4 minutes
Cooking Time: 16 minutes
Servings: 4
Ingredients:
- 4 tbsp. virgin olive oil
- 3 tbsp. lemon juice
- 1 garlic clove, minced
- 2 tbsp. chopped parsley
- ½ tsp. salt
- ½ tsp. black pepper
- 1 sliced zucchini
- 1 sliced yellow squash
- ½ red bell pepper
- ½ c. cherry tomatoes
- ½ c. pineapple chunks
- 4 wooden skewers

Directions:
1. In a large mixing bowl combine olive oil, garlic, parsley, lemon juice, pepper, and salt. Pour into large resalable plastic bag. Add zucchini, squash, bell pepper, and tomatoes. Seal bag, shake to coat vegetables, and place in refrigerator for a minimum of 1 hour.
2. Remove vegetables from marinade and thread onto skewers, along with pineapple, alternating among each item.
3. Place skewers on the 4-inch rack. Cook on High Power (350°C) for 8 minutes.
4. Flip skewers over and cook for another 6-8 minutes until veggies are desired level of doneness.

5. Remove from the air fryer, transfer to a plate, and serve.
Nutrition: Calories: 173 Fat 2.8 g Carbs 36.5g Protein 5g

471. Roasted Sweet Potatoes with Rosemary
Preparation Time: 15 minutes
Cooking Time: 22 minutes
Servings: 4
Ingredients:
- 1 ½ pound sweet potatoes, cubed
- 1 tsp. olive oil
- 1 dash chopped rosemary
- 1 dash lemon juice

Directions:
1. In a bowl, toss sweet potatoes with oil. Evenly spread on the 10-inch baking sheet, sprinkle with rosemary. Place on 1-inch rack and back on High power (350 degrees F) for 12 minutes. Flip sweet potatoes over and cook an additional 10 minutes.
2. Drizzle with lemon juice and serve.

Nutrition: Calories: 114 Total Fat 0g Carbs: 27g Protein 2g

472. Tangy Roasted Broccoli with Garlic
Preparation Time: 10 minutes
Cooking Time: 17 minutes
Servings: 4
Ingredients:
- 1 broccoli head
- 3 garlic cloves, minced
- 2 tsp. virgin olive oil
- 1 tsp. sea salt
- ½ tsp. black pepper
- ½ tsp. lemon juice

Directions:
1. In a mixing bowl, add oil, salt, garlic and black pepper. Add broccoli. Mix to coat. Evenly scatter broccoli on the 10-inch baking sheet. Place on 1-inch rack and roast on High power (350 degrees F) for about 10 minutes. Flip florets and cook another 5-7 minutes or until fork tender.
2. Plate and drizzle lemon juice. Serve at once.

Nutrition: Calories: 141 Carbs: 10g Fat 10 g Protein 5g

473. Roasted Carrots with Garlic
Preparation Time: 10 minutes
Cooking Time: 20 minutes
Servings: 2
Ingredients:
- 3 tbsp. olive oil
- 2 minced garlic cloves
- Sea salt, to taste
- 1-pound baby carrots

Directions:
1. In a medium bowl, mix carrots with olive oil, salt and garlic. Spread carrots in single layer on parchment or foil-lined baking sheet.
2. Place on 1-inch rack and cook on High power (350 F) for 15-20 minutes until carrots are tender.

Nutrition: Calories: 95 Fat 6.9g Carbs: 7.6g Protein 1g

474. Savory Roasted Balsamic Vegetables
Preparation Time: 20 minutes
Cooking Time: 30 minutes
Servings: 4
Ingredients:
- 1½ c. cubed butternut squash
- 1 c. chopped broccoli florets
- ½ chopped red onion
- 1 chopped zucchini
- 1 minced garlic clove
- 2 tbsp. virgin olive oil
- 1½ tsp. rosemary
- A pinch of salt, to taste
- 1 tbsp. balsamic vinegar

Directions:
1. In a mixing bowl, add oil, rosemary, vinegar, pepper, and salt; mix to blend. Mix in the vegetables, mix to coat evenly.
2. Evenly spread on a parchment-lined baking sheet.
3. Place on 1-inch rack and cook on High power (350 degrees F) for about 15 minutes. Flip vegetables and cook for another 15 minutes or until squash is just softened.

Nutrition: Calories 148 Fat 4.6g Carbs 25g Protein 7g

475. Baked Macaroni and Cheese
Preparation Time: 15 minutes
Cooking Time: 30 minutes
Servings: 4
Ingredients:
- ½ pound Cheddar cheese, shredded
- 4 tbsp. butter
- 2 eggs
- 1 tsp. Dijon mustard
- 12 oz. evaporated milk
- 1-pound elbow macaroni
- Salt and black pepper to taste
- ½ c. breadcrumbs

Directions:
1. Cook macaroni according to package directions.
2. Spray casserole dish with cooking spray.
3. Add all ingredients except for bread crumbs to a casserole dish and mix well to combine. Sprinkle with breadcrumbs.
4. Cover with foil and place pan on 1-inch rack. Bake on High (350 degrees F) for 15-20 minutes. Remove the foil then cook for another 5-10 minutes or until golden brown.

Nutrition: Calories: 480 Total Fat 19g Carbs: 31g Protein 24g

476. Curried Zucchini Chips
Preparation Time: 4 minutes
Cooking Time: 22 minutes
Servings: 2
Ingredients:

- 1 medium sliced zucchini
- 1 tbsp. virgin olive oil
- ⅛ tsp of garlic powder
- ¼ tsp of curry powder
- ⅛ tsp of salt

Directions:
1. Lightly grease paper-lined baking sheet. Arrange zucchini slices in one layer on the baking sheet. Sprinkle olive oil and dust with curry powder, salt, and garlic powder.
2. Place baking sheet on 1-inch rack and bake on High power (350 degrees F) for 12 minutes. Flip zucchini over and cook for another 10 minutes or till very crisp. Cool and store in airtight container

Nutrition: Calories 152 Carbs 17g Fat 3g Protein 2g

477. Lemony Okra

Preparation Time: 10 minutes
Cooking Time: 20 minutes
Servings: 2
Ingredients:
- 1 (10-ounce) bag frozen cut okra
- ¼ cup nutritional yeast
- 2 tablespoons fresh lemon juice
- Salt and ground black pepper, as required

Directions:
1. In a bowl, add the okra, nutritional yeast, lemon juice, salt, and black pepper and toss to coat well.
2. Arrange the okra into the greased air fryer basket in a single layer.
3. Turn on the air fryer and then adjust the temperature to 400 degrees F.
4. Set the timer for 20 minutes and press "Start/Stop" to begin cooking.
5. When the unit beeps to show that it is preheated, insert the basket in the air fryer.
6. When cooking time is complete, remove the okra.
7. Serve hot.

Nutrition: Calories 131 Fat 1.5 g Sodium 103 mg Carbs 20.1 g Fiber 9.6 g Sugar 2.4 g Protein 12.1 g

478. Buttered Broccoli

Preparation Time: 10 minutes
Cooking Time: 20 minutes
Servings: 4
Ingredients:
- 3 cups broccoli, cut into 1-inch pieces
- 1 tablespoon butter, melted
- Salt, as required

Directions:
1. In a bowl, add the broccoli, butter and salt and toss to coat well.
2. Arrange the broccoli pieces into the greased air fryer basket in a single layer.
3. Select "Air Fry" of Digital Air Fryer Oven and then adjust the temperature to 375 degrees F.
4. Set the timer for 20 minutes and press "Start/Stop" to begin cooking.
5. When the unit beeps to show that it is preheated, insert the basket in the Oven.
6. When cooking time is complete, remove the broccoli from Oven and serve hot.

Nutrition: Calories 49 Total Fat 3.1 g Saturated Fat 1.8 g Cholesterol 8 mg Sodium 82 mg Total Carbs 4.5 g Fiber 1.8 g Sugar 1.2 g Protein 1.9 g

479. Baked Sweet Potatoes

Preparation Time: 10 minutes
Cooking Time: 40 Minutes
Servings: 2
Ingredients:
- 2 large-size sweet potatoes
- 1 tablespoon of olive oil
- 1-2 teaspoons of sea salt

Directions:
1. Wash the sweet potatoes, and using a metal fork, prick the potatoes to make air holes. Sprinkle olive oil over the potatoes and rub with salt. Add the potatoes to the air fryer basket and bake at 390 degrees for 35-40 minutes, until fork-tender.

Nutrition: Calories 332 Fat 13g Protein 25g Sugar 12g

480. Beetroot Chips

Preparation Time: 15 minutes
Cooking Time: 25 Minutes
Servings: 2
Ingredients:
- 2 medium-size washed beetroot
- ½ tablespoon of olive oil
- Sea salt and freshly ground black pepper

Directions:
1. Peel the washed beetroot and set the skin to one side.
2. With a mandolin slicer, thinly slice the beets.
3. Spread the slices of beetroot on paper, placing another piece on top. Set to one side for 10 minutes, doing this will help to absorb any moisture from the beetroots.
4. Toss the beetroot slices in oil and season with salt.
5. Preheat the air fryer to 300 degrees F for 4 minutes.
6. Take the basket out of the air fryer. Add the beetroot to the basket and return to the air fryer.
7. Fry the beetroot for 15 minutes. You will need to shake the basket every 5 minutes or so.
8. When the chips are tender in the center and the outer edges are crisp, allow them to cool down for a while. Return the basket to the air fryer and heat at 355 degrees F for an additional 3 minutes.
9. Season it with salt and freshly ground black pepper and enjoy.

Nutrition: Calories 422 Fat 14g Protein 16g Sugar 4g

481. Buffalo Cauliflower

Preparation Time: 10 minutes
Cooking Time: 25 Minutes
Servings: 3-4

Ingredients:
- 2-3 tablespoons of hot sauce
- 1½ teaspoons of pure maple syrup
- 2 teaspoons of avocado oil
- 2-3 tablespoons of nutritional yeast
- ¼ teaspoon of sea salt
- 1 tablespoon of cornstarch
- 6 cups of ½ "cauliflower florets

Directions:
1. Set your air fryer to 360 degrees F.
2. Add the hot sauce, maple syrup, avocado oil, nutritional yeast, sea salt, and cornstarch to a large-size bowl. Whisk well to incorporate fully.
3. Add the cauliflower florets to the bowl and toss to coat well and evenly.
4. Add approximately half of the florets to your air fryer basket.
5. Cook in the air fryer for 12-14 minutes, shaking the basket halfway through cooking until the florets are your preferred consistency.
6. Repeat the process with the remaining cauliflower florets, for 8-10 minutes.
7. Serve and enjoy.

Nutrition: Calories 187 Fat 7g Protein 15g Sugar 2g

482. Buttermilk Fried Mushrooms
Preparation Time: 5 minutes
Cooking Time: 45 Minutes
Servings: 2
Ingredients:
- 2 cups of cleaned oyster mushrooms
- 1 cup of buttermilk
- 1½ cups of all-purpose flour
- 1 teaspoon of salt
- 1 teaspoon of black pepper
- 1 teaspoon of garlic powder
- 1 teaspoon of onion powder
- 1 teaspoon of smoked paprika
- 1 teaspoon of cumin
- 1 tablespoon of oil

Directions:
1. Preheat your air fryer to 375 degrees.
2. In a bowl, toss the mushrooms with the buttermilk and set aside to marinate for 15 minutes.
3. In a second larger bowl, combine the flour with the salt, pepper, garlic powder, onion powder, smoked paprika, cumin, and oil.
4. Take the mushrooms out of the buttermilk, setting the buttermilk to one side.
5. Dip each mushroom in the flour mixture, shaking off any excess flour. Dip the mushrooms once again in the buttermilk, then once again in the flour.
6. Liberally grease the bottom of the air fryer pan.
7. In a single layer, allowing space between the mushrooms, add the mushrooms to the pan. Cook for 5 minutes, before brushing them all over with a drop of oil.
8. Continue to cook for an additional 5-10 minutes, until crisp and golden.

Nutrition: Calories 602 Fat 8g Protein 24g Sugar 11g

483. Chinese Spring Rolls
Preparation Time: 10 minutes
Cooking Time: 35 Minutes
Servings: 8
Ingredients:
- 2 tablespoons of sesame oil
- ½ teaspoon of minced garlic
- 2 cups of shredded cabbage
- 1 cup of matchstick-cut carrots
- ½ of cup thinly sliced bamboo shoots
- 1 tablespoon of freshly squeezed lime juice
- 2 teaspoons of fish sauce
- 1 teaspoon of soy sauce
- 8 square spring roll wrappers
- Water
- Spray oil

Directions:
1. Firstly, heat the oven to 390 degrees F.
2. Over medium to high heat, heat sesame oil in a skillet or frying pan, add garlic and cook for 30 seconds, until fragrant.
3. Add chopped cabbage, carrots, and bamboo shoots and cook for 4-5 minutes, until smooth.
4. Remove the pan from the heat and add the fresh lime juice followed by the fish sauce and soy sauce.
5. Fill each of the 8 spring wrappers with the vegetable mix. The filling should be just below the middle of the wrapper. Fold the bottom of the wrap over the filling to close it and press down. Fold both sides and roll hard. Use a drop of cold water to seal.
6. Repeat the process with the remaining ingredients until you have collected the 8 spring rolls.
7. Spray the fryer basket and springs with cooking spray.
8. In a single layer, and if you work in batches, if necessary, add springs to the basket. Fry the rolls with a spring for 5 minutes, before turning them over and cook until golden, for an additional 5 minutes.
9. Remove from the fryer and serve.

Nutrition: Calories 378 Fat 18g Protein 19g Sugar 4g

484. Onion Pakoras
Preparation Time: 10 minutes
Cooking Time: 45 Minutes
Servings: 2-3
Ingredients:
- 2 cups of gram flour
- 2 cups of peeled and sliced red onions
- ½ teaspoon of carom seeds
- ¼ teaspoon of asafetida
- 1 teaspoon of red chili powder
- ⅛ Cup of rice flour
- ½ cup of water
- 1-2 teaspoons of oil, for brushing
- Chopped coriander leaves, to garnish
- Chopped green chilies, to garnish
- Salt, to taste

Directions:
1. Preheat the air fryer to 200 degrees F for 8-10 minutes.
2. Meanwhile, in a bowl, combine the flour with the red onions, carom seeds, asafetida, red chili powder, and rice flour.
3. Slowly stir in the water to create a sticky, thick batter.
4. Add 1 teaspoon of oil to the batter and mix thoroughly.
5. When the air fryer is at the required temperature, in small-size portions, place the batter on the Air Fryer mesh.
6. Lightly brush the pakoras with oil and air fry for 10 minutes.
7. Flip them over, brush with a little more oil and air fry for 8 minutes.
8. Remove and serve hot.
9. Repeat the process with the remaining batter.

Nutrition: Calories: 506 Fat 2g Protein 22g Sugar 12g

485. Onion Rings
Preparation Time: 10 minutes
Cooking Time: 25 Minutes
Servings: 2
Ingredients:
- ½ cup of all-purpose flour
- 1 teaspoon of paprika
- 1 teaspoon of salt
- ½ cup of buttermilk
- 1 medium-size egg
- 1 cup panko breadcrumbs
- 2 tablespoons of olive oil
- 1 large-size, peeled and sliced into ½" thick yellow sweet onion rings
- Spray oil

Directions:
1. Gather 3 shallow dishes or bowls.
2. In the first dish, combine the flour with the paprika and ½ a teaspoon of salt.
3. In the second dish, combine the buttermilk with the egg.
4. Add a ¼ cup of the seasoned flour mixture to the buttermilk-egg.
5. In the third dish or bowl, combine the breadcrumbs with ½ a teaspoon of salt, and the olive oil. Using a fork, mix until the oil is incorporated evenly.
6. Dredge the yellow onion rings first in the flour, second in the buttermilk mixture, and finally dredge them in the breadcrumb mixture.
7. In a single layer, add the coated onion rings to your air fryer basket. Try and leave space between the rings.
8. Cook the onion rings at 400 degrees F until golden and crisp. This will take approximately 12-15 minutes. You will need to spray the rings with spray oil after approximately 6 minutes of air frying.
9. Transfer to a kitchen paper towel-lined plate to absorb any excess oil.
10. Serve and enjoy with your favorite dip or as a side.

Nutrition: Calories 442 Fat 9g Protein 28g Sugar 7g

486. Roasted Green Beans
Preparation Time: 15 minutes
Cooking Time: 25 Minutes
Servings: 6 Servings
Ingredients:
- 1 pound of fresh green beans
- ½ pound of sliced fresh mushrooms
- 1 peeled and thinly slices red onion
- 2 tbsp. of extra-virgin olive oil
- 1 tsp of Italian seasoning
- ¼ tsp of salt
- ⅛ tsp of black pepper

Directions:
1. Preheat your air fryer to 375 degrees F.
2. First, cut the green beans into 2" pieces.
3. In a large-size bowl, combine the green beans with the mushrooms, red onions, oil, Italian seasoning, salt, and pepper.
4. In a single layer, arrange the veggie on a lightly greased tray in the air fryer basket. Cook for 8-10 minutes, until tender.
5. Toss the veggies and cook for 8-10 minutes, until browned.

Nutrition: Calories 542 Fat 16g Protein 38g Sugar 17g

487. Basil Tomatoes
Preparation Time: 10 minutes
Cooking Time: 10 minutes
Servings: 2
Ingredients:
- 3 tomatoes, halved
- Olive oil cooking spray
- Salt and ground black pepper, as required
- 1 tablespoon fresh basil, chopped

Directions:
1. Drizzle cut sides of the tomato halves with cooking spray evenly.
2. Sprinkle with salt, black pepper and basil.
3. Press "power button" of air fry and turn the dial to select the "air fry" mode.
4. Press the time button and again turn the dial to set the cooking time to 10 minutes.
5. Now push the temp button and rotate the dial to set the temperature at 320 degrees f.
6. Press "start/pause" button to start.
7. When the unit beeps to show that it is preheated, open the lid.
8. Arrange the tomatoes in "air fry basket" and insert in the oven.
9. Serve warm.

Nutrition: Calories 34 Fat 0.4 g Carbs 7.2 g Fiber 2.2 g Protein 1.7g

488. Pesto Tomatoes
Preparation Time: 15 minutes
Cooking Time: 14 minutes

Servings: 4
Ingredients:
- 3 large heirloom tomatoes cut into ½ inch thick slices.
- 1 cup pesto
- 8 oz. feta cheese, cut into ½ inch thick slices.
- ½ cup red onions, sliced thinly
- 1 tablespoon olive oil

Directions:
1. Spread some pesto on each slice of tomato.
2. Top each tomato slice with a feta slice and onion and drizzle with oil.
3. Press "Power Button" of Air Fry Oven and turn the dial to select the "Air Fry" mode.
4. Press the Time button and again turn the dial to set the cooking time to 14 minutes.
5. Now push the Temp button and rotate the dial to set the temperature at 390 degrees F.
6. Press "Start/Pause" button to start.
7. When the unit beeps to show that it is preheated, open the lid.
8. Arrange the tomatoes in greased "Air Fry Basket" and insert in the oven.
9. Serve warm.

Nutrition: Calories 480 Fat 41.9 g Total Carbs 13 g Protein 15.4 g

489. Sweet & Spicy Parsnips
Preparation Time: 15 minutes
Cooking Time: 44 minutes
Servings: 5
Ingredients:
- 1½ lbs. parsnip, peeled and cut into 1-inch chunks
- 1 tablespoon butter, melted
- 2 tablespoons honey
- 1 tablespoon dried parsley flakes, crushed
- ¼ teaspoon red pepper flakes, crushed
- Salt and ground black pepper, as required

Directions:
1. In a large bowl, mix together the parsnips and butter.
2. Press "Power Button" of Air Fry and turn the dial to select the "Air Fry" mode. Press the Time button and again turn the dial to set the cooking time to 44 minutes.
3. Now push the Temp button and rotate the dial to set the temperature at 355 degrees F. Press "Start/Pause" button to start. When the unit beeps to show that it is preheated, open the lid.
4. Arrange the squash chunks in greased "Air Fry Basket" and insert in the oven. Meanwhile, in another large bowl, mix together the remaining ingredients. After 40 minutes of cooking, press "Start/Pause" button to pause the unit.
5. Transfer the parsnips chunks into the bowl of honey mixture and toss to coat well. Again, arrange the parsnip chunks in "Air Fry Basket" and insert in the oven.
6. Serve hot.

Nutrition: Calories 149 Fat 2.7 g Carbs 31.5 g Protein 1.7 g

490. Caramelized Baby Carrots
Preparation Time: 10 minutes
Cooking Time: 15 minutes
Servings: 4
Ingredients:
- ½ cup butter, melted
- ½ cup brown Sugar
- 1 lb. bag baby carrots

Directions:
1. In a bowl, mix together the butter, brown sugar and carrots.
2. Press "Power Button" of air fry and turn the dial to select the "Air Fry" mode.
3. Press the Time button and again turn the dial to set the cooking time to 15 minutes.
4. Now push the Temp button and rotate the dial to set the temperature at 400 degrees F.
5. Press "Start/Pause" button to start.
6. When the unit beeps to show that it is preheated, open the lid.
7. Arrange the carrots in greased "Air Fry Basket" and insert in the oven.
8. Serve warm.

Nutrition: Calories 312 Fat 23.2 g Carbs 27.1 g Protein 1 g

491. Carrot with Spinach
Preparation Time: 15 minutes
Cooking Time: 35 minutes
Servings: 4
Ingredients:
- 4 teaspoons butter, melted and divided
- ¼ lb. carrots, peeled and sliced
- 1 lb. zucchinis, sliced
- 1 tablespoon fresh basil, chopped
- Salt and ground black pepper, as required

Directions:
1. In a bowl, mix together 2 teaspoons of the butter and carrots.
2. Press "Power Button" of Air Fry Oven and turn the dial to select the "Air Fry" mode.
3. Press the Time button and again turn the dial to set the cooking time to 35 minutes.
4. Now push the Temp button and rotate the dial to set the temperature at 400 degrees F.
5. Press "Start/Pause" button to start.
6. When the unit beeps to show that it is preheated, open the lid.
7. Arrange the carrots in greased "Air Fry Basket" and insert in the oven.
8. In a large bowl, mixed together remaining butter, zucchini, basil, salt and black pepper.
9. After 5 minutes of cooking, place the zucchini mixture into the basket with carrots.
10. Toss the vegetable mixture 2-3 times during the cooking.
11. Serve hot.

Nutrition: Calories 64 Fat 4 g Carbs 6.6 g Protein 1.7 g

492. Broccoli with Sweet Potatoes
Preparation Time: 15 minutes
Cooking Time: 20 minutes
Servings: 4
Ingredients:
- 2 medium sweet potatoes, peeled and cut in 1-inch cubes
- 1 head broccoli, cut in 1-inch florets
- 2 tablespoons vegetable oil
- Salt and ground black pepper, as required

Directions:
1. In a large bowl, add all the ingredients and toss to coat well.
2. Press "Power Button" of Air Fry and turn the dial to select the "Air Roast" mode.
3. Press the Time button and again turn the dial to set the cooking time to 20 minutes.
4. Now push the Temp button and rotate the dial to set the temperature at 415 degrees F.
5. Press "Start/Pause" button to start.
6. When the unit beeps to show that it is preheated, open the lid.
7. Arrange the carrots in greased "Air Fry Basket" and insert in the oven.
8. In a large bowl, mixes together remaining butter, zucchini, basil, salt and black pepper.
9. After 5 minutes of cooking, place the zucchini mixture into the basket with carrots.
10. Serve hot.

Nutrition: Calories 170 Fat 7.1 g Saturated Fat 1.4 g Cholesterol 0 mg Sodium 67 mg

493. Vegetable Air Fryer with Beans, Peppers and Carrots
Preparation Time: 5 minutes
Cooking Time: 10 minutes
Servings: 4
Ingredients:
- 100 g beans green
- 1 red fresh paprika
- 1 fresh green pepper
- 3 carrots (carrot, carrot) raw
- 2 cloves of garlic
- 2 tbsp. olive oil
- 1 tbsp. butter
- 1 pinch of sea salt
- 1 pinch of black pepper

Directions:
1. Wash the beans, clean them and put them in a pot.
2. Cover the beans with water and bring to a boil.
3. Simmer the beans for about 5 minutes, then strain into a sieve.
4. Halve the peppers, remove the cores and partitions and rinse the halves under running water
5. Cut the peppers into strips
6. Wash the carrots thoroughly, halve the carrots lengthwise
7. Peel the garlic and cut into thin slices.
8. Heat the butter and oil in the air fryer and add the carrots. Add the peppers, beans and garlic and fry everything in the air fryer for 2 - 3 minutes, stirring the vegetables several times.
9. Season the vegetable air fryer with salt and pepper.

Nutrition: Calories 202 Fat 10g Protein 28g Sugar 1g

494. Roasted Avocado in Bacon
Preparation Time: 5 minutes
Cooking Time: 5 minutes
Servings: 1
Ingredients:
- 2 mediums avocado fresh hate
- 1 lime freshly pressed
- 300 g bacon
- 1 tbsp. olive oil
- 1 pinch of sea salt
- 1 pinch of black pepper

Directions:
1. Halve and core the avocados
2. Quarter the avocados, remove the pulp from the skin and sprinkle with lime juice to prevent the pieces from turning brown.
3. Spread the bacon slices on a board and roll in the avocado pieces one after the other.
4. Heat the oil in the air fryer and fry the avocados wrapped in bacon on all sides.
5. Remove avocados in bacon from the air fryer, season with salt and pepper and serve hot.

Nutrition: Calories: 132 Fat 6g Protein 9g Sugar 2g

495. Fried Cauliflower with Fresh Herbs
Preparation Time: 5 minutes
Cooking Time: 5 minutes
Servings: 2
Ingredients:
- 600 g of cauliflower
- 2 cloves of garlic
- 2 tablespoons butter
- 2 stems of basil fresh
- 2 stems of parsley
- 1 tsp turmeric powder
- 1 pinch of sea salt
- 1 pinch of black pepper
- 2 tbsp. olive oil

Directions:
1. Cut the cauliflower florets from the stalk, then wash and drain.
2. Peel the garlic and finely chop it.
3. Add the olive oil, garlic, turmeric, salt and pepper to a bowl and mix.
4. Add the cauliflower to the spice mixture and swirl through.
5. Heat the butter in an air fryer and add cauliflower.
6. Fry the cauliflower florets from all sides.
7. Wash and dry the herbs, then chop and add to the cauliflower.

Nutrition: Calories 189 Fat 5g Protein 20g Sugar 5g

496. Fried Liver with Onion and Herbs
Preparation Time: 10 minutes
Cooking Time: 5 minutes
Servings: 2
Ingredients:
- 500 g calf's liver (alternatively beef liver)
- 1 big onion
- 4 stems of thyme
- 2 stems of sage
- 4 stalks of parsley
- 2 tablespoons butter
- 1 tsp olive oil
- Sea-salt
- Pepper

Directions:
1. Wash the liver and pat dry with kitchen paper, clean the liver and cut into pieces. peel the onion and cut into ring
2. Wash and dry the herbs, finely chop the parsley.
3. Heat the butter and oil in the air fryer and fry the onion until golden brown. remove the onion and set aside. put the liver, thyme and sage in the hot air fryer. fry the pieces of liver on all sides.
4. Remove the herbs from the air fryer and salt and pepper the meat. put the onions back into the air fryer and heat briefly. Put the fried liver with onions on two plates and sprinkle with parsley.

Nutrition: Calories 143 Fat 4g Protein 18g Sugar 4g

497. Green Asparagus with Salmon Fillet and Dill Butter
Preparation Time: 5 minutes
Cooking Time: 5 minutes
Servings: 3
Ingredients:
- 2 salmon fillet with skin of the fisherman á 250 g
- 400 g green asparagus
- 2 organic lemons
- 3 tablespoons butter
- 2 tbsp. olive oil
- 3 - 4 stalks Dill
- Pepper
- Sea salt

Directions:
1. Wash the green asparagus and cut off the ends.
2. Peel the bottom third of the rods if necessary. Wash and drain the dill, wash the salmon fillets and pat dry with a kitchen towel
3. Rinse the lemon hot, dry and cut into writing.
4. For the asparagus, heat 1 tablespoon of oil and 1 tablespoon of butter in the air fryer and fry the bars for several minutes.
5. Turn the bars several times so that they are fried from all sides.
6. In the second air fryer, melt 1 tbsp. Oil and 2 tbsp. Butter and fry the salmon on the side without skin for about two minutes, turn the fillets and fry on the skin side. Spoon the liquid oil-butter mixture over the fish with the spoon over and over,
7. Divide green asparagus into two plates and add one salmon fillet each. Pour liquid butter over the fish and serve with dill and lemon slices.

Nutrition: Calories 287 Fat 15g Protein 30g Sugar 12g

498. Chicken Breast Strips with Green Asparagus of Asian Style
Preparation Time: 15 minutes
Cooking Time: 20 minutes
Servings: 4
Ingredients:
- 300 g chicken breast fillet, organic quality
- 500 g green asparagus
- 2 cloves of garlic
- 1 shallot
- 150 ml of water
- 40 ml organic soy sauce
- 2 tablespoons of sesame oil
- 2 tsp honey
- Lemon zest from an organic lemon
- Bamboo salt
- Colorful pepper

Directions:
1. Cut the meat into thin strips, making sure that the cuts are transverse to the longitudinal Fibers. Wash the asparagus spears thoroughly and peel the lower third if necessary.
2. Cut the green asparagus into pieces. Peel and cut the shallot and garlic.
3. Heat the oil in an air fryer and fry the meat.
4. Remove the meat and set aside. Put the shallot and garlic in the hot air fryer and sauté.
5. Add green asparagus and stir. Mix the honey and soy sauce with 150 ml of warm water and add to the asparagus.
6. Put the meat strips back into the air fryer to the green asparagus and swing everything through. Add the lemon zest to the meat and season with salt and pepper.
7. Place the chicken breast strips with green asparagus of the Asian style on two plates and serve.

Nutrition: Calories 587 Fat 2g Protein 16g Sugar 8g

499. Salmon Fillet on Green Asparagus and Kohlrabi
Preparation Time: 5 minutes
Cooking Time: 10 minutes
Servings: 2
Ingredients:
- 2 salmon fillets á 200 g
- 500 g green asparagus
- 50 g lamb's lettuce
- 1 large kohlrabi
- 2 - 3 branches dill
- 2 tbsp. olive oil
- 1 tbsp. butter

- 1 teaspoon pink berries
- Sea-salt

Directions:
1. Wash salmon and dry with kitchen paper towel pat, salmon skin with your sharp knife, lettuce and wash dill and drain.
2. Cut off the asparagus leaves and peel the bottom as needed, peel and dice the kohlrabi
3. Place the kohlrabi and asparagus in a large pot with steamer insert and cook until crispy in the hot steam.
4. Heat the butter and olive oil in the air fryer and fry the salmon on the skin side. Then cover with the air fryer and cook the salmon covered over medium heat
5. Depending on how thick the filet is; the salmon must roast for 10 - 20 minutes.
6. Arrange corn salad on both plates
7. Add the asparagus and kohlrabi and lay the salmon on the plates
8. Sprinkle salmon with chopped dill and sea salt and serve hot.

Nutrition: Calories 96 Fat 23g Protein 12g Sugar 13g

500. Roasted trout with butter and lemon

Preparation Time: 15 minutes
Cooking Time: 20 minutes
Servings: 1
Ingredients:
- 100 g of butter
- 2 lemon / n
- 4 garlic toes
- 4 stalks of dill fresh
- 4 stems thyme, fresh
- 1 pinch of sea salt
- 1 pinch of black pepper
- 2 rainbow trout except with head

Directions:
1. Rinse the trout under running water and drain on the kitchen towel.
2. Wash the lemons hot, dry them, and then cut into slices and the second into small boats. Wash the herbs and shake dry.
3. Peel the garlic and chop it roughly.
4. Fill the trout with herbs, garlic and lemon slices. Cut the butter into pieces and melt about half of it in the air fryer. Fry the trout from both sides for a short time.
5. Place the trout in a refractory dish and cook in a preheated oven at 175 ° c for 15-20 minutes. Remove trout from the oven and butter. Salt and pepper the fish and serve with the lemon boat.

Nutrition: Calories 194 Fat 10g Protein 22g Sugar 11g

501. Steak on spring onions with cherry sauce

Preparation Time: 10 minutes
Cooking Time: 20 minutes
Servings: 4
Ingredients:
- 4 beef steaks à 180 g
- 1 bunch of spring onions
- 1 glass of cherries
- 1 shallot
- 6 stems of rosemary
- 2 tbsp. balsamic vinegar
- 2 tbsp. olive oil
- 2 tablespoons butter
- 1 tbsp. Sucker
- ½ tsp agar
- Sea salt (Fleur de sell)
- Pepper
- Cinnamon sticks
- 100 ml of water

Directions:
1. Clean spring onions and cut into strips at an angle,
2. Finely chop the rosemary, drain the cherries through a sieve, collecting the juice, peel the shallot and finely chop.
3. For the sauce, heat 1 tbsp. Butter and sauté shallot. Add sucker and deglaze with cherry juice, vinegar and water and bring to a boil. Simmer sauce for 5-10 minutes. Stir agar in a little water, add to the sauce, stir and bring to a boil again
4. Season the sauce with salt, pepper and freshly grated cinnamon.
5. Remove the pot from the heat and add the cherries to the sauce.
6. Heat the butter and oil in the air fryer and fry the steaks for 2 minutes.
7. Turn the steaks and roast on the other side for about 2 minutes. Put the steaks on a large plate and season.
8. Place a rosemary steak on each steak, with a second large plate cover steaks and let them rest in the oven at about 50 ° c for 5 minutes.
9. Add the spring onions to the air fryer and sauté from all sides, add the chopped rosemary, then season the onions with salt and pepper and divide into four plates. Remove the steaks from the oven and add to the spring onions.
10. Pour the meat with cherry sauce and serve.

Nutrition: Calories: 234 Fat 14g Protein 19g Sugar 18g

RICE RECIPES

502. Cheesy Rice with Artichoke Hearts
Preparation Time: 10 minutes
Cooking Time: 10 minutes
Servings: 4
Ingredients:
- Canned artichoke hearts - 15 oz. chopped
- 5 oz Arborio rice
- 16 oz cream cheese
- 1 tbsp extra-virgin olive oil
- 1 tbsp grated parmesan cheese
- 1 tbsp white wine
- 6 oz Graham cracker crumbs
- 1 ¼ cups of water
- 1 ½ tbsp of Thyme, chopped
- Garlic - 2 cloves, crushed
- 1 ¼ cups, chicken broth
- Seasoning - salt and black pepper

Directions:
1. Select Sauté in your instant pot and then put the oil to heat. Cook the rice for 2 minutes. Add the garlic, mix well and then cook for a minute. Place the rice mix in a bowl.
2. Pour over the stock, salt, pepper, wine, and crumbs on the bowl and then cover it with a tin foil. Put the bowl in a steamer basket and then put the basket on the instant pot.
3. Put water on the pot and then secure the lid. Cook for 8 minutes at high pressure. After cooking, do a quickly release and then remove the bowl from the pot.
4. Remove the tin foil and then put the cream cheese, artichoke hearts, thyme, and parmesan. Mix well and serve hot.

Nutrition: Calories: 412; Fat 12g Protein 33g Sugar 6g

503. Salty Jasmin Rice
Preparation Time: 15 minutes
Cooking Time: 10 minutes
Servings: 8
Ingredients:
- 2 cups jasmine rice
- 1/2 tsp sea salt
- 3 ¼ cups water
- 1/2 cup Millet

Directions:
1. Mix all the ingredients in your instant pot. Secure the lid and then press the Rice function.
2. Cook for 10 minutes and then serve right after.

Nutrition: Calories: 313 Fat 11g Protein 34g Sugar 2g

504. Rice with Salmon Fillets
Preparation Time: 10 minutes
Cooking Time: 5 minutes
Servings: 2
Ingredients:
- Wild salmon fillets – 2 pieces, frozen
- Jasmine rice - 1/2 cup
- Vegetable soup mix - 1/4 cup, dried
- Chicken stock - 1 cup
- Butter - 1 tbsp
- Saffron - a pinch only
- Seasoning - salt and black pepper

Directions:
1. Pour the stock in your instant pot and then add the rice, soup mix, butter, and saffron. Mix well.
2. Sprinkle salt and pepper on the salmon fillets and then put the steamer basket inside the pot. Secure the lid and then cook for 5 minutes at high pressure.
3. Do a quickly release and then serve the rice on separate plates.

Nutrition: Calories: 113; Fat 14g Protein 22g Sugar 8g

505. Savory Beef Soup Rice
Preparation Time: 15 minutes
Cooking Time: 10 minutes
Servings: 6
Ingredients:
- Beef meat - 1 lb. ground
- Garlic - 3 cloves, minced
- Yellow onion – 1 piece, chopped
- Canned garbanzo beans - 15 oz. rinsed
- Potato – 1 piece, cubed
- Frozen peas - 1/2 cup
- Canned tomatoes - 14 oz. crushed
- White rice - 1/2 cup
- Spicy V8 juice - 12 oz
- Carrots – 2 pieces, thinly sliced
- Vegetable oil - 1 tbsp
- Celery rib – 1 piece, chopped
- Canned beef stock - 28 oz.
- Seasoning - salt and black pepper

Directions:
1. Select Sauté in your instant pot and then add the beef. Mix well and then cook until the beef turns brown.
2. Put the oil on the pot and heat it. Add the onion and celery mix well and then cook for 5 minutes. Add the garlic and then cook for another minute.
3. Pour the V8 juice, rice, tomatoes, beans, potatoes, carrots, beef, salt, stock, and pepper. Mix them well and then secure the lid of the pot. Cook for 5 minutes at high pressure.
4. Do a quickly release and then gently open up the lid of the pot. Press Simmer and then add more salt and pepper if desired.
5. Put the peas and mix well. Serve the rice hot.

Nutrition: Calories: 216; Fat 17g Protein 22g Sugar 8g

506. Black Rice Pudding
Preparation Time: 15 minutes
Cooking Time: 45 minutes
Servings: 4
Ingredients:
- Black rice - 2 cups, washed and rinsed
- Water - 6 ½ cups
- Sugar - 3/4 cup
- Cardamom pods – 5 pieces, crushed
- Cloves – 3 pieces
- Coconut - 1/2 cup, grated
- Chopped mango
- Cinnamon - 2 sticks
- Salt - a pinch only

Directions:
1. Place the rice in your instant pot and then add a pinch of salt and water, mix well.
2. Using a cheesecloth bag, fill it with cardamom and cinnamon, mix them well and then add the cloves. Tie the bag.
3. Put the bag in the pot together with the rice. Secure the lid of the pot and then cook for 35 minutes at low pressure.
4. Do a natural release and then open up the pot's lid. Put the coconut and then select Sauté. Cook for 10 minutes and then after cooking, remove the cheesecloth bag.
5. Serve the rice in separate bowls.

Nutrition: Calories: 298 Fat 18g Protein 29g Sugar 12g

507. Buttered Brown Rice
Preparation Time: 8 minutes
Cooking Time: 22 minutes
Servings: 4
Ingredients:
- Vegetable stock - 1 ¼ cups
- Brown rice - 2 cups
- Butter - 1 stick
- French Onion soup - 1 ¼ cups

Directions:
1. Mix up all the ingredients inside your instant pot.
2. Secure the lid of the pot and then select manual. Cook the rice for 22 minutes at high pressure.
3. After cooking the rice, do a natural release. Serve the rice on separate plates.

Nutrition: Calories: 513; Fat 21g Protein 44g Sugar 12g

508. Hawaiian Style Rice
Preparation Time: 3 minutes
Cooking Time: 9 minutes
Servings: 4
Ingredients:
- Crushed pineapple - 8 oz
- Brown rice - 1 cup
- Pineapple juice - 1/4 cup
- Butter - 1 tbsp

Directions:
1. Place all the ingredients inside the instant pot and then secure the lid.
2. Press manual and then cook the rice for 7 minutes.
3. After cooking the rice, wait for about 2 minutes and then do a quickly release. Mix well and then serve hot.

Nutrition: Calories: 383; Fat 10g Protein 25g Sugar 15g

509. Brown Rice with Black Beans
Preparation Time: 7 minutes
Cooking Time: 28 minutes
Servings: 4
Ingredients:
- 1 cup onion, diced
- 2 cups Brown rice
- 2 cups Dry black beans
- Garlic - 4 cloves crushed and then minced.
- Water - 9 cups
- 1 tsp salt
- Lime – 1 or 2 pieces
- Avocado – 1 piece, sliced

Directions:
1. Place the garlic and onion in the Instant Pot. Add the brown rice and black beans and then pour the water and salt.
2. Select manual and then cook the rice for 28 minutes. After cooking the rice, do a natural release. Let it sit for about 20 minutes.
3. Serve the rice in separate bowls squeezed with lime wedges and then add the avocado slices.

Nutrition: Calories: 110; Fat 12g Protein 14g Sugar 11g

510. Rice Combo
Preparation Time: 10 minutes
Cooking Time: 23 minutes
Servings: 4
Ingredients:
- Sea salt - 1/2 tsp
- Short grain brown rice - 3/4 cup
- Red, wild or black rice - 2 to 4 tbsp
- Water - 1 tbsp
- Water - 1 ½ cups

Directions:
1. Put all the red, wild or brown rice or a mixture of the three in a 1-cup measuring cup. Put brown rice to fill the cup.
2. Rinse the rice and then put it in the instant pot. Add the 1 ½ cup and the 1 tbsp. water in the pot. Put some salt.
3. Mix and make sure that the rice is compressed in the pot. Secure the lid of the pot and then select Multigrain. Cook the rice for 23 minutes.
4. After cooking the rice, do a natural release for 5 minutes. You can also release the pressure naturally for 15 minutes but it is up to you.
5. Right after releasing the pressure, you can now serve the rice.

Nutrition: Calories: 714; Fat 31g Protein 44g Sugar 9g

511. Breakfast Rice
Preparation Time: 10 minutes
Cooking Time: 5 minutes
Servings: 2
Ingredients:
- Eggs – 2 pieces
- Water - 1 ⅓ cup
- Scallions – 2 pieces, finely chopped
- Seasoning - salt and black pepper
- Sesame seeds - a pinch only
- Garlic powder - a pinch only
- Hot rice

Directions:
1. Mix up the eggs and 1/3 cup of water in a bowl. Strain the mixture in a microwavable bowl.
2. Put salt, pepper, garlic powder, sesame seeds, and scallions. Mix them well and then pour 1 cup of water in the instant pot.
3. Put the microwavable bowl in a steamer basket and then secure the lid of the pot. Cook for 5 minutes at high pressure.

4. Do a quickly release and then gently open up the lid of the pot. Serve the rice in separate bowls and enjoy.
Nutrition: Calories: 309; Fat 3g Protein 33g Sugar 8g

512. Rice Veggies Stew
Preparation Time: 15 minutes
Cooking Time: 17 minutes
Servings: 6
Ingredients:
- Medium-sized onions – 3 pieces, peeled and sliced.
- Brown basmati rice - 6 oz. rinsed
- Cooked chickpeas - 30 oz
- Orange juice - 8 oz
- Olive oil - 1 tbsp
- Vegetable broth - 4 cups
- Chopped cilantro - 4 oz
- Sweet potato - 1 lb. peeled and diced.
- Salt - 1/4 tsp
- Ground black pepper - 1/4 tsp
- Ground cumin - 2 tsp
- Ground coriander -2 tsp

Directions:
1. Press Sauté in your instant pot and then put the oil and onion. Cook for 12 minutes. Add in the coriander and cumin while stirring it. Cook for 15 seconds more.
2. Put all the ingredients in the pot beside the black pepper and cilantro. Mix the ingredients well.
3. Select Cancel to stop sautéing. Secure the lid of the pot and then press manual. Cook for 5 minutes at high pressure.
4. After cooking, do a natural release for 10 minutes and then gently open up the lid of the pot.
5. Serve with cilantro and black pepper on top.
Nutrition: Calories: 204 Fat 6g Protein 30g Sugar 20g

513. Easy Brown Rice
Preparation Time: 8 minutes
Cooking Time: 22 minutes
Servings: 6
Ingredients:
- Brown rice - 2 cups
- Vegetable broth - 2 ½ cups
- Sea salt - 1/2 tsp

Directions:
1. Place the rice in your instant pot and then pour down the broth. Secure the lid and then select manual.
2. Cook the rice for 22 minutes and then after cooking, do a natural release for 10 minutes.
3. Gently open up the lid and then serve the rice hot.
Nutrition: Calories: 398; Fat 2g Protein 21g Sugar 1g

514. Rice and Vegetables Mix
Preparation Time: 5 minutes
Cooking Time: 15 minutes
Servings: 4
Ingredients:
- Basmati rice - 2 cups
- Garlic – 3 cloves, minced
- Butter - 2 tbsp
- Cinnamon – 1 stick
- Cumin seeds - 1 tbsp.
- Bay leaves – 2 pieces
- Whole cloves – 3 pieces
- Ginger, grated - 1/2 tsp
- Mixed frozen carrots, peas, corn, green beans - 1 cup
- Water - 2 cups
- Green chili - 1/2 tsp. minced
- Black peppercorns – 5 pieces
- Whole cardamoms – 2 pieces
- Sugar - 1 tbsp
- Seasoning - Salt

Directions:
1. Put the water inside the instant pot and then add the rice, mixed frozen veggies, green chili, grated ginger, garlic cloves, cinnamon stick, whole cloves, butter, cumin seeds, bay leaves, cardamoms, black peppercorns, salt, and sugar.
2. Mix the ingredients well and then secure the lid. Cook for 15 minutes at high pressure.
3. Do a quickly release and then serve right after?
Nutrition: Calories: 253; Fat 5g Protein 10g Sugar 12g

515. Spiced Natural Rice
Preparation Time: 11 minutes
Cooking Time: 9 minutes
Servings: 4
Ingredients:
- 3 ¾ cups veggie stock
- 2 pieces medium-sized halved acorn squash
- 1/2 cup quinoa
- 1/2 cup vegan cheese
- 2 cloves garlic, minced
- 1 tbsp earth balance spread
- 1 cup white rice
- 1 tsp chopped rosemary
- 1 tsp chopped thyme
- 1 tsp chopped sage
- 1 cup diced onion

Directions:
1. Select Sauté in your instant pot and then add the Earth Balance to melt. Put the onion and salt and then cook for 2 minutes.
2. Add the garlic and then cook for 1 minute. Put the rice, quinoa, herbs, and broth. Mix well.
3. Put the squash in the steamer basket with the cut-side up. Secure the lid and then press manual.
4. Cook for 6 minutes at high pressure. After cooking, do a quickly release and then drain the liquids from the steamer basket.
5. Put the vegan cheese in the pot. Mix well and then serve with the rice.
Nutrition: Calories: 419; Fat 8g Protein 4g Sugar 7g

SOUP AND STEW RECIPES

516. Creamy Pumpkin Soup
Preparation Time: 10 minutes
Cooking Time: 23 minutes
Servings: 8
Ingredients:
- ¼ cup unsalted butter
- ½ small onion, diced
- 1 celery stalk, diced
- 1 carrot, diced
- 2 garlic cloves, minced
- 1 (15-ounce) can pumpkin purée
- 1½ teaspoons poultry spice blend
- 3 cups chicken stock
- 1 (8-ounce) package cream cheese
- 1 cup heavy (whipping) cream
- ¼ cup maple syrup
- Sea salt
- Freshly ground black pepper

Directions:
1. Select sear/sauté and set to hi. Select start/stop to begin. Let preheat for 5 minutes.
2. Add the butter. Once melted, add the onions, celery, carrot, and garlic. Cook, stirring occasionally, for 3 minutes
3. Add the pumpkin, poultry spice, and chicken stock. Assemble pressure lid, making sure the pressure release valve is in the seal position.
4. Select pressure and set to hi. Set time to 15 minutes. Select start/stop to begin.
5. When pressure cooking is complete, quickly release the pressure by turning the pressure release valve to the vent position. Carefully remove lid when the unit has finished releasing pressure.
6. Whisk in the cream cheese, heavy cream, and maple syrup. Season it with salt and pepper. Purée the soup using an immersion blender and do it until it become smooth.

Nutrition: Calories: 334 Fat 28g Saturated Fat 18g Cholesterol: 90mg Sodium: 266mg Carbohydrates: 17g Fiber 2g Protein 6g

517. Goulash
Preparation Time: 15 minutes
Cooking Time: 55 minutes
Servings: 6
Ingredients:
- ½ cup all-purpose flour
- 1 tablespoon kosher salt
- ½ teaspoons freshly ground black pepper
- 2 pounds' beef stew meat
- 2 tablespoons canola oil
- 1 medium red bell pepper, seeded and chopped
- 4 garlic cloves, minced
- 1 large yellow onion, diced
- 2 tablespoons smoked paprika
- 1½ pounds small Yukon gold potatoes, halved
- 2 cups beef broth
- 2 tablespoons tomato paste
- ¼ cup sour cream
- Fresh parsley, for garnish

Directions:
1. Select sear/sauté and set to hi. Select start/stop to begin. Let preheat for 5 minutes.
2. Mix together the flour, salt, and pepper in a small bowl. Dip the pieces of beef into the flour mixture, shaking off any extra flour.
3. Add the oil and let heat for 1 minute. Place the beef in the pot and brown it on all sides, about 10 minutes.
4. Add the bell pepper, garlic, onion, and smoked paprika. Sauté for about 8 minutes or until the onion is translucent.
5. Add the potatoes, beef broth, and tomato paste and stir. Assemble pressure lid, making sure the pressure release valve is in the seal position.
6. Select pressure and set to lo. Set time to 30 minutes. Select start/stop to begin. When pressure cooking is complete, quickly release the pressure by moving the pressure release valve to the vent position. Carefully remove lid when unit has finished releasing pressure.
7. Add the sour cream and mix thoroughly. Garnish with parsley, if desired, and serve immediately.

Nutrition: Calories: 413 Fat 13g Saturated Fat 4g Cholesterol: 98mg Sodium: 432mg Carbohydrates: 64g Fiber 5g Protein 37g

518. Mushroom and Wild Rice Soup
Preparation Time: 10 minutes
Cooking Time: 30 minutes
Servings: 6
Ingredients:
- 5 medium carrots, chopped
- 5 celery stalks, chopped
- 1 onion, chopped
- 3 garlic cloves, minced
- 1 cup wild rice
- 8 ounces' fresh mushrooms, sliced
- 6 cups vegetable broth
- 1 teaspoon kosher salt
- 1 teaspoon poultry seasoning
- ½ teaspoon dried thyme

Directions:
1. Place all the ingredients in the pot. Assemble pressure lid, making sure the pressure release valve is in the seal position. Select pressure and set to hi. Set time to 30 minutes. Select start/stop to begin.
2. When pressure cooking is complete, quickly release the pressure by turning the pressure release valve to the vent position. Carefully remove lid when unit has finished releasing pressure.
3. Serve.

Nutrition: Calories: 175 Total Fat 2g Saturated Fat 0g Cholesterol: 0mg Sodium: 723mg Carbohydrates: 30g Fiber 4g Protein 11g

519. Loaded Potato Soup
Preparation Time: 15 minutes
Cooking Time: 30 minutes
Servings: 6
Ingredients:
- 5 slices bacon, chopped
- 1 onion, chopped
- 3 garlic cloves, minced
- 4 pounds' russet potatoes, peeled and chopped
- 4 cups chicken broth
- 1 cup whole milk
- ½ teaspoon sea salt
- ½ teaspoon freshly ground black pepper
- 1½ cups shredded cheddar cheese
- Sour cream, for serving (optional)
- Chopped fresh chives, for serving (optional)

Directions:
1. Select sear/sauté and set to hi. Select start/stop to begin. Let preheat for 5 minutes.
2. Add the bacon, onion, and garlic. Cook and stir it occasionally, for 5 minutes. Set aside some of the bacon for garnish.
3. Add the potatoes and chicken broth. Assemble pressure lid, making sure the pressure release valve is in the seal position.
4. Select pressure and set to hi. Set time to 10 minutes, then select start/stop to begin.
5. When pressure cooking is complete, quickly release the pressure by moving the pressure release valve to the vent position. Carefully remove lid when unit has finished releasing pressure.
6. Add the milk and mash the ingredients until the soup reaches your desired consistency. Season it with the salt and black pepper. Sprinkle the cheese evenly over the top of the soup. Close crisping lid.
7. Select broil and set time to 5 minutes. Select start/stop to begin.
8. When cooking is complete, top with the reserved crispy bacon and serve with sour cream and chives (if using).

Nutrition: Calories: 468 Total Fat 19g Saturated Fat 9g Cholesterol: 51mg Sodium: 1041mg Carbohydrates: 53g Fiber 8g Protein 23g

520. Italian Sausage, Potato, and Kale Soup
Preparation Time: 10 minutes
Cooking Time: 18 minutes
Servings: 8
Ingredients:
- 1 tablespoon extra-virgin olive oil
- 1½ pounds hot Italian sausage, ground
- 1 pound sweet Italian sausage, ground
- 1 large yellow onion, diced
- 2 tablespoons minced garlic
- 4 large russet potatoes cut in ½-inch thick quarters
- 5 cups chicken stock
- 2 tablespoons Italian seasoning
- 2 teaspoons crushed red pepper flakes
- Salt
- Freshly ground black pepper
- 6 cups kale, chopped
- ½ cup heavy (whipping) cream

Directions:
1. Select sear/sauté. Set temperature to md: hi. Select start/stop to begin. Let preheat for 5 minutes.
2. Add the olive oil and hot and sweet Italian sausage. Cook, by breaking up the sausage with a spatula, until the meat is cooked all the way through, about 5 minutes.
3. Add the onion, garlic, potatoes, chicken stock, Italian seasoning, and crushed red pepper flakes. Season it with salt and pepper. Stir to combine. Assemble pressure lid, making sure the pressure release valve is in the seal position.
4. Select pressure and set to hi. Set time to 10 minutes. Select start/stop to begin.
5. When pressure cooking is complete, quickly release the pressure by turning the pressure release valve to the vent position. Carefully remove lid when the unit has finished releasing pressure.
6. Stir in the kale and heavy cream. Serve.

Nutrition: Calories: 689 Total Fat 45g Saturated Fat 15g Cholesterol: 130mg Sodium: 1185mg Carbohydrates: 38g Fiber 5g Protein 33g

521. Butternut Squash, Apple, Bacon and Orzo Soup
Preparation Time: 10 minutes
Cooking Time: 28 minutes
Servings: 8
Ingredients:
- 4 slices uncooked bacon, cut into ½-inch pieces
- 12 ounces' butternut squash, peeled and cubed
- 1 green apple, cut into small cubes
- Kosher salt
- Freshly ground black pepper
- 1 tablespoon minced fresh oregano
- 2 quarts (64 ounces) chicken stock
- 1 cup orzo

Directions:
1. Select sear/sauté and set temperature to hi. Select start/stop to begin. Let preheat for 5 minutes.
2. Place the bacon in the pot and cook, stirring frequently, about 5 minutes, or until Fat is rendered and the bacon starts to brown. Using a slotted spoon, transfer the bacon to a paper towel-lined plate to drain, leaving the rendered bacon Fat in the pot.
3. Add the butternut squash, apple, salt, and pepper and sauté until partially soft, about 5 minutes. Stir in the oregano.
4. Add the bacon back into the pot along with the chicken stock. Bring to a boil for about 10 minutes, and

then add the orzo. Cook for about 8 minutes, until the orzo is tender. Serve.
Nutrition: Calories: 247 Total Fat 7g Saturated Fat 2g Cholesterol: 17mg Sodium: 563mg Carbohydrates: 33g Fiber 3g Protein 12g

522. Braised Pork and Black Bean Stew
Preparation Time: 15 minutes
Cooking Time: 30 minutes
Servings: 8
Ingredients:
- 2 pounds' boneless pork shoulder, cut into 1-inch pieces
- ¼ cup all-purpose flour
- ¼ cup unsalted butter
- ½ small onion, diced
- 1 carrot, diced
- 1 celery stalk, diced
- 2 garlic cloves, minced
- 1 tablespoon tomato paste
- 1 tablespoon cumin
- 1 tablespoon smoked paprika
- 4 cups chicken stock
- 1 (10-ounce) can diced tomatoes with chilies
- 1 (15-ounce) can black beans, rinsed and drained
- 1 (15-ounce) can hominy, rinsed and drained
- Sea salt
- Freshly ground black pepper

Directions:
1. In a large bowl, coat the pork pieces with the flour.
2. Select sear/sauté and set to hi. Select start/stop to begin. Let preheat for 5 minutes.
3. Add the butter. Once melted, add the pork and sear for 5 minutes, turning the pieces so they begin to brown on all sides.
4. Add the onion, carrot, celery, garlic, tomato paste, cumin, and paprika and cook, stirring occasionally, for 3 minutes.
5. Add the chicken stock and tomatoes. Assemble pressure lid, making sure the pressure release valve is in the seal position.
6. Select pressure and set to hi. Set time to 15 minutes. Select start/stop to begin.
7. When pressure cooking is complete, quickly release the pressure by turning the pressure release valve to the vent position. Carefully remove lid when the unit has finished releasing pressure.
8. Select sear/sauté and set to hi. Select start/stop to begin.
9. Whisk in the beans and hominy. Season it with salt and pepper and cook for 2 minutes. Serve.
Nutrition: Calories: 342 Total Fat 12g Saturated Fat 6g Cholesterol: 64mg Sodium: 638mg Carbohydrates: 27g Fiber 6g Protein 29g

523. Fish Chowder and Biscuits
Preparation Time: 15 minutes
Cooking Time: 30 minutes
Servings: 8
Ingredients:
- 5 strips bacon, sliced
- 1 white onion, chopped
- 3 celery stalks, chopped
- 4 cups chicken stock
- 2 russet potatoes, rinsed and cut in 1-inch pieces
- 4 (6-ounce) frozen haddock fillets
- Kosher salt
- ½ cup clam juice
- ⅓ Cup all-purpose flour
- 2 (14-ounce) cans evaporated milk
- 1 (14-ounce) tube refrigerated biscuit dough

Directions:
1. Select sear/sauté and set to hi. Select start/stop to begin. Let preheat for 5 minutes.
2. Add the bacon and cook, stirring frequently, for 5 minutes. Add the onion and celery and cook for an additional 5 minutes, stirring occasionally.
3. Add the chicken stock, potatoes, and haddock filets. Season it with salt. Assemble pressure lid, making sure the pressure release valve is in the seal position.
4. Select pressure and set to hi. Set time to 5 minutes. Select start/stop to begin.
5. Whisk together the clam juice and flour in a small bowl, ensuring there are no flour clumps in the mixture.
6. When pressure cooking is complete, quickly release the pressure by moving the pressure release valve to the vent position. Carefully remove lid when unit has finished releasing pressure.
7. Select sear/sauté and set to med. Select start/stop to begin. Add the clam juice mixture, stirring well to combine. Add the evaporated milk and continue to stir frequently for 3 to 5 minutes, until chowder has thickened to your desired texture.
8. Place the reversible rack in the pot in the higher position. Place the biscuits on the rack; it may be necessary to tear the last biscuit or two into smaller pieces in order to fit them all on the rack. Close crisping lid. Select bake/roast, set temperature to 350°f, and set time to 12 minutes. Select start/stop to begin.
9. After 10 minutes, check the biscuits for doneness. If desired, cook for up to an additional 2 minutes. When cooking is complete, open lid and remove rack from pot. Serve the chowder and top each portion with biscuits.
Nutrition: Calories: 518 Total Fat 22g Carbohydrates: 49g Fiber 2g Protein 33g

524. Coconut and Shrimp Bisque
Preparation Time: 10 minutes
Cooking Time: 15 minutes
Servings: 4
Ingredients:
- ¼ cup red curry paste
- 2 tablespoons water
- 1 tablespoon extra-virgin olive oil
- 1 bunch scallions, sliced

- 1-pound medium (21-30 count) shrimp, peeled and deveined
- 1 cup frozen peas
- 1 red bell pepper, diced
- 1 (14-ounce) can full-Fat coconut milk
- Kosher salt

Directions:
1. In a small bowl, whisk together the red curry paste and water. Set aside.
2. Select sear/sauté and set to med. Select start/stop to begin. Let preheat for 3 minutes.
3. Add the oil and scallions. Cook for 2 minutes.
4. Add the shrimp, peas, and bell pepper. Stir well to combine. Stir in the red curry paste. Cook for 5 minutes, until the peas are tender.
5. Stir in coconut milk and cook for an additional 5 minutes until shrimp is cooked through and the bisque is thoroughly heated.
6. Season it with salt and serve immediately.

Nutrition: Calories: 460 Total Fat 32g Saturated Fat 23g Cholesterol: 223mg Sodium: 902mg Carbohydrates: 16g Fiber 5g Protein 29g

525. Roasted Tomato and Seafood Stew

Preparation Time: 10 minutes
Cooking Time: 46 minutes
Servings: 6
Ingredients:
- 2 tablespoons extra-virgin olive oil
- 1 yellow onion, diced
- 1 fennel bulb, tops removed and bulb diced
- 3 garlic cloves, minced
- 1 cup dry white wine
- 2 (14.5-ounce) cans fire-roasted tomatoes
- 2 cups chicken stock
- 1-pound medium (21-30 count) shrimp, peeled and deveined
- 1-pound raw white fish (cod or haddock), cubed
- Salt
- Freshly ground black pepper
- Fresh basil, torn, for garnish

Directions:
1. Select sear/sauté and set to med. Select start/stop to begin. Let preheat for 3 minutes.
2. Add the olive oil, onions, fennel, and garlic. Cook for about 3 minutes, until translucent.
3. Add the white wine and deglaze, scraping any stuck bits from the bottom of the pot using a silicone spatula. Add the roasted tomatoes and chicken stock. Simmer for 25 to 30 minutes. Add the shrimp and white fish.
4. Select sear/sauté and set to md: lo. Select start/stop to begin.
5. Simmer for 10 minutes, stirring frequently, until the shrimp and fish are cooked through. Season it with salt and pepper.
6. Ladle into bowl and serve topped with torn basil.

Nutrition: Calories: 301 Total Fat 8g Saturated Fat 1g Cholesterol: 99mg Sodium: 808mg Carbohydrates: 21g Fiber 4g Protein 26g

526. Chicken Enchilada Soup

Preparation Time: 5 minutes
Cooking Time: 30 minutes
Servings: 8
Ingredients:
- 1 tablespoon extra-virgin olive oil
- 1 small red onion, diced
- 2 (10-ounce) cans fire-roasted tomatoes with chilies
- 1 (15-ounce) can corn
- 1 (15-ounce) can black beans, rinsed and drained
- 1 (10-ounce) can red enchilada sauce
- 1 (10-ounce) can tomato paste
- 3 tablespoons taco seasoning
- 2 tablespoons freshly squeezed lime juice
- 2 (8-ounce) boneless, skinless chicken breasts
- Salt
- Freshly ground black pepper

Directions:
1. Select sear/sauté and set temperature to md: hi. Select start/stop to begin. Let preheat for 5 minutes.
2. Place the olive oil and onion in the pot. Cook until the onions are translucent, about 2 minutes.
3. Add the tomatoes, corn, beans, enchilada sauce, tomato paste, taco seasoning, lime juice, and chicken. Season it with salt and pepper and stir. Assemble pressure lid, making sure the pressure release valve is in the seal position.
4. Select pressure and set to hi. Set time to 9 minutes. Select start/stop to begin.
5. When pressure cooking is complete, allow pressure to naturally release for 10 minutes. After 10 minutes, quickly release remaining pressure by moving the pressure release valve to the vent position. Carefully remove lid when unit has finished releasing pressure.
6. Transfer the chicken breasts to a cutting board. Using two forks shred the chicken. Return the chicken back to the pot and stir. Serve in a bowl with toppings of choice, such as shredded cheese, crushed tortilla chips, sliced avocado, sour cream, cilantro, and lime wedges, if desired.

Nutrition: Calories: 257 Total Fat 4g Saturated Fat 0g Cholesterol: 33mg Sodium: 819mgCarbohydrates: 37g Fiber 7g Protein 20g

527. Chicken Noodle Soup

Preparation Time: 10 minutes
Cooking Time: 19 minutes
Servings: 8
Ingredients:
- 2 tablespoons unsalted butter
- 1 large onion, chopped
- 2 carrots, chopped
- 2 celery stalks, chopped
- 2 pounds' boneless chicken breast

- 4 cups chicken broth
- 4 cups water
- 1 tablespoon chopped fresh parsley
- 1 teaspoon dried thyme
- 1 teaspoon dried oregano
- ½ teaspoon sea salt
- ½ teaspoon freshly ground black pepper
- 5 ounces' egg noodles

Directions:
1. Select sear/sauté and set to hi. Select start/stop to begin. Let preheat for 5 minutes.
2. Add the butter. Once melted, add the onion, carrots, and celery. Cook, stir it occasionally, for 5 minutes.
3. Add the chicken, chicken broth, water, parsley, thyme, oregano, salt, and pepper. Assemble pressure lid, making sure the pressure release valve is in the seal position.
4. Select pressure and set to hi. Set time to 8 minutes. Select start/stop to begin.
5. When pressure cooking is complete, quickly release the pressure by moving the pressure release valve to the vent position. Carefully remove lid when unit has finished releasing pressure.
6. Remove the chicken from the soup and shred it with two forks. Set aside.
7. Add the egg noodles. Select sear/sauté and set to med. Select start/stop to begin.
8. Cook it for 6 minutes, uncovered, or until the noodles are tender. Stir the shredded chicken back into the pot. Serve.

Nutrition: Calories: 237 Total Fat 5g Saturated Fat 2g Cholesterol: 87mg Sodium: 413mg Carbohydrates: 17g Fiber 2g Protein 30g

528. Chicken Potpie Soup

Preparation Time: 15 minutes
Cooking Time: 1 hour
Servings: 6
Ingredients:
- 4 (8-ounce) chicken breasts
- 2 cups chicken stock
- 2 tablespoons unsalted butter
- 1 yellow onion, diced
- 16 ounces frozen mixed vegetables
- 1 cup heavy (whipping) cream
- 1 (10.5-ounce) can condensed cream of chicken soup
- 2 tablespoons cornstarch
- 2 tablespoons water
- Salt
- Freshly ground black pepper
- 1 (16.3-ounce) tube refrigerated biscuit dough

Directions:
1. Place the chicken and stock in the pot. Assemble pressure lid, making sure the pressure release valve is in the seal position.
2. Select pressure and set to hi. Set time to 15 minutes. Select start/stop to begin.
3. Once pressure cooking is complete, quickly release the pressure by turning the pressure release valve to the vent position. Carefully remove lid when the unit has finished releasing pressure.
4. Using a silicone-tipped utensil shred the chicken.
5. Select sear/sauté and set to med. add the butter, onion, mixed vegetables, cream, and condensed soup and stir. Select start/stop to begin. Simmer for 10 minutes.
6. In a small bowl, whisk together the cornstarch and water. Slowly whisk the cornstarch mixture into the soup. Set temperature to low and simmer for 10 minutes more. Season it with salt and pepper.
7. Carefully arrange the biscuits on top of the simmering soup. Close crisping lid.
8. Select bake/roast, set temperature to 325°f, and set time to 15 minutes. Select start/stop to begin.
9. When cooking is complete, remove the biscuits. To serve, place a biscuit in a bowl and ladle soup over it.

Nutrition: Calories: 731 Total Fat 26g Saturated Fat 17g Cholesterol: 169mg Sodium: 1167mg Carbohydrates: 56g Fiber 5g Protein 45g

529. Tex-Mex Chicken Tortilla Soup

Preparation Time: 10 minutes
Cooking Time: 20 minutes
Servings: 8
Ingredients:
- 1 tablespoon extra-virgin olive oil
- 1 onion, chopped
- 1 pound boneless, skinless chicken breasts
- 6 cups chicken broth
- 1 (12-ounce) jar salsa
- 4 ounces' tomato paste
- 1 tablespoon chili powder
- 2 teaspoons cumin
- ½ teaspoon sea salt
- ½ teaspoon freshly ground black pepper
- 1 pinch of cayenne pepper
- 1 (15-ounce) can black beans, rinsed and drained
- 2 cups frozen corn
- Tortilla strips, for garnish

Directions:
1. Select sear/sauté and set to temperature to hi. Select start/stop to begin. Let preheat for 5 minutes.
2. Place the olive oil and onions into the pot and cook, stirring occasionally, for 5 minutes.
3. Add the chicken breast, chicken broth, salsa, tomato paste, chili powder, cumin, salt, pepper, and cayenne pepper. Assemble pressure lid, making sure the pressure release valve is in the seal position.
4. Select pressure and set to hi. Set time to 10 minutes. Select start/stop to begin.
5. When pressure cooking is complete, allow pressure to naturally release for 10 minutes. After 10 minutes, quickly release remaining pressure by moving the pressure release valve to the vent position. Carefully remove lid when unit has finished releasing pressure.

6. Transfer the chicken breasts to a cutting board and shred with two forks. Set aside.
7. Add the black beans and corn. Select sear/sauté and set to mi. Select start/stop to begin. Cook until heated through, about 5 minutes.
8. Add shredded chicken back to the pot. Garnish with tortilla strips, serve, and enjoy!

Nutrition: Calories: 186 Total Fat 4g Saturated Fat 0g Cholesterol: 33mg Sodium: 783mg Carbohydrates: 23g Fiber 6g Protein 19g

530. Chicken Tomatillo Stew

Preparation Time: 15 minutes
Cooking Time: 46 minutes
Servings: 4
Ingredients:
- 3 medium onions, quartered
- 3 garlic cloves, whole
- 2 poblano peppers, seeded and quartered
- ½ pound tomatillos
- 2 small jalapeño peppers, seeded and quartered (optional)
- 2 tablespoons canola oil, divided
- Kosher salt
- Freshly ground black pepper
- 2½ pounds boneless, skinless chicken thighs (6 to 8 pieces)
- 1 cup chicken stock
- 1 teaspoon cumin
- 1 tablespoon oregano
- 1 tablespoon all-purpose flour
- 1 cup water

Directions:
1. Place cook & crisp basket in pot and close crisping lid. Select air crisp and set to high. Set time to 25 minutes. Select start/stop to begin. Let preheat for 5 minutes.
2. Place the onions, garlic, poblano peppers, tomatillos, jalapeños, 1 tablespoon of canola oil, salt, and pepper in a medium-sized bowl and mix until vegetables are evenly coated.
3. Once unit has preheated, open lid and place the vegetables in the basket. Close lid and cook for 20 minutes.
4. After 10 minutes, open lid, then lift basket and shake the vegetables or toss them with silicone-tipped tongs. Lower the basket back into pot and close lid to continue cooking.
5. When cooking is complete, remove basket and vegetables and set aside.
6. Select sear/sauté and set to hi. Select start/stop to begin. Let preheat for 5 minutes.
7. Season the chicken thighs with salt and pepper.
8. After 5 minutes, add the remaining 1 tablespoon of oil and chicken. Sear the chicken, about 3 minutes on each side.
9. Add the chicken stock, cumin, and oregano. Scrape the pot with a rubber or wooden spoon to release any pieces that are sticking to the bottom. Assemble pressure lid, making sure the pressure release valve is in the seal position.
10. Select pressure and set to hi. Set time to 10 minutes. Select start/stop to begin.
11. Remove the vegetables from the basket and roughly chop.
12. In a small bowl, add the flour and water and stir.
13. When pressure cooking is complete, quickly release the pressure by turning the pressure release valve to the vent position. Carefully remove lid when unit has finished releasing pressure.
14. Remove the chicken and shred it using two forks.
15. Select sear/sauté and set to med. Select start/stop to begin. Return the chicken and vegetables and stir with a rubber or wooden spoon, being sure to scrape the bottom of the pot. Slowly stir in the flour mixture. Bring to a simmer and cook for 10 minutes, or until the broth becomes clear and has thickened.
16. When cooking is complete, serve as is or garnish with sour cream, lime, cilantro, and a flour tortilla for dipping.

Nutrition: Calories: 487 Total Fat 20g Saturated Fat 3g Cholesterol: 239mg Sodium: 382mg Carbohydrates: 19g Fiber 4g Protein 59g

SNACKS RECIPES

531. Classic French Fries
Preparation Time: 5 minutes
Cooking Time: 30 minutes
Servings: 6
Ingredients:
- 3 large russet potatoes
- 1 tablespoon canola oil
- 1 tablespoon extra-virgin olive oil
- Salt
- Pepper

Directions:
1. Peel the potatoes and cut lengthwise to create French fries.
2. Place the potatoes in a large bowl of cold water. Allow the potatoes to soak in the water for at least 30 minutes, preferably an hour.
3. Spread the fries onto a baking sheet (optional: lined with parchment paper) and coat them with the canola oil, olive oil, and salt and pepper to taste.
4. Transfer half of the fries to the air fryer basket. Cook for 10 minutes.
5. Cook for an additional 5 minutes.
6. When the first half finishes, remove the cooked fries, then repeat steps 4 and 5 for the remaining fries.
7. Cool before serving.

Nutrition: Calories: 168;Total Fat 5g Saturated Fat 1g Cholesterol: 0mg Sodium: 38mg Carbohydrates: 29g Fiber 4g Protein 3g

532. Olive Oil Sweet Potato Chips
Preparation Time: 10 minutes
Cooking Time: 20 minutes
Servings: 5
Ingredients:
- 3 sweet potatoes
- 2 teaspoons extra-virgin olive oil
- 1 teaspoon cinnamon (optional)
- Salt
- Pepper

Directions:
1. shred the sweet potatoes using a vegetable peeler. Cut the potatoes crosswise into thin slices. You can also use a mandolin to slice the potatoes into chips.
2. Place the sweet potatoes in a large bowl of cold water for 30 minutes. This helps remove the starch from the sweet potatoes, which promotes crisping.
3. Drain the sweet potatoes. Dry the slices thoroughly with paper towels or napkins.
4. Place the sweet potatoes in another large bowl. Add the olive oil and sprinkle with the cinnamon, if using, and salt and pepper to taste. Toss to fully coat.
5. Place the sweet potato slices in the air fryer. It is okay to stack them, but do not overcrowd. You may need to cook the chips in two batches. Cook the potatoes for 10 minutes.
6. Cook the chips for an additional 10 minutes.
7. Cool before serving.

Nutrition: Calories: 94; Total Fat 2g Saturated Fat 0g Cholesterol: 0mg Sodium: 58mg Carbohydrates: 20g Fiber 2g Protein 1g

533. Parmesan Breaded Zucchini Chips
Preparation Time: 15 minutes
Cooking Time: 20 minutes
Servings: 5
Ingredients:
For the zucchini chips:
- 2 medium zucchini
- 2 eggs
- ⅓ cup bread crumbs
- ⅓ cup grated Parmesan cheese
- Salt
- Pepper
- Cooking oil

For the lemon aioli:
- ½ cup mayonnaise
- ½ tablespoon olive oil
- Juice of ½ lemon
- 1 teaspoon minced garlic
- Salt
- Pepper

Directions:
1. To make the zucchini chips:
2. Slice the zucchini into thin chips (about ⅛ inch thick) using a knife or mandolin.
3. In a small bowl, beat the eggs. In another small bowl, combine the bread crumbs, Parmesan cheese, and salt and pepper to taste.
4. Spray the air fryer basket with cooking oil.
5. Dip the zucchini slices one at a time in the eggs and then the bread crumb mixture. You can also sprinkle the bread crumbs onto the zucchini slices with a spoon.
6. Place the zucchini chips in the air fryer basket, but do not stack. Cook in batches. Spray the chips with cooking oil from a distance (otherwise, the breading may fly off). Cook for 10 minutes.
7. Remove the cooked zucchini chips from the air fryer, then repeat step 5 with the remaining zucchini.
8. To make the lemon aioli:
9. While the zucchini is cooking, combine the mayonnaise, olive oil, lemon juice, and garlic in a small bowl, adding salt and pepper to taste. Mix well until fully combined.
10. Cool the zucchini and serve alongside the aioli.

Nutrition: Calories: 192; Total Fat 13g Saturated Fat 3g Cholesterol: 97mg Sodium: 254mg Carbohydrates: 12g Fiber 4g Protein 6g

534. Low-Carb Cheese-Stuffed Jalapeño Poppers
Preparation Time: 10 minutes
Cooking Time: 5 minutes
Servings: 5

Ingredients:
- 10 jalapeño peppers
- 6 ounces' cream cheese
- ¼ cup shredded Cheddar cheese
- 2 tablespoons panko bread crumbs
- Cooking oil

Directions:
1. recommend you wear gloves while handling jalapeños. Halve the jalapeños lengthwise. Remove the seeds and the white membrane.
2. Place the cream cheese in a small, microwave-safe bowl. Microwave for 15 seconds to soften.
3. Remove the bowl from the microwave. Add the Cheddar cheese. Mix well.
4. Stuff each of the jalapeño halves with the cheese mixture, then sprinkle the panko bread crumbs on top of each popper.
5. Place the poppers in the air fryer. Spray them with cooking oil. Cook for 5 minutes.
6. Cool before serving.

Nutrition: Calories: 156; Total Fat 14g Saturated Fat 9g Cholesterol: 43mg Sodium: 874mg Carbohydrates: 3g Fiber 1g Protein 4g

535. Vidalia Onion Blossom
Preparation Time: 10 minutes
Cooking Time: 25 minutes
Servings: 4
Ingredients:
- 1 large Vidalia onion
- 1½ cups all-purpose flour
- 1 teaspoon garlic powder
- 1 teaspoon paprika
- Salt
- Pepper
- 2 eggs
- 1 cup milk
- Cooking oil

Directions:
1. Cut off the pointy stem end of the onion. Leave the root end intact. Peel the onion and place it cut-side down. The root end of the onion should be facing up.
2. Starting about ½ inch from the root end, cut downward to make 4 evenly spaced cuts. In each section, make 3 additional cuts. There should be 16 cuts in the onion.
3. Turn the onion over and fluff out the "petals."
4. Place the flour in a large bowl and season it with the garlic powder, paprika, and salt and pepper to taste.
5. In another large bowl, whisk the eggs. Add the milk and stir. This will form a batter.
6. Place the onion in the bowl with the flour mixture. Use a large spoon to cover the onion petals in flour.
7. Transfer the onion to the batter. Use a spoon or basting brush to cover the onion completely.
8. Return the onion to the flour mixture. Cover completely.
9. Wrap the battered onion in foil and place in the freezer for 45 minutes.
10. Spray the air fryer basket with cooking oil. Unwrap the foil covering and place the onion in the air fryer basket. Cook for 10 minutes.
11. Open the air fryer. Spray the onion with cooking oil. If areas of the onion are still white from the flour, focus the spray on these areas.
12. Cook for an additional 10 to 15 minutes, or until crisp.

Nutrition: Calories: 253; Total Fat 4g; Saturated Fat 2g Cholesterol: 87mg Sodium: 101mg Carbohydrates: 43g Fiber 2g Protein 10g

536. Crispy Fried Pickle Chips
Preparation Time: 10 minutes
Cooking Time: 10 minutes
Servings: 4
Ingredients:
- 1-pound whole dill pickles
- 2 eggs
- ⅓ cup all-purpose flour
- ⅓ cup bread crumbs
- Cooking oil

Directions:
1. Cut the pickles crosswise into ½-inch-thick slices. Dry the slices completely using a paper towel.
2. In a small bowl, beat the eggs. In another small bowl, add the flour. Place the bread crumbs in a third small bowl.
3. Spray the air fryer basket with cooking oil.
4. Dip the pickle slices in the flour, then the egg, and then the bread crumbs.
5. Place the breaded pickle slices in the air fryer. It is okay to stack them. Spray them with cooking oil. Cook for 6 minutes.
6. Open the air fryer and flip the pickles. Cook for an additional 2 to 3 minutes, or until the pickles are crisp.

Nutrition: Calories: 137; Total Fat 3g Saturated Fat 1g Cholesterol: 82mg Sodium: 2372mg Carbohydrates: 21g Fiber 4g Protein 7g

537. Spiced Nuts
Preparation Time: 5 minutes
Cooking Time: 15 minutes
Servings: 4
Ingredients:
- ½ teaspoon cinnamon
- ½ teaspoon stevia
- Pepper
- 1 cup nuts (walnuts, pecans, and almonds work well)
- 1 egg white
- Cooking oil

Directions:
1. In a small bowl, combine the cinnamon, stevia, and pepper to taste.
2. Place the nuts in another bowl with the egg white. Add the spices to the nuts.

3. Spray the air fryer basket with cooking oil.
4. Place the nuts in the air fryer. Spray them with cooking oil. Cook for 10 minutes.
5. Open the air fryer and shake the basket. Cook for an additional 3 to 4 minutes.
6. Serve warm.

Nutrition: Calories: 210; Total Fat 18g Saturated Fat 2g Cholesterol: 0mg Sodium: 237mg Carbohydrates: 9g Fiber 3g Protein 7g

538. Pigs in a Blanket
Preparation Time: 10 minutes
Cooking Time: 20 minutes
Servings: 1
Ingredients:
- 1 (8-ounce) can crescent rolls or croissant biscuit rolls
- 16 cocktail franks or mini smoked hot dogs
- Cooking oil

Directions:
1. Separate the crescent roll dough into 8 triangles and place them on a flat work surface. Cut each triangle in half to make 16 triangles.
2. Dry the franks with a paper towel. Place 1 frank on the bottom of a triangle. This should be the widest part of the dough. Roll up the dough. Repeat for the remaining franks and triangles.
3. Spray the air fryer basket with cooking oil.
4. Place 8 pigs in a blanket in the air fryer. It is okay to stack them, but do not overcrowd the basket. Spray them with cooking oil. Cook for 8 minutes.
5. Remove the cooked pigs in a blanket from the air fryer, then repeat step 4 for the remaining 8 pigs in a blanket.
6. Cool before serving.

Nutrition: Calories: 75; Total Fat 5g Saturated Fat 2g Cholesterol: 5mg Sodium: 170mg Carbohydrates: 6g Fiber 0g Protein 2g

539. Breaded Artichoke Hearts
Preparation Time: 15 minutes
Cooking Time: 10 minutes
Servings: 1
Ingredients:
- 14 whole artichoke hearts packed in water
- 1 egg
- ½ cup all-purpose flour
- ⅓ cup panko bread crumbs
- 1 teaspoon Italian seasoning
- Cooking oil

Directions:
1. Squeeze excess water from the artichoke hearts and place them on paper towels to dry.
2. In a small bowl, beat the egg. In another small bowl, place the flour. In a third small bowl, combine the bread crumbs and Italian seasoning, and stir.
3. Spray the air fryer basket with cooking oil.
4. Dip the artichoke hearts in the flour, then the egg, and then the bread crumb mixture.
5. Place the breaded artichoke hearts in the air fryer. It is okay to stack them. Spray them with cooking oil. Cook for 4 minutes.
6. Open the air fryer and flip the artichoke hearts. I recommend flipping instead of shaking because the hearts are small, and this will help keep the breading intact. Cook for an additional 4 minutes, or until the artichoke hearts have browned and are crisp.
7. Cool before serving.

Nutrition: Calories: 54; Total Fat 1g Saturated Fat 0g Cholesterol: 12mg Sodium: 248mg Carbohydrates: 9g Fiber 1g Protein 3g

540. Crunchy Pork Egg Rolls
Preparation Time: 15 minutes
Cooking Time: 15 minutes
Servings: 1
Ingredients:
- Cooking oil
- 2 garlic cloves, minced
- 1 teaspoon sesame oil
- ¼ cup soy sauce
- 2 teaspoons grated fresh ginger
- 12 ounces ground pork
- ½ cabbage, shredded (2 cups)
- 4 scallions, green parts (white parts optional), chopped
- 24 egg roll wrappers

Directions:
1. Spray a skillet with cooking oil and place over medium-high heat. Add the garlic. Cook for 1 minute, until fragrant.
2. Add the ground pork to the skillet. Using a spoon, break the pork into smaller chunks.
3. In a small bowl, combine the sesame oil, soy sauce, and ginger. Mix well to combine.
4. Add the sauce to the skillet. Stir to combine. Continue cooking for 5 minutes, until the pork is browned.
5. When the pork has browned, add the cabbage and scallions. Mix well.
6. Transfer the pork mixture to a large bowl.
7. Lay the egg roll wrappers on a flat surface. Dip a basting brush in water and glaze each of the egg roll wrappers along the edges with the wet brush. This will soften the dough and make it easier to roll.
8. Stack 2 egg roll wrappers (it works best if you double-wrap the egg rolls). Scoop 1 to 2 tablespoons of the pork mixture onto the center.
9. Roll one long side of the wrappers up over the filling. Press firmly on the area with the filling, tucking it in lightly to secure it in place. Next, fold in the left and right sides.
10. Continue rolling to close. Use the basting brush to wet the seam and seal the egg roll.
11. Place the egg rolls in the basket of the air fryer. It is okay to stack them. Spray them with cooking oil. Cook for 8 minutes.
12. Flip the egg rolls. Cook for an additional 4 minutes.

13. Cool before serving.
Nutrition: Calories: 244; Total Fat 4g Saturated Fat 1g Cholesterol: 27mg Sodium: 683mg Carbohydrates: 39g Fiber 2g Protein 12g

541. Air Fry Bacon
Preparation Time: 5 minutes
Cooking Time: 10 minutes
Servings: 11
Ingredients:
- 11 bacon slices

Directions:
1. Place half bacon slices in air fryer basket.
2. Cook at 400 F for 10 minutes.
3. Cook remaining half bacon slices using same steps.
4. Serve and enjoy.

Nutrition: Calories 103 Fat 7.9 g Carbohydrates 0.3 g Sugar 0 g Protein 7 g Cholesterol 21 mg

542. Crunchy Bacon Bites
Preparation Time: 5 minutes
Cooking Time: 10 minutes
Servings: 4
Ingredients:
- 4 bacon strips, cut into small pieces
- 1/2 cup pork rinds, crushed
- 1/4 cup hot sauce

Directions:
1. Add bacon pieces in a bowl.
2. Add hot sauce and toss well.
3. Add crushed pork rinds and toss until bacon pieces are well coated.
4. Transfer bacon pieces in air fryer basket and cook at 350 F for 10 minutes.
5. Serve and enjoy.

Nutrition: Calories 112 Fat 9.7 g Carbohydrates 0.3 g Sugar 0.2 g Protein 5.2 g Cholesterol 3 mg

543. Easy Jalapeno Poppers
Preparation Time: 10 minutes
Cooking Time: 13 minutes
Servings: 5
Ingredients:
- 1/2 tsp garlic, minced
- 2 tbsp. salsa
- 4 oz. goat cheese, crumbled
- 5 jalapeno peppers, slice in half and deseeded
- 1/4 tsp chili powder
- Salt
- Pepper

Directions:
1. In a small bowl, mix together cheese, sauce, chili, garlic, pepper, and salt.
2. Place the cheese mixture in each jalapeño half and place it in the fryer basket.
3. Cook the jalapeños at 350 F for 13 minutes.
4. Serve and enjoy.

Nutrition: Calories 111 Fat 8.3 g Carbohydrates 2.1 g Sugar 1.2 g Protein 7.3 g Cholesterol 24 mg

544. Perfect Crab Dip
Preparation Time: 5 minutes
Cooking Time: 7 minutes
Servings: 4
Ingredients:
- 1 cup crabmeat
- 2 tbsp. parsley, chopped
- 2 tbsp. fresh lemon juice
- 2 tbsp. hot sauce
- 1/2 cup green onion, sliced
- 2 cups cheese, grated
- 1/4 cup mayonnaise
- 1/4 tsp pepper
- 1/2 tsp salt

Directions:
1. In a 6-inch dish, mix together crabmeat, hot sauce, cheese, mayo, pepper, and salt.
2. Place dish in air fryer basket and cook dip at 400 F for 7 minutes.
3. Remove dish from air fryer.
4. Drizzle dip with lemon juice and garnish with parsley.
5. Serve and enjoy.

Nutrition: Calories 313 Fat 23.9 g Carbohydrates 8.8 g Sugar 3.1 g Protein 16.2 g Cholesterol 67 mg

545. Spinach Dip
Preparation Time: 10 minutes
Cooking Time: 40 minutes
Servings: 8
Ingredients:
- 8 oz. cream cheese, softened
- 1/4 tsp garlic powder
- 1/2 cup onion, minced
- 1/3 cup water chestnuts, drained and chopped
- 1 cup mayonnaise
- 1 cup parmesan cheese, grated
- 1 cup frozen spinach, thawed and squeeze out all liquid
- 1/2 tsp pepper

Directions:
1. Spray air fryer baking dish with cooking spray.
2. Add all ingredients into the bowl and mix until well combined.
3. Transfer bowl mixture into the prepared baking dish and place dish in air fryer basket.
4. Cook at 300 F for 35-40 minutes. After 20 minutes of cooking stir dip.
5. Serve and enjoy.

Nutrition: Calories 220 Fat 20.5 g Carbohydrates 9.3 g Sugar 2.3 g Protein 3.8 g Cholesterol 41 mg

546. Sweet Potato Tots
Preparation Time: 10 minutes
Cooking Time: 31 minutes
Servings: 24
Ingredients:
- 2 sweet potatoes, peeled
- 1/2 tsp Cajun seasoning

- Salt

Directions:
1. Add water in large pot and bring to boil. Add sweet potatoes in pot and boil for 15 minutes. Drain well.
2. Grated boil sweet potatoes into a large bowl using a grated.
3. Add Cajun seasoning and salt in grated sweet potatoes and mix until well combined.
4. Spray air fryer basket with cooking spray.
5. Make small tot of sweet potato mixture and place in air fryer basket.
6. Cook at 400 F for 8 minutes. Turn tots to another side and cook for 8 minutes more.
7. Serve and enjoy.

Nutrition: Calories 15 Fat 0 g Carbohydrates 3.5 g Sugar 0.1 g Protein 0.2 g Cholesterol 0 mg

547. Herb Zucchini Slices

Preparation Time: 10 minutes
Cooking Time: 15 minutes
Servings: 4
Ingredients:
- 2 zucchinis, slice in half lengthwise and cut each half through middle
- 1 tbsp. olive oil
- 4 tbsp. parmesan cheese, grated
- 2 tbsp. almond flour
- 1 tbsp. parsley, chopped
- Pepper
- Salt

Directions:
1. Preheat the air fryer to 350 F.
2. In a bowl, mix together cheese, parsley, oil, almond flour, pepper, and salt.
3. Top zucchini pieces with cheese mixture and place in the air fryer basket.
4. Cook zucchini for 15 minutes at 350 F.
5. Serve and enjoy.

Nutrition: Calories 157 Fat 11.4 g Carbohydrates 5.1 g Sugar 1.7 g Protein 11 g Cholesterol 20 mg

548. Ranch Kale Chips

Preparation Time: 5 minutes
Cooking Time: 5 minutes
Servings: 4
Ingredients:
- 4 cups kale, stemmed
- 1 tbsp. nutritional yeast flakes
- 2 tsp ranch seasoning
- 2 tbsp. olive oil
- 1/4 tsp salt

Directions:
1. Add all ingredients into the large mixing bowl and toss well.
2. Spray air fryer basket with cooking spray.
3. Add kale in air fryer basket and cook for 4-5 minutes at 370 F. Shake halfway through.
4. Serve and enjoy.

Nutrition: Calories 102 Fat 7 g Carbohydrates 8 g Sugar 0 g Protein 3 g Cholesterol 0 mg

549. Curried Sweet Potato Fries

Preparation Time: 10 minutes
Cooking Time: 20 minutes
Servings: 3
Ingredients:
- 2 small sweet potatoes, peel and cut into fry's shape
- 1/4 tsp coriander
- 1/2 tsp curry powder
- 2 tbsp. olive oil
- 1/4 tsp sea salt

Directions:
1. Add all ingredients into the large mixing bowl and toss well.
2. Spray air fryer basket with cooking spray.
3. Transfer sweet potato fries in the air fryer basket.
4. Cook for 20 minutes at 370 F. Shake halfway through.
5. Serve and enjoy.

Nutrition: Calories 118 Fat 9 g Carbohydrates 9 g Sugar 2 g Protein 1 g Cholesterol 0 mg

550. Roasted Almonds

Preparation Time: 5 minutes
Cooking Time: 8 minutes
Servings: 8
Ingredients:
- 2 cups almonds
- 1/4 tsp pepper
- 1 tsp paprika
- 1 tbsp. garlic powder
- 1 tbsp. soy sauce

Directions:
1. Add pepper, paprika, garlic powder, and soy sauce in a bowl and stir well.
2. Add almonds and stir to coat.
3. Spray air fryer basket with cooking spray.
4. Add almonds in air fryer basket and cook for 6-8 minutes at 320 F. Shake basket after every 2 minutes.
5. Serve and enjoy.

Nutrition: Calories 143 Fat 11.9 g Carbohydrates 6.2 g Sugar 1.3 g Protein 5.4 g Cholesterol 0 mg

551. Pepperoni Chips

Preparation Time: 2 minutes
Cooking Time: 8 minutes
Servings: 6
Ingredients:
- 6 oz. pepperoni slices

Directions:
1. Place one batch of pepperoni slices in the air fryer basket.
2. Cook for 8 minutes at 360 F.
3. Cook remaining pepperoni slices using same steps.

4. Serve and enjoy.
Nutrition: Calories 51 Fat 1 g Carbohydrates 2 g Sugar 1.3 g Protein 0 g Cholesterol 0 mg

552. Crispy Eggplant
Preparation Time: 5 minutes
Cooking Time: 20 minutes
Servings: 4
Ingredients:
- 1 eggplant, cut into 1-inch pieces
- 1/2 tsp Italian seasoning
- 1 tsp paprika
- 1/2 tsp red pepper
- 1 tsp garlic powder
- 2 tbsp. olive oil

Directions:
1. Add all ingredients into the large mixing bowl and toss well.
2. Transfer eggplant mixture into the air fryer basket.
3. Cook at 375 F for 20 minutes. Shake basket halfway through.
4. Serve and enjoy.

Nutrition: Calories 99 Fat 7.5 g Carbohydrates 8.7 g Sugar 4.5 g Protein 1.5 g Cholesterol 0 mg

553. Steak Nuggets
Preparation Time: 10 minutes
Cooking Time: 15 minutes
Servings: 4
Ingredients:
- 1 lb. beef steak, cut into chunks
- 1 large egg, lightly beaten
- 1/2 cup pork rind, crushed
- 1/2 cup parmesan cheese, grated
- 1/2 tsp salt

Directions:
1. Add egg in a small bowl.
2. In a shallow bowl, mix together pork rind, cheese, and salt.
3. Dip each steak chunk in egg then coat with pork rind mixture and place on a plate. Place in refrigerator for 30 minutes.
4. Spray air fryer basket with cooking spray.
5. Preheat the air fryer to 400 F.
6. Place steak nuggets in air fryer basket and cook for 15-18 minutes or until cooked. Shake after every 4 minutes.
7. Serve and enjoy.

Nutrition: Calories 609 Fat 38 g Carbohydrates 2 g Sugar 0.4 g Protein 63 g Cholesterol 195 mg

554. Cheese Bacon Jalapeno Poppers
Preparation Time: 10 minutes
Cooking Time: 5 minutes
Servings: 5
Ingredients:
- 10 fresh jalapeno peppers, cut in half and remove seeds
- 2 bacon slices, cooked and crumbled
- 1/4 cup cheddar cheese, shredded
- 6 oz. cream cheese, softened

Directions:
1. In a bowl, combine together bacon, cream cheese, and cheddar cheese.
2. Stuff each jalapeno half with bacon cheese mixture.
3. Spray air fryer basket with cooking spray.
4. Place stuffed jalapeno halved in air fryer basket and cook at 370 F for 5 minutes.
5. Serve and enjoy.

Nutrition: Calories 195 Fat 17.3 g Carbohydrates 3.2 g Sugar 1 g Protein 7.2 g Cholesterol 52 mg

555. Cabbage Chips
Preparation Time: 10 minutes
Cooking Time: 30 minutes
Servings: 6
Ingredients:
- 1 large cabbage head, tear cabbage leaves into pieces
- 2 tbsp. olive oil
- 1/4 cup parmesan cheese, grated
- Pepper
- Salt

Directions:
1. Preheat the air fryer to 250 F.
2. Add all ingredients into the large mixing bowl and toss well.
3. Spray air fryer basket with cooking spray.
4. Divide cabbage in batches.
5. Add one cabbage chips batch in air fryer basket and cook for 25-30 minutes at 250 F or until chips are crispy and lightly golden brown.
6. Serve and enjoy.

Nutrition: Calories 96 Fat 5.1 g Carbohydrates 12.1 g Sugar 6.7 g Protein 3 g Cholesterol 1 mg

556. Fried Calzones
Preparation Time: 10 minutes
Cooking Time: 30 minutes
Servings: 2
Ingredients:
- 1 tsp olive oil
- ¼ cup red onion, finely chopped
- 3 cups baby spinach leaves
- 1/3 cup shredded rotisserie chicken breast
- 1/3 cup lower-sodium marinara sauce
- 6 oz. fresh prepared whole-wheat pizza dough
- 1½ oz. pre-shredded part-skim mozzarella cheese (about 6 tbsp.)
- Cooking spray

Directions:
1. Get a medium-sized non-stick skillet and in it, heat the oil over medium-high. Toss in the onions, and cook while stirring oc-casionally. Stop cooking when the onions are tender - this takes about 2 minutes.
2. Now toss in the spinach, and allow to cook until wilted, while covering the skil-let. This takes about

1.5 minutes. With-draw the pan from the heat and stir in the chicken and the marinara sauce.
3. Halve the dough into four and roll each piece on a lightly floured surface to form a circle of 6 inches. Place ¼ of the spinach mixture over half of each dough circle, and top with ¼-th of the cheese. Form half-moons by folding the dough over the filling, and crimp the edges to seal.
4. Transfer the calzones into the air fryer basket and allow cooking for 12 minutes at 325 F, or until you have the golden brown dough. Turn the calzones to the other side after the first 8 minutes.
5. Serve.
Nutrition: Calories: 200 Fat 15g Protein 22g Sugar 7g

557. Reuben Calzones
Preparation Time: 10 minutes
Cooking Time: 30 minutes
Servings: 6
Ingredients:
- Cooking spray
- 1 tube (13.8 oz.) refrigerated pizza crust
- 4 slices Swiss cheese
- 1 cup sauerkraut, rinsed and well drained
- ½ lb. sliced cooked corned beef
- Thousand Island salad dressing

Directions:
1. Ensure that your air fryer is preheated to 400 F.
2. Drizzle some cooking spray over the air fryer basket.
3. Prepare a lightly floured surface, and on it, unroll the pizza crust dough while patting into a 12-inches square.
4. Cut the dough into four squares. Layer a slice of the cheese, 1/4 of the sauerkraut, and the corned beef diagonally over half of each square to within 0.5 inches of edges.
5. Form a triangle by folding one corner over filling to the opposite corner. Seal by pressing the edges with your fork.
6. Arrange two calzones in a single layer in the sprayed air fryer basket.
7. Allow cooking for about 8-12 minutes or until the calzones are golden brown. Turn the sides after 4-6 minutes of cooking.
8. When fully cooked, withdraw and keep warm while preparing the other calzones.
9. Serve alongside salad dressing.
Nutrition: Calories: 176 Fat 8g Protein 15g Sugar 10g

558. Popcorn
Preparation Time: 10 minutes
Cooking Time: 30 minutes
Servings: 6
Ingredients:
- 3 tbsp. corn kernels, dried
- Spray avocado oil (Substitutes: safflower oil; co-conut oil; peanut oil)
- Sea salt and ground black pepper to taste
- Garnish:
- 2 tbsp. nutritional yeast
- Dried chives

Directions:
1. Ensure that your air fryer is set to 390F.
2. In the air fryer basket, arrange the ker-nels gently and light-spray some coconut or avocado oil. You may line the tray sides with aluminum foil - this ensures that the popped popcorn does not escape the bas-ket.
3. Return the air fryer basket into the air fryer and allow cooking for 15 minutes. Pay close attention to the cooking kernels to ensure that they do not burn.
4. At the sound of popping sounds, monitor closely until they do not pop anymore - or until the 15 minutes' lapses.
5. Withdraw the basket immediately and transfer the contents into a large bowl.
6. Spray the cooked kernels with some avo-cado or coconut oil.
7. Dust with garnish according to your pref-erence.
8. Serve warm or at room temperature.
Nutrition: Calories: 242 Fat 13g Protein 17g Sugar 8g

559. Mexican-Style Corn on the Cob
Preparation Time: 15 minutes
Cooking Time: 25 minutes
Servings: 4
Ingredients:
- 4 ears fresh corn (about 1½ lbs.), shucked
- Cooking spray
- 1½ tbsp. unsalted butter
- 1 tsp lime zest
- 2 tsp chopped garlic
- 1 tbsp. fresh juice (from 1 lime)
- ½ tsp black pepper
- 2 tbsp. chopped fresh cilantro
- ½ tsp kosher salt

Directions:
1. Coat your corn mildly with some cooking spray before placing in the air fryer bas-ket following a single layer. Allow cooking at 400 F until the corn is tender or mildly charred - this takes about 14 minutes. Turn the corn over after the first 7 minutes of cooking.
2. While cooking the corn, get a small bowl that is suitable for microwaving and in it, combine the butter, lime zest, garlic, and lime juice.
3. Set the microwave to 'high' and mi-crowave the mixture until the butter is melted and the fragrance of the garlic ob-vious - this takes about 30 seconds.
4. Transfer the corn on a platter, and pour the butter mixture on it.
5. Add sprinkles of pepper, cilantro, and salt to taste.
6. Serve immediately.
Nutrition: Calories: 198 Fat 9g Protein 22g Sugar 2g

560. Salt and Vinegar Chickpeas
Preparation Time: 25 minutes
Cooking Time: 55 minutes

Servings: 2
Ingredients:
- 1 (15 oz.) can chickpeas, drained and rinsed
- 1 cup white vinegar
- ½ tsp sea salt
- 1 tbsp. olive oil

Directions:
1. Get a clean small saucepan, and in it, com-bine chickpeas and vinegar. Bring to a simmer over high heat. Once simmering, withdraw and allow to stand for 30 min-utes.
2. Drain the chickpeas and get rid of all loose skins.
3. Ensure that your air fryer is preheated to 390 F.
4. With the chickpeas spread evenly in the air fryer basket, allow cooking for about 4 minutes or until the chickpeas dry out.
5. Move the dried chickpeas into a heat-proof bowl. Drizzle with sea salt and oil and stir to coat evenly.
6. Place the coated chickpeas into the air fryer again and allow cooking for about 8 minutes. Endeavor to shake the basket at 2 or 3 minutes' intervals. Withdraw once you have lightly browned chickpeas.
7. Serve instantly.

Nutrition: Calories: 386 Fat 11g Protein 22g Sugar 7g

561. Curry Chickpeas
Preparation Time: 15 minutes
Cooking Time: 35 minutes
Servings: 4
Ingredients:
- 1 (15-oz) can no-salt-added chickpeas (garbanzo beans), drained and rinsed (about 1½ cups)
- 2 tbsp. olive oil
- 2 tbsp. red wine vinegar
- ¼ tsp ground coriander
- ¼ tsp plus
- 1/8 tsp ground cinnamon
- ¼ tsp ground cumin
- 2 tsp curry powder
- ½ tsp ground turmeric
- Thinly sliced fresh cilantro
- ½ tsp Aleppo pepper
- ¼ tsp kosher salt

Directions:
1. Smash the chickpeas mildly in a medium bowl with your hands. Remove the chick-pea skins.
2. Pour over the oil and vinegar into the chickpeas. Stir to coat evenly, and add co-riander, cinnamon, cumin, curry powder and turmeric. Stir the mixture gently to combine.
3. In the air fryer basket, arrange the chick-peas in a single layer and allow cooking at 400 F for about 15 minutes or until the chickpeas are crispy. Ensure that you shake the chickpeas after the first 7 or 8 minutes of cooking.
4. Move the cooked chickpeas into a bowl, while sprinkling the cilantro, Aleppo pep-per, and salt - toss to coat.

Nutrition: Calories: 409 Fat 16.6g Protein 38.6g Sugar 17.2g

562. Buffalo-Ranch Chickpeas
Preparation Time: 15 minutes
Cooking Time: 35 minutes
Servings: 2
Ingredients:
- 2 tbsp. Buffalo wing sauce
- 1 (15 oz.) can chickpeas, rinsed and drained
- 1 tbsp. dry ranch dressing mix

Directions:
1. Ensure that your air fryer is preheated to 350 F
2. After lining your baking sheet with paper towels, spread the chickpeas over the lined paper towels. Cover the chickpeas with another layer of paper towels, and press gently to drain any excess moisture.
3. Add the can chickpeas in a container and pour in the wing sauce. Stir the mixture to com-bine.
4. Add ranch dressing powder and mix well to combine.
5. Arrange the air fryer in an even layer in the air fryer basket.
6. Allow cooking for 8 minutes. Stop, shake, and cook for an extra 5 minutes, shake again, and cook for 5 minutes more, and shake again for the last time, before cook-ing for the final 2 minutes.
7. Set aside the cooked chickpeas for about 5 minutes to allow cooling.
8. Serve immediately.

Nutrition: Calories: 106 Fat 13g Protein 26g Sugar 19g

563. Whole-Wheat Pizzas
Preparation Time: 10 minutes
Cooking Time: 20 minutes
Servings: 2
Ingredients:
- 2 whole-wheat pita rounds
- ¼ cup lower-sodium marinara sauce
- 1 cup baby spinach leaves (1 oz.)
- 1 oz. pre-shredded part-skim mozzarella cheese (about ¼ cup)
- 1 small garlic clove, thinly sliced
- 1 small plum tomato, cut into 8 slices
- ¼ oz. shaved Parmigiano-Reggiano cheese (about 1 tbsp.)

Directions:
1. Lay out your pita bread.
2. Spread the marina sauce evenly over the side facing upwards. Add half of the spinach leaves, cheeses, garlic, and tomato slices as toppings.
3. Transfer each pita into the air fryer basket, and allow cooking at 350 F for about 4-5 minutes or until you have melted cheese.
4. Do the same for other pitas.

Nutrition: Calories: 300 Fat 10g Protein 33g Sugar 9g

564. Basic Hot Dogs
Preparation Time: 10 minutes

Cooking Time: 15 minutes
Servings: 4
Ingredients:
- 4 hot dog buns
- 4 hot dogs

Directions:
1. Ensure that your air fryer is preheated to 390 F.
2. Move your burns into the air fryer basket and allow cooking for 2 minutes.
3. Withdraw the cooked buns to a plate.
4. Replace the buns with the hot dogs, and allow cooking for 3 minutes.
5. Withdraw and place in the same plate as the buns.
6. Serve.

Nutrition: Calories: 190 Fat 7g Protein 29g Sugar 13g

565. Feta Cheese Dough Balls
Preparation Time: 10 minutes
Cooking Time: 25 minutes
Servings: 8
Ingredients:
- Leftover pizza dough gets the recipe here
- 1 tbsp. Greek yoghurt
- 2 oz. soft cheese
- 1 tsp mustard
- 1 tsp garlic puree
- 1 tbsp. olive oil
- 2 tsp rosemary
- Salt and ground black pepper to taste
- 2 oz. feta cheese

Directions:
1. After removing it from the fridge, allow the pizza dough acclimatize to the room temperature so that working with it is easy.
2. Combine the dough with some flour and knead for a while. This makes the dough soft and gives it the local dough feel. Set aside.
3. In a clean mixing bowl, combine all the in-gredients, except the feta and the dough. Mix thoroughly to form a creamy paste.
4. Make eight equal sized pieces from the dough and flatten each piece out like a pancake.
5. Top each flat piece with about 1/3 tea-spoon of the ingredients mix. Now, add a little square of feta and seal it up.
6. Repeat the same process for the other seven flatten pieces, so that you have 8 top nice little balls.
7. Now transfer them into the air fryer and allow cooking for 10 minutes at 360 F.
8. Reduce the heat to 320 F and allow cook-ing for an additional 5 minutes.

Nutrition: Calories: 245 Fat 2g Protein 18g Sugar 1.3g

566. Flourless Crunchy Cheese Straws
Preparation Time: 20 minutes
Cooking Time: 50 minutes
Servings: 8
Ingredients:
- 4 oz. gluten free oats
- 1 large cauliflower
- 1 large egg
- 6 oz. cheddar cheese
- 1 red onion peeled and thinly diced
- 1 tsp mustard
- 1 tsp mixed herbs
- Salt and ground black pepper to taste

Directions:
1. Blitz your oats in a food processor until you have the appearance of fine bread-crumbs.
2. Place your cauliflower florets in the steamer and allow to steam for 20 min-utes. Immediately after steaming, drain and allow the florets to cool. Get rid of all excess water by squeezing out using a clean pillowcase.
3. Divide the cauliflower into two, and move the half into a separate bowl, alongside the other ingredients. Mix well to form a dough and if necessary add some more cauliflower to ensure even combination.
4. Twist the mixture into straw strips and move them into the air fryer baking mat.
5. Allow cooking for 10 minutes at 360 F.
6. Switch sides and allow cooking for an-other 10 minutes at 360 F.
7. Serve.

Nutrition: Calories: 109 Fat 23g Protein 45g Sugar 0g

567. Veggie Wontons
Preparation Time: 10 minutes
Cooking Time: 15 minutes
Servings: 10
Ingredients:
- Cooking spray
- ½ cup white onion, grated
- ½ cup mushrooms, chopped
- ½ cup carrot, grated
- ¾ cup red pepper, chopped
- ¾ cup cabbage, grated
- 1 tablespoons chili sauce
- 1 teaspoon garlic powder
- Salt and pepper to taste
- 30 vegan wonton wrappers
- Water

Directions:
1. Spray oil in a pan.
2. Put the pan over medium heat and cook the onion, mushrooms, carrot, red pepper and cabbage until tender.
3. Stir in the chili sauce, garlic powder, salt and pepper.
4. Let it cool for a few minutes.
5. Add a scoop of the mixture on top of the wrappers.
6. Fold and seal the corners using water.
7. Cook in the air fryer at 320 degrees F for 7 minutes or until golden brown.

Nutrition: Calories 290 Total Fat 1.5g Saturated Fat 0.3g Cholesterol 9mg Sodium 593mg Total

Carbohydrate 58g Dietary Fiber 2.3g Total Sugars 1.3g Protein 9.9g Potassium 147mg

568. Avocado Rolls
Preparation Time: 20 minutes
Cooking Time: 25 minutes
Servings: 5
Ingredients:
- 10 rice paper wrappers
- 3 avocados, sliced
- 1 tomato, diced
- Salt and pepper to taste
- 1 tablespoon olive oil
- 4 tablespoons sriracha
- 2 tablespoons Sugar
- 1 tablespoon rice vinegar
- 1 tablespoon sesame oil

Directions:
1. Mash avocados in a bowl.
2. Stir in the tomatoes, salt and pepper.
3. Mix well.
4. Arrange the rice paper wrappers.
5. Scoop mixture on top.
6. Roll and seal the edges with water.
7. Cook in the oven at 350 degrees F for 5 minutes.
8. Mix the rest of the ingredients.
9. Serve rolls with the sriracha dipping sauce.

Nutrition: Calories 422 Saturated Fat 5.8g Cholesterol 0mg Sodium 180mg Total Carbohydrate 38.7g Dietary Fiber 8.8g Total Sugars 6.5g Protein 3.8g Potassium 633mg

569. Fried Ravioli
Preparation Time: 15 minutes
Cooking Time: 8 minutes
Servings: 4
Ingredients:
- ½ cup panko breadcrumbs
- Salt and pepper to taste
- 1 teaspoon garlic powder
- 1 teaspoon dried oregano
- 1 teaspoon dried basil
- 2 teaspoons nutritional yeast flakes
- ¼ cup Aquafina liquid
- 8 oz. frozen vegan ravioli
- Cooking spray
- ½ cup marinara sauce

Directions:
1. Mix the breadcrumbs, salt, pepper, garlic powder, oregano, basil and nutritional yeast flakes on a plate.
2. In another bowl, pour the aquafaba liquid.
3. Dip each ravioli into the liquid and then coat with the breadcrumb mixture.
4. Put the ravioli in the air fryer.
5. Spray oil on the raviolis.
6. Cook at 390 degrees F for 6 minutes.
7. Flip each one and cook for another 2 minutes.
8. Serve with marinara sauce.

Nutrition: Calories 154 Total Fat 3.8g Saturated Fat 0.6g Cholesterol 7mg Sodium 169mgTotal Carbohydrate 18.4g Dietary Fiber 1.5g Total Sugars 3g Protein 4.6g Potassium 154mg

570. Corn Fritters
Preparation Time: 15 minutes
Cooking Time: 10 minutes
Servings: 4
Ingredients:
- ¼ cup ground cornmeal
- ¼ cup flour
- Salt and pepper to taste
- ½ teaspoon baking powder
- ¼ teaspoon garlic powder
- ¼ teaspoon onion powder
- ¼ teaspoon paprika
- ¼ cup parsley, chopped
- 1 cup corn kernels mixed with 3 tablespoons almond milk
- 2 cups fresh corn kernels
- 4 tablespoons vegan mayonnaise
- 2 teaspoons grainy mustard

Directions:
1. Mix the cornmeal, flour, salt, pepper, baking powder, garlic powder, onion powder, paprika and parsley in a bowl.
2. Put the corn kernels with almond milk in a food processor.
3. Season it with salt and pepper.
4. Pulse until well blended.
5. Add the corn kernels.
6. Transfer to a bowl and stir into the cornmeal mixture.
7. Pour a small amount of the batter in the air fryer pan.
8. Pour another a few centimeters away from the first fritter.
9. Cook in the air fryer at 350 degrees for 10 minutes or until golden.
10. Flip halfway through.
11. Serve with mayo mustard dip.

Nutrition: Calories 135 Total Fat 4.6g Saturated Fat 0.2g Cholesterol 0mg Sodium 136mg Carbohydrate 22.5g Dietary Fiber 2.5g Total Sugars 2.7g Protein 3.5g Potassium 308mg

571. Mushroom Pizza
Preparation Time: 15 minutes
Cooking Time: 10 minutes
Servings: 4
Ingredients:
- 4 large Portobello mushrooms, stems and gills removed
- 1 teaspoon balsamic vinegar
- Salt and pepper to taste
- 4 tablespoons vegan pasta sauce
- 1 clove garlic, minced
- 3 oz. zucchini, chopped
- 4 olives, sliced

- 2 tablespoons sweet red pepper, diced
- 1 teaspoon dried basil
- ½ cups hummus
- Fresh basil, minced

Directions:
1. Coat the mushrooms with balsamic vinegar and Season it with salt and pepper.
2. Spread pasta sauce inside each mushroom.
3. Sprinkle with minced garlic.
4. Preheat your air fryer to 330 degrees F.
5. Cook mushrooms for 3 minutes.
6. Take the mushrooms out and top with zucchini, olives, and peppers.
7. Season it with salt, pepper and basil.
8. Put them back to the air fryer and cook for another 3 minutes.
9. Serve mushroom pizza with hummus and fresh basil.

Nutrition: Calories 70 Total Fat 1.56g Saturated Fat 0.5g Cholesterol 12 mg Sodium 167 mg Total Carbohydrate 11g Dietary Fiber 3.4g Total Sugars 3.8g Protein 4.3g Potassium 350 mg

572. Onion Appetizers

Preparation Time: 10 minutes
Cooking Time: 4 minutes
Servings: 4
Ingredients:
- 2 lb. onions, sliced into rings
- 2 vegan eggs
- 1 cup almond milk
- 2 cups flour
- 1 tablespoon paprika
- Salt and pepper to taste
- 1 teaspoon garlic powder
- 1 teaspoon cayenne pepper
- Cooking spray
- ¼ cup vegan mayo
- ¼ cup vegan sour cream
- 1 tablespoon ketchup

Directions:
1. Combine the eggs and milk in one plate.
2. In another plate, mix the flour, paprika, salt, pepper, garlic powder and cayenne pepper.
3. Dip each onion into the egg mixture before coating with the flour mixture.
4. Spray with oil.
5. For 4 minutes or until golden and crispy.
6. Serve with the dipping sauces.

Nutrition: Calories 364 Total Fat 14.5g Saturated Fat 10.3g Cholesterol 0mg Sodium 143mg Carbohydrate 52.7g Dietary Fiber 7.2g Total Sugars 9.3g Protein 8.1g Potassium 434mg

573. Crispy Brussels Sprouts

Preparation Time: 5 minutes
Cooking Time: 1 minutes
Servings: 2
Ingredients:
- 2 cups Brussels sprouts, sliced
- 1 tablespoon olive oil
- 1 tablespoon balsamic vinegar
- Salt to taste

Directions:
1. Toss all the ingredients in a bowl.
2. Cook in the air fryer at 400 degrees F for 10 minutes, shake once or twice during the cooking process.
3. Check to see if crispy enough.
4. If not, cook for another 5 minutes.

Nutrition: Calories 100 Total Fat 7.3g Saturated Fat 1.1g Cholesterol 0mg Sodium 100mg Total Carbohydrate 8.1g Dietary Fiber 3.3g Total Sugars 1.9g Protein 3g Potassium 348mg

574. Sweet Potato Tots

Preparation Time: 10 minutes
Cooking Time: 12 minutes
Servings: 10
Ingredients:
- 2 cups sweet potato puree
- ½ teaspoon salt
- ½ teaspoon cumin
- ½ teaspoon coriander
- ½ cup breadcrumbs
- Cooking spray
- Vegan mayo

Directions:
1. Preheat your air fryer to 390 degrees f.
2. Combine all ingredients in a bowl.
3. Form into balls.
4. Arrange on the air fryer pan.
5. Spray with oil.
6. Cook for 6 minutes or until golden.
7. Serve with vegan mayo.

Nutrition: Calories 77 Total Fat 0.8g Saturated Fat 0.1g Cholesterol 0mg Sodium 205mg Total Carbohydrate 15.9g Dietary Fiber 1.1g Total Sugars 3.1g Protein 1.8g Potassium 120mg

575. Popcorn Tofu

Preparation Time: 15 minutes
Cooking Time: 12 minutes
Servings: 4
Ingredients:
- ½ cup cornmeal
- ½ cup quinoa flour
- 1 tablespoon vegan bouillon
- 2 tablespoons nutritional yeast
- 1 teaspoon garlic powder
- 1 teaspoon onion powder
- 1 tablespoon mustard
- Salt and pepper to taste
- ¾ cup almond milk
- 1 ½ cups breadcrumbs
- 14 oz. tofu, sliced into small pieces
- ½ cup vegan mayo
- 2 tablespoons hot sauce

Directions:

1. In the first bowl, mix the first 8 ingredients.
2. In the second bowl, pour the almond milk.
3. In the third bowl, add the breadcrumbs.
4. Dip each tofu slice into each of the bowls starting from the flour mixture, then the almond milk and finally in the breadcrumbs.
5. Cook in the air fryer at 350 degrees F for 12 minutes, shaking halfway through.
6. Mix the mayo and hot sauce and serve with tofu.

Nutrition: Calories 261 Total Fat 5.5g Saturated Fat 1g Cholesterol 12 mg Sodium 120 mg Total Carbohydrate 37.5g Dietary Fiber 4.8g Total Sugars 3g Protein 16g Potassium 430 mg

576. Black Bean Burger
Preparation Time: 10 minutes
Cooking Time: 25 minutes
Servings: 6
Ingredients:
- 1 ¼ cup rolled oats
- 16 oz. black beans, rinsed and drained
- ¾ cup salsa
- 1 tablespoon soy sauce
- 1 ¼ teaspoons chili powder
- ¼ teaspoon chipotle chili powder
- ½ teaspoon garlic powder

Directions:
1. Pulse the oats inside a food processor until powdery.
2. Add all necessary ingredients and pulse until well blended.
3. Transfer to a bowl and refrigerate for 15 minutes.
4. Form into burger patties.
5. Cook in the air fryer at 375 degrees' f for 15 minutes.

Nutrition: Calories 158 Total Fat 2g Saturated Fat 1g Cholesterol 10 mg Sodium 690 mg Total Carbohydrate 30g Dietary Fiber 9g Total Sugars 2.7g Protein 8g Potassium 351 mg

577. Crisp Sweet Potato Fries
Preparation Time: 5 minutes
Cooking Time: 16 minutes
Servings: 2 to 4
Ingredients:
- 2 sweet potatoes sliced to own preference (peeling is optional)
- ½ tbsp. chili powder (optional)
- ½ tbsp. garlic powder
- 2 tsp onion powder
- 2 tsp paprika
- 1 tbsp. olive oil or canola oil
- salt and pepper to taste
- vegetable oil to spray

Directions:
1. Thoroughly rinse and dry the sweet potatoes. Slice into circles (⅛-inch), keeping thickness even.
2. Pat the slices dry with paper towels and place into a large mixing bowl and add the olive oil. Toss the sweet potato slices so that both sides are coated in oil.
3. Add the chili powder, garlic powder, paprika, onion powder, salt, and pepper to the mixing bowl and gently mix to ensure the sweet potato slices are evenly coated in the spices and herbs.
4. Spray the rotisserie basket with cooking oil and place a single layer of sweet potato fries inside the basket.
5. Place the rotisserie basket inside the Vortex air fryer.
6. Press rotate and heat the oven to 360° F and set the cooking time for 22 minutes.
7. The sweet potato fries are ready when the edges have started crisping and golden.
8. Place the fries on a paper towel-lined cooling rack. Please note that the fries crisp during the cooling downtime.
9. Repeat the cooking process with the next batch of fries.
10. Sweet potato chips are best eaten fresh on the day. They can be stored in an airtight container but may lose their crispness.

Nutrition: Calories: 187 Fat 10g Protein 12g Sugar 2g

578. Snack-Sized Calzones
Preparation Time: 25 minutes
Cooking Time: 12-15 minutes
Servings: 16
Ingredients:
- 1 lb. pizza dough (at room temperature for 1 hour before use)
- all-purpose flour to roll out the pizza dough
- 8 oz. mozzarella cheese, shredded
- 1 cup of pizza sauce of own choice
- extra pizza sauce as a dip, or dip sauce of own choice
- 6 oz. of pepperoni, sliced thinly

Directions:
1. Lightly flour a workspace and place pizza dough on it. Roll dough out to a ¼-inch thickness. Cut out 8 circles with a 3-inch biscuit cutter (or use a large glass). Place the circles on a baking sheet lined with parchment paper.
2. Shape leftover dough into a ball and roll out to a ¼-inch thickness until you have 16 dough circles altogether.
3. Place 1 tsp of pepperoni, 1 tbsp. cheese, and 2 tsp cheese on top of each dough circle.
4. Fold each dough circle over and press edges together. To ensure that the calzones are fully sealed, crimp the edges of the dough with a fork.
5. Place the calzones on 2 cooking trays, making sure that they do not touch, and place cooking trays into the oven using the middle and bottom positions.
6. Heat your air fryer to 375° F and cook calzones for about 8 minutes; they should be golden and crisp.

7. If you have any calzones left over, repeat the air frying process.
8. Place calzones on a cooling rack to cool down slightly and serve with dipping sauce.
9. Calzones can be stored for up to 5 days in an airtight container in the fridge.
Nutrition: Calories: 376 Fat 11g Protein 28g Sugar 4g

579. Jalapeno and Cheese Balls
Preparation Time: 15 minutes
Cooking Time: 10 minutes
Servings: 22
Ingredients:
- 1 cup diced jalapenos (if this is too hot, use ½ cup jalapenos and ½ bell peppers)
- ½ cup all-purpose flour
- 12 bacon slices
- 3 eggs
- ½ cup scallions
- 2 cups breadcrumbs Panko, or as per your own preference
- 8 oz. cream cheese brought to room temperature to soften
- ¼ tsp onion powder
- 2 cups shredded cheddar cheese, sharp flavored
- ¼ tsp garlic powder
- 3 tbsp. green pepper sauce (Tabasco mild green pepper sauce)
- 2 tbsp. milk
- salt and pepper to taste

Directions:
1. Prepare two cooking trays and spray with vegetable oil of your own choice.
2. Line a flat baking sheet with wax paper and set aside.
3. Cook bacon in a skillet until cooked through and cut into small pieces.
4. Cut jalapenos (and bell pepper if using) and slice scallions thinly.
5. Place the chopped bacon, softened cream cheese, garlic powder, jalapenos, shredded cheddar cheese, green pepper sauce, onion powder, scallions, and salt and pepper into a mixing bowl and mix to combine all the ingredients.
6. Use an ice cream scoop to make balls of roughly 1 ½ to 2 inches and place the balls on the wax paper-lined baking sheet. Place the baking sheet with the balls into the freezer for about 15 minutes. You can omit this step, but freezing the balls for a while makes them much easier to work with when you start dredging them.
7. Preheat the air fryer oven to 400° F on the air fryer mode.
8. Place three mixing bowls on a work surface for dredging.
9. Place the flour into the first bowl, whisk the milk and eggs in a second bowl, and place the breadcrumbs into the third bowl.
10. Roll each ball first in the flour, then in the egg mixture, and lastly in the breadcrumbs. If you prefer a thicker crust, you can repeat the dredging procedure with each ball.
11. Place the balls on the prepared cooking trays, making sure that they don't touch.
12. Cook the balls for 10-12 minutes; they must be golden brown and crisp on the outside.
13. Remove jalapeno balls from the cooking trays with silicone tongs and serve with a dipping sauce.
14. Dip sauce suggestions: marinara sauce, sour cream with smoky paprika chipotle seasoning, or homemade guacamole.
Nutrition: Calories: 342 Fat 12g Protein 21g Sugar 22g

580. Parmesan Chicken Nuggets
Preparation Time: 10 minutes
Cooking Time: 8 minutes
Servings: 2 to 4
Ingredients:
- 2 skinned and filleted chicken breasts
- 1 ½ cups dried breadcrumbs (panko or own preference, can also be substituted with crushed cornflakes)
- vegetable oil spray
- ¼ to ½ cup parmesan cheese
- 1 tsp Italian seasoning
- 2 tsp sweet paprika
- ⅓ cup olive oil (more can be added as needed)
- salt and pepper to taste

Directions:
1. Set out two mixing bowls. Add olive oil to one mixing bowl and add the rest of the ingredients to the other bowl.
2. Cut chicken roughly into 1½-inch cubes (can be slightly smaller if preferred).
3. Lightly spray two of the oven's cooking trays and make sure that the drip tray is in place inside the oven.
4. Place chicken cubes one by one into the olive oil and then into the bowl holding the coating ingredients, making sure that each nugget is fully coated.
5. Place the coated chicken cubes onto the cooking trays without the cubes touching each other.
6. Turn the fryer oven to 400° F and cook the chicken cubes for about 8 minutes until crisp (internal temp should be 165° F).
7. Serve with your own choice of dip sauces.
Nutrition: Calories: 254 Fat 10g Protein 16g Sugar 2g

581. Date Tapas
Preparation Time: 5 minutes
Cooking Time: 7 minutes
Servings: 2
Ingredients:
- 1 packet pitted dates (variations pitted prunes or maraschino cherries)
- 1 packet bacon (or more, depends on the number of tapas you wish to make)

Directions:

1. Cut all the bacon slices in half.
2. Wrap each pitted prune in a half slice of bacon and place it on the cooking tray. You can pack two cooking trays to cook at a time.
3. Heat the air fryer oven to 500° F and cook the tapas for 7 minutes on the air fryer setting of the oven.
4. It can be served warm or cold.
Nutrition: Calories: 398 Fat 5g Protein 15g Sugar 4g

582. Hush Puppies
Preparation Time: 10 minutes
Cooking Time: 10 minutes
Servings: 12
Ingredients:
- ¾ cup all-purpose flour (can be substituted with gluten-free flour)
- 1 cup cornmeal, yellow
- ¼ tsp sugar
- ½ tsp salt
- 1 ½ tsp baking powder
- 1 egg
- ¼ cup onion, finely chopped
- ¾ milk (whole milk, reduced-Fat milk, Fat-free or low-Fat milk works equally well)
- vegetable oil for spraying

Directions:
1. Place flour, baking powder, cornmeal, salt, and sugar into a large mixing bowl and stir to combine. Add in the chopped onion.
2. Add milk and egg to the mixture and whisk until all ingredients are combined.
3. Set batter aside to rest and for the dough to firm up for about 5 minutes.
4. Spray 2 cooking trays with non-stick spray
5. Divide the dough into 12 balls and form small balls with your hands.
6. Set temperature to 390° F for the air fryer function.
7. Place dough balls well-spaced on the cooking trays and insert them into the oven using the center and bottom positions.
8. Cook for 5 minutes, then use silicone tongs to turn hush puppies over, spray them with oil spray, and continue cooking for another 5 minutes.
9. When they are crisp, check to make sure they are cooked through and return to the oven for a few minutes if necessary.
10. Remove from cooking trays and place them on a wire cooling rack.
11. It can be served hot or cold with a dipping sauce of your preference.
Nutrition: Calories: 173 Fat 2g Protein 40g Sugar 2g

583. Flavorful Salsa
Preparation Time: 10 minutes
Cooking Time: 30 minutes
Servings: 8
Ingredients:
- 12 cups fresh tomatoes, peeled, seeded, and diced
- 3 tbsp. cayenne pepper
- 2 tbsp. garlic powder
- 3 tbsp. Sugar
- 1/2 cup vinegar
- 12 oz. can tomato paste
- 1 cup jalapeno pepper, chopped
- 3 onions, chopped
- 2 green peppers, chopped
- 1 tbsp. salt

Directions:
1. Add all ingredients into the instant pot and stir well.
2. Seal pot with lid and cook on manual high pressure for 30 minutes.
3. Once done then allow to release pressure naturally then open the lid.
4. Allow to cool completely then serve or store.
Nutrition: Calories 145 Fat 1.1 g Carbohydrates 32.5 g Sugar 20.3 g Protein 5.1 g Cholesterol 0 mg

584. Cheddar Cheese Dip
Preparation Time: 10 minutes
Cooking Time: 9 minutes
Servings: 16
Ingredients:
- 1 lb. bacon slices, cooked and crumbled
- 1 green onion, sliced
- 1/4 cup heavy cream
- 2 cups cheddar cheese, shredded
- 1 cup non-alcoholic beer
- 1 tsp garlic powder
- 1 1/2 tbsp. Dijon mustard
- 1/4 cup sour cream
- 18 oz. cream cheese, softened

Directions:
1. Add cream cheese, bacon, beer, garlic powder, mustard, and sour cream into the instant pot and stir well.
2. Seal pot with lid and cook on manual high pressure for 5 minutes.
3. Once done then release pressure using the quick-release method than open the lid.
4. Stir in heavy cream and cheese and cook on sauté mode for 3-4 minutes.
5. Garnish with green onion and serve.
Nutrition: Calories 195 Fat 17.4 g Carbohydrates 2 g Sugar 0.2 g Protein 6.3 g Cholesterol 54 mg

585. Creamy Eggplant Dip
Preparation Time: 10 minutes
Cooking Time: 20 minutes
Servings: 4
Ingredients:
- 1 eggplant
- 1/8 tsp paprika
- 1/2 tbsp. olive oil
- 1/2 lemon juice
- 2 tbsp. tahini
- 1 garlic clove

- 1 cup of water
- 1/8 tsp salt

Directions:
1. Pour water into the instant pot then place eggplant into the pot.
2. Seal pot with lid and cook on manual mode for 20 minutes.
3. Once done then release pressure using the quick-release method than open the lid.
4. Remove eggplant from the pot and let it cool.
5. Remove the skin of the eggplant and place eggplant flesh into the food processor.
6. Add remaining ingredients into the food processor and process until smooth.
7. Serve and enjoy.

Nutrition: Calories 91 Fat 6.1 g Carbohydrates 8.7 g Sugar 3.6 g Protein 2.5 g Cholesterol 0 mg

586. Delicious Nacho Dip

Preparation Time: 10 minutes
Cooking Time: 20 minutes
Servings: 10
Ingredients:
- 1 lb. ground beef
- 1 cup Mexican cheese
- 4 oz. cream cheese
- 14 oz. salsa
- 15 oz. can black beans, drained
- 1/4 cup water
- 2 tsp cayenne pepper
- 1 1/2 tsp ground cumin
- 1 1/2 tsp chili powder
- 3 garlic cloves, chopped
- 1 jalapeno pepper, chopped
- 1 small onion, chopped
- 1 tbsp. olive oil
- 1 tsp salt

Directions:
1. Add oil into the instant pot and set the pot on sauté mode.
2. Add jalapeno peppers and onion and sauté for 5 minutes.
3. Add garlic and sauté for a minute.
4. Add ground beef, cayenne, cumin, chili powder, and salt and sauté until browned.
5. Add water and stir well.
6. Add salsa and beans and stir well.
7. Seal pot with lid and cook on manual high pressure for 10 minutes.
8. Once done then allow to release pressure naturally then open the lid.
9. Stir in cheese and sour cream.
10. Serve and enjoy.

Nutrition: Calories 214 Fat 10.4 g Carbohydrates 12.1 g Sugar 2 g Protein 19 g Cholesterol 58 mg

587. Spinach Dip

Preparation Time: 10 minutes
Cooking Time: 4 minutes
Servings: 10
Ingredients:
- 1 lb. fresh spinach
- 1 tsp onion powder
- 1 cup mozzarella cheese, shredded
- 7.5 oz. cream cheese, cubed
- 1/2 cup mayonnaise
- 1/2 cup sour cream
- 1/2 cup chicken broth
- 1 tbsp. olive oil
- 2 garlic cloves, minced
- 1/4 tsp pepper
- 1/2 tsp salt

Directions:
1. Add oil into the instant pot and set the pot on sauté mode.
2. Add spinach and garlic and sauté until spinach is wilted. Drain excess liquid.
3. Add remaining ingredients and stir well.
4. Seal pot with lid and cook on manual high pressure for 4 minutes.
5. Once done then release pressure using the quick-release method than open the lid.
6. Stir well and serve.

Nutrition: Calories 179 Fat 15.9 g Carbohydrates 6.1 g Sugar 1.1 g Protein 4.5 g Cholesterol 33 mg

588. Chipotle Bean Dip

Preparation Time: 10 minutes
Cooking Time: 43 minutes
Servings: 6
Ingredients:
- 1 cup dry pinto beans, rinsed
- 1/2 tsp cumin
- 1 tsp liquid smoke
- 1/2 cup salsa
- 2 garlic cloves, peeled
- 2 chipotle peppers in adobo sauce
- 5 cups of water
- 1/4 tsp pepper
- 1 tsp salt

Directions:
1. Add water, beans, chipotle peppers, and garlic into the instant pot.
2. Seal pot with lid and cook on manual high pressure for 43 minutes.
3. Once done then allow to release pressure naturally then open the lid.
4. Transfer beans to the blender and blends until smooth.
5. Add remaining ingredients and blend until just mixed.
6. Serve and enjoy.

Nutrition: Calories 124 Fat 0.8 g Carbohydrates 22.3 g Sugar 1.4 g Protein 7.7 g Cholesterol 2 mg

589. Asian Boiled Peanuts

Preparation Time: 10 minutes
Cooking Time: 60 minutes
Servings: 4
Ingredients:

- 1 lb. raw peanuts
- 3 dried red chili peppers
- 3 garlic cloves
- 2 cinnamon stick
- 3 whole star anise
- 3 tbsp. kosher salt

Directions:
1. Add all ingredients into the instant pot and stir well.
2. Pour enough water to the pot to cover peanuts
3. Seal pot with lid and cook on manual high pressure for 60 minutes.
4. Once done then allow to release pressure naturally then open the lid.
5. Serve and enjoy.

Nutrition: Calories 672 Fat 55.9 g Carbohydrates 24.3 g Sugar 4.8 g Protein 30.3 g Cholesterol 0 mg

590. Mexican Pinto Bean Dip

Preparation Time: 10 minutes
Cooking Time: 45 minutes
Servings: 6
Ingredients:
- 1 cup dry pinto beans
- 1 1/2 tsp chili powder
- 4 chilies
- 4 cups of water
- 1 tsp salt

Directions:
1. Add water, chilies, and beans into the instant pot.
2. Seal pot with lid and cook on manual high pressure for 45 minutes.
3. Once done then allow to release pressure naturally for 10 minutes then release using quick-release method. Open the lid.
4. Transfer beans into the blender along with chili powder and salt and blends until smooth.
5. Serve and enjoy.

Nutrition: Calories 115 Fat 0.5 g Carbohydrates 20.7 g Sugar 0.9 g Protein 7 g Cholesterol 0 mg

591. Perfect Cinnamon Toast

Preparation Time: 10 minutes
Cooking Time: 5 minutes
Servings: 6
Ingredients
- 2 tsp. Pepper
- 1 ½ tsp. Vanilla extract
- 1 ½ tsp. Cinnamon
- ½ c. Sweetener of choice
- 1 c. Coconut oil
- 12 slices whole wheat bread

Directions:
1. Preparing the ingredients. Melt coconut oil and mix with sweetener until dissolved. Mix in remaining ingredients minus bread till incorporated.
2. Spread mixture onto bread, covering all area.
3. Air frying. Place coated pieces of bread in your instant crisp air fryer. Close air fryer lid and cook 5 minutes at 400 degrees.
4. Remove and cut diagonally. Enjoy!

Nutrition: Calories: 124 Fat 2g Protein 0g Sugar 4g

592. Easy Baked Chocolate Mug Cake

Preparation Time: 5 minutes
Cooking Time: 15 minutes
Servings: 3
Ingredients:
- ½ cup cocoa powder
- ½ cup stevia powder
- 1 cup coconut cream
- 1 package cream cheese, room temperature
- 1 tablespoon vanilla extract
- Tablespoons butter

Directions:
1. Preparing the ingredients. Preheat the instant crisp air fryer for 5 minutes.
2. In a mixing bowl, combine all ingredients.
3. Use a hand mixer to mix everything until fluffy.
4. Pour into greased mugs.
5. Place the mugs in the fryer basket.
6. Air frying. Close air fryer lid and bake for 15 minutes at 350°f.
7. Place in the fridge to chill before serving.

Nutrition: Calories: 744 Fat 69.7g Protein 13.9g Sugar 4g

593. Angel Food Cake

Preparation Time: 5 minutes
Cooking Time: 30 minutes
Servings: 12
Ingredients:
- ¼ cup butter, melted
- 1 cup powdered erythritol
- 1 teaspoon strawberry extract
- 12 egg whites
- 2 teaspoons cream of tartar
- A pinch of salt

Directions:
1. Preparing the ingredients. Preheat the instant crisp air fryer for 5 minutes.
2. Mix the egg whites and cream of tartar.
3. Use a hand mixer and whisk until white and fluffy.
4. Add the rest of the ingredients except for the butter and whisk for another minute.
5. Pour into a baking dish.
6. Air frying. Place in the instant crisp air fryer basket, close air fryer lid and cook for 30 minutes at 400°f or if a toothpick inserted in the middle comes out clean.
7. Drizzle with melted butter once cooled.

Nutrition: Calories: 65 Fat 5g Protein 3.1g Fiber 1g

594. Fried Peaches

Preparation Time: 2 hours 10 minutes
Cooking Time: 15 minutes

Servings: 4
Ingredients:
- 4 ripe peaches
- 1 1/2 cups flour
- Salt
- 2 egg yolks
- 3/4 cups cold water
- 1 1/2 tablespoons olive oil
- 2 tablespoons brandy
- 4 egg whites
- Cinnamon/sugar mix

Directions:
1. Preparing the ingredients. Mix flour, egg yolks, and salt in a mixing bowl.
2. Slowly mix in water, then add brandy.
3. Set the mixture aside for 2 hours and go do something for 1 hour 45 minutes.
4. Boil a large pot of water and cut and x at the bottom of each peach.
5. While the water boils fill another large bowl with water and ice.
6. Boil each peach for about a minute, then plunge it in the ice bath.
7. Now the peels should basically fall off the peach.
8. Beat the egg whites and mix into the batter mix.
9. Dip each peach in the mix to coat.
10. Air frying. Close air fryer lid and cook at 360 degrees for 10 minutes.
11. Prepare a plate with cinnamon/sugar mix, roll peaches in mix and serve.

Nutrition: Calories: 306 Fat 3g Protein 10g Fiber 2.7g

595. Easy Donuts

Preparation Time: 5 minutes
Cooking Time: 10 minutes
Servings: 8
Ingredients:
- Pinch of allspice
- 4 tbsp. Dark brown Sugar
- ½ - 1 tsp. Cinnamon
- 1/3 c. Granulated sweetener
- 3 tbsp. Melted coconut oil
- 1 can of biscuits

Directions:
1. Preparing the ingredients. Preheat the unit by selecting bake/roast, setting the temperature to 300°f, and setting the time to 5 minutes.
2. Press start/stop to begin.
3. Mix allspice, sugar, sweetener, and cinnamon together.
4. Take out biscuits from can and with a circle cookie cutter, cut holes from centers and place into instant crisp air fryer.
5. Air frying the dish. Close the air fryer lid.
6. Select bake, set the temperature to 350°f, and set the time to 5 minutes.
7. Select start to begin. As batches are cooked, use a brush to coat with melted coconut oil and dip each into sugar mixture.
8. Serve warm!

Nutrition: Calories: 242 Fat 6g Protein 28g Sugar 18g

596. Apple Pie in Air Fryer

Preparation Time: 5 minutes
Cooking Time: 35 minutes
Servings: 4
Ingredients:
- ½ teaspoon vanilla extract
- 1 beaten egg
- 1 large apple, chopped
- 1 Pillsbury refrigerator pie crust
- 1 tablespoon butter
- 1 tablespoon ground cinnamon
- 1 tablespoon raw Sugar
- 2 tablespoon Sugar
- 2 teaspoons lemon juice
- Baking spray

Directions:
1. Preparing the ingredients. Lightly grease baking pan of instant crisp air fryer with cooking spray. Spread pie crust on bottom of pan up to the sides.
2. In a bowl, mix vanilla, sugar, cinnamon, lemon juice, and apples. Pour on top of pie crust. Top apples with butter slices.
3. Cover apples with the other pie crust. Pierce with knife the tops of pie.
4. Spread beaten egg on top of crust and sprinkle sugar.
5. Cover with foil.
6. Air frying. Close air fryer lid. For 25 minutes, cook on 390°f.
7. Remove foil cook for 10 minutes at 330of until tops are browned.
8. Serve and enjoy.

Nutrition: Calories: 372 Fat 19g Protein 4.2g Sugar 5g

597. Raspberry Cream Roll-Ups

Preparation Time: 10 minutes
Cooking Time: 25 minutes
Servings: 4
Ingredients:
- 1 cup of fresh raspberries, rinsed and patted dry
- ½ cup of cream cheese, softened to room temperature
- ¼ cup of brown Sugar
- ¼ cup of sweetened condensed milk
- 1 egg
- 1 teaspoon of corn starch
- 6 spring roll wrappers (any brand will do, we like blue dragon or tasty joy, both available through target or Walmart, or any large grocery chain
- ¼ cup of water

Directions:
1. Preparing the ingredients.

2. Cover the basket of the instant crisp air fryer with a lining of tin foil, leaving the edges uncovered to allow air to circulate through the basket.
3. Preheat the instant crisp air fryer to 350 degrees.
4. In a mixing bowl, combine the cream cheese, brown sugar, condensed milk, cornstarch, and egg.
5. Beat or whip thoroughly, until all ingredients are completely mixed and fluffy, thick and stiff.
6. Spoon even amounts of the creamy filling into each spring roll wrapper, then top each dollop of filling with several raspberries.
7. Roll up the wraps around the creamy raspberry filling, and seal the seams with a few dab of water.
8. Place each roll on the foil-lined instant crisp air fryer basket, seams facing down.
9. Air frying. Close air fryer lid. Set the instant crisp air fryer timer to 10 minutes.
10. During cooking, shake the handle of the fryer basket to ensure a nice even surface crisp.
11. After 10 minutes, when the instant crisp air fryer shuts off, the spring rolls should be golden brown and perfect on the outside, while the raspberries and cream filling will have cooked together in a glorious fusion.
12. Remove with tongs and serve hot or cold.

Nutrition: Calories 251 Fat 12 Protein 23 Fiber 2

BREAD RECIPES

598. Sourdough Bread
Preparation Time: 20 minutes
Cooking Time: 20 minutes
Servings: 8
Ingredients:
- 1 cup sourdough starter
- 1 cup unbleached all-purpose flour
- ¼ cup whole-wheat flour
- 1 tablespoon white sugar
- ½ teaspoon salt
- 1 tablespoon canola oil

Directions:
1. In the baking pan of a bread machine, place all the ingredients in the order recommended by the manufacturer.
2. Place the baking pan in bread machine and close with the lid.
3. Select the Dough cycle and press Start button.
4. Once the cycle is completed, remove the paddles from bread machine but keep the dough inside for about 4 hours to proof.
5. Now, transfer the dough into a floured proofing basket and set aside to rise for about 3 hours.
6. Set the temperature of air fryer to 390 degrees F. Carefully, arrange the dough onto the grill insert of an air fryer.
7. Air fries it for about 20 minutes, turning the pan once halfway through.
8. Remove the bread from air fryer and place onto a wire rack for about 2-3 hours before slicing.
9. Cut the bread into desired size slices and serve.

Nutrition: Calories: 162 Carbohydrate: 25.3g Protein 11.3g Fat 3.1g Sugar 1.6g Sodium: 160mg

599. Cream Bread
Preparation Time: 20 minutes
Cooking Time: 55 minutes
Servings: 12
Ingredients:
- 1 cup milk
- ¾ cup whipping cream
- 1 large egg
- 4½ cups bread flour
- ½ cup all-purpose flour
- 2 tablespoons milk powder
- 1 teaspoon salt
- ¼ cup fine sugar
- 3 teaspoons dry yeast

Directions:
1. In the baking pan of a bread machine, place all the ingredients in the order recommended by the manufacturer.
2. Place the baking pan in bread machine and close with the lid.
3. Select the Dough cycle and press Start button.
4. Once the cycle is completed, remove the paddles from bread machine but keep the dough inside for about 45-50 minutes to proof.
5. Set the temperature of air fryer to 375 degrees F. Grease 2 loaf pans.
6. Remove the dough from pan and place onto a lightly floured surface.
7. Divide the dough into four equal-sized balls and then, roll each into a rectangle.
8. Tightly, roll each rectangle like a Swiss roll.
9. Place two rolls into each prepared loaf pan.
10. Set aside for about 1 hour.
11. Arrange the loaf pans into an air fryer basket.
12. Air fry for about 50-55 minutes or until a toothpick inserted in the center comes out clean.
13. Remove the pans from air fryer and place onto a wire rack for about 10-15 minutes.
14. Then, remove the bread rolls from pans and place onto a wire rack until they are completely cool before slicing.
15. Cut each roll into desired size slices and serve.

Nutrition: Calories: 215 Carbohydrate: 36.9g Protein 6.5g Fat 3.1g Sugar 5.2g Sodium: 189mg

600. Sunflower Seeds Bread
Preparation Time: 15 minutes
Cooking Time: 18 minutes
Servings: 4
Ingredients:
- 2/3 cup whole-wheat flour
- 2/3 cup plain flour
- 1/3 cup sunflower seeds
- ½ sachet instant yeast
- 1 teaspoon salt
- 2/3-1 cup lukewarm water

Directions:
1. In a bowl, mix together the flours, sunflower seeds, yeast, and salt.
2. Slowly, add in the water, stirring continuously until a soft dough ball forms.
3. Now, move the dough onto a lightly floured surface and knead for about 5 minutes using your hands.
4. Make a ball from the dough and place into a bowl.
5. With a plastic wrap, cover the bowl and place at a warm place for about 30 minutes.
6. Set the temperature of air fryer to 390 degrees F. Grease a cake pan. (6"x 3")
7. Coat the top of dough with water and place into the prepared cake pan.
8. Arrange the cake pan into an air fryer basket.
9. Air fry for about 18 minutes or until a toothpick inserted in the center comes out clean.
10. Remove from air fryer and place the pan onto a wire rack for about 10-15 minutes.
11. Carefully, take out the bread from pan and put onto a wire rack until it is completely cool before slicing.
12. Cut the bread into desired size slices and serve.

Nutrition: Calories: 177 Carbohydrate: 33g Protein 5.5g Fat 2.4g Sugar 0.2g Sodium: 580mg

601. Date Bread
Preparation Time: 15 minutes
Cooking Time: 22 minutes
Servings: 10
Ingredients:
- 2½ cup dates, pitted and chopped

- ¼ cup butter
- 1 cup hot water
- 1½ cups flour
- ½ cup brown sugar
- 1 teaspoon baking powder
- 1 teaspoon baking soda
- ½ teaspoon salt
- 1 egg

Directions:
1. In a large bowl, add the dates, butter and top with the hot water.
2. Set aside for about 5 minutes.
3. In a separate bowl, mix together the flour, brown sugar, baking powder, baking soda, and salt.
4. In the same bowl of dates, mix well the flour mixture, and egg.
5. Set the temperature of air fryer to 340 degrees F. Grease an air fryer non-stick pan.
6. Place the mixture into the prepared pan.
7. Arrange the pan into an air fryer basket.
8. Air fry for about 22 minutes or until a toothpick inserted in the center comes out clean.
9. Remove from air fryer and place the pan onto a wire rack for about 10-15 minutes.
10. Carefully, take out the bread from pan and put onto a wire rack until it is completely cool before slicing.
11. Cut the bread into desired size slices and serve.

Nutrition: Calories: 269 Carbohydrate: 55.1g Protein 3.6g Fat 5.4g Sugar 35.3 Sodium: 585mg

602. Banana Bread
Preparation Time: 10 minutes
Cooking Time: 20 minutes
Servings: 8
Ingredients:
- 1 1/3 cups flour
- 2/3 cup sugar
- 1 teaspoon baking soda
- 1 teaspoon baking powder
- 1 teaspoon ground cinnamon
- 1 teaspoon salt
- ½ cup milk
- ½ cup olive oil
- 3 bananas, peeled and sliced

Directions:
1. Take the bowl of a stand mixer and mix well all the listed ingredients.
2. Set the temperature of air fryer to 330 degrees F. Grease a loaf pan.
3. Place the mixture into the prepared pan.
4. Arrange the loaf pan into an air fryer basket.
5. Air fry for about 20 minutes or until a toothpick inserted in the center comes out clean.
6. Remove from air fryer and place the pan onto a wire rack for about 10-15 minutes.
7. Carefully, take out the bread from pan and put onto a wire rack until it is completely cool before slicing.
8. Cut the bread into desired size slices and serve.

Nutrition: Calories: 295 Carbohydrate: 44g Protein 3.1g Fat 13.3g Sugar 22.8g Sodium: 458mg

603. Nutty Banana Bread
Preparation Time: 15 minutes
Cooking Time: 25 minutes
Servings: 10
Ingredients:
- 1½ cups self-rising flour
- ¼ teaspoon bicarbonate of soda
- 5 tablespoons plus 1 teaspoon butter
- 2/3 cup plus ½ tablespoon caster sugar
- 2 medium eggs
- 3½ ounces walnuts, chopped
- 2 cups bananas, peeled and mashed

Directions:
1. In a bowl, mix together the flour and bicarbonate of soda.
2. In another bowl, add the butter, and sugar. Beat until pale and fluffy.
3. Put the eggs, one at a time along with a little flour and mix them well.
4. Stir in the remaining flour and walnuts.
5. Now, add the bananas and mix until well combined.
6. Set the temperature of air fryer to 355 degrees F. Grease a loaf pan.
7. Place the mixture evenly into the prepared pan.
8. Arrange the loaf pan into an air fryer basket.
9. Air fry it for 10 minutes on 355 degrees F, then 15 minutes for 338 degrees F.
10. Once done, remove from air fryer and place the pan onto a wire rack for about 10-15 minutes.
11. Carefully, take out the bread from pan and put onto a wire rack until it is completely cool before slicing.
12. Cut the bread into desired size slices and serve.

Nutrition: Calories: 337 Carbohydrate: 44.5g Protein 7.3g Fat 16g Sugar 21.6g Sodium: 106mg

604. Yogurt Banana Bread
Preparation Time: 15 minutes
Cooking Time: 35 minutes
Servings: 5
Ingredients:
- ½ cup all-purpose flour
- ¼ cup whole-wheat flour
- ¼ teaspoon baking soda
- ½ teaspoon salt
- 1 large egg
- ½ cup granulated sugar
- ¼ cup plain yogurt
- ¼ cup vegetable oil
- ½ teaspoon pure vanilla extract
- 2 ripe bananas, peeled and mashed
- 2 tablespoons turbinado sugar

Directions:
1. In a bowl, sift together the flours, baking soda, and salt.
2. In another large bowl, mix well the egg, granulated sugar, yogurt, oil, and vanilla extract.
3. Add in the bananas and beat until well combined.
4. Now, add the flour mixture and mix until just combined.
5. Set the temperature of Air Fryer to 310 degrees F.

6. Place the mixture evenly into a cake pan and sprinkle with the turbinado sugar.
7. Arrange the cake pan into an Air Fryer basket.
8. Air Fry for about 30-35 minutes or until a toothpick inserted in the center comes out clean, turning the pan once halfway through.
9. Carefully, take out the bread from pan and put onto a wire rack until it is completely cool before slicing.
10. Cut the bread into desired size slices and serve
Nutrition: Calories: 317 Carbohydrate: 49.2g Protein 7.3g Fat 16g Sugar 21.6g Sodium: 106mg

605. Peanut Butter Banana Bread
Preparation Time: 15 minutes
Cooking Time: 40 minutes
Servings: 6
Ingredients:
- 1 cup plus 1 tablespoon all-purpose flour
- 1 teaspoon baking powder
- ¼ teaspoon baking soda
- ¼ teaspoon salt
- 1 large egg
- 1/3 cup granulated sugar
- ¼ cup canola oil
- 2 tablespoons creamy peanut butter
- 2 tablespoons sour cream
- 1 teaspoon vanilla extract
- 2 medium ripe bananas, peeled and mashed
- ¾ cup walnuts, roughly chopped

Directions:
1. Take a bowl and mix together the flour, baking powder, baking soda, and salt.
2. In another large bowl, add the egg, sugar, oil, peanut butter, sour cream, and vanilla extract. Beat until well combined.
3. Add in the bananas and beat until well combined.
4. Now, add the flour mixture and mix until just combined.
5. Gently, fold in the walnuts.
6. Set the temperature of Air Fryer to 330 degrees F. Grease a non-stick baking dish.
7. Transfer the mixture evenly into the prepared baking dish.
8. Arrange the baking dish in an Air Fryer basket.
9. Air Fry for about 30-40 minutes or until a toothpick inserted in the center comes out clean.
10. Remove the dish from Air Fryer and place onto a wire rack for about 10-15 minutes.
11. Carefully, take out the bread from dish and place onto a wire rack until it is completely cool before slicing.
12. Cut the bread into desired size slices and serve.
Nutrition: Calories: 384 Carbohydrate: 39.3g Protein 8.9g Fat 2.6g Sugar 16.6g Sodium: 189mg

606. Soda Brad
Preparation Time: 15 minutes
Cooking Time: 30 minutes
Servings: 10
Ingredients:
- 3 cups whole-wheat flour
- 1 tablespoon sugar
- 2 teaspoon caraway seeds
- 1 teaspoon baking soda
- 1 teaspoon sea salt
- ¼ cup chilled butter, cubed into small pieces
- 1 large egg, beaten
- 1½ cups buttermilk

Directions:
1. In a large bowl, mix together the flour, sugar, caraway seeds, baking soda and salt and mix well.
2. With a pastry cutter, cut in the butter flour until coarse crumbs like mixture is formed.
3. Make a well in the center of flour mixture.
4. In the well, add the egg, followed by the buttermilk and with a spatula, mix until well combined.
5. With floured hand, shape the dough into a ball.
6. Place the dough onto a floured surface and lightly knead it.
7. Shape the dough into a 6-inch ball.
8. With a serrated knife, score an X on the top of the dough.
9. Press "Power Button" of Air Fry Oven and turn the dial to select the "Air Crisp" mode.
10. Press the Time button and again turn the dial to set the cooking time to 30 minutes.
11. Now push the Temp button and rotate the dial to set the temperature at 350 degrees F.
12. Press "Start/Pause" button to start.
13. When the unit beeps to show that it is preheated, open the lid.
14. Arrange the dough in lightly greased "Air Fry Basket" and insert in the oven.
15. Place the pan onto a wire rack to cool for about 10 minutes.
16. Carefully, invert the bread onto wire rack to cool completely before slicing.
17. Cut the bread into desired-sized slices and serve.
Nutrition: Calories 205 Total Fat 5.9 g Saturated Fat 3.3 g Cholesterol 32 mg Sodium 392 mg Total Carbs 31.8 g Fiber 1.2 g Sugar 3.1 g Protein 5.9 g

607. Baguette Bread
Preparation Time: 15 minutes
Cooking Time: 20 minutes
Servings: 8
Ingredients:
- ¾ cup warm water
- ¾ teaspoon quick yeast
- ½ teaspoon demerara sugar
- 1 cup bread flour
- ½ cup whole-wheat flour
- ½ cup oat flour
- 1¼ teaspoons salt

Directions:
1. In a large bowl, place the water and sprinkle with yeast and sugar.
2. Set aside for 5 minutes or until foamy.
3. Add the bread flour and salt mix until a stiff dough forms.
4. Put the dough onto a floured surface and with your hands, knead until smooth and elastic.
5. Now, shape the dough into a ball.

6. Place the dough into a slightly oiled bowl and turn to coat well.
7. With a plastic wrap, cover the bowl and place in a warm place for about 1 hour or until doubled in size.
8. With your hands, punch down the dough and form into a long slender loaf.
9. Place the loaf onto a lightly greased baking sheet and set aside in warm place, uncovered, for about 30 minutes.
10. Press "Power Button" of Air Fry Oven and turn the dial to select the "Air Bake" mode.
11. Press the Time button and again turn the dial to set the cooking time to 20 minutes.
12. Now push the Temp button and rotate the dial to set the temperature at 450 degrees F.
13. Press "Start/Pause" button to start.
14. When the unit beeps to show that it is preheated, open the lid.
15. Carefully, arrange the dough onto the "Wire Rack" and insert in the oven.
16. Carefully, invert the bread onto wire rack to cool completely before slicing.
17. Cut the bread into desired-sized slices and serve.

Nutrition: Calories 114 Total Fat 0.8 g Saturated Fat 0.1 g Cholesterol 0 mg Sodium 366 mg Total Carbs 22.8 g Fiber 2.1 g Sugar 0.3 g Protein 3.8 g

608. Yogurt Bread

Preparation Time: 20 minutes
Cooking Time: 40 minutes
Servings: 10
Ingredients:
- 1½ cups warm water, divided
- 1½ teaspoons active dry yeast
- 1 teaspoon sugar
- 3 cups all-purpose flour
- 1 cup plain Greek yogurt
- 2 teaspoons kosher salt

Directions:
1. Add ½ cup of the warm water, yeast and sugar in the bowl of a stand mixer, fitted with the dough hook attachment and mix well.
2. Set aside for about 5 minutes.
3. Add the flour, yogurt, and salt and mix on medium-low speed until the dough comes together.
4. Then, mix on medium speed for 5 minutes.
5. Place the dough into a bowl.
6. With a plastic wrap, cover the bowl and place in a warm place for about 2-3 hours or until doubled in size.
7. Transfer the dough onto a lightly floured surface and shape into a smooth ball.
8. Place the dough onto a greased parchment paper-lined rack.
9. With a kitchen towel, cover the dough and let rest for 15 minutes.
10. With a very sharp knife, cut a 4x½-inch deep cut down the center of the dough.
11. Press "Power Button" of Air Fry Oven and turn the dial to select the "Air Roast" mode.
12. Press the Time button and again turn the dial to set the cooking time to 40 minutes.
13. Now push the Temp button and rotate the dial to set the temperature at 325 degrees F.
14. Press "Start/Pause" button to start.
15. When the unit beeps to show that it is preheated, open the lid.
16. Carefully, arrange the dough onto the "Wire Rack" and insert in the oven.
17. Carefully, invert the bread onto wire rack to cool completely before slicing.
18. Cut the bread into desired-sized slices and serve.

Nutrition: Calories 157 Total Fat 0.7 g Saturated Fat 0.3 g Cholesterol 1 mg Sodium 484 mg Total Carbs 31 g Fiber 1.1 g Sugar 2.2 g Protein 5.5 g

609. Banana & Raisin Bread

Preparation Time: 15 minutes
Cooking Time: 40 minutes
Servings: 6
Ingredients:
- 1½ cups cake flour
- 1 teaspoon baking soda
- ½ teaspoon ground cinnamon
- Salt, to taste
- ½ cup vegetable oil
- 2 eggs
- ½ cup sugar
- ½ teaspoon vanilla extract
- 3 medium bananas, peeled and mashed
- ½ cup raisins, chopped finely

Directions:
1. In a large bowl, mix together the flour, baking soda, cinnamon, and salt.
2. In another bowl, beat well eggs and oil.
3. Add the sugar, vanilla extract, and bananas and beat until well combined.
4. Add the flour mixture and stir until just combined.
5. Place the mixture into a lightly greased baking pan and sprinkle with raisins.
6. With a piece of foil, cover the pan loosely.
7. Press "Power Button" of Air Fry Oven and turn the dial to select the "Air Bake" mode.
8. Press the Time button and again turn the dial to set the cooking time to 30 minutes.
9. Now push the Temp button and rotate the dial to set the temperature at 300 degrees F.
10. Press "Start/Pause" button to start.
11. When the unit beeps to show that it is preheated, open the lid.
12. Arrange the pan in "Air Fry Basket" and insert in the oven.
13. After 30 minutes of cooking, set the temperature to 285 degrees F for 10 minutes.
14. Place the pan onto a wire rack to cool for about 10 minutes.
15. Carefully, invert the bread onto wire rack to cool completely before slicing.
16. Cut the bread into desired-sized slices and serve.

Nutrition: Calories 448 Total Fat 20.2 g Saturated Fat 4.1 g Cholesterol 55 mg Sodium 261 mg Total Carbs 63.9 g Fiber 2.9g Sugar 31.3 g Protein 6.1 g

610. Brown Sugar Banana Bread

Preparation Time: 15 minutes
Cooking Time: 30 minutes
Servings: 4
Ingredients:
- 1 egg
- 1 ripe banana, peeled and mashed
- ¼ cup milk
- 2 tablespoons canola oil
- 2 tablespoons brown Sugar
- ¾ cup plain flour
- ½ teaspoon baking soda

Directions:
1. Line a very small baking pan with a greased parchment paper.
2. In a small bowl, add the egg and banana and beat well.
3. Add the milk, oil and sugar and beat until well combined.
4. Add the flour and baking soda and mix until just combined.
5. Place the mixture into prepared pan.
6. Press "Power Button" of Air Fry Oven and turn the dial to select the "Air Crisp" mode.
7. Press the Time button and again turn the dial to set the cooking time to 30 minutes.
8. Now push the Temp button and rotate the dial to set the temperature at 320 degrees F.
9. Press "Start/Pause" button to start.
10. When the unit beeps to show that it is preheated, open the lid.
11. Arrange the pan in "Air Fry Basket" and insert in the oven.
12. Place the pan onto a wire rack to cool for about 10 minutes.
13. Carefully, invert the bread onto wire rack to cool completely before slicing.
14. Cut the bread into desired-sized slices and serve.

Nutrition: Calories 214 Total Fat 8.7 g Saturated Fat 1.1 g Cholesterol 42 mg Sodium 183 mg Total Carbs 29.9 g Fiber 1.4 g Sugar 8.8 g Protein 4.6 g

611. Date & Walnut Bread

Preparation Time: 15 minutes
Cooking Time: 35 minutes
Servings: 5
Ingredients:
- 1 cup dates, pitted and sliced
- ¾ cup walnuts, chopped
- 1 tablespoon instant coffee powder
- 1 tablespoon hot water
- 1¼ cups plain flour
- ¼ teaspoon salt
- ½ teaspoon baking powder
- ½ teaspoon baking soda
- ½ cup condensed milk
- ½ cup butter, softened
- ½ teaspoon vanilla essence

Directions:
1. In a large bowl, add the dates, butter and top with the hot water.
2. Set aside for about 30 minutes.
3. Drain well and set aside.
4. In a small bowl, add the coffee powder and hot water and mix well.
5. In a large bowl, mix together the flour, baking powder, baking soda and salt.
6. In another large bowl, add the condensed milk and butter and beat until smooth.
7. Add the flour mixture, coffee mixture and vanilla essence and mix until well combined.
8. Fold in dates and ½ cup of walnut.
9. Line a baking pan with a lightly greased parchment paper.
10. Place the mixture into the prepared pan and sprinkle with the remaining walnuts.
11. Press "Power Button" of Air Fry Oven and turn the dial to select the "Air Crisp" mode.
12. Press the Time button and again turn the dial to set the cooking time to 35 minutes.
13. Now push the Temp button and rotate the dial to set the temperature at 320 degrees F.
14. Press "Start/Pause" button to start.
15. When the unit beeps to show that it is preheated, open the lid.
16. Arrange the pan in "Air Fry Basket" and insert in the oven.
17. Place the pan onto a wire rack to cool for about 10 minutes.
18. Carefully, invert the bread onto wire rack to cool completely before slicing.
19. Cut the bread into desired-sized slices and serve.

Nutrition: Calories 593 Total Fat 32.6 g Saturated Fat 14 g Cholesterol 59 mg Sodium 414 mg Total Carbs 69.4 g Fiber 5 g Sugar 39.6 g Protein 11.2 g

DESSERTS RECIPES

612. Easy Lava Cake
Preparation Time: 10 minutes
Cooking Time: 9 minutes
Servings: 2
Ingredients:
- 1 egg
- 1/2 tsp baking powder
- 1 tbsp. coconut oil, melted
- 1 tbsp. flax meal
- 2 tbsp. erythritol
- 2 tbsp. water
- 2 tbsp. unsweetened cocoa powder
- Pinch of salt

Directions:
1. Whisk all ingredients into the bowl and transfer in two ramekins.
2. Preheat the air fryer to 350 F.
3. Place ramekins in air fryer basket and bake for 8-9 minutes.
4. Carefully remove ramekins from air fryer and let it cool for 10 minutes.
5. Serve and enjoy.

Nutrition: Calories 119 Fat 11 g Carbohydrates 4 g Sugar 0.3 g Protein 5 g Cholesterol 82 mg

613. Tasty Cheese Bites
Preparation Time: 10 minutes
Cooking Time: 2 minutes
Servings: 16
Ingredients:
- 8 oz. cream cheese, softened
- 2 tbsp. erythritol
- 1/2 cup almond flour
- 1/2 tsp vanilla
- 4 tbsp. heavy cream
- 1/2 cup erythritol

Directions:
1. Add cream cheese, vanilla, 1/2 cup erythritol, and 2 tbsp. heavy cream in a stand mixer and mix until smooth.
2. Scoop cream cheese mixture onto the parchment lined plate and place in the refrigerator for 1 hour.
3. In a small bowl, mix together almond flour and 2 tbsp. erythritol.
4. Dip cheesecake bites in remaining heavy cream and coat with almond flour mixture.
5. Place prepared cheesecake bites in air fryer basket and air fry for 2 minutes at 350 F.
6. Make sure cheesecake bites are frozen before air fry otherwise they will melt.
7. Drizzle with chocolate syrup and serve.

Nutrition: Calories 80 Fat 7 g Carbohydrates 2 g Sugar 1 g Protein 2 g Cholesterol 16 mg

614. Apple Chips with Dip
Preparation Time: 10 minutes
Cooking Time: 12 minutes
Servings: 4
Ingredients:
- 1 apple, thinly slice using a mandolin slicer
- 1 tbsp. almond butter
- 1/4 cup plain yogurt
- 2 tsp olive oil
- 1 tsp ground cinnamon
- 4 drops liquid stevia

Directions:
1. Add apple slices, oil, and cinnamon in a large bowl and toss well.
2. Spray air fryer basket with cooking spray.
3. Place apple slices in air fryer basket and cook at 375 F for 12 minutes. Turn after every 4 minutes.
4. Meanwhile, in a small bowl, mix together almond butter, yogurt, and sweetener.
5. Serve apple chips with dip and enjoy.

Nutrition: Calories 86 Fat 4.9 g Carbohydrates 10 g Sugar 7.1 g Protein 1.9 g Cholesterol 1 mg

615. Delicious Spiced Apples
Preparation Time: 10 minutes
Cooking Time: 10 minutes
Servings: 6
Ingredients:
- 4 small apples, sliced
- 1 tsp apple pie spice
- 1/2 cup erythritol
- 2 tbsp. coconut oil, melted

Directions:
1. Add apple slices in a mixing bowl and sprinkle sweetener, apple pie spice, and coconut oil over apple and toss to coat.
2. Transfer apple slices in air fryer dish. Place dish in air fryer basket and cook at 350 F for 10 minutes.
3. Serve and enjoy.

Nutrition: Calories 73 Fat 4.6 g Carbohydrates 8.2 g Sugar 5.4 g Protein 0 g Cholesterol 0 mg

616. Easy Cheesecake
Preparation Time: 10 minutes
Cooking Time: 10 minutes
Servings: 6
Ingredients:
- 2 eggs
- 16 oz. cream cheese, softened
- 2 tbsp. sour cream
- 1/2 tsp fresh lemon juice
- 1 tsp vanilla
- 3/4 cup erythritol

Directions:
1. Preheat the air fryer to 350 F.
2. Add eggs, lemon juice, vanilla, and sweetener in a large bowl and beat using a hand mixer until smooth.
3. Add cream cheese and sour cream and beat until fluffy.

4. Pour batter into the 2 four-inch spring-form pan and place in air fryer basket and cook for 8-10minutes at 350 F.
5. Remove from air fryer and let it cool completely.
6. Place in refrigerator for overnight.
7. Serve and enjoy.
Nutrition: Calories 296 Fat 28 g Carbohydrates 2.4 g Sugar 0.4 g Protein 7.7 g Cholesterol 139 mg

617. Coconut Pie
Preparation Time: 10 minutes
Cooking Time: 12 minutes
Servings: 6
Ingredients:
- 2 eggs
- 1/2 cup coconut flour
- 1/2 cup erythritol
- 1 cup shredded coconut
- 1 1/2 tsp vanilla
- 1/4 cup butter
- 1 1/2 cups coconut milk

Directions:
1. Add all ingredients into the large bowl and mix until well combined.
2. Spray a 6-inch baking dish with cooking spray.
3. Pour batter into the prepared dish and place in the air fryer basket.
4. Cook at 350 F for 10-12 minutes.
5. Slice and serve.
Nutrition: Calories 282 Fat 28.9 g Carbohydrates 6.3 g Sugar 3.2 g Protein 4 g Cholesterol 75 mg

618. Strawberry Muffins
Preparation Time: 10 minutes
Cooking Time: 15 minutes
Servings: 12
Ingredients:
- 3 eggs
- 1 tsp ground cinnamon
- 2 tsp baking powder
- 2 1/2 cups almond flour
- 2/3 cup fresh strawberries, diced
- 1/3 cup heavy cream
- 1 tsp vanilla
- 1/2 cup Swerve
- 5 tbsp. butter

Directions:
1. Preheat the air fryer 325 F.
2. Add butter and sweetener in a bowl and beat using a hand mixer until smooth.
3. Add eggs, cream, and vanilla and beat until frothy.
4. In another bowl, sift together almond flour, cinnamon, baking powder, and salt.
5. Add almond flour mixture to wet ingredients and mix until well combined.
6. Add strawberries and fold well.
7. Pour batter into the silicone muffin molds and place into the air fryer basket in batches.
8. Cook muffins for 15 minutes.
9. Serve and enjoy.
Nutrition: Calories 205 Fat 18 g Carbohydrates 6 g Sugar 1.5 g Protein 6 g Cholesterol 58 mg

619. Pecan Muffins
Preparation Time: 10 minutes
Cooking Time: 15 minutes
Servings: 12
Ingredients:
- 4 eggs
- 1 tsp vanilla
- 1/4 cup almond milk
- 2 tbsp. butter, melted
- 1/2 cup swerve
- 1 tsp psyllium husk
- 1 tbsp. baking powder
- 1/2 cup pecans, chopped
- 1/2 tsp ground cinnamon
- 2 tsp allspice
- 1 1/2 cups almond flour

Directions:
1. Preheat the air fryer to 370 F.
2. Beat eggs, almond milk, vanilla, sweetener, and butter in a bowl using a hand mixer until smooth.
3. Add remaining ingredients and mix until well combined.
4. Pour batter into the silicone muffin molds and place into the air fryer basket in batches.
5. Cook muffins for 15 minutes.
6. Serve and enjoy.
Nutrition: Calories 204 Fat 18 g Carbohydrates 6 g Sugar 1.2 g Protein 5 g Cholesterol 60 mg

620. Chocolate Brownie
Preparation Time: 10 minutes
Cooking Time: 16 minutes
Servings: 4
Ingredients:
- 1 cup bananas, overripe
- 1 scoop Protein powder
- 2 tbsp. unsweetened cocoa powder
- 1/2 cup almond butter, melted

Directions:
1. Preheat the air fryer to 325 F.
2. Spray air fryer baking pan with cooking spray.
3. Add all ingredients into the blender and blend until smooth.
4. Pour batter into the prepared pan and place in the air fryer basket.
5. Cook brownie for 16 minutes.
6. Serve and enjoy.
Nutrition: Calories 80 Fat 2.1 g Carbohydrates 11.4 g Protein 7 g Sugars 5 g Cholesterol 15 mg

621. Blueberry Muffins
Preparation Time: 10 minutes
Cooking Time: 20 minutes
Servings: 12
Ingredients:

- 3 large eggs
- 1/3 cup coconut oil, melted
- 1 1/2 tsp gluten-free baking powder
- 1/2 cup erythritol
- 2 1/2 cups almond flour
- 3/4 cup blueberries
- 1/2 tsp vanilla
- 1/3 cup unsweetened almond milk

Directions:
1. Preheat the air fryer to 325 F.
2. In a large bowl, stir together almond flour, baking powder, erythritol.
3. Mix in the coconut oil, vanilla, eggs, and almond milk. Add blueberries and fold well.
4. Pour batter into the silicone muffin molds and place into the air fryer basket in batches.
5. Cook muffins for 20 minutes.
6. Serve and enjoy.

Nutrition: Calories 215 Fat 19 g Carbohydrates 5 g Sugar 2 g Protein 7 g Cholesterol 45 mg

622. Pumpkin Muffins

Preparation Time: 10 minutes
Cooking Time: 20 minutes
Servings: 10
Ingredients:
- 4 large eggs
- 1/2 cup pumpkin puree
- 1 tbsp. pumpkin pie spice
- 1 tbsp. baking powder, gluten-free
- 2/3 cup erythritol
- 1 tsp vanilla
- 1/3 cup coconut oil, melted
- 1/2 cup almond flour
- 1/2 cup coconut flour
- 1/2 tsp sea salt

Directions:
1. Preheat the air fryer to 325 F.
2. In a large bowl, stir together coconut flour, pumpkin pie spice, baking powder, erythritol, almond flour, and sea salt.
3. Stir in eggs, vanilla, coconut oil, and pumpkin puree until well combined.
4. Pour batter into the silicone muffin molds and place into the air fryer basket in batches.
5. Cook muffins for 20 minutes.
6. Serve and enjoy.

Nutrition: Calories 150 Fat 13 g Carbohydrates 7 g Sugar 2 g Protein 5 g Cholesterol 75 mg

623. Cappuccino Muffins

Preparation Time: 10 minutes
Cooking Time: 20 minutes
Servings: 12
Ingredients:
- 4 eggs
- 2 cups almond flour
- 1/2 tsp vanilla
- 1 tsp espresso powder
- 1/2 cup sour cream
- 1 tsp cinnamon
- 2 tsp baking powder
- 1/4 cup coconut flour
- 1/2 cup Swerve
- 1/4 tsp salt

Directions:
1. Preheat the air fryer to 325 F.
2. Add sour cream, vanilla, espresso powder, and eggs in a blender and blend until smooth.
3. Add almond flour, cinnamon, baking powder, coconut flour, sweetener, and salt. Blend again until smooth.
4. Pour batter into the silicone muffin molds and place into the air fryer basket. (Cook in batches)
5. Cook muffins for 20 minutes.
6. Serve and enjoy.

Nutrition: Calories 150 Fat 13 g Carbohydrates 5.3 g Sugar 0.8 g Protein 6 g Cholesterol 59 mg

624. Moist Cinnamon Muffins

Preparation Time: 10 minutes
Cooking Time: 12 minutes
Servings: 20
Ingredients:
- 1 tbsp. cinnamon
- 1 tsp baking powder
- 2 scoops vanilla Protein powder
- 1/2 cup almond flour
- 1/2 cup coconut oil
- 1/2 cup pumpkin puree
- 1/2 cup almond butter

Directions:
1. Preheat the air fryer to 325 F.
2. In a large bowl, combine together all dry ingredients and mix well.
3. Add wet ingredients into the dry ingredients and mix until well combined.
4. Pour batter into the silicone muffin molds and place into the air fryer basket. (Cook in batches)
5. Cook muffins for 12 minutes.
6. Serve and enjoy.

Nutrition: Calories 80 Fat 7.1 g Carbohydrates 1 g Sugar 0.4 g Protein 3 g Cholesterol 0 mg

625. Cream Cheese Muffins

Preparation Time: 10 minutes
Cooking Time: 16 minutes
Servings: 10
Ingredients:
- 2 eggs
- 1/2 cup erythritol
- 8 oz. cream cheese
- 1 tsp ground cinnamon
- 1/2 tsp vanilla

Directions:
1. Preheat the air fryer to 325 F.
2. In a bowl, mix together cream cheese, vanilla, erythritol, and eggs until soft.

3. Pour batter into the silicone muffin molds and sprinkle cinnamon on top.
4. Place muffin molds into the air fryer basket and cook for 16 minutes.
5. Serve and enjoy.
Nutrition: Calories 90 Fat 8.8 g Carbohydrates 13 g Sugar 12.2 g Protein 2.8 g Cholesterol 58 mg

626. Cinnamon Apple Chips
Preparation Time: 10 minutes
Cooking Time: 8 minutes
Servings: 6
Ingredients:
- 3 Granny Smith apples, wash, core and thinly slice
- 1 tsp ground cinnamon
- Pinch of salt

Directions:
1. Rub apple slices with cinnamon and salt and place into the air fryer basket.
2. Cook at 390 F for 8 minutes. Turn halfway through.
3. Serve and enjoy.
Nutrition: Calories 41 Fat 0 g Carbohydrates 11 g Sugar 8 g Protein 0 g Cholesterol 0 mg

627. Sweet Pumpkin Loaf
Preparation Time: 20 minutes
Cooking Time: 20 minutes
Servings: 2
Ingredients:
- ½ teaspoon baking soda
- 2 tablespoon pumpkin seeds
- 1 egg
- ¼ cup milk
- 1/3 cup flour
- 2 tablespoon brown sugar
- 1 teaspoon vanilla extract
- ½ teaspoon olive oil
- 1 teaspoon fresh lemon juice
- 1 teaspoon lime zest
- 1 pinch salt

Directions:
1. Combine together baking soda, flour, brown sugar, vanilla extract, fresh lemon juice, lime zest, and salt in the bowl.
2. Beat the egg in the flour mixture.
3. Add milk and stir the mixture gently with the help of the fork.
4. Crush the pumpkin seeds gently and put them in the flour mixture.
5. Then knead the soft and elastic dough. Add more flour if desired.
6. Let the dough rest for 10 minutes.
7. Preheat the air fryer to 350 F.
8. Spray the loaf tin with the olive oil and put the dough there.
9. Cook the pumpkin seeds loaf for 15 minutes.
10. After this, reduce the temperature to 320 F and cook the loaf for 5 minutes more.
11. Check if the meal is cooked – and transfer it to the serving plate.
12. Slice the sweet pumpkin seeds loaf.
13. Enjoy!
Nutrition: Calories 221 Fat 8.2 Fiber 1 Carbs 28.4 Protein 8.1

628. Milky Egg Custard
Preparation Time: 15 minutes
Cooking Time: 20 minutes
Servings: 2
Ingredients:
- 1 egg yolk
- ¼ cup milk
- ½ teaspoon potato starch
- 1 teaspoon white sugar
- ¼ teaspoon vanilla extract

Directions:
1. Preheat the air fryer to 210 F.
2. Preheat the milk until it starts to boil.
3. Then whisk together the egg yolk and white sugar.
4. Pour the egg yolk mixture into the hot milk slowly. Whisk it constantly.
5. Add vanilla extract and potato starch. Whisk it well until the mixture is homogenous.
6. Pour the egg mixture into 2 ramekins.
7. Place the ramekins in the air fryer basket.
8. Cook the egg custard for 20 minutes.
9. When the dessert is cooked – let it chill to the room temperature.
10. Enjoy!
Nutrition: Calories 55 Fat 2.9 Fiber 0 Carbs 4.9 Protein 2.4

629. Raisins Carrot Pie
Preparation Time: 20 minutes
Cooking Time: 35 minutes
Servings: 2
Ingredients:
- 3 tablespoon flour
- 2 oz. carrot, grated
- 1 tablespoon raisins
- ¼ teaspoon baking soda
- ½ teaspoon apple cider vinegar
- ¼ teaspoon ground cinnamon
- 1 pinch salt
- 2 teaspoon brown sugar
- 1 egg
- 2 tablespoon milk

Directions:
1. Sift the flour into the bowl.
2. Add grated carrot, raisins, baking soda, apple cider vinegar, ground cinnamon, salt, brown sugar, and milk.
3. Stir the mixture gently.
4. Beat the egg in the separate bowl and whisk it.
5. Pour the whisked egg into the flour mixture.
6. Mix it up until homogenous. The mixture should look like a thick batter.

7. Preheat the air fryer to 350 F.
8. Cover the air fryer tray with the parchment and pour the dough there.
9. Cover the dough with the foil.
10. Pin the foil to give the dough the opportunity to "breath".
11. Put the pie in the air fryer and cook for 35 minutes.
12. Then discard the foil and cook the pie for 2 minutes more at 400 F.
13. When the pie is cooked – chill it till the room temperature.
14. Serve!

Nutrition: Calories 119 Fat 2.6 Fiber 1.3 Carbs 19.4 Protein 4.9

630. Cracker Cheesecake

Preparation Time: 15 minutes
Cooking Time: 17 minutes
Servings: 2
Ingredients:
- 1 teaspoon butter
- 3 oz. graham crackers
- 3 oz. cream cheese
- 1 tablespoon brown sugar
- 1 egg
- ¼ teaspoon vanilla extract

Directions:
1. Preheat the air fryer to 360 F.
2. Crush the graham crackers and combine them with the butter.
3. Then cover the air fryer tray with the parchment and put the cracker mixture.
4. Press it gently and slide the tray into the air fryer.
5. Cook the cheesecake crust for 2 minutes.
6. Then beat the egg in the cream cheese.
7. Add brown sugar and vanilla extract.
8. Mix the mixture carefully until smooth.
9. Pour the cream cheese mixture over the cheesecake crust and flatten it with the help of the spatula.
10. Reduce the air fryer temperature to 310 F.
11. Put the cheesecake in the air fryer and cook for 15 minutes.
12. After this, chill the cheesecake well.
13. Serve it!

Nutrition: Calories 109 Fat 8.8 Fiber 0.8 Carbs 3.8 Protein 5.2

631. Ginger Apricot Tart

Preparation Time: 15 minutes
Cooking Time: 10 minutes
Servings: 2
Ingredients:
- 2 tablespoon butter
- 4 tablespoons flour
- 1 pinch salt
- 2 teaspoon sugar
- 2 big apricots
- 1 teaspoon butter
- ¼ teaspoon ground ginger

Directions:
1. Combine together the butter, flour, and salt in the mixing bowl.
2. Knead the soft, elastic dough.
3. Roll the dough and separate it into 2 parts.
4. Make the rounds from the dough with the help of the cutter.
5. Then halve the apricots and remove the stones from them.
6. Slice the apricots.
7. Place the apricots in the center of the dough.
8. Roll the edges of the tarts.
9. Add ½ teaspoon of butter on the top of every tart.
10. Then sprinkle the tarts with the ground ginger and sugar.
11. Preheat the air fryer to 360 F.
12. Place the apricot tarts there and cook for 10 minutes.
13. Chill the cooked tarts till the room temperature.
14. Enjoy!

Nutrition: Calories 217 Fat 14.8 Fiber 1.1 Carbs 19.9 Protein 2.2

632. Banana Oatmeal Bites

Preparation Time: 10 minutes
Cooking Time: 8 minutes
Servings: 2
Ingredients:
- 2 bananas
- 1 egg white
- 1 teaspoon coconut sugar
- 1 tablespoon oatmeal flour
- 2 tablespoon panko breadcrumbs
- 1 teaspoon ground cinnamon
- ¼ teaspoon ground nutmeg

Directions:
1. Peel the bananas and cut them into the bites.
2. Combine together coconut sugar, panko bread crumbs, ground cinnamon, and ground nutmeg.
3. Then whisk the egg white gently.
4. Coat the banana bites with the oatmeal flour.
5. Then dip them in the whisked egg white.
6. After this, coat the banana bites with the coconut sugar mixture.
7. Place the banana bites in the air fryer basket.
8. Cook the banana bites at 360 F for 8 minutes.
9. Let the cooked dessert chill briefly.
10. Enjoy!

Nutrition: Calories 159 Fat 1.1 Fiber 4.3 Carbs 35.7 Protein 4.5

633. Honey Pumpkin Delights

Preparation Time: 20 minutes
Cooking Time: 7 minutes
Servings: 2
Ingredients:

- ¼ teaspoon ground anise
- ¼ teaspoon vanilla extract
- 2 teaspoon honey
- ¼ teaspoon ground cinnamon
- ½ teaspoon ground ginger
- 1 teaspoon butter
- 10 oz. pumpkin

Directions:
1. Peel the pumpkin and cut it into 4 pieces.
2. Combine together vanilla extract, ground anise, honey, ground cinnamon, ground ginger, and butter,
3. Churn the mixture. Preheat it if desired.
4. Then sprinkle the pumpkin pieces with the spice mixture and leave them for 15 minutes or till the pumpkin gives the juice.
5. Then preheat the air fryer to 400 F.
6. Put the pumpkin pieces in the air fryer basket.
7. Sprinkle the pumpkin pieces with the remaining juice mixture.
8. Cook the pumpkin pieces for 7 minutes.
9. Shake the pumpkin pieces after 3 minutes of cooking.
10. When the pumpkin pieces are cooked – they should be tender.
11. Let the cooked pumpkin pieces cool briefly.
12. Serve the dessert immediately or keep it in the fridge.
13. Enjoy!

Nutrition: Calories 91 Fat 2.4 Fiber 4.4 Carbs 18 Protein 1.7

634. Nutmeg Blueberry Crumble

Preparation Time: 15 minutes
Cooking Time: 15 minutes
Servings: 2
Ingredients:
- 3 tablespoon blueberry
- 1 tablespoon brown sugar
- 1 teaspoon lemon juice
- ¼ teaspoon ground nutmeg
- 2 tablespoon butter, soft
- 4 tablespoons flour
- ¼ teaspoon olive oil
- 2 teaspoons white sugar

Directions:
1. Mash the blueberries with the help of the fork.
2. Add lemon juice and brown sugar.
3. Mix the mixture up and add ground nutmeg.
4. Then combine together flour, soft butter, and white sugar.
5. Knead the soft dough.
6. Crumble the dough with the help of the fingertips.
7. Separate the crumbled dough into 2 parts.
8. Then cover the cake tin with the parchment.
9. Place the first part of the crumbled dough in the cake tin,
10. After this, spread the blueberry mixture over the dough.
11. Sprinkle the blueberry mixture with the second part of the dough.
12. Preheat the air fryer to 360 F.
13. Put the crumble in the air fryer and cook for 15 minutes.
14. When the dessert is cooked – let it chill briefly.
15. Enjoy!

Nutrition: Calories 206 Fat 12.4 Fiber 0.8 Carbs 22.5 Protein 1.9

635. Cherry Crust Pie

Preparation Time: 15 minutes
Cooking Time: 10 minutes
Servings: 2
Ingredients:
- 6 oz. pie crust, uncooked
- 2 oz. cherry, pitted
- 1 teaspoon brown sugar
- 1 teaspoon water
- ¼ teaspoon turmeric

Directions:
1. Roll the pie crust and place the cherries there.
2. Sprinkle the cherries with the brown sugar and turmeric.
3. Place the pie in the air fryer basket and sprinkle the edges of the pie with water.
4. Preheat the air fryer to 360 F.
5. Cook the pie for 10 minutes.
6. Then chill the cherry pie to the room temperature.
7. Enjoy!

Nutrition: Calories 157 Fat 5 Fiber 2.6 Carbs 28 Protein 2.6

636. Cream Cheesecake Soufflé

Preparation Time: 15 minutes
Cooking Time: 10 minutes
Servings: 2
Ingredients:
- 5 oz. cream cheese
- 1 egg yolk
- 1 egg
- 1 teaspoon butter
- 2 tablespoons brown sugar
- ½ teaspoon vanilla extract
- ½ teaspoon almond flakes

Directions:
1. Beat the egg in the bowl.
2. Add the egg yolk and brown sugar.
3. Mix the mixture with the help of the hand mixer.
4. Then add butter, cream cheese, and vanilla extract.
5. Mix the mixture with the help of the hand mixer for 2 minutes at the maximum speed.
6. After this, pour the cream cheese mixture into 2 ramekins.
7. Preheat the air fryer to 350 F.
8. Place the ramekins in the air fryer basket and cook for 10 minutes.

9. The soufflé is cooked when you get the light brown color of the surface.
10. Let the soufflé chill for 5 minutes.
11. Then sprinkle the soufflé with the almond flakes.
12. Enjoy!
Nutrition: Calories 363 Fat 31.3 Fiber 0.1 Carbs 11.4 Protein 9.6

637. Creamy Chocolate Profiteroles
Preparation Time: 15 minutes
Cooking Time: 10 minutes
Servings: 2
Ingredients:
- 3 tablespoons flour
- 1 tablespoon butter
- 1 egg
- 2 tablespoon water
- 2 tablespoon whipped cream

Directions:
1. Boil the water and melt the butter.
2. Combine together boiled water, butter, and flour.
3. Mix the mixture and beat the egg.
4. Then mix the dough with the help of the mixer.
5. When you get the plastic dough – transfer it to the pastry bag.
6. Preheat the air fryer to 360 F.
7. Make the profiteroles with the help of the special nozzle and transfer them in the air fryer basket.
8. Cook the profiteroles for 10 minutes,
9. Then chill the profiteroles and cut them crosswise.
10. Fill the profiteroles with the whipped cream.
11. Enjoy!
Nutrition: Calories 338 Fat 25.4 Fiber 0.6 Carbs 19.1 Protein 8.7

638. Oats Cookies
Preparation Time: 10 minutes
Cooking Time: 9 minutes
Servings: 2
Ingredients:
- 3 tablespoon oatmeal flour
- 2 tablespoons sour cream
- 1 tablespoon brown sugar
- 1 teaspoon butter
- 1 pinch salt
- ½ teaspoon ground cardamom
- 1 egg

Directions:
1. Beat the egg in the bowl and whisk it.
2. Add the oatmeal flour and flour in the whisked egg.
3. After this, add sour cream, brown sugar, butter, salt, and ground cardamom.
4. Mix the mixture to get the homogenous dough.
5. Preheat the air fryer to 360 F.
6. Cover the air fryer basket with the parchment.
7. Make the medium cookies from the dough. Use the spoon for this step.
8. Place the cookies in the air fryer basket and cook for 9 minutes.
9. When the cookies are cooked – chill them well.
10. Taste and enjoy!
Nutrition: Calories 115 Fat 7 Fiber 0.8 Carbs 9.3 Protein 4.2

639. Avocado Cream
Preparation Time: 5 minutes
Cooking Time: 20 minutes
Servings: 6
Ingredients:
- 2 cups avocado, peeled, pitted and mashed
- 1 cup heavy cream
- 1 cup blueberries
- 3 tablespoons sugar
- 1 cup coconut cream

Directions:
1. In a bowl, mix the avocado with the cream and the other ingredients and whisk well.
2. Divide this into 6 ramekins, put them in your air fryer and cook at 320 degrees F for 20 minutes.
3. Cool down and serve.
Nutrition: Calories 100 Fat 1 Fiber 1 Carbs 2 Protein 2

640. Cocoa Brownies
Preparation Time: 10 minutes
Cooking Time: 30 minutes
Servings: 8
Ingredients:
- 2 tablespoons cocoa powder
- 2 eggs, whisked
- 4 tablespoons butter, melted
- 1 cup coconut flour
- ¼ teaspoon baking powder
- ½ cup almond milk
- Cooking spray

Directions:
1. Grease a cake pan that fits the air fryer with the cooking spray.
2. In a bowl, mix the cocoa with the eggs and the other ingredients, whisk well and pour into the pan.
3. Put the pan in your air fryer, cook at 370 degrees F for 30 minutes, cool the brownies down, slice and serve.
Nutrition: Calories 182 Fat 12 Fiber 2 Carbs 4 Protein 6

641. Cocoa Cream
Preparation Time: 10 minutes
Cooking Time: 30 minutes
Servings: 4
Ingredients:
- 1 cup heavy cream
- 2 eggs, whisked
- 2 tablespoons cocoa powder
- ½ teaspoon vanilla extract
- 4 tablespoons cocoa powder
- 3 tablespoons ghee, melted

- 2 tablespoons Sugar

Directions:
1. In a bowl, mix the cream with the eggs and the other ingredients, whisk and divide into 4 ramekins.
2. Put them the air fryer and cook at 350 degrees F for 30 minutes.
3. Serve the cream cold.

Nutrition: Calories 155 Fat 6 Fiber 2 Carbs 6 Protein 4

642. Coconut Ramekins

Preparation Time: 5 minutes
Cooking Time: 15 minutes
Servings: 4
Ingredients:
- 2 tablespoons ghee, melted
- 1 cup coconut, shredded
- 1 cup heavy cream
- ½ cup coconut cream
- 3 tablespoons sugar
- 3 eggs
- ½ teaspoon vanilla extract

Directions:
1. In a bowl, mix the ghee with the coconut and the other ingredients, whisk really well and divide into 4 ramekins.
2. Put them in the fryer's basket and cook at 320 degrees F for 15 minutes.
3. Serve cold.

Nutrition: Calories 164 Fat 4 Fiber 2 Carbs 5 Protein 5

643. Carrot Bars

Preparation Time: 10 minutes
Cooking Time: 20 minutes
Servings: 10
Ingredients:
- 2 tablespoons butter, melted
- 4 eggs, whisked
- 2 cups carrots, peeled and grated
- ½ cup coconut cream
- ½ cup cream cheese, soft
- ½ cup almond flour
- 2 teaspoons vanilla extract
- ½ teaspoon baking powder
- 3 tablespoons sugar

Directions:
1. In a bowl, combine the melted butter with the carrots and the other ingredients and whisk well.
2. Pour this into a baking dish that fits your air fryer lined with parchment paper, introduce in the fryer and cook at 360 degrees F, bake for 20 minutes.
3. Cut into bars and serve cold.

Nutrition: Calories 178 Fat 8 Fiber 3 Carbs 4 Protein 5

644. Pecan Bars

Preparation Time: 5 minutes
Cooking Time: 20 minutes
Servings: 4
Ingredients:
- 3 eggs, whisked
- 1 cup pecans, chopped
- 3 tablespoons sugar
- 4 tablespoons butter, melted
- 1 teaspoon almond extract
- ½ cup coconut flour
- ½ teaspoon baking soda

Directions:
1. In a bowl, mix the eggs with the pecans and the other ingredients and stir well.
2. Spread this on a baking sheet that fits your air fryer lined with parchment paper put it in the fryer and cooks at 330 degrees F and bakes for 20 minutes.
3. Cut into bars, cool down and serve.

Nutrition: Calories 182 Fat 12 Fiber 1 Carbs 3 Protein 6

645. Chocolate Cream

Preparation Time: 5 minutes
Cooking Time: 20 minutes
Servings: 4
Ingredients:
- 3 eggs, whisked
- ½ cup heavy cream
- 3 tablespoons butter, melted
- ½ cup dark chocolate, melted
- 3 tablespoons Sugar

Directions:
1. In a bowl, mix the chocolate with the eggs and the rest of the ingredients, whisk well, divide into ramekins, put them in the fryer and cook at 360 degrees F for 20 minutes.
2. Serve cold.

Nutrition: Calories 150 Fat 2 Fiber 2 Carbs 4 Protein 7

646. Walnut and Pecan Bars

Preparation Time: 5 minutes
Cooking Time: 15 minutes
Servings: 12
Ingredients:
- 1 teaspoon almond extract
- ½ cup walnuts, chopped
- ¼ cup pecans, chopped
- ½ cup almond flour
- 1 cup almond butter, soft
- 3 eggs, whisked
- 4 tablespoons sugar

Directions:
1. In a bowl, mix the walnuts with the pecans and the other ingredients and whisk really well.
2. Spread this on a cookie sheet that fits the air fryer lined with parchment paper, introduce in the fryer and cook at 370 degrees F and bake for 15 minutes.
3. Cool down, cut into bars and serve.

Nutrition: Calories 130 Fat 12 Fiber 1 Carbs 3 Protein 5

647. Yogurt and Berries Cream

Preparation Time: 5 minutes
Cooking Time: 20 minutes
Servings: 4
Ingredients:
- 4 eggs, whisked
- 1 cup blackberries

- ½ cup blueberries
- 1 teaspoon vanilla extract
- 3 tablespoons sugar
- 8 ounces' Greek yogurt

Directions:
1. In a blender, mix the eggs with the berries and the other ingredients and pulse well.
2. Pour this into 4 ramekins, put them in the air fryer and cook at 330 degrees F for 20 minutes.
3. Serve cold.

Nutrition: Calories 181 Fat 13 Fiber 2 Carbs 4 Protein 5

648. Cream Cheese Pudding

Preparation Time: 10 minutes
Cooking Time: 20 minutes
Servings: 6
Ingredients:
- 2 cups cream cheese, soft
- ½ cup heavy cream
- ½ cup coconut cream
- 4 tablespoons sugar
- 2 eggs, whisked
- ¼ cup almond flour
- 1 tablespoon vanilla extract
- 3 tablespoons cocoa powder

Directions:
1. In a bowl mix the cream cheese with the cream and the other ingredients and whisk well.
2. Divide this into 6 ramekins, put them in your air fryer and cook at 350 degrees F for 20 minutes.
3. Serve the puddings cold.

Nutrition: Calories 200 Fat 7 Fiber 2 Carbs 4 Protein 6

649. Rhubarb Cake

Preparation Time: 10 minutes
Cooking Time: 30 minutes
Servings: 6
Ingredients:
- 4 tablespoons butter, melted
- 3 eggs, whisked
- 4 tablespoons sugar
- 1 cup rhubarb, sliced
- ½ teaspoon vanilla extract
- 2 cups almond flour
- 2 teaspoons baking powder
- 1 cup almond milk
- ½ cup heavy cream

Directions:
1. In a bowl, mix the melted butter with the eggs and the other ingredients and whisk well.
2. Pour this into a cake pan that fits the air fryer lined with parchment paper, put the pan in the machine and cook at 360 degrees F for 30 minutes.
3. Cool the cake down, slice and serve.

Nutrition: Calories 183 Fat 4 Fiber 3 Carbs 4 Protein 7

650. Mango and Plums Bowls

Preparation Time: 5 minutes
Cooking Time: 15 minutes
Servings: 4
Ingredients:
- 1 cup mango, peeled and roughly cubed
- 1 cup plums, pitted and halved
- 2 tablespoons sugar
- ½ teaspoon vanilla extract
- ¼ cup apple juice
- Zest of 1 lemon, grated
- Juice of ½ lemons

Directions:
1. In a pan that fits the air fryer, combine the mango with the plums and the rest of the ingredients, toss gently, put the pan in the air fryer and cook at 360 degrees F for 15 minutes.
2. Divide into bowls and serve.

Nutrition: Calories 170 Fat 5 Fiber 1 Carbs 3 Protein 5

651. Rhubarb Cream

Preparation Time: 5 minutes
Cooking Time: 20 minutes
Servings: 4
Ingredients:
- 2 cups rhubarb, sliced
- 2 tablespoons sugar
- ½ cup heavy cream
- ½ cup coconut cream
- ¼ teaspoon vanilla extract
- 1 tablespoon lemon juice
- 1 tablespoon lemon zest, grated

Directions:
1. In a blender, combine the rhubarb with the other ingredients and pulse well.
2. Divide this into 4 ramekins, put them in the air fryer and cook at 340 degrees F for 20 minutes.
3. Serve the cream cold.

Nutrition: Calories 171 Fat 4 Fiber 2 Carbs 4 Protein 4

652. Lime Cake

Preparation Time: 10 minutes
Cooking Time: 30 minutes
Servings: 4
Ingredients:
- 3 eggs, whisked
- 3 tablespoons butter, melted
- 3 tablespoons sugar
- Juice of 1 lime
- Zest of 1 lime, grated
- ½ cup heavy cream
- ¼ cup almond milk
- 2 cups almond flour
- ½ teaspoon baking powder

Directions:
1. In a bowl, mix the eggs with the melted butter and the other ingredients and whisk well.
2. Pour this into a cake pan that fits the air fryer lined with parchment paper, put the cake pan in your air fryer and cook at 360 degrees F for 30 minutes.
3. Cool the cake down, slice and serve.

Nutrition: Calories 193 Fat 5 Fiber 1 Carbs 4 Protein 4

653. Cinnamon Apple Bowls

Preparation Time: 5 minutes
Cooking Time: 20 minutes
Servings: 4
Ingredients:
- 1 pound apples, cored and cut into wedges
- ½ cup heavy cream
- 3 tablespoons sugar
- 1 tablespoon butter, melted
- 1 tablespoon cinnamon powder
- 1 teaspoon vanilla extract

Directions:
1. In a pan that fits your air fryer, mix the apples with the cream and the rest of the ingredients, toss, put the pan in the air fryer and cook at 360 degrees F for 20 minutes.
2. Divide into bowls and serve warm.

Nutrition: Calories 162 Fat 3 Fiber 2 Carbs 4 Protein 5

654. Instant Pot Chocolate Chip Cookie in Air Fryer

Preparation Time: 10 minutes
Cooking Time: 10 minutes
Servings: 2
Ingredients:
- 2 large eggs
- 16 oz. cream cheese, softened at room temperature
- ½ tsp. lemon juice
- 2 tbsp sour cream
- 1 tsp. vanilla extract
- ¾ cup zero-calorie sweetener

Directions
1. Add eggs, vanilla, sweetener and lemon juice in a blender. Process until smooth and add the sour cream along with the cheese. Continue to free until silky and free of lumps. The creamier, the better
2. Line the air fryer basket with parchment paper and pour the batter into it. Place inside the instant pot and cover with the air fryer lid.
3. Bake for 8-10 minutes at 350 degrees F.
4. Allow to cool in a wire rack and leave in the fridge overnight or at least 2-3 hours.

Nutrition: Calories – 752 Carbohydrates – 9.87 g; Fat – 70.65 g;Protein – 19.22 g Fiber - 0 g Sugar – 38.36 g Sodium – 1020 mg

655. Air Fried Chocolate Chips

Preparation Time: 15 minutes
Cooking Time: 12 minutes
Servings: 8
Ingredients:
- 1 cup chocolate chips or chunks
- ½ tsp. baking soda
- ½ cup butter, softened
- 1 egg
- 1 tsp. vanilla
- ½ cup light brown Sugar
- 1½ cups all-purpose flour
- ¼ tsp. salt
- A scoop of vanilla ice cream to serve

Directions
1. Line 2 layers of the air fryer basket with parchment paper.
2. Cream altogether the butter and brown sugar. Then add the egg and vanilla along with the baking soda, flour, and salt. Stir in chocolate chunks.
3. Press cookie dough into the bottom of the air fryer. Attach the air fryer lid and bake for 10-12 minutes until edges are lightly browned.
4. Top with a scoop of vanilla ice cream to serve.

Nutrition: Calories – 286 kcal; Carbohydrates – 24.79 g Fat – 18.64 g Protein – 4.82 g Fiber - 2 g Sugar – 3.52 g Sodium – 262 mg

656. Flourless Chocolate Almond Cupcakes

Preparation Time: 10 minutes
Cooking Time: 18 minutes
Servings: 5
Ingredients:
- ⅓ Cup of chocolate chips
- 3 tablespoons butter
- ½ cup almond flour
- 1 egg
- 2 tablespoons maple syrup
- ½ teaspoon vanilla
- Cupcake pan and silicone liners
- Shredded coconuts

Directions:
1. In the AIR FRY mode, set the Instant Pot Air Fryer temperature to 320°F and timer for 5 minutes for preheating.
2. Press START to begin preheating.
3. Beat the egg in a small bowl.
4. In a clean non-stick saucepan, combine butter, maple syrup, and chocolate chip in a low-medium temperature until it starts to melt.
5. When the chocolate starts to melt, remove it from the heat and continue to stir until it melts completely.
6. Once the chocolate melted completely, allow it to settle down the heat.
7. Now add the remaining ingredients and stir well.
8. Place silicone liners in the cupcake pan and scoop the batter into it.
9. Put the air fryer basket in the inner pot and place the cupcake pan in the inner pot of the Instant Pot Air Fryer.
10. Close crisp cover.
11. In the BAKE mode select the temperature to 320°F and set the timer to 12 minutes.
12. Press START to begin baking.
13. When the timer elapses, open the crisp cover and insert a toothpick in the cake and check if it comes out clean.
14. If not, continue cooking for another 4 minutes.
15. After finished cooking, remove it from the air fryer and top it with shredded coconut.
16. Allow it to cool down for 10 minutes and serve.

Nutrition: Calories: 177, Total Fat 9.2g, Saturated Fat 5g, Trans Fat 0.3g, Cholesterol: 142mg, Sodium: 94mg, Total Carbs: 21g, Dietary Fiber 1g, Sugars: 17g, Protein 2g

657. Air Fryer Gluten-Free Chocolate Lava Cake

Preparation Time: 5 minutes
Cooking Time: 9 minutes
Servings: 1
Ingredients:
- 2 tablespoons cocoa powder
- 1 egg
- 2 tablespoons erythritol
- 2 tablespoons water
- ⅛ Tsp Stevie
- 1 tablespoon flax meal
- 1 tablespoon coconut oil
- ½ teaspoon baking powder
- ½ teaspoon vanilla essence
- ⅛ Tsp salt

Directions:
1. In an oven-safe medium glass bowl whisk all the ingredients.
2. In the AIR FRY mode, set the Instant Pot Air Fryer temperature to 350°F and timer to 2 minutes for preheating.
3. Press START to begin the preheating.
4. Place the glass bowl with the batter in the inner pot of the Air fryer.
5. Close the crisp cover.
6. In the AIR FRY mode, maintain the temperature at 350°F and set the cooking time to 9 minutes.
7. Press START to begin the cooking.
8. When the timer is off, remove the bowl from the air fryer.
9. Allow it to settle down the heat for a few minutes and serve.

Nutrition: Calories: 379, Total Fat 25g, Saturated Fat 15.2g, Trans Fat 0.1g, Cholesterol: 619mg, Sodium: 426mg, Total Carbs: 38g, Dietary Fiber 3g, Sugars: 24g, Protein 11g

658. Air Fried Sweet Potato Dessert

Preparation Time: 5 minutes,
Cooking Time: 18 minutes,
Servings: 4
Ingredients:
- 2 sweet potatoes, medium size
- 1 tablespoon arrowroot powder
- 2 teaspoons butter, melted
- ½ tablespoon coconut oil
- ¼ cup of coconut Sugar
- 1 tablespoon ground cinnamon
- 2 tablespoons sugar, powdered
- ½ cup vanilla yogurt
- ½ cup dessert hummus
- ½ cup maple frosting

Directions:
1. Peel the potatoes, wash and pat dry.
2. Julienne the peeled potatoes in half-inch thickness
3. Put the julienned potatoes in a large bowl and add coconut oil and arrowroot powder.
4. Toss them to mix thoroughly.
5. Transfer the coated julienned potatoes into a baking tray and put in the inner pot of the Instant Pot Air Fryer.
6. Close the crisp cover and set the temperature to 370°F in the AIR FRY mode.
7. Set the timer for 18 minutes.
8. Press START to begin the baking process.
9. Halfway through the cooking, open the crisp cover, and stir the potatoes.
10. Close the crisp cover to resume baking for the remaining period.
11. After cooking, transfer it into a bowl.
12. Drizzle 2 tablespoons of melted butter, sprinkle the cinnamon powder and sugar powder. Toss it to mix thoroughly.
13. Serve along with the dipping sauce.

Nutrition: Calories: 360, Total Fat 15.6g, Saturated Fat 6.4g, Trans Fat 1.4g, Cholesterol: 7mg, Sodium: 173mg, Total Carbs: 52g, Dietary Fiber 9g, Sugars: 28g, Protein 6g

659. Gluten-Free Easy Coconut Pie in Air Fryer

Preparation Time: 7 minutes,
Cooking Time: 12 minutes,
Servings: 6
Ingredients:
- 1 cup shredded coconut
- 2 eggs
- 1½ cup of coconut milk
- 1½ teaspoon vanilla extract
- ¼ cup butter
- ½ cup shredded Monk fruit
- Non-stick vegetable oil spray

Directions:
1. Combine all the ingredients in a large bowl using a wooden/steel spatula.
2. Spray some non-stick cooking oil into a 6" pie plate.
3. Transfer the prepared batter into it.
4. Place the pie plate with the batter in the air fryer basket and put in the inner pot of the Instant Pot Air Fryer.
5. Close the crisp cover and set the temperature to 350°F in the BAKE mode
6. Select the timer to 12 minutes, and press START to begin the baking.
7. After cooking, check the doneness by inserting a toothpick.
8. If it comes out clean, then it is ready to serve. Otherwise, bake it another 4 minutes.
9. When the cooking is over, remove it from the air fryer and allow it to settle down the heat.

10. Cut the coconut pie into 6 pieces and serve.
Nutrition: Calories: 275, Total Fat 25.3g, Saturated Fat 18.5g, Trans Fat 0.3g, Cholesterol: 227mg, Sodium: 147mg, Total Carbs: 9g, Dietary Fiber 2g, Sugars: 7g, Protein 5g

660. Air Fryer Brownies
Preparation Time: 5 minutes
Cooking: 18 minutes
Servings: 2
Ingredients:
- ⅓ Cup of cocoa powder
- ¼ cup all-purpose flour
- ½ cup sugar, granulated
- ¼ teaspoon baking powder
- ⅛ Teaspoon kosher salt
- 1 egg, large
- ¼ cup butter, melted
- Non-stick cooking oil spray

Directions:
1. Combine flour, sugar, baking powder, cocoa powder, and salt in a large bowl.
2. Take a round cake pan that can put inside the air fryer basket of the Instant Pot Air Fryer and grease it with cooking spray.
3. Combine egg and melted butter in a small bowl thoroughly.
4. Pour the wet ingredient mixture into the dry ingredient mixture and combine thoroughly.
5. Transfer the batter into the cake pan and flatten the surface.
6. Put the cake pan in the air fryer basket and place the basket in the inner pot of the Instant Pot Air Fryer. Close the crisp cover.
7. In the BAKE mode, set the temperature to 350°F and set the cooking time to 18 minutes.
8. Press START for baking. After cooking, allow it to settle down the temperature. Slice and serve.

Nutrition: Calories: 417, Total Fat 27.3g, Saturated Fat 16.5g, Trans Fat 0.9g, Cholesterol: 153mg, Sodium: 346mg, Total Carbs: 46g, Dietary Fiber 5g, Sugars: 25g, Protein 6g

661. Air Fryer Doughnuts
Preparation Time: 10 minutes
Cooking Time: 1 hour & 40 minutes
Servings: 6
Ingredients:
- 2 cup all-purpose flour
- ½ cup milk
- ¼ cup + 1 teaspoon granulated Sugar
- 2¼ teaspoon active-dry east
- 4 tablespoons melted butter
- 1 egg, large
- 1 teaspoon vanilla essence
- ½ teaspoon kosher salt
- Vegetable oil, cooking spray
- For the Vanilla Glaze:
- ½ teaspoon vanilla extract
- 2 ounces' milk
- 1 cup of sugar powder

For the Chocolate Glaze:
- ¼ cup cocoa powder, unsweetened
- ¾ cup of sugar powder
- 3 tablespoons milk

For the Cinnamon Sugar
- 2 tablespoons ground cinnamon
- ½ cup granulated Sugar
- 2 tablespoons melted butter

Directions:
1. For making the Doughnuts:
2. Microwave the milk for 40 seconds in an oven-safe glass bowl.
3. Add sugar and stir until it dissolves.
4. After that, drizzle some yeast and keep it aside to froth. Within 8-10 minutes, it will froth.
5. Combine salt and flour in a medium bowl.
6. Spray some cooking oil in a large bowl and combine butter, ¼ sugar, vanilla, and egg.
7. Transfer the yeast mixture into it and combine it thoroughly.
8. After that add, the dry mixture kept ready in the medium bowl. Combine the mix to become rough dough.
9. Drizzle some flour on your kitchen working table and transfer the dough onto it.
10. Knead it gently for 5 minutes until it becomes soft and change to elastic texture.
11. Maintain the consistency of the dough by adding the flour.
12. Shape the dough into a ball and transfer into a greased bowl.
13. Cover it with a dish towel and keep it in a warm place for 1 hour to raise the dough to its double size.
14. Take a baking tray and line with a parchment paper.
15. Sprits cooking oil and place the dough on it
16. Place the dough on a floured working table and spread the dough, pressing with your palm and make it into a ½" thick flat sheet.
17. Using a 3" diameter doughnut cutter, make doughnuts with holes
18. Transfer the doughnuts into the parchment paper.
19. You can use the remaining dough and knead it make fresh doughnuts.
20. Place the baking tray in the air fryer basket and place the air fryer basket into the inner pot of the Instant Pot Air Fryer.
21. Close the crisp cover and set the temperature to 375°F in the BAKE mode.
22. Set the timer to 6 minutes.
23. Press START to begin baking and continue cooking until it becomes golden brown.
24. For making the vanilla glaze, whisk milk, vanilla, and sugar powder in a medium bowl until it turns smooth. Dip the doughnuts in the glaze.

25. For making the chocolate glaze, combine cocoa powder, milk, and powdered sugar in a medium bowl, until it becomes soft. Dip the doughnuts in the glaze.
26. For making the cinnamon sugar, whisk sugar, and ground cinnamon in a large shallow bowl. Apply butter on the doughnuts and sprinkle the cinnamon sugar on it.
27. After glazing and sugaring, allow the doughnuts to settle down the heat before you serve.
Nutrition: Calories: 472, Total Fat 14.6g, Saturated Fat 8.7g, Trans Fat 0.5g, Cholesterol: 65mg, Sodium: 307mg, Total Carbs: 80g, Dietary Fiber 4g, Sugars: 43g, Protein 8g

662. Perfect Cinnamon Toast
Preparation Time: 10 Minutes
Cooking Time: 5 Minutes
Servings: 6
Ingredients:
- 2 tsp. pepper
- 1 ½ tsp. vanilla extract
- 1 ½ tsp. cinnamon
- ½ C. sweetener of choice
- 1 C. coconut oil
- 12 slices whole wheat bread

Directions:
1. Melt coconut oil and mix with sweetener until dissolved. Mix in remaining ingredients minus bread till incorporated.
2. Spread mixture onto bread, covering all area.
3. Pour the coated pieces of bread into the Oven rack/basket. Place the Rack on the middle-shelf of the Smart Air Fryer Oven. Set temperature to 400°F, and set time to 5 minutes.
4. Remove and cut diagonally. Enjoy!
Nutrition: Calories: 124; Fat 2g Protein 0g Sugar 4g

663. Easy Baked Chocolate Mug Cake
Preparation Time: 5 Minutes
Cooking Time: 15 Minutes
Servings: 3
Ingredients:
- ½ cup cocoa powder
- ½ cup Stevie powder
- 1 cup coconut cream
- 1 package cream cheese, room temperature
- 1 tablespoon vanilla extract
- 1 tablespoon butter

Directions:
1. Preheat the Smart Air Fryer Oven for 5 minutes.
2. In a mixing bowl, combine all ingredients.
3. Use a hand mixer to mix everything until fluffy.
4. Pour into greased mugs.
5. Place the mugs in the fryer basket.
6. Bake for 15 minutes at 350°F.
7. Place in the fridge to chill before serving.
Nutrition: Calories: 744; Fat 69.7g Protein 13.9g Sugar 4g

664. Angel Food Cake
Preparation Time: 5 Minutes
Cooking Time: 30 Minutes
Servings: 12
Ingredients:
- ¼ cup butter, melted
- 1 cup powdered erythritol
- 1 teaspoon strawberry extract
- 12 egg whites
- 1 teaspoon of cream of tartar
- A pinch of salt

Directions:
1. Preheat the Smart Air Fryer Oven for 5 minutes.
2. Mix the egg whites and cream of tartar.
3. Use a hand mixer and whisk until white and fluffy.
4. Add the rest of the ingredients except for the butter and whisk for another minute.
5. Pour into a baking dish.
6. Place in the air fryer basket and cook for 30 minutes at 400°F or if a toothpick inserted in the middle comes out clean.
7. Drizzle with melted butter once cooled.
Nutrition: Calories: 65; Fat 5g Protein 3.1g Fiber 1g

665. Fried Peaches
Preparation Time: 2 Hours 10 Minutes
Cooking Time: 15 Minutes
Servings: 4
Ingredients:
- Ripe peaches (1/2 a peach = 1 serving)
- 1 1/2 cups flour
- Salt
- Egg yolks
- 3/4 cups cold water
- 1 1/2 tablespoons olive oil
- 1 tablespoon brandy
- Egg whites
- Cinnamon/sugar mix

Directions:
1. Mix flour, egg yolks, and salt in a mixing bowl. Slowly mix in water, and then add brandy. Set the mixture aside for 2 hours and go do something for 1 hour 45 minutes.
2. Boil a large pot of water and cut and X at the bottom of each peach. While the water boils fill another large bowl with water and ice. Boil each peach for about a minute, and then plunge it in the ice bath. Now the peels should basically fall off the peach. Beat the egg whites and mix into the batter mix. Dip each peach in the mix to coat.
3. Pour the coated peach into the Oven rack/basket. Place the Rack on the middle-shelf of the Smart Air Fryer Oven. Set temperature to 360°F, and set time to 10 minutes.
4. Prepare a plate with cinnamon/sugar mix, roll peaches in mix and serve.
Nutrition: Calories: 306; Fat 3g Protein 10g Fiber 2.7g

666. Apple Dumplings
Preparation Time: 10 Minutes
Cooking Time: 25 Minutes
Servings: 4
Ingredients:
- 1 tbsp melted coconut oil
- Puff pastry sheets
- 1 tbsp. brown Sugar
- 2 tbsp. raisins
- 2 small apples of choice

Directions:
1. Ensure your Smart Air Fryer Oven is preheated to 356 degrees.
2. Core and peel apples and mix with raisins and sugar.
3. Place a bit of apple mixture into puff pastry sheets and brush sides with melted coconut oil.
4. Place into the air fryer. Cook 25 minutes, turning halfway through until its golden brown.

Nutrition: Calories: 367; Fat 7g Protein 2g Sugar 5g

667. Apple Pie in Air Fryer
Preparation Time: 5 Minutes
Cooking Time: 35 Minutes
Servings: 4
Ingredients:
- ½ teaspoon vanilla extract
- 1 beaten egg
- 1 large apple, chopped
- 1 Pillsbury Refrigerator pie crust
- 1 tablespoon butter
- 1 tablespoon ground cinnamon
- 1 tablespoon raw Sugar
- 1 tablespoon Sugar
- 2 teaspoons lemon juice
- Baking spray

Directions:
1. Lightly grease baking pan of Smart Air Fryer Oven with cooking spray. Spread pie crust on bottom of pan up to the sides.
2. In a bowl, mix vanilla, sugar, cinnamon, lemon juice, and apples. Pour on top of pie crust. Top the apples with butter slices.
3. Cover apples with the other pie crust. Pierce with knife the tops of pie.
4. Spread beaten egg on top of crust and sprinkle sugar.
5. Cover with foil.
6. For 25 minutes, cook it on 390°F.
7. Remove foil cook for 10 minutes at 330oF until tops are browned.
8. Serve and enjoy.

Nutrition: Calories: 372; Fat 19g Protein 4.2g Sugar 5g

668. Raspberry Cream Roll-Ups
Preparation Time: 10 Minutes
Cooking Time: 25 Minutes
Servings: 4
Ingredients:
- 1 cup of fresh raspberries, rinsed and patted dry
- ½ cup of cream cheese, softened to room temperature
- ¼ cup of brown sugar
- ¼ cup of sweetened condensed milk
- 1 egg
- 1 teaspoon of corn starch
- Spring roll wrappers (any brand will do, we like Blue Dragon or Tasty Joy, both available through Target or Walmart, or any large grocery chain)
- ¼ cup of water

Directions:
1. Cover the basket of the Smart Air Fryer Oven with a lining of tin foil, leaving the edges uncovered to allow air to circulate through the basket. Preheat the Smart Air Fryer Oven to 350 degrees.
2. In a mixing bowl, combine the cream cheese, brown sugar, condensed milk, cornstarch, and egg. Beat or whip thoroughly, until all ingredients are completely mixed and fluffy, thick and stiff.
3. Spoon even amounts of the creamy filling into each spring roll wrapper, then top each dollop of filling with several raspberries.
4. Roll up the wraps around the creamy raspberry filling, and seal the seams with a few dab of water.
5. Place each roll on the foil-lined air fryer basket, seams facing down.
6. Set the Smart Air Fryer Oven timer to 10 minutes. During cooking, shake the handle of the fryer basket to ensure a nice even surface crisp.
7. After 10 minutes, when the Smart Air Fryer Oven shuts off, the spring rolls should be golden brown and perfect on the outside, while the raspberries and cream filling will have cooked together in a glorious fusion. Remove with tongs and serve hot or cold.

Nutrition: Calories: 54; Fat 6g Protein 8g Sugar 1g

669. Air Fryer Chocolate Cake
Preparation Time: 5 Minutes
Cooking Time: 35 Minutes
Servings: 8-10
Ingredients:
- ½ C. hot water
- 1 tsp. vanilla
- ¼ C. olive oil
- ½ C. almond milk
- 1 egg
- ½ tsp. salt
- ¾ tsp. baking soda
- ¾ tsp. baking powder
- ½ C. unsweetened cocoa powder
- C. almond flour
- 1 C. brown Sugar

Directions:
1. Preheat your Smart Air Fryer Oven to 356 degrees.

2. Stir all dry ingredients together. Then stir in wet ingredients. Add hot water last.
3. The batter will be thin, no worries.
4. Pour cake batter into a pan that fits into the fryer. Cover with foil and poke holes into the foil.
5. Bake 35 minutes.
6. Discard foil and then bake another 10 minutes.
Nutrition: Calories: 378; Fat 9g Protein 4g Sugar 5g

670. Banana-Choco Brownies
Preparation Time: 5 Minutes
Cooking Time: 30 Minutes
Servings: 12
Ingredients:
- cups almond flour
- teaspoons baking powder
- ½ teaspoon baking powder
- ½ teaspoon baking soda
- ½ teaspoon salt
- 1 over-ripe banana
- large eggs
- ½ teaspoon stevia powder
- ¼ cup coconut oil
- 1 tablespoon vinegar
- 1/3 cup almond flour
- 1/3 cup cocoa powder

Directions:
1. Preheat the Smart Air Fryer Oven for 5 minutes.
2. Combine all ingredients in a food processor and pulse until well-combined.
3. Pour into a baking dish that will fit in the air fryer.
4. Place in the air fryer basket and cook for 30 minutes at 350°F or if a toothpick inserted in the middle comes out clean.
Nutrition: Calories: 75; Fat 6.5g Protein 1.7g Sugar 2g

671. Chocolate Donuts
Preparation Time: 5 Minutes
Cooking Time: 20 Minutes
Servings: 8-10
Ingredients:
- (8-ounce) can jumbo biscuits
- Cooking oil
- Chocolate sauce, such as Hershey's

Directions:
1. Separate the biscuit dough into 8 biscuits and place them on a flat work surface. Use a small circle cookie cutter or a biscuit cutter to cut a hole in the center of each biscuit. You can also cut the holes using a knife.
2. Spray the air fryer basket with cooking oil.
3. Place 4 donuts in the Smart Air Fryer Oven and do not stack. Spray with cooking oil. Cook for 4 minutes.
4. Open the air fryer and flip the donuts. Cook for an additional 4 minutes.
5. Remove the cooked donuts from the Smart Air Fryer Oven, and then repeat for the remaining 4 donuts.
6. Drizzle chocolate sauce over the donuts and enjoy while warm.
Nutrition: Calories: 181; Fat 98g Protein 3g Fiber 1g

672. Easy Air Fryer Donuts
Preparation Time: 5 Minutes
Cooking Time: 5 Minutes
Servings: 8
Ingredients:
- Pinch of allspice
- 1 tbsp dark brown Sugar
- ½ - 1 tsp. cinnamon
- 1/3 C. granulated sweetener
- 1 tbsp melted coconut oil
- 1 can of biscuits

Directions:
1. Mix allspice, sugar, sweetener, and cinnamon together.
2. Take out biscuits from can and with a circle cookie cutter, cut holes from centers and place into air fryer.
3. Cook 5 minutes at 350 degrees. As batches are cooked, use a brush to coat with melted coconut oil and dip each into sugar mixture.
4. Serve warm!
Nutrition: Calories: 209; Fat 4g Protein 0g Sugar 3g

673. Chocolate Soufflé for Two
Preparation Time: 5 Minutes
Cooking Time: 14 Minutes
Servings: 2
Ingredients:
- 1 tbsp. almond flour
- ½ tsp. vanilla
- 1 tbsp sweetener
- 2 separated eggs
- ¼ C. melted coconut oil
- 1 ounces of semi-sweet chocolate, chopped

Directions:
1. Brush coconut oil and sweetener onto ramekins.
2. Melt coconut oil and chocolate together.
3. Beat egg yolks well, adding vanilla and sweetener. Stir in flour and ensure there are no lumps.
4. Preheat the Smart Air Fryer Oven to 330 degrees.
5. Whisk egg whites till they reach peak state and fold them into chocolate mixture.
6. Pour batter into ramekins and place into the Smart Air Fryer Oven.
7. Cook 14 minutes.
8. Serve with powdered sugar dusted on top.
Nutrition: Calories: 238; Fat 6g Protein 1g Sugar 4g

674. Fried Bananas with Chocolate Sauce
Preparation Time: 10 Minutes
Cooking Time: 10 Minutes
Servings: 2
Ingredients:
- 1 large egg

- ¼ cup cornstarch
- ¼ cup plain bread crumbs
- Bananas, halved crosswise
- Cooking oil
- Chocolate sauce (see Ingredient tip)

Directions:
1. In a small bowl, beat the egg. In another bowl, place the cornstarch. Place the bread crumbs in a third bowl. Dip the bananas in the cornstarch, then the egg, and then the bread crumbs.
2. Spray the air fryer basket with cooking oil. Place the bananas in the basket and spray them with cooking oil.
3. Cook for 5 minutes. Open the air fryer and flip the bananas. Cook for an additional 2 minutes. Transfer the bananas to plates.
4. Drizzle the chocolate sauce over the bananas, and serve.
5. You can make your own chocolate sauce using 2 tablespoons milk and ¼ cup chocolate chips. Heat a saucepan over medium-high heat. Add the milk and stir for 1 to 2 minutes. Add the chocolate chips. Stir it for 2 minutes, or until the chocolate has melted.

Nutrition: Calories: 203; Fat 6g Protein 3g Fiber 3g

675. Apple Hand Pies

Preparation Time: 5 Minutes
Cooking Time: 8 Minutes
Servings: 6
Ingredients:
1. 15-ounces no-sugar-added apple pie filling
2. 1 store-bought crust

Directions:
1. Lay out pie crust and slice into equal-sized squares.
2. Place 2 tablespoons filling into each square and then seal crust with a fork.
3. Pour into the Oven rack/basket. Place the Rack on the middle-shelf of the Smart Air Fryer Oven. Set temperature to 390°F, and set time to 8 minutes until golden in color.

Nutrition: Calories: 278 Fat 10g Protein 5g Sugar 4g

OTHER OMNI AIR FRYER LID FAVORITES

676. Deviled Eggs with Bacon
Preparation Time: 10 minutes
Cooking Time: 20 minutes
Servings: 3
Ingredients:
- 6 eggs
- 3 slices bacon
- 2 tablespoons green onions, chopped
- 2 tablespoons mayonnaise
- 1 tablespoon pickle relish
- ½ teaspoon Worcestershire sauce
- 1 teaspoon hot sauce
- Salt and ground black pepper, to taste
- 1 teaspoon smoked paprika

Directions:
1. Arrange the bacon slices in the basket. Put the lid on and bake at 375ºF for 8 minutes, flipping once when it shows 'TURN FOOD' on the lid screen halfway through.
2. Remove the bacon slices from the basket to the cutting board. Cut them into mince. Set aside.
3. Place the eggs in the air fryer basket. Put the air fryer lid on and air fry in the preheated instant pot at 275ºF for 15 minutes. Meanwhile, prepare a bowl of ice water.
4. Remove the eggs from the basket into the ice water. Under cold running water, peel the eggs.
5. Slice them in half on a cutting board. Scoop the egg yolks out and mash them in a bowl.
6. Stir in the green onions, mayo, pickle relish, Worcestershire sauce, hot sauce, salt, and pepper. Add the minced bacon and gently stir.
7. Spoon the yolk mixture into the egg whites. Sprinkle with the smoked paprika before serving.

Nutrition: Calories: 513, Fat 43g Carbs: 5.2g, Protein 25.3g, Sugars: 3.7g

677. Quick Greek Revithokeftedes
Preparation Time: 10 minutes
Cooking Time: 25minutes
Servings: 3
Ingredients:
- 12 ounces canned chickpeas, drained
- 1 chili pepper
- 1 tablespoon fresh coriander
- 2 cloves garlic
- 1 red onion, sliced
- 2 tablespoons all-purpose flour
- Sea salt and freshly ground pepper, to taste
- ½ teaspoon cayenne pepper
- 3 large (6½-inch) of pita bread
- Cooking spray

Directions:
1. To make revithokeftedes, in a food processor, put the chickpeas, chili pepper, coriander, garlic, and onion. Process until the chickpeas is grated. Set aside.
2. In a large bowl, whisk the all-purpose flour, black pepper, salt, and cayenne pepper until well blended.
3. Spoon the chickpea mixture into the bowl. Stir to mix well. Shape the mixture into balls.
4. Sprits the air fryer basket with cooking sprays. Place the balls in the air fryer basket, and then sprits it again with the cooking spray.
5. Put the air fryer lid on and bake in the preheated instant pot at 375ºF for approximately 15 minutes, shaking the basket occasionally to make sure to cook evenly.
6. Remove the revithokeftedes from the basket, and bake the pita bread in the basket at 400ºF for approximately 5 minutes.
7. Serve the revithokeftedes in pita bread on a plate.

Nutrition: Calories: 352, Fat 4.2g, Carbs: 65.4g, Protein 14.4g, Sugars: 6.4g

678. Baked Philadelphia Mushroom Omelet
Preparation Time: 10 minutes
Cooking Time: 15minutes
Servings: 2
Ingredients:
- 6 ounces' button mushrooms, thinly sliced
- 1 bell pepper, deseeded and thinly sliced
- ½ cup scallions, chopped
- 1 tablespoon olive oil
- 2 tablespoons milk
- 4 eggs, beaten
- Sea salt and freshly ground black pepper, to taste
- 1 tablespoon fresh chives

Directions:
1. In a skillet, heat the olive oil over moderate heat until shimmering. Add and sauté the peppers and scallions for 3 minutes or until fragrant. Add the mushrooms and sauté for an additional 3 minutes or until soft. Set aside.
2. Grease a 6×6×2-inch baking pan with olive oil.
3. To make omelet, add the milk, beaten eggs, salt, and black pepper in the pan. Stir to combine well. Arrange the pan in the air fryer basket.
4. Put the air fryer lid on and bake in the preheated instant pot at 350ºF for 10 minutes. Flip the omelet with tongs when the lid screen indicates 'TURN FOOD' halfway through. Cool for a few minutes.
5. On one side of the omelet, spoon in the prepared vegetables and fold up your omelet and transfer onto a serving plate. Sprinkle with fresh chives for garnish. Enjoy!

Nutrition: Calories: 273, Fat 19.2g Carbs: 8.2g Protein 18.4g Sugars: 4.6g

679. Spiced and Baked Mixed Nuts
Preparation Time: 5 minutes
Cooking Time: 20minutes
Servings: 6

Ingredients:
- ½ cup hazelnuts
- ½ cup pine nuts
- 2 tablespoons butter, softened
- 1 cup pecans
- 1 teaspoon coarse sea salt
- ½ teaspoon paprika
- 1 tablespoon dried rosemary

Directions:
1. Combine all ingredients well in a bowl.
2. Spoon the coated nuts in a single layer in the air fryer basket lined with parchment paper.
3. Put the air fryer lid on and bake in the preheated instant pot at 350ºF for 6 to 8 minutes, giving the basket a shake once or twice during the cooking.
4. Remove the nuts from the basket and serve on a plate.

Nutrition: Calories: 294, Fat 30.1g, Carbs: 5.7g, Protein 4.6g, Sugars: 1.5g

680. Fingerling Potatoes with Cashew Sauce

Preparation Time: 10 minutes
Cooking Time: 15 minutes
Servings: 4
Ingredients:
- 1-pound fingerling potatoes, peeled, rinsed, and drained
- 1 tablespoon butter, melted
- 1 teaspoon garlic powder
- 1 teaspoon onion powder
- Sea salt and ground black pepper, to taste
- Cooking spray
- Cashew Sauce:
- ½ cup raw cashews
- 1 teaspoon cayenne pepper
- 3 tablespoons nutritional yeast
- 2 teaspoons white vinegar
- 4 tablespoons water
- ¼ teaspoon dried rosemary
- ¼ teaspoon dried dill

Directions:
1. Combine the fingerling potatoes with the butter, garlic powder, onion powder, salt, and pepper in a bowl. Sprits the air fryer basket with cooking sprays. Arrange the fingerling potatoes in the basket.
2. Put the air fryer lid on and cook in batches in the preheated instant pot at 375ºF for 8 minutes, shaking the basket, and cook for 6 minutes more. Meanwhile, to make the cashew sauce, in a food processor or a blender, pulse to combine all the ingredients.
3. Spoon the cashew sauce on the potatoes. Put the air fryer lid on and cook at 375ºF for an additional 3 minutes. Remove the potatoes from the basket and serve warm on a large platter.

Nutrition: Calories: 342, Fat 20.3g, Carbs: 34.3g, Protein 9.9g Sugars: 4.7g

681. Brown Rice Bowl

Preparation Time: 15 minutes
Cooking Time: 15 minutes
Servings: 4
Ingredients:
- 1 cup brown rice
- 2½ cups of water
- 1 tablespoon peanut oil
- 2 tablespoons soy sauce
- ½ cup scallions, chopped
- 2 bell pepper, chopped
- 2 eggs, beaten
- Sea salt and ground black pepper, to taste
- ½ teaspoon garlic, granulated
- Nonstick cooking spray

Directions:
1. In a saucepan, put the brown rice and water. Bring it to a boil over high heat. Lower heat and simmer for 35 minutes.
2. Use the nonstick cooking spray to sprits a 6×6×2-inch baking pan. Put in the hot rice and the remaining ingredients. Place the pan in the air fryer basket. Put the air fryer lid on and cook in the preheated instant pot at 375ºF for 14 minutes or until cooked through. Stir the mixture occasionally. Remove the pan from the basket and serve warm in a bowl with broth, if desired.

Nutrition: Calories: 301, Fat 10.9g, Carbs: 41.1g Protein 9.3g, Sugars: 3.6g

682. Greek-style Fruit Skewers

Preparation Time: 5 minutes
Cooking Time: 5 minutes
Servings: 2
Ingredients:
- ¼ pineapple, peeled and cubed
- 1 banana, peeled and sliced
- 6 strawberries, halved
- 1 teaspoon fresh lemon juice
- ¼ cup Greek-Style yoghurt, optional
- 1 teaspoon vanilla
- 2 tablespoons honey
- 2 wooden skewers, soaked in the water for at least 30 minutes

Directions:
1. Combine the fruits with lemon juice in a bowl and arrange the fruit slices on skewers. Place the fruit skewers in the air fryer basket.
2. Put the air fryer lid on and cook in the preheated instant pot at 325ºF for 6 minutes. Flip the fruit skewers halfway through the cooking time.
3. Meanwhile, combine the Greek yogurt, vanilla, and honey in a separate small bowl. Stir to mix well.
4. Remove the fruit skewers from the basket and serve with the Greek sauce.

Nutrition: Calories: 195, Fat 0.6g, Carbs: 49.3g, Protein 3.2g, Sugars: 38g

683. Yummy Hot Fruit Bake

Preparation Time: 15 minutes
Cooking Time: 35 minutes

Servings: 4
Ingredients:
- 2 cups blueberries
- 2 cups raspberries
- 1 tablespoon cornstarch
- 2 tablespoons coconut oil
- A pinch of nutmeg, grated
- A pinch of salt
- 3 tablespoons maple syrup
- 1 vanilla bean
- 1 cinnamon stick
- Cooking spray

Directions:
1. Sprits a 6×6×2-inch baking pan with cooking spray. Put in the berries and cornstarch.
2. Combine well the coconut oil, nutmeg, salt, and maple syrup in a bowl. Spoon the mixture over the pan, whisking slowly to blend well.
3. Top the mixture with the vanilla bean and cinnamon stick. Arrange the pan in the air fryer basket.
4. Put the air fryer lid on and bake in the preheated instant pot at 375ºF for 35 minutes. Stir the mixture two or three times during the cooking.
5. Remove the pan from the basket. Discard the vanilla bean and cinnamon stick before serving.

Nutrition: Calories: 333, Fat 7.3g, Carbs: 69.9g, Protein 1.8g, Sugars: 60.8g

684. Cornmeal Puddings with Jamaican Flair

Preparation Time: 20 minutes
Cooking Time: 25 minutes
Servings: 6
Ingredients:
- 2 ounces' butter, softened
- 3 cups coconut milk
- 1 cup sugar
- ½ teaspoon fine sea salt
- ½ teaspoon nutmeg, grated
- 1 teaspoon cinnamon
- ¼ cup all-purpose flour
- ½ cup water
- 1½ cups yellow cornmeal
- 1 teaspoon vanilla extract
- 1 teaspoon rum extract
- ½ cup raisins
- Cooking spray
- Custard:
- ½ cup full-Fat coconut milk
- ¼ cup honey
- A dash of vanilla
- 1 ounce (or two tablespoons) butter

Directions:
1. In a large saucepan, put the butter, coconut milk, sugar, salt, nutmeg, and cinnamon. Bring to a boil. Turn off the heat and set aside.
2. In a medium bowl, combine the flour, water, and cornmeal. Whisk until well incorporated.
3. To make puddings, pour the flour mixture into the butter mixture. Stir until well combined. Bring to a boil, and then cook over low heat for about 7 minutes, stirring constantly.
4. Turn off the heat. Add the vanilla extract, rum extract, and raisins and gently stir.
5. Sprits a 6×6×2-inch baking pan with cooking spray. Pour the mixture in the pan. Arrange the pan in the air fryer basket.
6. Put the air fryer lid on and bake in the preheated instant pot at 325ºF for 12 minutes.
7. Meanwhile, to make the custard, in a saucepan, stir the coconut milk, honey, vanilla, and butter. Cook for 2 to 3 minutes over low heat.
8. After the custard is ready, using a fork to poke your puddings in the basket. Spoon the custard on top.
9. Continue cooking for an additional 35 minutes or until a toothpick that has been inserted into the center of the puddings comes out clean. Transfer the pudding to the refrigerator. Chill for a few minutes before serving.

Nutrition: Calories: 537, Fat 21.4g, Carbs: 82.3g, Protein 8.1g, Sugars: 49.3g

685. Mushroom Frittata with Mozzarella

Preparation Time: 10 minutes
Cooking Time: 25 minutes
Servings: 3
Ingredients:
- 6 ounces' wild mushrooms, sliced
- ½ cup mozzarella cheese, shredded
- 1 yellow onion, finely chopped
- ¼ cup heavy cream
- 6 eggs, beaten
- 2 cups kale, chopped
- 1 tablespoon butter, melted
- 2 tablespoons fresh Italian parsley, chopped
- ½ teaspoon cayenne pepper
- Sea salt and ground black pepper, to taste
- Cooking spray

Directions:
1. Use the cooking spray to sprits a 6×6×2-inch baking pan.
2. Add the wild mushrooms and onions into the pan. Arrange the pan in the air fryer basket.
3. Put the air fryer lid on and bake in the preheated instant pot at 350ºF for 5 to 6 minutes.
4. Meanwhile, stir the heavy cream and beaten eggs in a bowl until foamy. Add the kale, butter, parsley, cayenne pepper, salt, and black pepper. Whisk to combine well.
5. To make the frittata, top the baking pan with the cream mixture and mozzarella cheese. Put the air fryer lid on and bake for 10 minutes more. Stir occasionally during the cooking.
6. Remove the frittata from the basket and serve warm.

Nutrition: Calories: 290, Fat 19.7g, Carbs: 9.3g, Protein 20g, Sugars: 5.1g

DEHYDRATOR AND CASSEROLE RECIPES

686. Eggplant Jerky
Preparation Time: 10 minutes
Cooking Time: 12 hours
Servings: 4
Ingredients:
- 1 eggplant, sliced
- 1 tsp paprika
- 1/2 tsp black pepper
- 1 garlic clove, minced
- 1/2 cup vinegar
- 1/2 cup olive oil
- 1/2 tsp sea salt

Directions:
1. Add eggplant slices into the large bowl.
2. Add remaining ingredients and toss well. Cover and set aside for 2 hours.
3. Place the dehydrating tray in a multi-level air fryer basket and place basket in the instant pot.
4. Arrange marinated eggplant slices on dehydrating tray.
5. Seal pot with air fryer lid and select dehydrate mode then set temperature to 115 F and timer for 12 hours.
6. Serve and enjoy.

Nutrition: Calories 254 Fat 25.5 g Carbohydrates 7.7 g Sugar 3.6 g Protein 1.3 g Cholesterol 0 mg

687. Dehydrated Pear Slices
Preparation Time: 10 minutes
Cooking Time: 5 hours
Servings: 3
Ingredients:
- 2 pears cut into 1/4-inch thick slices
- 1 tbsp. lemon juice

Directions:
1. In a large bowl, mix lemon juice and 2 cups of water
2. Add pear slices into the lemon water and soak for 10 minutes.
3. Place the dehydrating tray in a multi-level air fryer basket and place basket in the instant pot.
4. Place pear slices on the dehydrating tray.
5. Seal pot with air fryer lid and select dehydrate mode then set temperature to 160 F and timer for 5 hours.
6. Serve and enjoy.

Nutrition: Calories 82 Fat 0.2 g Carbohydrates 21.3 g Protein 0.5 g

688. Sausage Casserole
Preparation Time: 10 minutes
Cooking Time: 30 minutes
Servings: 8
Ingredients:
- 1 lb. ground sausage
- 1/2 tsp garlic powder
- 8 oz. Velveeta cheese
- 1 cup milk
- 10 oz. cream of mushroom soup
- 10 oz. cream of chicken soup
- 2 cups cooked macaroni
- Pepper

Directions:
1. Add sausage into the instant pot and sauté until browned. Turn off the sauté mode.
2. Add remaining ingredients and stir everything well.
3. Seal pot with air fryer lid and select bake mode then set the temperature to 350 F and timer for 30 minutes.
4. Serve and enjoy.

Nutrition: Calories 414 Fat 26.2 g Carbohydrates 24.1 g Protein 21 g

689. Squash Casserole
Preparation Time: 10 minutes
Cooking Time: 35 minutes
Servings: 8
Ingredients:
- 4 1/2 lbs. yellow squash, cut into bite-size pieces
- 2 tbsp. mayonnaise
- 1 1/2 cups cheddar cheese, shredded
- 1 egg, lightly beaten
- 10 oz. cream of celery soup
- 1 cup onion, chopped
- Pepper
- Salt

For topping:
- 1/2 cup butter, melted
- 1 cup crushed crackers

Directions:
1. Add squash pieces into the boiling water and boil until tender. Drain well and set aside.
2. Mix together squash, onion, celery soup, egg, mayonnaise, pepper, and salt and pour into the instant pot.
3. Sprinkle cheddar cheese on top.
4. Seal pot with air fryer lid and select bake mode then set the temperature to 350 F and timer for 20 minutes.
5. Mix together butter and crushed crackers and sprinkle on top.
6. Seal pot with air fryer lid and select bake mode then set the temperature to 350 F and timer for 15 minutes.
7. Serve and enjoy.

Nutrition: Calories 281 Fat 22.4 g Carbohydrates 13.6 g Protein 9.8 g

690. Apple Chips
Preparation Time: 10 minutes
Cooking Time: 8 hours
Servings: 2
Ingredients:
- 1 apple, cut into 1/8-inch thick slices
- 1/4 tbsp. ground cinnamon
- 1/4 tbsp. granulated Sugar

Directions:
1. Add apple slices, cinnamon, and sugar into the large bowl and mix well.
2. Place the dehydrating tray in a multi-level air fryer basket and place basket in the instant pot.
3. Arrange apple slices on dehydrating tray.

4. Seal pot with air fryer lid and select dehydrate mode then set temperature to 130 F and timer for 8 hours.
5. Serve and enjoy.
Nutrition: Calories 66 Fat 0.2 g Carbohydrates 17.6 g Protein 0.3 g

691. Apple Sweet Potato Fruit Leather
Preparation Time: 10 minutes
Cooking Time: 4 hours
Servings: 2
Ingredients:
- 1/2 cup mashed sweet potatoes
- 1/4 tsp cinnamon
- 1 tbsp. honey
- 1/2 cup applesauce

Directions:
1. Add all ingredients into the blender and blend until smooth.
2. Place the dehydrating tray in a multi-level air fryer basket and place basket in the instant pot.
3. Line dehydrating tray with parchment paper.
4. Spread blended mixture on dehydrating tray.
5. Seal pot with air fryer lid and select dehydrate mode then set temperature to 110 F and timer for 4 hours or until leathery.
6. Serve and enjoy.
Nutrition: Calories 123 Fat 0.2 g Carbohydrates 30.6 g Protein 1.4 g

692. Dehydrated Mango
Preparation Time: 10 minutes
Cooking Time: 14 hours
Servings: 3
Ingredients:
- 1 mango, peel and sliced 1/4-inch thick

Directions:
1. Place the dehydrating tray in a multi-level air fryer basket and place basket in the instant pot.
2. Arrange mango slices on dehydrating tray.
3. Seal pot with air fryer lid and select dehydrate mode then set temperature to 135 F and timer for 14 hours.
4. Serve and enjoy.
Nutrition: Calories 67 Fat 0.4 g Carbohydrates 16.8 g Protein 0.9 g

693. Sausage Zucchini Casserole
Preparation Time: 10 minutes
Cooking Time: 45 minutes
Servings: 8
Ingredients:
- 12 eggs
- 2 small zucchinis, shredded
- 1 lb. ground Italian sausage
- 3 tomatoes, sliced
- 3 tbsp. coconut flour
- 1/4 cup coconut milk
- Pepper
- Salt

Directions:
1. Spray instant pot from inside with cooking spray.
2. Add sausage into the instant pot and cook on sauté mode until browned.
3. Spread shredded zucchini and sliced tomatoes on top of sausage.
4. In a bowl, whisk eggs, coconut flour, milk, pepper, and salt and pour over sausage mixture.
5. Seal pot with air fryer lid and select bake mode then set the temperature to 350 F and timer for 45 minutes.
6. Serve and enjoy.
Nutrition: Calories 306 Fat 21.8 g Carbohydrates 6.6 g Protein 19.6 g

694. Broccoli Rice Casserole
Preparation Time: 10 minutes
Cooking Time: 20 minutes
Servings: 8
Ingredients:
- 2 cups cooked rice
- 10 oz. cream of chicken soup
- 1 cup Velveeta cheese, diced
- 3 tbsp. butter
- 1/2 cup onion, chopped
- 16 oz. broccoli, steam & chopped

Directions:
1. Add butter into the instant pot and set the pot on sauté mode.
2. Add onion and sauté until softened. Turn off the sauté mode.
3. Add broccoli, soup, cheese, and rice and stir well.
4. Seal pot with air fryer lid and select bake mode then set the temperature to 350 F and timer for 20 minutes.
5. Serve and enjoy.
Nutrition: Calories 293 Fat 9.3 g Carbohydrates 45.2 g Protein 7.9 g

695. Cheesy Mashed Potato Casserole
Preparation Time: 10 minutes
Cooking Time: 20 minutes
Servings: 8
Ingredients:
- 4 cups mashed potatoes
- 3/4 cup cheddar cheese, shredded
- 1 cup French onion rings
- 1 tsp dried parsley
- 1 tsp dried chives
- 3/4 cup sour cream

Directions:
1. Spray instant pot from inside with cooking spray.
2. Add mashed potatoes, sour cream, chives, and parsley into the instant pot stir well.
3. Sprinkle cheese and onion rings on top.
4. Seal pot with air fryer lid and select bake mode then set the temperature to 350 F and timer for 20 minutes.
5. Serve and enjoy.
Nutrition: Calories 204 Fat 10.2 g Carbohydrates 22.4 g Protein 6.3 g

696. Corn Gratin
Preparation Time: 10 minutes
Cooking Time: 30 minutes
Servings: 8
Ingredients:

- 2 cups corn
- 1 cup cheddar cheese, shredded
- 1 cup milk
- 1 tbsp. flour
- 1 tbsp. butter
- 1 cup crushed crackers

Directions:
1. Add butter into the instant pot and set the pot on sauté mode.
2. Add flour and milk and stir until smooth. Turn off the sauté mode.
3. Add corn and cup cheese and stir well.
4. Sprinkle remaining cheese and crushed crackers on top.
5. Seal pot with air fryer lid and select bake mode then set the temperature to 350 F and timer for 15 minutes.
6. Serve and enjoy.

Nutrition: Calories 137 Fat 8 g Carbohydrates 11.6 g Protein 6.1 g

697. Flavors Crab Casserole

Preparation Time: 10 minutes
Cooking Time: 30 minutes
Servings: 5
Ingredients:
- 8 oz. crabmeat
- 1 onion, sliced
- 1/4 tsp garlic powder
- 1/4 tsp onion powder
- 1 tsp Worcestershire sauce
- 1 cup Swiss cheese, shredded
- 1 cup cheddar cheese, shredded
- 1/4 cup sour cream
- 5 oz. cream cheese

Directions:
1. Spray instant pot from inside with cooking spray.
2. Add all ingredients except cheddar cheese into the instant pot and stir well.
3. Sprinkle cheddar cheese on top.
4. Seal pot with air fryer lid and select bake mode then set the temperature to 350 F and timer for 30 minutes.
5. Serve and enjoy.

Nutrition: Calories 350 Fat 26 g Carbohydrates 11.9 g Protein 17.7 g

698. Broccoli Chicken Casserole

Preparation Time: 10 minutes
Cooking Time: 25 minutes
Servings: 6
Ingredients:
- 3 chicken breasts, boneless, cooked and diced
- 1/2 cup breadcrumbs
- 1 cup cheddar cheese, shredded
- 2 tbsp. parmesan cheese, grated
- 1 tsp lemon juice
- 3/4 cup milk
- 10 oz. broccoli florets, cooked and drained
- 10 oz. cream of chicken soup

Directions:
1. Spray instant pot from inside with cooking spray.
2. Add chicken, lemon juice, milk, broccoli, and soup into the instant pot and stir well.
3. Sprinkle cheddar cheese, parmesan cheese, and breadcrumbs on top.
4. Seal pot with air fryer lid and select bake mode then set the temperature to 350 F and timer for 25 minutes.
5. Serve and enjoy.

Nutrition: Calories 330 Fat 16.1 g Carbohydrates 14.8 g Protein 31.1 g

699. Asian Mushroom Jerky

Preparation Time: 10 minutes
Cooking Time: 12 hours
Servings: 4
Ingredients:
- 2 large portabella mushroom caps, sliced into 1/8-inch thick pieces
- 1 tsp ginger, grated
- 1 garlic clove, grated
- 1 tsp sriracha
- 1 1/2 tsp sesame oil
- 2 tbsp. brown Sugar
- 3 tbsp. vinegar
- 1/4 cup soy sauce, low-sodium

Directions:
1. Add mushrooms sliced into the large bowl.
2. Add remaining ingredients and mix well and marinate for 8 hours.
3. Place the dehydrating tray in a multi-level air fryer basket and place basket in the instant pot.
4. Arrange marinated mushroom pieces on dehydrating tray.
5. Seal pot with air fryer lid and select dehydrate mode then set temperature to 125 F and timer for 12 hours.
6. Serve and enjoy.

Nutrition: Calories 60 Fat 1.8 g Carbohydrates 9.1 g Sugar 5.6 g Protein 2.3 g Cholesterol 0 mg

700. Banana Fruit Leather

Preparation Time: 10 minutes
Cooking Time: 4 hours
Servings: 2
Ingredients:
- 1 small banana
- 1 tbsp. Novella

Directions:
1. Add banana and Novella into the blender and blend until smooth.
2. Place the dehydrating tray in a multi-level air fryer basket and place basket in the instant pot.
3. Line dehydrating tray with parchment paper
4. Spread banana mixture on dehydrating tray.
5. Seal pot with air fryer lid and select dehydrate mode then set temperature to 125 F and timer for 4 hours.
6. Serve and enjoy.

Nutrition: Calories 94 Fat 2.9 g Carbohydrates 17.1 g Protein 1 g

www.ingramcontent.com/pod-product-compliance
Lightning Source LLC
Chambersburg PA
CBHW081110080526
44587CB00021B/3530